Hope you enjoy the video

Best wishes

[signature]

Retail Revolution

Will Your Brick-and-Mortar Store **Survive?**

Rajiv Lal, José Alvarez
and Dan Greenberg

To my parents, who gave me the courage to speak my mind,
To my mentor, Walter Salmon, for his wisdom and friendship, and
To my wife, Suruchi, for unconditional love and support

—Rajiv Lal

To Sue, Mario, Gabe, and Santi, for their patience and love

—José Alvarez

To my parents, my siblings, and Kim, for your love and support

—Dan Greenberg

Contents

Chapter 1
Introduction

The perception of the online threat to brick-and-mortar retailers has ping-ponged between apocalyptic pronouncements of doom and encouraging hopes that brick-and-mortar retailers are actually more capable of exploiting eCommerce than their pure-play online counterparts. During both the dot com boom of the late 1990's and immediately after the introduction of the Home Shopping Network in the 1980's, "Retail is dead" was, to some, a going assumption.[1] Then, following the dot com bust, retailers realized that the web would "not make their physical assets obsolete."[2] Fears were rekindled in the recent Great Recession with the fall of both Blockbuster and Borders.

Currently, we're likely somewhere in the middle of this range of opinion. It is widely acknowledged that online retail, or eCommerce, is a threat to brick-and-mortar retailers; however, there remains much debate about 1) the scale of this threat, 2) which retailers are at greatest peril and why, 3) the defenses retailers can erect against eCommerce penetration, and 4) what responses are available to tackle the threat given a retailer's position. Much of this debate over the online threat suffers from an assumption that brick-and-mortar retailers are homogeneous. In reality, there is a wide variety in the types of threats brick-and-mortar retailers face, in the current impact of eCommerce on brick-and-mortar retailers, and in the solutions brick-and-mortar retailers can employ. The solutions available depend on what retail category, or vertical, a retailer specializes in as well as the legacy a retailer brings with it in terms of store operations, formats, locations, employees, and customer relationships. These solutions all rely on the harmonious interaction of the four assets that brick-and-mortar retailers directly control, what we've termed TIPS: Technology, Inventory, People, and the Store itself (both the physical space it provides as well as its location). Through the examples of several category killers (retailers that specialize in a single retail vertical) and mass merchandisers, we explore the differences between retailers and the impacts of these differences on retailers' option sets when responding to the eCommerce threat. Without this clear understanding of how eCommerce can impact specific types of retailers, individual retailers are unable to develop coherent strategies to diagnose and respond to the particular online threats they face. While we focus on category killers and mass merchandisers, we introduce a framework that any retailer, large or small, focused or with a broad assortment, dealing in commodity or luxury items, can apply to their business. As the threats are not identical across all retail segments, the responses cannot be one size fits all. Under our framework, retailers first identify the specific types of threats they face, evaluate any unique advantages they have relative to eCommerce competitors, and based on these answers, adopt one of three strategies: Wind Down, Shrink and Transform the Format, or Enhance the Value of the Box, and the associated TIPS tactics that go with them.

Problem? What Problem?

Before we can define this framework, however, our first challenge lies in convincing some readers that an eCommerce threat exists, and that it is very deadly for many retailers. Those who consider the eCommerce threat overblown have a number of arguments on their side. Online retail is still a small part of the retail industry, with electronic shopping generating 5.4% of retail sales in 2013 after nearly 20 years of existence.[3] By comparison, in 2009, 20 years after Walmart introduced its first supercenter and began the last major retail revolution, supercenters accounted for almost 7% of retail sales. Despite eCommerce's advantages in asset efficiency, supercenters as a channel amassed 25% more share in their first 20 years. Even crediting Amazon with its third-party Gross Merchandise Value (the total dollar value of all sales on Amazon's retail platform, regardless of whether the seller was Amazon or a third-party), the company has slightly over a 1.6% share of retail industry sales.[4] Compared to Walmart's US market share of almost 8%, Amazon is still a relatively small player.[5] While eCommerce has certainly been growing rapidly, at a compound annual rate of 20% per year since 2000, brick-and-mortar has not shrunk. It has continued to grow at almost 3.9% a year on a base of $2.2 trillion.

As for brick-and-mortar retailers that have gone out of business or are underperforming, analysts at JP Morgan point out that these retailers have also had to deal with significant product issues. Neither Blockbuster nor Borders managed the shift to digital media well. Best Buy is stuck at the end of a television replacement cycle as HD TVs have saturated American households while customers haven't been convinced to trade up to 3D TVs and Smart TVs. Similarly the office supply superstores are facing an environment where paper is gradually losing its place in the modern office.[6]

Optimists also point to signs that brick-and-mortar retailers that have stuck around are successfully competing in an online world. One indication of this is that many retailers' online sales are growing rapidly. Macy's reported 2012 online sales growth rates of over 40%,[7] Nordstrom achieved its third consecutive year of greater than 30% online same-store sales growth in 2013,[8] imperiled Best Buy's online sales growth far exceeds its comp store sales, and Walmart believes it will hit 30% online growth in 2014.[9] These growth rates are far higher than Amazon's owned and operated (excluding sales from Amazon Marketplace) retail sales growth of 23% in 2012 and 18% in 2013. After years against the ropes, many retailers are fighting out of the corner: revisiting store layouts and shifting particularly hard-hit merchandise categories or sub-categories online. Best Buy, for example, allots floor space only to higher-end televisions—commodity-level TVs are mostly merchandised online. Virtually all major retailers have rolled out or are experimenting with programs, such as buy-online-pick-up-in-store (BOPIS) and ship-from-store (SFS), to increase their store productivity and expand their integrated presence across multiple retail channels (i.e. brick-and-mortar store, web, and mobile; also known as omnichannel retailing).

The Scale of the Threat

Nonetheless, we hold that these arguments admire the forest while forgoing an inspection of the trees. And many trees in the retail forest, that is, many brick-and-mortar stores, are in ill health. Like trees, retail stores are long-lived, often with leases lasting ten or more years, and are unable to rapidly adapt to meet a changing environment. Online sales, no matter if they come from pure-play online retailers or omnichannel retailers, suck volume out of a store and often lead to more intense price competition. For reasons we'll cover later in this book, neither BOPIS nor SFS are enough to save these categories. The online threat is different from what retailers have faced in the past. Although Walmart took an enormous amount of market share in a diverse set of categories, many retailers were able to respond to and effectively co-exist with Walmart. However, with eCommerce we believe we are now at a tipping point for many retailers.

Category killers are highly focused retailers specializing in a category of goods that succeeded against Walmart due to their deep assortment, aggressive pricing, large stores, extensive store network, and knowledgeable salespeople with "deep expertise in the categories they served."[10] Against Amazon and other online retailers, these advantages fade. Online retailers have appropriated the strengths of category killers: they can offer wider assortments than any store, have driven prices to new lows, and replace associate knowledge with editorials, professional and customer reviews, and ratings systems. Expanding fulfillment networks get products to customers in increasingly shorter time windows, defeating any convenience advantage that category killers might have. Additionally, online retail is open 24 hours a day, 7 days a week and is available from one's own home without a trip. While Amazon has been compared to Walmart, it's probably most apt to compare Amazon to category killers.

Amazon's sales are only a fraction of Walmart's, but like category killers, its market share in some categories, like books, is enormous. Later in this chapter, we've modeled the levels of gross margin or same-store sales declines, which, everything else equal, retailers in categories particularly hard hit by eCommerce could incur before their stores are in serious trouble. We found that small declines in same-store sales or gross margin could turn a profitable store base into one that is best left to wither.

Understanding how online retailers can cause these same-store sales and gross margin declines by affecting the operating metrics of a retail store is fundamental to understanding the threat brick-and-mortar retailers face. Margin compression is where most studies of the online threat begin. In most, though not all, retail verticals, online retailers can offer lower prices than brick-and-mortar retailers because of their lower cost structures. In the face of this price competition, brick-and-mortar retailers find themselves either lowering their prices across the board, instituting price-match policies with online retailers, or accepting that they will lose sales to customers who are showrooming. In all of these circumstances, either because of price reductions or fixed cost deleveraging (when low or negative sales growth reduces the amount earned on fixed costs), the brick-and-mortar retailer finds itself with shrinking margins.

Online retailers' lower cost structures are driven by a variety of cost efficiencies. From an employee perspective, positions such as cashiers and sales clerks are eliminated. Automated check-out procedures take their place and the need for stocking or tidying up merchandise at store level doesn't exist. Without a store network, real estate costs are confined to a handful of distribution centers. Inventory aggregation at a few key points of distribution rather than throughout a store network means that forecasting can be more accurate and replenishment more timely, and thus markdowns, shrink costs, and working capital needs are reduced.

Online fulfillment and home delivery also create traffic problems for brick-and-mortar retailers. Brick-and-mortar retailers have long benefitted from merchandise lines that matched needs and trip-drivers with impulses and wants within their stores. If shoppers can get their primary purchases online, brick-and-mortar retailers can't sell them the rest. For example, if customers cease buying their high-ticket electronics in-store, Best Buy associates can neither upsell the customer to a device that may suit their needs better or make complementary sales of cables and ancillary devices that may improve the experience, and that customers are unlikely to buy online themselves. On a broader scale, while still a very small part of the total market, online fulfillment of basic needs, such as Consumer Product Goods and apparel basics, is growing. With customers increasingly ordering these and other products online, potential shoppers have fewer reasons to leave their homes, and the clothing store collocated with the supermarket can't benefit from grocery trips that don't happen. As a result of increased online shopping, traffic across the retail sector is falling (by as much as 50% when the holiday months of 2010 are compared to those of 2013).[11] Exacerbating the traffic decline, when shoppers do leave their homes, they have often already researched online the products that they are interested in purchasing. This makes them less likely to browse, research, and compare prices across brick-and-mortar locations, and thus shoppers visit fewer stores per trip, resulting in a decline in overall traffic. This same behavior also leads to more targeted buying both online and in-store, which can reduce stores' ability to upsell, make complementary sales (recall the Best Buy example), and make impulse sales (think candy at the checkout), resulting in smaller shopping baskets. This basket disruption could cause the business models of many retailers to fall apart.

Taken all together, lower price points, decreased traffic, and smaller baskets means lower sales and margins for brick-and-mortar stores. Given recent promotional intensity and continued declines in retail store asset productivity since 2007, these issues become even more pertinent. Compounding the issue, most retailers have already reduced their in-store labor to such an extent that further cost-cutting has a negative impact, and thus the costs of operating a store today are largely fixed. Retailers arrived at this point in part due to the recession when many retailers reduced headcounts as customers focused more on price and less on service, but also as a result of long-term initiatives like self-checkout, which eliminated many cashier positions; inventory, ordering and logistics systems implementations, which reduced merchandise handling; labor scheduling systems coupled with a greater use of part-time labor sector-wide, which aligned employee levels closely with customer visits and left little spare capacity; and through outsourcing many tasks that used to be performed in-store, such as pre-packaged meat eliminating butchers in supermarkets and apparel goods retailers contracting third parties to sort, hang, and tag incoming products so that they are shelf-ready. As a consequence, the ordinary levers that retailers could pull to respond to crises have already been used, and, barring radical changes, stores with long-term leases are largely at the mercy of the deteriorations in same-store sales and gross margin caused by eCommerce.

As brick-and-mortar sales per store decline, fixed assets become less productive, and retailers face declining profitability. As prices are lowered, gross margin declines directly eat into net margins. Although this dynamic does not necessarily send retailers directly to bankruptcy, falling store profits will force many retailers to a point where the return from continuing investments in stores is less than investors could achieve elsewhere. Pursuing higher returns, retailers then enter a vicious cycle of reduced investment and cost cutting that leads to customer dissatisfaction and a lack of differentiation. Supervalu's Jewel and Albertsons stores went through this vicious cycle when, due to Supervalu's high cost structure and heavy interest payments, the chains cut store investments during the recession, leaving many stores unremodeled for years and "cluttered," which turned off shoppers.[12] If this cycle continues, whole retail chains can quickly become full of zombie stores.

Zombie stores still generate cash flow, but reinvesting in the store base – to paint the walls, introduce new fixtures, and spruce up the establishment – doesn't make financial sense. Instead, the zombie stores continue to exist, eating away at sales that their healthier, competitive counterparts could instead capture. When these chains eventually enter bankruptcy, they are allowed to break leases and shut down their unprofitable stores. The newly reorganized chain generally has not solved the basic underlying issues created by the online threat. However, it now has a smaller, healthier set of stores that begin anew the downward spiral. A&P provides a strong example of this spiral, and, remarkably, is still around, and still not on solid ground, after numerous rounds of store closures and selloffs.

Both of these points in a retailer's death cycle can be predicted, and in Figure 1.1, Figure 1.2, and Figure 1.3, we've modeled the gross margin and same-store sales impacts brick-and-mortar retailers can withstand before facing bankruptcy and before further store investments no longer make financial sense (the method is explained in the technical appendix at the end of this book). Bankruptcy is entered when a company can no longer support itself as-is (and can't find the resources for a turnaround without entering bankruptcy). Retailers reach this point when their average store provides zero earnings before interest, taxes, depreciation, and amortization (EBITDA) contribution; when this has happened, it no longer makes sense to operate the stores. Average same-store sales for most of the retailers in our sample have been positive, if only slightly so, and, with the exception of JC Penney which needs same-store sales to increase substantially to survive, these retailers can withstand significant declines before the average store reaches zero EBITDA contribution (see Figure 1.1 – declines to zero store contribution). (Note that in Figure 1.1, Figure 1.2, and Figure 1.3, negative numbers for the changes in same-store sales and gross margins needed to reach the hurdle point (the blue bars) are good things, but negative numbers in the three year average same-store sales rates (the green line) are bad.)

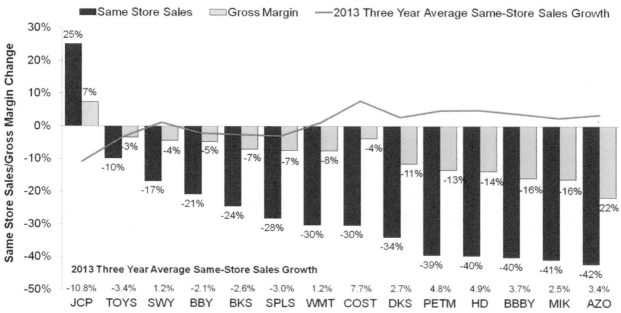

Figure 1.1 Source: Company Statements. Notes: Only Barnes & Noble's retail business is included, Nook is excluded. For further explanation of these calculations please see the technical appendix at the back of this book. A description of the abbreviations used in the table is provided below:

Abbreviation	Company Name	Abbreviation	Company Name
JCP	JC Penney	DKS	Dicks Sporting Goods
SWY	Safeway	HD	Home Depot
BBY	Best Buy	PETM	PetSmart
TOYS	Toys "R" Us	MIK	Michaels
BKS	Barnes & Noble	AZO	AutoZone
WMT	Walmart	BBBY	Bed Bath & Beyond
SPLS	Staples		

While these retailers likely have a long time to go before they're bankrupt, whether or not they have the ability to avoid that fate is an unresolved question. To do so, many would have to make substantial investments to transform their legacy store assets and operations into something suitable for an omnichannel world. In order to access the capital to fund these transformations, retailers would need to show investors a reasonable return. If they can't demonstrate this return, these retailers are likely to become zombie chains, and will eventually enter bankruptcy. This is why we've also modeled the level of declines retailers can withstand until investing in the average store no longer makes financial sense, when investors would rather abandon the chains to become zombies (see Figure 1.2 – return on invested capital below cost of capital).

In this model, we set a long-term weighted average cost of capital (WACC) of 10% across the board to reflect expected increases in long-term interest rates. This is the hurdle rate which a firm's return on invested capital (ROIC) must exceed. ROIC measures the return a dollar invested into the business will generate from its operations, and is defined as net operating profit after tax (NOPAT) divided by invested capital. As such, ROIC examines a company's operating income after tax relative to the operating assets for which, either through interest-bearing debt or equity, it has had to pay. If a firm can't generate an ROIC above its WACC, investors not only don't want to provide it with further investment, they'd also rather take any cash the retailer generates out of its business and have it redistributed to themselves. This is the first step to becoming a zombie chain. From an ROIC perspective, many retailers now begin to appear perilously close to the point where, with a few more years of negative same-store sales, it may no longer be tenable to continue investing in their store base.

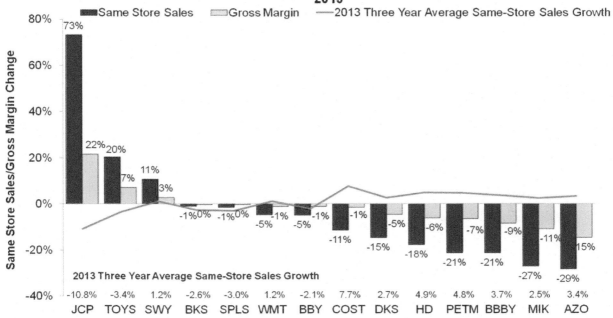

Figure 1.2

We also look at this 10% ROIC hurdle scenario when retailers operating leases are capitalized (Figure 1.3 – ROIC below cost of capital, Capitalized Operating Leases). We exhibit this capitalized operating leases scenario because long-term lease payments impose the same kind of obligations as interest payments, and we consider these operating leases a form of debt. Capitalizing operating leases makes these retailers appear even worse off from a returns perspective because it more accurately portrays the amount of invested capital in the firm.

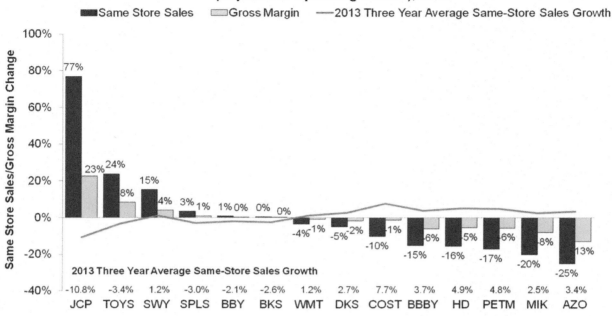

Figure 1.3

With such thin margins for some retailers before they enter zombie store territory, the shift of a single category, even a sub-category, within a retail vertical to either digital media or online fulfillment can doom a chain. Consider the example of Borders. While Barnes & Noble had quickly followed Amazon into online book retailing and eBook reading devices, Borders was always the late entrant. Until 2008, Amazon.com had been managing Borders' online book retailing presence. As a result, Borders was in a much weaker position than Barnes & Noble when the medium for books shifted to digital. Using the same-store sales deterioration analysis described above, if we look at Borders in 2005, just before the introduction of the Sony eBook reader in 2006 and the Amazon Kindle which followed a year later, we see that, keeping SG&A fixed and varying COGs with sales, Borders had a 27% cushion on same-store sales before the average store would no longer be profitable. However, the transition to eBooks occurred rapidly after the introduction of the Kindle, iBookstore, and Nook, with publisher sales of eBooks as a share of total books growing from 3% in 2009 to 23% in 2013. With Borders poorly staked in both online physical book sales and digital eBook sales, the transition to online retail and digital media severely hurt the chain's same-store sales, and, consequently, store-level contribution margins. Borders declining contribution margin is shown in Figure 1.4.

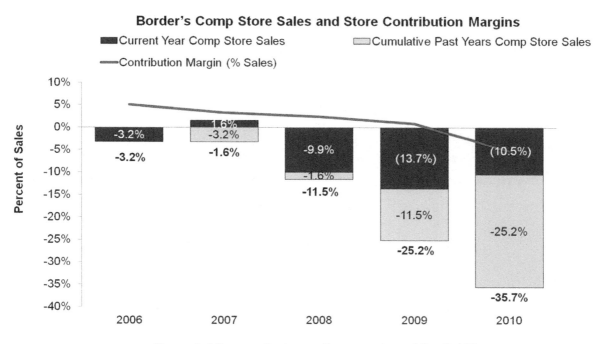

Figure 1.4 Source: Company Documents and Capital IQ

In-line with the estimate from the average store zero EBITDA contribution model, Borders declared bankruptcy in early 2011.

Category killers are most at risk of gross margin and same-store sales declines, and the product cycle imperiled category killers described by JP Morgan (Barnes & Noble, Staples, and Best Buy) have little breathing room. Unlike mass merchandisers and department stores which frequently rearrange store space and emphasize various parts of their broad assortment according to the season, when a sub-category (such as DVDs or computers) at a category killer goes online, the retailer can't simply flex their assortment to cover the shortfall. Instead, they are left with an empty space in their store. The lack of diversification in the product portfolio of these stores leads to many fewer degrees of freedom and a much reduced option set for solving the online threat.

Surprisingly, Walmart, the company that has dominated much of retailing over the past three decades, is also on the edge, with only a 5% same-store sales and 1% gross margin buffer between it and the 10% ROIC hurdle. In addition to online competitors, Walmart also faces resurgent supermarkets and rising dollar stores that take trips out of its grocery departments. While category killers lack the ability to flex their assortment to cover holes in their stores and are heavily exposed to trends within their specialist category, over the long term they can shrink store sizes such as Best Buy is doing with Best Buy Mobile and the office supply companies are doing with their new stores. Walmart's business model, however, relies on its massive supercenters offering a broad selection of categories with a shallow assortment within each category: the one-stop-shop. Walmart may not want to risk this one-stop promise and lose segments of customers (like mothers lured by low diaper prices) by dropping items from its already shallow assortment, dropping entire departments from its stores, or shrinking its format. Because of this, Walmart's store format choices and how it makes use of dead space and dying categories within its stores will be of particular interest in how it plans its future. We will discuss this further in Chapter Six: "Is Anybody Safe?"

In the face of the online threat, many brick-and-mortar retailers' responses look uncoordinated, short-term focused, and intent on improving key operational metrics like traffic, basket size, and margins while ignoring the long-term viability of the enterprise. It is rare that retailers are developing a cohesive, organization-wide strategy. For example, much has been made of brick-and-mortar retailers offering BOPIS and SFS programs. However, these programs are inherently less efficient than the distribution system that Amazon is building. These programs are useful as a short-term solution to increase inventory turns and capture incremental sales, but often do not point to a coordinated long-term survival strategy. Similarly, a number of third parties are happy to offer services to brick-and-mortar retailers that make them look more like online players. Shopkick, for example, will help retailers attract traffic to their stores, and eBay Enterprise will run brick-and-mortar retailers' eCommerce operations. But the value of these services cannot be maximized unless retailers put their brick-and-mortar and online assets to work in a cohesive way. Shopkick traffic won't necessarily convert to sales if in-store merchandise can be had for less online. Retailers' online sites are only partially about selling goods, they're also for educating shoppers and protecting key merchandise categories. Other retailers have turned to exclusive private-label products to compete with online retailers' price efficiency and to prevent customers from showrooming. However, if retailers cannot build traffic to their stores in the absence of national brands' advertising campaigns, such efforts do not guarantee a sound future. These tactics focus on increasing store productivity, without asking the question of whether stores need to be reimagined entirely based on evolving customer demands and the changing competitive landscape.

The result is that, on an industry average, retail sales per square foot have not improved significantly, and the ROICs of many of the retailers profiled in this book have not recovered since the recession of 2008. Meanwhile, eCommerce continues to grow at a much faster pace than brick-and-mortar retail, and several categories, such as consumer electronics, office supplies, toys, and baby products, have experienced such significant levels of eCommerce penetration that the incumbents are in peril of bankruptcy.

Changing Consumer Behavior

The trends in margin compression, falling traffic, and shrinking tickets are also likely to continue due to broader generational trends. As Millennials age and take Generation X's position as the largest shopper cohort, their current Recession-induced frugal behavior may moderate, but will likely still shift the average towards more price comparison, lower traffic, and smaller tickets. Many of these trends are being driven by Millennials' increased use of technology.

Millennials, as Digital Natives, use technology as an integral part of their shopping experience, and activities such as showrooming, downloading coupons off the internet, searching for deals online, and researching potential purchases online before going to a store are more common with them than in older generations. What this means for retailers is that prices will likely flatten across channels, and an inability to compete at the lowest price, barring some immediate fulfillment need on the part of the customer, is a recipe for being uncompetitive. Retailers can respond to this by implementing new operational models to lower prices (such as the dramatically different supply chain and retail infrastructure envisioned by Walmart where supercenters act as distribution centers and small satellite stores act as eCommerce pickup points), or by dreaming up new business models that take price out of the equation (such as Best Buy's relationships with its store-within-a-store brands).

Fueled by smart-phone apps and online platforms, Millennials also show a greater predisposition to buying services and renting, rather than owning things directly. Such behavior could give stores fresh life as service centers, or contribute to their fall if the products they sell are consumed in lesser quantity.

Consumers' more targeted shopping, coupled with the growing ubiquity of free two-day delivery, means that retailers who want to survive must offer a compelling reason for shoppers to leave their homes. It also means that shoppers will increasingly be able to easily get what they want from anywhere, which may lead them to segment their purchases between channels in a way that wasn't possible when each purchase required a different trip. This, in turn, may mean the end of the once-compelling one-stop-shop promise. However, this need not necessarily be bad for every retailer. Without a consumer need for the convenience of buying everything in one place, category killers and other retailers can dispense with merchandise lines that may have been 'sacred cows' in former days. Indeed, if income inequality trends in the US continue and the divide between high and low income grows, many retailers may have no choice but to abandon some price-points and products to eCommerce. It is nearly impossible to be 'all things to all customers' at a time when the middle class is disappearing.

Millennials' technology use is also bringing them closer to brands. Compared to previous generations, they rely more on word-of-mouth and social networks to discover new products. They are also forging connections with brands over online media, and desire to be a part of the creation process. Retailers have long served as the intermediary between customers and brands: helping brands to understand consumer trends, design and launch new products, plan production, and create and target advertising. As manufacturers develop closer direct relationships with their end-customers, retailers will have to ask what benefits they provide brands and explore how to maximize those benefits. Best Buy is doing this now by providing spaces for manufacturers to interact directly with customers in Best Buy's stores-within-a-store.

Readers should keep these retailer-specific trends in mind as they read the descriptions of each eCommerce threat below and as they discover how retailers are dealing with these challenges throughout this book.

Unpacking the eCommerce Threat, Store by Store

We believe there are some fundamental principles related to asset utilization that apply regardless of what retail segment a company inhabits. Because brick-and-mortar retail is an asset-heavy sector, this book will look closely at return on invested capital for retailers and how the eCommerce threat impacts the ability to get acceptable returns. Examining how well a retailer is utilizing its key assets in the TIPS framework: technology, inventory, people, and the store itself (including both its store space and its location)—and exploring how these assets might be best transformed and combined to deliver value to consumers and brand partners will lead to a stronger basis for strategy development in the rapidly evolving world of retailing.

To appropriately create strategy, respond to both the online threat and shifting consumer behavior, and effectively deploy brick-and-mortar assets and the employees, inventory, and technology within them, retailers must first define the specific threat they face from eCommerce. There are three types of threats that we use to categorize brick-and-mortar retailers, largely based on the products that category-killers sell: 1) a digitization of or disappearance of demand for the core category within the store, 2) a situation in which online retailers have large cost, inventory, and selection advantages in core categories, and 3) a situation where, for a variety of reasons, most categories in the store are relatively protected from an online threat. We define these categories below and list attributes of product verticals and companies that typically fall within these categories to help readers decide what threats they may face.

The first threat occurs when a fundamental shift in the core category of the store eliminates the need for physical distribution. Such is the case when physical categories shift to digital consumption, as happened with Blockbuster's movies and games and Barnes & Noble's books. In other cases, demand for a retailer's core product evaporates, as is ongoing with the office supply superstores (as offices digitize and both businesses and consumers simply uses less paper) and the toy vertical (as children rely more on digital games than physical toys). Retailers specializing in these categories can expect to see continuous same-store sales declines in these core areas.

The second threat occurs in categories where high selling prices and large gross profits are used to support brick-and-mortar assets, salespeople, and mark-downs. Online retailers can slash these high prices as, with the efficiency of aggregated inventory, the use of other retailers as showrooms, and a world of online reviews, they don't bear these costs and can get by with lower gross profits. These advantages are heightened when the products involved are also small and light-weight, making the cost of shipping a small fraction of the overall price. They are further heightened when selection matters as online retailers, who don't have disaggregated store inventory or store space limitations, can appeal to customers with a wider selection in one location: their website, and don't suffer as much from a long tail of items that have to be marked down at the end of the season. Online retailers have a similar advantage when categories have short product cycles and they can more readily avoid inventory overhangs than can brick-and-mortar retailers. Best Buy faces these issues in its technology departments, and CompUSA (remember them?) failed as online retailers outpriced it.

The third threat is relatively small. For these retailers, eCommerce may chip away at sales on the margin, but is unlikely to impact the store heavily. Low selling prices can make the cost of picking and shipping greater than the cost of stocking the product in stores. This is especially true of high-turn, commodity products, like food consumables, that best leverage the fixed assets of shelf space. When products are large and heavy, shipping costs are even more expensive, and products like sheet rock and lumber at Home Depot and Lowe's, and pet food at PetSmart and Petco, are best sold out of their stores. Channel exclusivity, such as brick-and-mortar pet stores maintain with many premium brands, has helped prevent showrooming behavior. In other categories, customer buying behavior such as a proclivity for impulse purchases, an immediate need for the item, a need to touch and feel a product, or a need for in-store help has also helped brick-and-mortar retailers compete with online competitors. For brick-and-mortar retail stores that also act as forward inventory points, such as with Lowe's and Home Depot's contractor business and auto parts stores' commercial business, the professional customers' need to have products delivered or picked-up right away, not just same-day, has also been an advantage for brick-and-mortar stores. In-store services, such as copy centers at the office supply superstores and the whole raft of services at PetSmart, cannot be duplicated by online retailers and have remained the domain of brick-and-mortar retailers.

In many situations, retailers will face a combination of these threats. For instance, Best Buy suffers from both the digitization of its media business as well as from competition from online retailers in its technology department. While mostly protected, Home Depot does suffer from the second threat described above in its décor and power tools business. However, due to the make-up of the product verticals they compete in, one of these three threats is usually predominant. On the other hand, broad assortment retailers that aggregate categories, like supermarkets and mass merchandisers, often face all three threat categorizations to varying degrees across their product portfolio. For example, greeting cards have been going digital for some time, mass merchandisers' technology departments face the same threat as Best Buy's, but their food and CPG lines are not experiencing massive share grab from online retailers. In addition to this amalgam of category-killer threats, these retailers often face the threat of losing whole segments of customers that support their volume-based retailing. For instance, supermarkets, once the destinations where everyone bought their groceries, are experiencing a bifurcation where the highest-income shoppers are going to online delivery and premium stores, while lower-income shoppers are going to dollar stores and supercenters, leaving supermarkets with a shrinking middle class.

Whatever type of threat a retailer is experiencing, the solutions will depend on a careful consideration of what value the brick-and-mortar store creates for suppliers and customers. The brick-and-mortar store, and the company's other assets and operations, should be positioned to best capture that value. Retailers should ask themselves whether: 1)brands in their retail vertical need a physical showroom for their goods; 2) customers need face-to-face education on products that the internet cannot provide; 3) customers rely on personal relationships with store personnel to help them choose between products; 4) the stores' merchandise mix is composed of non-commodity products where the retailer can influence customers' choices on brands, styles, features, functions, etc.; 5) the retailer has some other unique advantage relative to pure-play online retailers that they can leverage to reimagine their offer (e.g. services like pet grooming).

Once the nature of the threat has been appropriately diagnosed, we can move on to prescriptions for a potential fix. In our review of current and potential retailer strategies, across product verticals, we identify three strategies that retailers are, or could be, employing based on their answers to the above questions. The first, "Wind Down," focuses on maximizing the cash that can be returned to investors. This is achieved by not betting the farm on trying to drastically reinvent brick-and-mortar stores (unless there is a clear, achievable, near-term payback period), but rather by acknowledging the realities of the situation as online retailers or product shifts replace the need for a store network. While the end result is very likely a closing of the company, this strategy is not a race to bankruptcy but a continuous rationalization of the organization and its stores to maximize shareholder value. As an example, A&P's New York City locations are still operating after multiple corporate bankruptcies. The Wind Down strategy fits those retailers who are in danger from eCommerce, but have no compelling advantages. It works because retailers' store portfolios are very rarely all bad, rather they are often composed of stores with very different return profiles.

The second strategy, "Shrink and Transform the Format," involves transforming brick-and-mortar stores and other elements of retailers' operations to focus on the most value-creating activities, while simultaneously ensuring that these activities are paid for by those who most benefit from them. Some retailers face the necessity of a wholesale reimagining of their business: from their stores, to the way they interact with customers, to their supply chain in order to remain relevant and competitive. These retailers should, indeed, bet the farm as the shift to online retail could quickly drive their current stores to unprofitability. This is a strategy for retailers who are in danger from eCommerce, but have a competitive proposition to build a new store format around. For retailers adopting one of these first two solutions, maintaining flexibility in inventory, interior fixtures, leases, and finances will be incredibly important as the retailing world continues to change rapidly.

A third strategy, which we call "Enhancing the Value of the Box," is for those retailers who, for various reasons, have largely been protected from the vicissitudes of eCommerce. It includes further protections of the brick-and-mortar store through a variety of strategies, as well as shrewd leverage of retailers' online operations to direct sales to a largely unchanged brick-and-mortar store. For some of these retailers, a blind adoption of online retail should be approached with caution as their core product, for example pet food, is better fulfilled in-store. The decision framework just described is laid out in Figure 1.5, and we will use it at the end of each chapter to summarize how this framework has worked for the retailer discussed.

Steps of the Online Threat Decision Framework

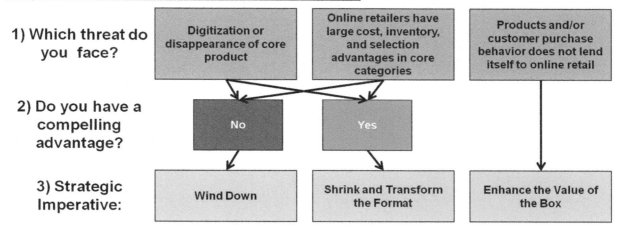

Figure 1.5

Structure of this Book

In this book, we will take the reader through the stories of retailers in five different retail verticals that typify the different eCommerce threats—office supplies, consumer electronics, groceries, pet products, and building supplies—to illustrate how their history and decisions fit into the framework we've discussed above. We will also visit two mass market retailers that have dominated retailers' dreams and nightmares for the last twenty years: Amazon and Walmart. The following chapter, "Driving the Retail Revolution," describes the nature and magnitude of the threat posed by Amazon and the aspects of its business model that make it such a competitive powerhouse. This chapter frames the discussion for the rest of the book.

This is followed by a chapter on the office supplies retail vertical, where we ask the question of whether a retailer should "Wind Down or Reinvent?" when faced with fundamental shifts taking place in their core categories. We then move on to analyzing the future of retailers where internet operators have huge cost, inventory, and selection advantages in core categories. In "Is Showrooming a Problem or a Solution?" we explore Best Buy's challenges, and those of retailers like it, and argue for a new approach to vendor relations as a way of fighting the significant threat from Amazon.

Next, we take a look at a retail vertical many assume is safe from an internet threat, and ask "Will the Internet Push Grocery Retailers Over the Edge?" Grocery categories do not lend themselves to delivery, and no internet retailer has been successful here on a significant scale. Even before Amazon Fresh, Amazon had been trying to deliver food and CPG items for a long time with limited success. Peapod and Fresh Direct also deliver groceries at home and are similarly limited in their geographical scope. However, we find that in groceries, while the internet may not appear to be a potent threat at first blush, the supermarket format of 40,000-60,000 square feet is ripe for disruption given consumer eating trends and the plethora of competitors (e.g. dollar stores, warehouse stores, drug stores, office supply stores) constantly eating away at sales in grocery categories. Consequently, we believe retailers need to be very alert to the possibilities of major threats even when the internet is only a small part of the overall competitive space. When everyone is out to get you, paranoia is just smart thinking.

We use the chapter on grocery retailing as a springboard for an analysis of the future of Walmart in the age of Amazon. In, "Is Anybody Safe?" we explain our firm belief that the Walmart business model is under extreme duress in the developed world. Although Walmart is working hard to change their model to survive the new realities of the marketplace, we believe they have their work cut out for them given the enormous amount of real estate and product inventory that they carry. We see this in the surprising ROIC tables in Figure 1.1, Figure 1.2, and Figure 1.3. As the Dollar stores and others steal shopping trips from Walmart and eCommerce disrupts the money-making categories that provide the profit to their model, Walmart finds itself in a compromised position.

While Walmart isn't safe, we end by looking at two retailers who have positioned themselves well. In "Skating to Where the Puck is Going to Be," we examine PetSmart, who foresaw the significance of the threat from Internet retailers very early on and took proactive steps to stop the competition in their tracks. Courageous leadership in addition to a proactive approach allowed PetSmart to introduce new services and exclusive merchandise while taking full advantage of general trends in the pet supplies industry. These actions have not only allowed PetSmart to flourish, but also created significant growth in the category. While PetSmart has done a tremendous job building defenses around its brick-and-mortar stores, it has not fully implemented the "Enhance the Value of the Box" strategy because it has failed to create a compelling omnichannel experience that drives store traffic. The final chapter, "Embracing eCommerce: a New Retail Model for Customer Engagement," fills in this gap. In it, we detail how Home Depot took a merchandise line by merchandise line look at its business in order to develop a comprehensive strategy to compete against online retail, leverage the internet to bring more business to its stores, and enhance overall customer satisfaction. While some categories at Home Depot were shored up dramatically through investments in private label products, price discounts and an online offering, the entire store has benefited from online efforts to help the customer dream even bigger when it comes to remodeling projects in the home and by making the life of a contractor more time- and cost-efficient.

We close with a concluding chapter that summarizes our recommendations and outlines continuing challenges and opportunities for the retail sector in light of emerging technology and consumer trends. In the conclusion, we also highlight the consequences of these shifts in retail for the United States and the communities that retailers serve.

Chapter 2
Amazon, Driving the Retail Revolution

The introduction to this book made the case that eCommerce, in all its forms, is a serious threat for many retailers. In this chapter, we focus on the biggest player in eCommerce, Amazon, and describe the ways in which Amazon is out-competing brick-and-mortar retailers in price, selection, service, and execution; explore how Amazon is evolving, and what its Marketplace and Prime programs mean for brick-and-mortar retailers; and also discuss the difficulty for brick-and-mortar retailers in competing directly with Amazon. We draw on Amazon's initial confrontation with media category-killers Barnes & Noble and Borders to highlight many of these points. Finally, we discuss Amazon's future prospects: focusing on what happens when growth slows down, Amazon's prospects of profitability, and the transformation it is undertaking in its approach to retailing. We end by placing the Amazon story in the wider context of this book.

We begin by exploring in more depth the sources of online retailers' advantages in efficiency (and by extension, price), assortment, and service.

Online retail is more efficient for a number of reasons. The two major assets on most retailers' balance sheets are stores and inventory. Amazon is able to avoid the cost of building stores by operating out of a relatively small number of fulfillment centers. This distribution system aggregates inventory in a few fulfillment centers rather than thousands of stores, which reduces the amount of inventory in Amazon's overall supply chain. In Figure 2.1 below, we have calculated the assets to sales ratio (the inverse of asset turnover) for each operating asset on retailers' balance sheets (ex-cash) to compare how efficient each retailer is at using its assets. In this ratio, lower numbers mean that a retailer is more efficient at asset utilization. For Amazon, note that not only is its overall asset to sales ratio among the lowest in this retailer sample, the absence of a store network enables Amazon to create each dollar of sales with less inventory and PP&E assets than other retailers.

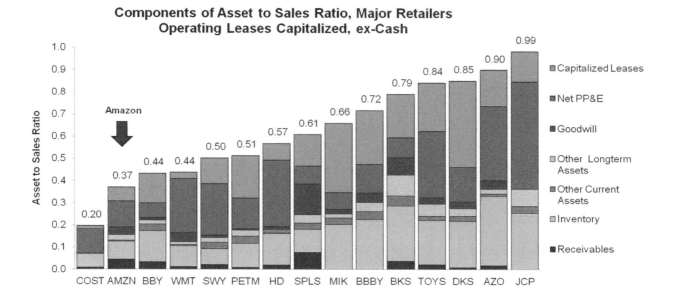

Figure 2.1 Source: Financial Statements from Cap IQ, Author's Calculations. Note: Operating Leases Capitalized Based on Estimated Future Minimum Payments and Interest Rate on Debt. No adjustments made to Barnes & Noble for Nook business.

Amazon also has a number of advantages on its income statement. It doesn't operate stores, and doesn't bear the operating costs of doing so, such as utilities and store personnel. Amazon's fulfillment centers are set up as efficient and controlled picking and packing centers, whereas stores have wide aisles, low shelves, and poor data capture. These benefits help Amazon maintain higher sales per employee than both Walmart and Costco, and as Amazon has grown, its advantage has become greater, as shown in Figure 2.2.

| | 2000 | | | 2003 | | | 2006 | | | 2009 | | | 2012 | | |
	AMZN	WMT	COST	AMZN	WMT	COST	AMZN	WMT	COST	AMZN	WMT	COST	AMZN	WMT	COST
Sales per Employee (thousands)	$333	$162	$435	$688	$178	$436	$827	$188	$508	$1,089	$194	$512	$845	$213	$587

Figure 2.2 Source: Company Financial Reports and Author Calculations

Because Amazon often relies on contracting and staffing services to run its fulfillment centers, these numbers must be taken with a grain of salt. However, we also estimated sales per fulfillment center employee and hourly store associate for both Walmart and Amazon (using estimates for full-time and part-time hours worked for Walmart and stowing, picking, packing, and home delivery via FedEx and UPS rates as inputs for Amazon), and Amazon still had four times as many sales per FTE as Walmart.

Greater efficiency also delivers better customer service. Amazon consistently outscores its brick-and-mortar peers on the American Customer Satisfaction Index, and is wholly focused on being customer-centric. Amazon's improving delivery speeds are one example of this. When Amazon first started in 1994, it was not uncommon for a book order, particularly an uncommon one, to take anywhere from one to five weeks to reach a customer. Today, orders with free shipping arrive in as little as three to five days, and Prime members can receive an unlimited number of orders in two days. With Amazon's continuing fulfillment center buildout, delivery times will only decrease.

These efficiencies all translate to lower prices for Amazon customers across a wide variety of goods. This assortment is another reason why Amazon has been so successful at gaining market share. While Amazon began in books, its founder, Jeffrey Bezos, had conducted an analysis of 20 product categories he thought could be sold online before starting the company. Amazon used this category plan as a roadmap, and has continuously entered new categories and begun new businesses. Entering these new categories was relatively easy, as Bezos "believed that having invested enough in customer acquisition, by building a brand name [and] a reliable logistics and distribution system, the marginal cost of adding extra lines was minimal and certainly less costly than in the physical world."[13] Its category-by-category approach has been especially damaging to traditional retailers because the shift of a single category online can often imperil a retailer's entire store. Amazon's ability to drive these online shifts in each category is impressive.

From a company with almost 80% of its sales in Media (Books, Video, and Music) in 2002, by 2013 Amazon's scope had expanded so that less than 30% of its revenue was generated by Media, with the balance made up of Electronics and General Merchandise (EGM) and a handful of services such as Amazon Web Services (AWS), Amazon Ad Network, etc. This evolution is shown in Figure 2.3. With every new merchandise line, Amazon expands its economies of scope and scale: increasing customer lifetime value, making fulfillment more efficient, and leveraging its fixed costs and massive investments in technology and fulfillment infrastructure across a greater share of its customers' wallets.

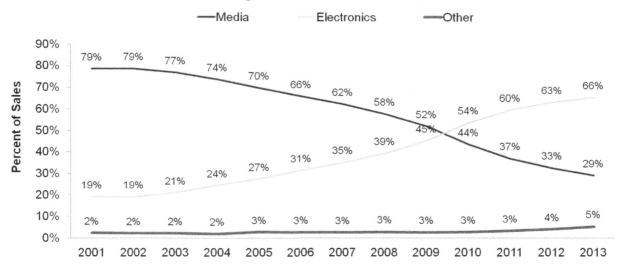

Figure 2.3 Source: Company Reports

This ongoing transformation to a general merchandise retailer, combined with Amazon's intense focus on cost efficiency and logistics, has sparked descriptions of Amazon as the 'Walmart of the Internet.' However, comparisons to another brick-and-mortar retailer, Costco, might be more apt, and specific initiatives of Amazon's are firmly rooted in the online space and draw no easy comparisons. We think all of these characterizations make sense for different reasons, and explain why in Figure 2.4.

Amazon is like ...	Amazon (AMZN)
Costco	Prime memberships, like warehouse club memberships, lead customers to devote more of their wallet share to Amazon. Amazon has also created a sense of trust with Prime customers, and many now assume that Amazon has the best price. Amazon's launch of Prime Pantry, where Prime members can pay a fixed amount for a certain-sized box, and then stuff whatever non-bulk sized CPG items they want into it, will enable Amazon to further compete for these stock-up trips. Previously, like Costco, Amazon relied on bulk-sized products to make its model work.
Walmart	Whereas Costco works hard to maximize value, Amazon and Walmart focus more on offering the broadest selection at the best price through logistics investments
Native to the Internet	Amazon Marketplace and Fulfillment by Amazon services are unique offerings, and ones with no easy comparison in brick-and-mortar retail

Figure 2.4

What makes Amazon so dangerous, however, is that all these descriptions of it are true. Amazon combines the characteristics of a category killer (low prices, deep assortment, and review-based knowledge) with the economies of scale and scope found at general merchandise retailers like Walmart, and supports both with powerful search tools and a great fulfillment system to help customers get exactly what they want. Such scope and scale advantages were part of Bezos' strategy to become an "electronic commerce destination." By grouping the product lines of multiple category-killers in one place, Amazon became "more relevant to more people."[14] This strategy paid off in Amazon's first fight against brick-and-mortar stores, when Amazon was able to reach more people at lower cost and at a greater lifetime value than media-focused Barnesandnoble.com and Borders.com as a result of Amazon's multi-category strategy. These results are seen in Figure 2.5, where Amazon consistently spent less than Barnes & Noble as measured by marketing spending relative to sales, yet attracted a greater percent (17.8%) of online customers, who spent more time and viewed more pages on Amazon's website.

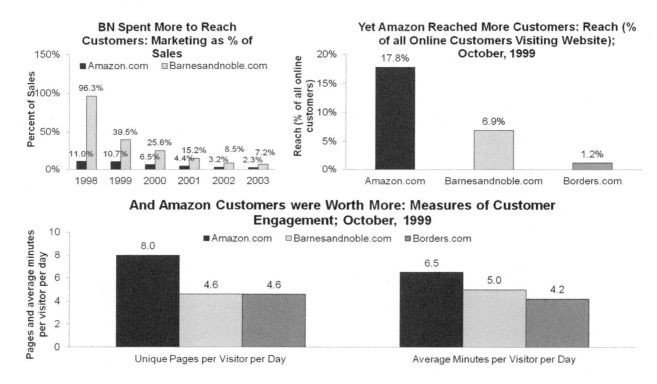

Figure 2.5 Source: Applegate, Linda, "Amazon.com: 1994-2000," HBS case number 9-801-194, Boston: Harvard Business School Publishing, 2002. Note: An etailer's 'reach' is defined as the percent of total online customers (online users who have bought anything from any online site) in a given period in a given geography that have purchased something from the specified etailer.

In the face of Amazon's key advantages in many, but not all, retail verticals, a host of arguments have arisen to defend brick-and-mortar stores on grounds that do not involve price or assortment. However, there are reasons to believe that Amazon will be able to invent itself around these arguments in favor of physical stores' enduring benefits, which we've summarized in Figure 2.6.

Brick-and-Mortar Advantage	Amazon Digital Replacement
Shopping Experience	Amazon's smartphone app lets customers enjoy the experience in-store but still purchase online. Amazon has learned lessons from Zappos about how to improve the online browsing experience, such as detailed photos of products from multiple angles. While still in its early stages and in limited geographies, Amazon's Lockers program delivers orders to a central, convenient location rather than to individual households. The logistics savings from this could be enough to fund free returns, making a try-before-you-buy program possible, and removing the need to go to a store to try on a dress or view a TV's image quality in person.
Purchase Immediacy	Amazon's rollout of same-day delivery partly eliminates this advantage.
Ease of Returns	Amazon's reverse logistics operations could become much more cost-effective and more consumer-friendly through Amazon Lockers.
Security of Purchase	Amazon Lockers cater to consumers who may not want expensive TVs sitting in front of their houses or in the entryways of their apartment buildings.
'Unbanked' Customers	Amazon Lockers could be outfitted with cash-accepting vending machine components that would facilitate a cash-on-demand delivery arrangement
Product issues (e.g. high weight, low price)	The logistics savings from Lockers or AmazonFresh memberships could be enough that items like pet food become a profitable, or at least not as costly, offering.

Figure 2.6

It may seem outlandish that Amazon Lockers (on which many of the arguments in Figure 2.6 depend) could provide many of the benefits of brick-and-mortar stores; indeed, the program has faced hurdles and both Staples and Radio Shack removed Amazon's Lockers from their stores. However, one should consider how well Amazon recreated the book superstore experience online before assuming that Amazon Lockers won't be able to replicate the store functions discussed in Figure 2.6. In the mid-90s, Barnes & Noble and Borders had become important mainstays in many of the communities where their stores were located. They hosted literary events such as author book signings, intimate music concerts, and lectures and seminars from experts. The two companies also tailored single-store inventories to local sales patterns.

A consummate technologist, Jeffrey Bezos sought to replicate a traditional bookstore digitally, as well as add new, compelling reasons to shop online. Amazon's book-focused early website provided hyperlinks to genres to mimic how aisles were divided in a traditional bookstore. To replicate the in-store reading experience, customers could digitally preview a book's table of contents and some excerpts. To create a community similar to what customers found in superstores, Amazon.com introduced discussion boards that provided places for customers to interact and build a community online. And while Amazon.com couldn't duplicate in-person book signings, they found ways to create new interactions with authors. For example, in one event customers could submit paragraphs to be included in the beginning of a new John Updike story,[15] in other events Amazon featured web interviews with authors.[16] Whereas the two book superstore chains could only personalize a store for an area, Amazon was able to personalize its website for every customer.

Amazon has proven adept at making it easy for customers to transition to online purchasing, and its Amazon Lockers program, while still new, could be enough to overcome many retailers' lingering brick-and-mortar advantages. If Amazon can come up with close enough and cost-efficient enough proxies for shopping in a brick-and-mortar environment, will there be any reasons left for customers to go to physical stores? And if customers cease going to stores, can brick-and-mortar retailers still serve them online? Because of Amazon's scope and scale in eCommerce, which we detail in the next section, we believe that the answer to this latter question is no, and for brick-and-mortar retailers to survive (at least those that can), they must find ways to continue to attract shoppers to their locations.

Why Can't Most Traditional Brick-and-Mortar Retailers Compete in eCommerce?

As discussed in the introduction, in the face of the Amazon threat, retailers at risk really have three broad strategic options. They can admit defeat, accept the "Wind Down" strategy, and prepare for a long process of gradually downsizing their operations while maintaining flexibility by avoiding long leases. Throughout this process, their goal will be to maximize the cash drawn out of the store assets for the benefit of investors. Or they can reimagine their stores and other aspects of their businesses to create and capture their most compelling values in the "Shrink and Transform the Format" strategy. These efforts may include dramatically altered store formats and/or changing deployments of in-store assets such as people, technology, and inventory (TIPS). Finally, in the "Enhance the Value of the Box" strategy, retailers can try to create more compelling omnichannel experiences by building additional defenses for their largely safe brick-and-mortar stores while improving their online experience.

A fourth option is to attempt to compete head-to-head with Amazon in eCommerce. However, with the exception of office supply retailers that have legacy businesses in this space, the advantages of Amazon's scope and scale should dissuade most retailers from this route, and we discuss it only briefly as so few brick-and-mortar retailers have the ability to pursue it. Comparing Amazon's online fulfillment distribution center locations to brick-and-mortar retailers' in Figure 2.7, we see the advantages of Amazon's scale. Amazon's 60-plus fulfillment centers across the country drive down shipping cost and delivery time, while most brick-and-mortar retailers often have only one or two distribution centers capable of fulfilling online orders, and only a handful of distribution centers in total.

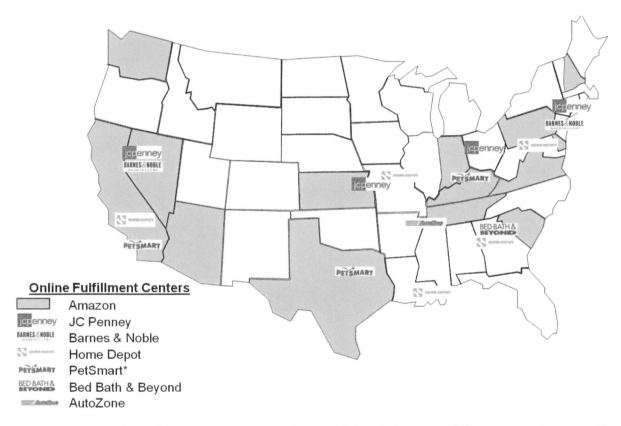

Online Fulfillment Centers

	Amazon
JC Penney	JC Penney
BARNES & NOBLE	Barnes & Noble
Home Depot	Home Depot
PETSMART	PetSmart*
BED BATH & BEYOND	Bed Bath & Beyond
AutoZone	AutoZone

Figure 2.7 Source: Consolidated. Note: Amazon has multiple DCs in many of these states. *PetSmart's California and Kentucky fulfillment centers are owned and run by eBay Enterprise.

The major exceptions are Office Depot, which has now completed renovations across its distribution centers (DCs) to make each one capable of handling single-item, consumer-driven, online orders; Staples, which is in the process of doing the same; and Best Buy, which is converting its 24 DCs to handle online fulfillment. Walmart, while it has more than 130 DCs across the US, currently only has three dedicated to eCommerce.

Of course, retailers could fulfill orders out of their stores through initiatives like buy-online-pick-up-in-store (BOPIS) and ship-from-store (SFS), but these are more short-term solutions than lasting advantages. BOPIS generates trips to stores and saves customers delivery fees, both when the order is picked in-store and also when the order must be shipped by a third party as "shipping to a commercial location is cheaper than a residential address."[17] SFS programs, such as those used by Nordstrom's and Macy's, increase inventory turnover and in so doing help retailers both free up working capital and reduce markdowns. SFS also helps retailers speed up delivery and save on zone charges (many shippers charge extra fees, or zone charges, if a package crosses a specified boundary or if a package must travel a long distance) that their relatively sparse distribution center shipping networks would otherwise incur.

Neither program, however, is an ideal solution or a long-term competitive advantage against Amazon. The store trips generated by BOPIS may give the brick-and-mortar retailer an opportunity for add-on sales, but the retailer's ability here is likely diminished, and they have little chance, if any, of conducting an upsell. BOPIS service desk employees are not trained in every department of the store, and won't be able to give all customers the targeted and relevant advice that staff in the store's departments are versed in. The targeted purchasing behavior of BOPIS customers also likely means that they just want to get in and out of the store, not be talked to by a sales associate; after all, they've already bought their main purchase.

While SFS programs may utilize unproductive store assets and be more cost-effective for brick-and-mortar retailers, they take customer trips out of the store entirely and so suffer from the same disadvantages as BOPIS programs. Long-term, as Amazon continues its fulfillment center expansion, it will drive down its cost of delivery to the point where any shipping cost or delivery time advantage from BOPIS or SFS is negligible. Amazon's fulfillment centers, designed for rapid and efficient each-picking and packaging at scale will likely have a lower overall cost than inefficient retail stores where pickers often wander the spacious store aisles looking for items. If the online threat really does boil down to price-competition and delivery time, BOPIS and SFS buy time for brick-and-mortar retailers but don't change the fundamentals and, long-term, are not a sufficient defense.

Brick-and-mortar retailers do have access to third-party services that enable them to gain efficiencies in online fulfillment. eBay Enterprise (formerly GSI Commerce) not only creates and manages end-to-end online websites for brick-and-mortar retailers, but also runs its own fulfillment and customer service centers for these online retailers. GSI, however, is not at Amazon's scale, with only six DCs compared to Amazon's expanding multitude in the US. Indeed, two of the DCs shown in Figure 2.7 as PetSmart's are in reality GSI Commerce (eBay Enterprise) fulfillment centers.

Kynetic (also formerly GSI Commerce, but was carved out of eBay's acquisition) runs a competing Prime-type service called Shoprunner for many brick-and-mortar and online retailers. However, the program is much weaker than Prime. Shoprunner, which continues to cost $79 per year, has an assortment that's limited to its member stores versus Amazon's open Marketplace. Most importantly, however, rather than offer a superior logistics operation like Amazon, ShopRunner merely pushes the cost and responsibility for two-day shipping on to its retail partners,[18] who are often ill-suited to perform the task.

In addition to its great scale, Amazon's supply chain is also highly-flexible. The company is able to take an online order and fulfill it in any number of ways through its own systems or through those of third parties. The number of paths Amazon has to receive and fulfill orders is shown in Figure 2.8.

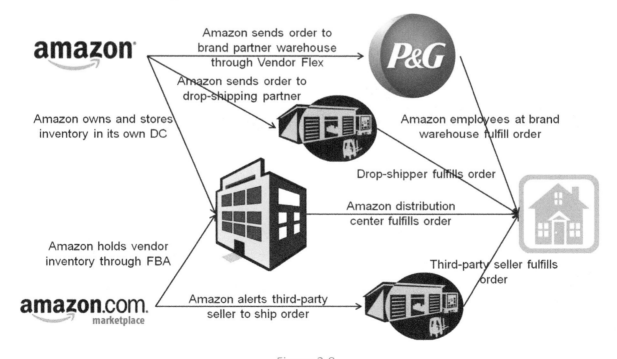

Figure 2.8

In fact, Amazon's online retail buying and logistics operations are superior in almost every respect. The online sales operations of brick-and-mortar retailers and Amazon are contrasted in Figure 2.9.

Cost of Online Sales – Brick & Mortar Retailers vs. Amazon

Category	Advantage	Brick & Mortar (B&M)	Amazon (AMZN)
Cost of Goods	B&M	Individual big box retailers' category shares range from 20% to 35%, often surpassing online retail's entire channel share	Shares for all online retail as a channel generally range from 2%-10% across categories
Factory Gate Pricing/Direct Supplier Pick-up	AMZN	Suppliers largely deliver to retailer distribution centers	Amazon freight network picks up goods directly from suppliers Under Vendor Flex, Amazon even embeds at suppliers' mixing centers
Inventory Control	AMZN	Online and store inventories held separately, DCs designed to deliver to stores	Efficient DC inventory distribution
Outbound Fulfillment	AMZN	Limited DC availability, most B&M retailers have 3-4 DCs capable of online fulfillment whereas Amazon has multiples of ten Ship-from-store is a high labor cost model compared to a distribution center	Lots of DCs, many located close to major population centers using Zone 0-1 shipping Better pricing from third-party shippers due to volume Programs like Subscribe & Save allow Amazon to elect the most cost-effective shipping method

Figure 2.9 Source: Author analysis and McKinsey Research

Even for those retailers with capable online fulfillment operations, challenges exist. Amazon increasingly serves as the first point of consideration for online product research and purchase,[19] and the company's technology base continues to grow. In addition to its fulfillment infrastructure, Amazon has invested significantly in customer-facing systems for search, personalization, and ease of ordering. In 1999-2000 alone, the company invested almost 10% of its sales on product development to further personalize customers' online stores.[20] It has used some features to build a moat against the online arms of the superstores and other eCommerce retailers. One example is Amazon One-Click, which gives Amazon the patented and exclusive ability to enable customers to use predefined payment and shipping information to purchase an order with just a click. The same scale and scope advantages that positioned Amazon well against brick-and-mortar book retailers get stronger by the day.

As Amazon evolves, it is becoming a platform for other retailers and brands to sell their wares. The advantages that Amazon brandishes in the current environment become amplified as they move to a platform business. As we will show later in this chapter, Amazon Marketplace, Fulfillment by Amazon, and Amazon Prime create an ecosystem with synergistic affects that make it difficult for many retailers to compete. It is instructive to compare brick-and-mortar retailers, Amazon, and a platform business (i.e. an evolved Amazon) in: how they create value; the key decisions that each are required to make; and the risks that are inherent in each type of business.

Figure 2.10 lays out the differences between these business model types along these three dimensions. The key point to take away from this exhibit is that the brick-and-mortar business is by far the most costly creator of value to consumers, with many more complex decisions to be made. Brick-and-mortar retailers also have exposure to a great deal more risk from many components of the physical retail store business structure. [It is important to note that consumers do not look under the hood to understand or appreciate the functioning of a retail organization. These are matters that are irrelevant to them. They are solely looking for a good experience: how the machine works or how retailers think about these issues is of no importance to them. There is no consumer appreciation for or willingness to pay for any difficulty or cost derived from differences in business models. Therefore, these additional risks and costs are not something consumers can be expected to pay for.]

A few examples will help to illustrate these points. Let's say that a retailer is in the women's fashion shoe business. With limited store shelf and warehouse space, a brick-and-mortar retailer cannot carry all shoe styles that are available from the many vendors that exist in this space. They have to curate the selection that they will carry. This is done by buyers who have been trained and have experience in the vicissitudes of fashion footwear. Inventory is purchased based on the expertise (guesses?) of the expert shoe buyers. Getting this decision right is critical to maximize sales and minimize markdowns. The retailer pays handsomely for this expertise and must support its buyers with significant amounts of historical data to support the decision making required not only for the overall buy made by the buyer but also for the allocation of the appropriate quantity of each product by store (which is usually done by another employee, the allocation manager for this category.) In the end though, the forecasts of the buyers and allocation managers tend to have significant error causing inventory imbalances at each store leading to out of stocks in some stores and markdowns in others. There is enormous risk, cost, and complexity involved in this seemingly straightforward buying example.

In the Amazon world this is much different. Amazon does not curate the selection. The company's buyers generally try to create the most comprehensive list of women's fashion footwear available to display to the consumer. Since store space is not a limiting factor, Amazon can offer tens of thousands of different styles in the widest available set of sizes. The buyers thus require much less training and experience in the category since they do not need to determine what the hot shoe of the season will be. There is also a much lower risk of inventory mismatch. Amazon does not need to pre-position inventory in individual stores and thus can be inventory light. The consumer can buy the same shoe from either retailer (likely at a much lower price at Amazon) but in the background, Amazon has a far simpler, more efficient set of processes that significantly reduce the costs and risks to the company. The simplicity, risk mitigation, and cost reduction are even greater when Amazon acts as a platform. When a third party retailer places these same shoes on the Amazon Marketplace, Amazon owns no inventory and no buying staff. Amazon acts as the enabler of the transaction for the retailer and receives a fee for its service without any of the attendant costs or risks!

Similar complexity, cost, and risk asymmetries exist in other key areas of retail. For example, Amazon does not have to contend with the difficult, risky, and expensive decisions involved in selecting a retail store location. Retailers have highly paid experienced personnel who do this work in their organizations. Yet, poor locations plague every retailer. The forecasting process for new stores is not a perfect science. Brick-and-mortar retailers are thus faced with significant risk related to an illiquid asset that is subject to the vagaries of consumer behavior. (Amazon does have to decide where to place distribution centers much like other retailers do but these are much more scientific endeavors. The key determinants in these decisions do not have to do with the vagaries of consumer behavior but rather with things like adequacy of the road network and traffic which are usually pretty well defined parameters.)

Another example will be helpful to understand the essence of Figure 2.10 and to further highlight the vast differences between these models. Amazon does not have to bother with labor forecasts for stores since it has none. Brick-and-mortar retailers however have a very tricky problem to solve in this regard. If you have too few people available in a retail location when customers are present it is entirely possible that you will lose sales either because customers cannot find what they need or because they abandon their shopping carts because they do not wish to wait in long lines. If you work too hard on the other side of this problem and increase labor hours too much you wind up with costly, inefficient use of personnel. You have too many people on hand for the sales being generated. Predicting sales not only for a given day of the week but for a 4 or 8 hour shift during that day is hard. Doing this a week or more before the fact is almost impossible. Factors like weather or promotional events can wreak havoc on even the best researched and calculated forecast of labor needs. The Amazon and platform business models have none of the risk or cost associated with this problem and no need for all of those store managers and employees.

Finally, eCommerce businesses are attractive places for technologists. Amazon hires an abundance of people who are expert at technology because they see Amazon as being on the cutting edge of innovation. These innovators allow Amazon to constantly improve its already industry leading customer experience. This is in sharp contrast to most brick-and-mortar retailers who have a very difficult time hiring people with strong technology backgrounds. When Walmart decided to revamp its eCommerce business, it had to decouple it from the main business in Bentonville, Arkansas and move it to the San Francisco area in order to attract the right talent. Even with this change in location, it struggled mightily to attract talented technology innovators to the company because the company culture was centered on retailing and not technological innovation. Retailers do not have a reputation for being technology pioneers and are thus at a significant disadvantage not just to Amazon but even eCommerce startups in attracting top technology talent that can drive their eCommerce and other technology innovations.

As we have explained earlier, eCommerce businesses live in an asset light world that is very nimble while brick-and-mortar players are in asset intensive businesses where change can take significant amounts of time, management attention, and money. As you think about the four key assets that retailers need to manage (people, inventory, space, and technology) you begin to realize the difficulties encountered when competing against eCommerce. But as you further explore these different models you realize that the way they create value, the types of talent that they require, and the level of risk that they take on is fundamentally different as well. eCommerce businesses are formidable competitors not solely because they are more capital efficient but because they can rapidly experiment and evolve without adding significant risk (e.g. by entering new categories where they may not currently have expertise). Brick-and-mortar retailers, on the other hand, need to weigh very closely how they will create value, the talent that will be required, and the significant additional real estate, inventory, and labor risk that they will take on when they enter new realms. The advantages in flexibility and nimbleness in the eCommerce and platform models are often overwhelming.

	Traditional Retailer	Internet Retailer	eComm Platform/Enabler
How They Create Value	▪ Break bulk ▪ Reduce transport costs for customers (e.g. act as one-stop-shop) ▪ Create showroom and selling point for brands ▪ Provide services to customers for which they are willing to pay ▪ Provide channel for convenience and impulse buying	▪ Lower operating costs than B&M (people, occupancy, depreciation) ▪ Lower working capital than B&M (consolidated inventory + payment days) ▪ Efficient transport to end consumer ▪ Lowest prices ▪ Widest assortment for customers ▪ Create place for small brands to thrive	▪ Become first point of consideration (i.e. drive traffic to site) ▪ Charge vendors for use of platform ▪ Keep platform costs low while continuing to develop capabilities ▪ Eliminate risk: weather, obsolescence, execution, and real estate
Key Decisions	▪ Format design ▪ Store location and network design ▪ Determination of curated assortment ▪ Negotiation of buys and determination of buy volumes ▪ Determination of pricing ▪ Allocation of buys to stores ▪ Scheduling of store personnel ▪ Warehouse locations ▪ Transportation infrastructure ▪ Hiring and development of buyers ▪ Hiring and development of store operations personnel	▪ Fulfillment center locations ▪ Shipping partners (e.g. UPS vs. USPS vs. FedEx) ▪ Negotiation of buys ▪ Determination of pricing ▪ Fulfillment center technology development and infrastructure ▪ Hiring of key management for intellectual property development (e.g. CRM algorithm developers, machine learning experts)	▪ Platform technology ▪ Partner acquisition ▪ Hiring of relationship managers for platform customers ▪ Hiring of key management for intellectual property development (e.g. CRM algorithm developers, machine learning experts)
Risks Inherent in Model	▪ Real estate ▪ Missed sales from out of stocks ▪ Inventory obsolescence (perishability/fashion as well as customer traffic issues) ▪ Weather ▪ Theft and robbery ▪ Execution: store locations as multiple points of failure and under/over allocation of store personnel	▪ Fulfillment center location ▪ Inventory obsolescence (but significantly reduced from B&M) ▪ Technology obsolescence ▪ Hacking of site ▪ Loss of consumer appeal ▪ Missed sales from out of stocks (but significantly reduced from B&M)	▪ Technology obsolescence ▪ Loss of consumer appeal ▪ Hacking of site

Figure 2.10

Considering the purchase funnel customers go through and how they experience each channel further defines the differences between these retail models. Aside from circulars, in-store product displays, some broad market, event driven advertising like back-to-school campaigns, and suggestions from store employees, brick-and-mortar stores largely cede Discovery to national brands or rely on commodities that customers already know they need. eCommerce operators, by contrast, use marketing emails, digital circulars, online clubs, flash sales, and, most importantly, data-driven product ads (based on past customer history and the purchases of similar customers) to stimulate purchases from potential customers. Hybrid, omnichannel retailers can blend both realms, issuing emailed invitations to workshops, such as banks do with their in-branch seminars, and using store and online environments to suggest product uses, such as merging online education with in-store displays.

In the Familiarity and Consideration stages, brick-and-mortar stores can capture a purchase by virtue of already having the customer in the store, by providing products for customers to try, and through the skillful active selling of store associates. Online retailers can use search engine optimization and other forms of digital advertising to attract customers' interest, and they also rely on their reputations for price and selection beyond what a brick-and-mortar store can offer. The product reviews hosted on online retailers' sites are also an important part of this phase as customers seek out information on their potential purchase. Omnichannel retailers, for their part, actively encourage showrooming and sampling, paired with online education and purchase capabilities. Warby Parker and Bonobos, for example, have opened small boutiques across the US that don't sell product in the store, but rather provide customers the opportunity to get comfortable with the products they are ordering before having them shipped.

In the Purchase phase, the sale is really the retailer's to lose. Brick-and-mortar stores can lose sales due to time-consuming checkout lines, whereas online retailers can lose sales if shipping is either too expensive or will take too long. Omnichannel retailers, with ship-to-store policies, can get over the shipping hurdles that strike online retailers. Similar constraints apply to after-sales service, where brick-and-mortar and omnichannel retailers can easily accept, repair, and replace returns or deal with other customer issues through in-store services, but customers face a number of hurdles in dealing with an online retailer after purchase.

Brick-and-mortar retailers are not eCommerce natives, and mostly lack the orientation and skill set that has made Amazon so successful. Over the last two decades, this has left most brick-and-mortar retailers too far behind to catch up. Amazon has compounded its advantage with two interlinked and mutually reinforcing initiatives, Marketplace and Prime, that are new and disruptive forces that together will further increase pressure on brick-and-mortar stores.[i]

Amazon Marketplace

Every retailer, both brick-and-mortar and online, should consider the possibility that Amazon Marketplace may be an end-run around the very concept of retail itself. While Marketplace began as a way to reinforce Amazon's guiding principles of selection and price, today it offers a turn-key online retail solution available to all, and allows Amazon to strengthen its advantages over brick-and-mortar retailers with third-party vendors helping to pick up the tab.

Third-party sellers are an incredibly important part of Amazon's business. They are responsible for many of the over 238 million items available through the Amazon website. By opening their website to third-parties, ranging from individuals to large companies, Amazon gained access to categories they had neither the experience nor the resources to enter themselves, and to different price points, particularly in used goods as Amazon found itself competing against other online participants like eBay in the early 2000's.[21]

In its early days, Amazon relegated its third-party sellers to separate areas of the Amazon website that were only reached if customers clicked on the relevant tab, such as for auctions, zShops (Amazon's original retail pages for its third-party sellers), and partner retailer relationships as with living.com and pets.com. For example, Amazon's books were sold under the 'Books' tab, but used books, exclusively sold by third parties at the time, were sold under the

---

[i] Amazon would likely also call Amazon Web Services transformational, but while it provides support for Amazon's retail business, we don't believe it to be essential or necessarily revolutionary to retail. The service began as a way to assist manufacturers interested in reaching Amazon's marketplace by providing full-featured cloud computing services, but Amazon Web Services now has expanded to many firms that are not part of its retail supply chain, providing "elastic information technology infrastructure services" flexibly as required. While this offering is now not closely related to the core retail business, the continued ability of Amazon to find other companies to subsidize its growing infrastructure gives it scale in information technology, which is core to its business.[i] For instance, AWS powers Amazon's Prime and media services, and improves Amazon's processing abilities and customers' web experience. Source: Deighton, John and Kornfeld, Leora, "Amazon, Apple, Facebook, and Google," HBS No. 9-513-060, Boston: Harvard Business School Publishing, 2013.

zShops tab.[22] Given its focus on customer-centricity and the importance Amazon assigned to its brand and customer relationships, the company wanted to make clear that these third party products were not fulfilled by Amazon in the event that outside vendors could not match Amazon's high standards in picking and shipping times and after-sales service.

However, by 2000, Amazon had realized that what third-party sellers really wanted was access to its customers, and the tab-segregated marketplace was not fulfilling the goal of introducing users to other product offerings. The company then moved to the 'Single-Store strategy,' which would display third-party and Amazon offerings alongside each other on product detail pages. Now, when customers searched for a product on Amazon, they'd be taken to a single unified listing that featured all the available options: new and used product sold by Amazon and third-party sellers. Describing the Single-Store strategy, Bezos explained, "One of the keys to making this work is to try to get our economics to the point where we are agnostic about whether customers buy from us or from a third party. In the end, if we satisfy our customers and partners, they'll remain loyal to us, and we should have no angst about cannibalizing our own business ... Our primary concern is the customer experience, not short-term economics."[23] The move to a Single-Store strategy increased the benefit of Amazon's marketplace to third-party sellers, and third-party sellers responded by signing up on Amazon's marketplace in droves. Amazon now has more than two million third-party sellers on its site, who collectively are responsible for around 40% of Amazon's unit sales and half of total sales.[24] Third party sales are growing much faster than Amazon's owned and operated sales (as shown in Figure 2.11), and Amazon is increasingly looking more like a platform than a retailer.

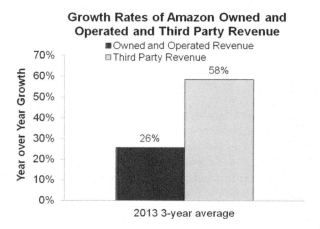

Figure 2.11 Source: Company Reports

Whereas the gross margins on Amazon's owned and operated sales look like those of a traditional retailer, the gross margins on its third-party sales are those of a technology company, a full 100%. Amazon can use these third-party fees to subsidize its owned-and-operated retail, furthering its price advantage relative to traditional brick-and-mortar stores. Third-party sellers have also helped Amazon get around many external constraints. Brands that refuse to sell to or on Amazon often find their products on Amazon's site sold through third parties. Brands that vigorously enforce minimum pricing on traditional retailers have a hard time corralling the plethora of small resellers on Amazon, making it possible for Amazon, through these third-parties, to offer lower prices than any other retailer. Indeed, the competition between third-party sellers (as well as between third-party sellers and Amazon) results in the lowest prices for Amazon's customers. Third-party sellers also offer a back-up supply of inventory. If Amazon is out of inventory on a product, customers can always turn to a third-party seller to fulfill their order.

A large concern in introducing the single-store strategy was the possibility of brand dilution from third parties unable to satisfy Amazon customers' high expectations of rapid delivery and great service. To help third party sellers overcome these challenges, Amazon opened up its own delivery infrastructure. In 2006, Amazon introduced "Fulfillment by Amazon," (FBA) a program that, for a fee, stocks third-party vendors' inventory and fulfills orders placed both on Amazon's site and on third-party vendors' separate online stores. When a third-party vendor opts to use FBA, they also gain access to all of Amazon's high-spending Prime users. Amazon benefits from higher service-based margins and also through greater leverage of its distribution system. Adding volume allows Amazon to build more distribution centers, which decreases shipping cost and delivery time and strengthens Amazon's online logistics superiority over brick-and-mortar chains.

Despite the benefits Amazon gains from hosting third-party sellers as a platform, it appears to be alienating at least a few of them. Many have made allegations that Amazon is using Marketplace as its personal lab, and that it eventually takes over third party sellers' best-selling products directly.[25] Such may be the lot of independent resellers of goods. Amazon, for its part, appears to be moving beyond them directly to the product source.

Amazon is pushing for brands to join its marketplace and use FBA services. The company introduced "Amazon Pages" in 2012, which allows brands to set up their own custom Amazon destinations (e.g. www.amazon.com/brandname) and pairs this with marketing and analytics tools to help brands increase sales.[26] The targets for these services are smaller brands, which can outperform large brands on Amazon's website. Smaller brands do particularly well at Amazon. For example, niche toothbrush brands Radius Totz and Dr. Collins Perio are among the top five purchased manual toothbrushes at Amazon, while Colgate and Procter & Gamble brands rule brick-and-mortar stores.[27]

Larger brands also find value in selling direct to consumers; they just do it without using Amazon's platform. P&G sells products through its own e-store, QR code shopping walls, pop-up locations, and other channels.[28] The benefits of selling direct-to-consumer are significant: the ability to set final price in the market (especially since many brands complain about third parties undercutting their recommended prices online due to supply chain leaks[29]), the ability to communicate directly with customers asking product questions, and better data on real-time product sales to feed demand forecasting, tailor promotions, and inform product development.

Amazon is not writing these larger brands off its platform, however. While not Marketplace vendors, P&G and other CPG companies have deepened their ties with Amazon. Amazon's Vendor Flex program, which has counted P&G as a partner for the past three years, is one more step towards closer partnerships with large brands. Under Vendor Flex, Amazon receives pallets of goods at small, Amazon-run fulfillment centers located inside brands' warehouses. When Amazon receives an order, "Amazon employees then package, label, and ship the items directly to the people who ordered them."[30] Amazon gets to extend its fulfillment network by using brands' warehouses: reducing its fulfillment costs (and end-customer prices) and speeding up delivery. The reduction in fulfillment costs helps Amazon move into household products, a category where most items' sizes and shipping costs relative to their low prices have precluded online retail, and a category in which only 2% of goods are bought online.[31] This 'just-in-time fulfillment' from within brands' own warehouses also reduces inventory in Amazon's supply chain.

P&G, for its part, is spared the costs of hauling products to Amazon's regional distribution centers and gains a prominent partner to help it grow its online sales. Online retail of household staples is a focus for consumer goods companies as the channel is growing rapidly and offers a new way to keep customers and protect share. One example of this is Amazon's "Subscribe & Save" program, through which customers can elect to receive a specific item on a periodic basis, thus locking them into specific brands.[32]

As Amazon develops deeper partnerships with small and major brands alike, it's possible that, in some far away future state, it can cut out other retailers entirely. One argument for retailers' endurance has been that they provide important value-added services, such as logistics ability, customer aggregation, and marketing. However, Amazon is coming to the point where it can provide all of these in a turn-key, automated system that reaches beyond Amazon to manage a brand's entire fulfillment and online presence. In effect, Amazon is handing the keys to a brand's online retail business directly to the brand itself. Brands, especially those smaller brands lacking the clout to gain presence in physical store aisles, may increasingly choose to go direct instead. While Alice.com, which sought to offer a similar service to major home good brands like P&G, recently went bankrupt, Amazon's focus on smaller brands, its far greater size, and its close partnerships with large brands, will likely help it succeed where Alice.com failed.

Amazon Prime

While Marketplace has the potential to help small brands go direct to customers, Amazon Prime is ensuring that high-spending online customers will be there to greet them. For $99 per year, Amazon Prime provides customers not only with free two-day shipping on Prime-eligible products at Amazon, but also with a Netflix-style service for movies and TV shows, and free book rentals from the Kindle store.

The program is, in many ways, similar to membership-warehouse stores like Costco. Like Costco members, Amazon Prime members tend to be more affluent than the average Amazon customer (who is already more affluent than the average American consumer), with 49% of Prime customers having incomes above $60,000 compared to 46% of regular Amazon customers, as shown in Figure 2.12.

Figure 2.12 Source: Pace, Matt, "Attention Retailers: Amazon Prime Members are Located in Aisle 5," Compete Pulse, April 17, 2013, available at https://blog.compete.com/2013/04/17/attention-retailers-amazon-prime-members-are-located-in-aisle-5/.

With similar demographics and the same value-pack merchandising, Amazon Prime probably poses a larger immediate threat to warehouse clubs than supercenters. However, its effects are ones that every retailer, both brick-and-mortar and Amazon's online competitors, should be worried about. Analysts estimate that Prime customers spend almost 150% more at Amazon after they become Prime customers than they did before.[33] Customers' desire to "get their money back" on their membership fee is one reason for this growth. More importantly, however, the Prime membership positions Amazon as a trusted source, and makes it the first point of consideration for many Prime subscribers. From that point, most take it for granted that Amazon's prices are competitive, and so many Prime subscribers don't bother price-shopping, despite how easy it is to compare prices online.[34] According to one member of the original team that developed Prime, the program was "really about changing people's mentality so they wouldn't shop anywhere else."[35] Possibly motivated by their new access to fast, free shipping, Prime customers' increased shopping isn't confined to their traditional categories, but takes place over more categories, often replacing convenience occasions for things like "batteries and coffee beans"[36] that help drive trips to traditional retailers. Describing the program, Robbie Schwietzer, vice-president of Amazon Prime said, "In all my years here, I don't remember anything that has been as successful at getting customers to shop in new product lines."[37]

All current signs point to Prime's continued success as well. The program has experienced rapid growth, from 4 million subscribers in the fall of 2011, to around 7 million subscribers in early 2012, to 10 million members in early 2013,[38] to over 20 million globally at the end of 2013.[39] The program looks to be accelerating: Amazon has reported that millions signed up for the service over its 2013 third quarter alone, and that more than a million members signed up in the third week of December 2013.[40] The company is heavily promoting the service, offering free trials to anyone buying a Kindle and offering half-priced memberships to students and mothers, and reports that retention in the service is "very good."[41]

Amazon generates significant incremental profit from its Prime program and is fully committed to expanding Prime. While offering free shipping and digital media to customers is expensive, Amazon makes enough gross profit off of incremental sales to more than cover the cost. Figure 2.13 explains this added profit for a typical Prime customer, with the incremental membership fee and product revenue greater than the added COGs, shipping costs, and media costs.

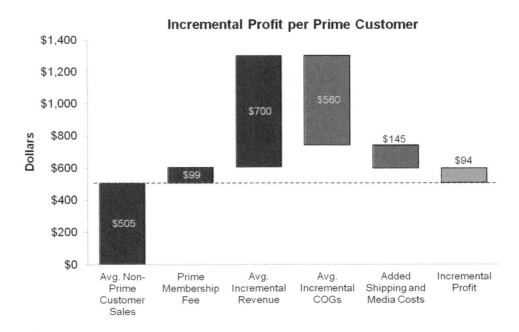

Figure 2.13 Source: Conversation with RJ Hottovy, Morningstar, December, 2014. Note: Assumed full-priced Prime subscription, no discounts given for students or moms.

And while one could think that the end of minimum order values to qualify for free shipping would mean that Prime members would disaggregate their baskets and begin buying only one item at a time whenever the urge struck, and consequently drive up shipping costs, data from *Compete* shows that this has not happened. Instead, Prime members "actually purchase 11% more items per order than non-Prime shoppers" while the average order value is 17% less for Prime members.[42] This data points to Prime members using the program exactly as Amazon appears to have intended: a replacement for those store trips meant to refill low-priced paper towels or laundry detergent. Low-priced items that previously did not make sense for Amazon shoppers to order online do get ordered under Prime, and are combined with other purchases. Prime may have worked too well, as Amazon now finds itself struggling with the costs of quick shipping on an expanded assortment, and has even gone so far as to offer Prime members $1 video rental coupons if they choose slower shipping.

Prime also isn't a service that's easily copied. Amazon can offer two-day delivery because it owns its fulfillment network and has achieved a scale and scope where it has located distribution centers close to population areas. With Amazon ready to begin collecting sales tax, the company has free rein to locate fulfillment centers closer to customers. This will reduce both shipping cost and shipping time. By way of comparison, most brick-and-mortar retailers use only one or two distribution centers to fulfill online orders (see Figure 2.7).

Independently, both Marketplace and Prime are dangerous for every other retailer. But, together with Amazon's Kindle hardware business, Marketplace and Prime form a re-enforcing cycle that will continue to grow. Amazon is widely-believed to sell its Kindle tablets at a loss and to make up the balance on media sales. This encourages tablet shoppers to buy Kindles. Amazon also introduces these tablet users to Prime with a free trial. The tablets are much more useful with the Prime media offerings, and so customers choose to continue the service (Morningstar believes Prime membership ramped sharply higher when the Kindle Fire, with its ability to watch movies and TV shows, was introduced). Data from Cowen and Company confirms this behavior, with their ongoing survey revealing that Kindle Fire ownership was at 36% for Prime members in February 2013, while only 13% of the survey's general population owned a Kindle Fire.[43] Prime members also get free shipping, and end up spending more at Amazon because of it. As more customers sign up for Prime, more vendors are inspired to join Amazon's FBA service to gain access to high-spending Prime members who concentrate their shopping at Amazon. With more products eligible for Prime, more customers want to become Prime subscribers. With additional Prime revenues, Amazon can invest more in content for its Prime media offerings. This dynamic is pictured in Figure 2.14.

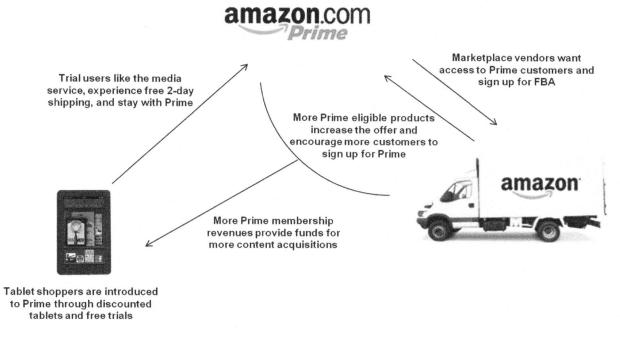

Figure 2.14

What Do Marketplace and Prime Mean for Brick-and-Mortar Retailers?

Could Amazon, a company with North American sales one-tenth the size of Walmart's, really impact these retailers? We'll ignore Amazon's business in grocery, and treat Amazon as just a general merchandise, electronics, and media retailer. Let's look at what it might take to cut 100 bps of same-store sales off of every retailer in our sample on average (save Safeway), a number which would drive some of the retailers in our ROIC charts perilously close to the cash-flow negative threshold. In 2012, US sales from brick-and-mortar retailers of this type (so excluding food service, grocery, motor vehicle dealers, gasoline sales, and non-store retailers) were $1.94 trillion. Amazon would have to remove $19.4 billion (1% of $1.94 trillion) from the brick-and-mortar channel, assuming an overall flat sales environment, to remove 1% of sales from brick-and-mortar retailers. While obviously a huge number, and one that would make Amazon half again as large as it is today in North America, it can be reached if Amazon signs up only 28 million more US Prime members. This assumes that Prime membership continues to generate $700 more in incremental sales from new members. 28 million new members constitutes an almost 150% increase over Prime's estimated 18.75 million US members at the end of the second quarter of 2014,[44] to a user base of 47 million members. However, Prime appears to have grown at least 20% globally in the third quarter of 2013 alone, and doubling its estimated worldwide membership base in 2013. In comparison, Costco has an estimated 51 million members in the United States[45] and Netflix reported 35 million total US subscribers in its third quarter of 2013,[46] but is growing at a rate closer to 20% annually rather than 20% quarterly. If US Prime membership can sustain its Q3 2013 growth of 20% per quarter, from a base of 18.75 million US members, Amazon could add 28 million new members in just 5 quarters, as depicted in Figure 2.15. A recent estimate of 30 million to 40 million US Prime subscribers as of September, 2014 suggests that Amazon is well along this path.[47]

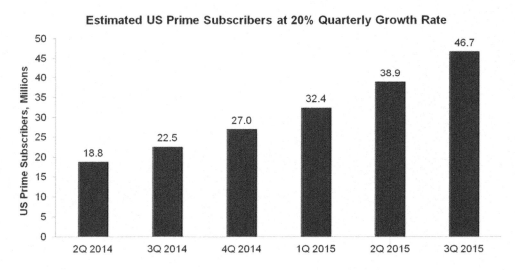

Figure 2.15 Source: Author Calculations.

There are also reasons to think that this scenario may be conservative. Amazon could get to this point faster if it restricts sharing of Prime accounts, as Netflix has done,[48] and forces second, third, fourth, or fifth users of Prime accounts to purchase their own memberships. Alternatively, Amazon could lower the price of Prime memberships to encourage user growth. While Amazon has recently raised the price of Prime membership to reflect increased "fuel and transportation costs,"[49] this was also done in the context of strong Prime subscriber growth. With estimates of Prime's incremental profit ranging from $78 to $133, in the event that membership growth slows down, Amazon could conceivably reduce the cost of Prime memberships in the future and still end up ahead.

Prime members may also come to buy more than an incremental $700 from Amazon. John Replogle, President and CEO of Seventh Generation, believes that consumers themselves are changing, and that fewer people want the traditional suburban experience of hauling bulky consumer products in their cars. As he describes today's, and increasingly the future's, consumer, "it tends to be young and well-educated ... Their shopping behavior is shifting increasingly to online and in urban centers."[50] If Amazon's prices on household staples become more competitive as a result of Vendor Flex and other assortment-extending Marketplace initiatives, and if Prime members increasingly value the convenience of buying household goods from Amazon through new programs like Prime Pantry, incremental sales per Prime member could increase from its present level. This would reduce the number of Prime members Amazon needs to sign up to take away an incremental one percent of the retail market from its brick-and-mortar competitors.

Apart from any efforts by Amazon, trips to online retailers and trips to brick-and-mortar retailers have different follow-on effects. Online retailers like Amazon, with sophisticated search technology, make it easy for a consumer to buy the specific item he or she is looking for, but brick-and-mortar stores generally do a better job of introducing the consumer to new products and rounding out a basket. Consider how much of brick-and-mortar retailing has been about the art of balancing out a customer's needs and wants, and how that affects most every aspect of a retailer's operations, from store layouts, to merchandising, to promotion. PetSmart, for instance, draws customers into their stores with routine purchases and services like dog food and grooming, located deep within the store. A large part of the business model rests on customers also picking up a high-margin dog toy while they are there. Or consider Walmart's supercenters, which offer grocery products that customers need at a low-margin, in the hope that Walmart can also sell them a higher-margin want, like a new shirt.

An example from Oliver Wyman demonstrates how the online retail model can drastically alter customer purchasing behavior to the detriment of this traditional need-want business model. Purchasers of a particular household item checked out with only 1.3 items ($45) on average in their online basket, while purchasers of the same item at brick-

and-mortar retailers had 4.8 items ($103) in their shopping cart.[51] If we assume that a customer who now buys their coffee and paper towels on Amazon no longer makes impulse purchases in the candy and magazine racks at the supermarket or that a customer who buys a TV on Amazon is no longer being upsold with audio upgrades like speakers and cables, the impact of a growing online market on brick-and-mortar retailers could be much more severe. Using the dollar value basket size numbers in the Oliver Wyman example above, Amazon would need to increase its sales only $8.2 billion to take $18.8 billion out of the brick-and-mortar channel. This would require only 11.4 million more new Prime members, as compared to 26.1 million incremental members.

Just as targeted online trips generate smaller baskets, Prime taking routine trips out of the ecosystem also has follow-on effects for brick-and-mortar retailers as consumers often consolidate a trip to one store with trips to others. There is evidence that this is occurring. Overall retail shopping trips in the US have fallen from 18.8 billion in 2008 to 17.5 billion in 2012.[52] To make matters worse, shoppers are also visiting fewer stores on each trip, having visited an average of five stores per mall trip in 2007 and now visiting only three.[53] Prime shows the potential to put brick-and-mortar stores already experiencing slow to negative same-store sales growth up against the ropes.

And if it can do so, the benefits to Amazon are significant. Below is a chart of Amazon's North American Media sales growth year-over-year by quarter. While the Borders liquidation near the end of Amazon's third quarter appears to have depressed sales growth in Q4 2011, from the beginning of Borders' declaration of Chapter 11 through most of 2012, Amazon outperformed corresponding Q2-Q4 quarters in 2010, as shown in Figure 2.16.

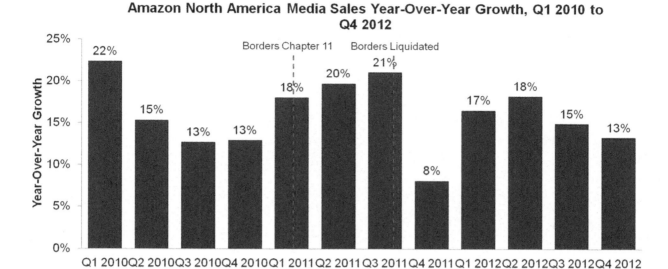

Figure 2.16 Source: Company Reports.

With so many big box retailers either being the last or one of the last large, dedicated, high market share retailers that can price within range of Amazon in their retail vertical, the sales benefit (and possibly later profit benefit) to Amazon of putting them out of business is enormous. Amazon will likely be more than willing to endure long-term low profits in order to do so. The question many brick-and-mortar retailers ask is whether Amazon will survive long enough to put more brick-and-mortar retailers out of business? We see two challenges that Amazon will have to overcome in the future: dealing with a lower growth rate and making a sustainable profit. However, we also believe that Amazon has a number of ways to overcome both these challenges, and is, in fact, already on the way to doing so.

What Happens to Amazon When Growth Slows Down?

Amazon's model has depended on its ability to generate increasing levels of accounts payable in order to fund its expansion. And in a virtuous cycle, as Amazon expanded, its accounts payable balance grew larger, enabling it to fund further expansion. This model depends on two attributes: a negative cash conversion cycle and consistent growth.

Amazon's pursuit of growth is rooted in its history as one of the first online retailers. When Jeffrey Bezos was researching the Internet in 1994 he ran across a statistic reporting that the growth rate of Web usage was 2,300% per year. In Bezos' words, "If something is growing that fast ... then it's going to be ubiquitous very quickly."[54] Driven by a decrease in the price of personal computers, lower average internet access costs, growth of higher bandwidth connections, and an increased availability of compelling content, the internet (and eCommerce) got 'very big very fast.'[55]

Similarly, Amazon has relied on accounts payable and a negative cash conversion cycle since the company began selling books online. Instead of buying books in bulk and then warehousing them like Barnes & Noble and Borders,[56] Amazon instead relied heavily on distributors and book resellers who would hold the books and ship them to Amazon upon request. The exception was a small selection of less than 2,000 titles that were "usually the best-selling items."[57] Amazon.com bought these directly from publishers so as to receive volume discounts, knowing that it could turn the books quickly, and, if it couldn't, could return them to publishers. This inventory structure meant that Amazon had dramatically higher inventory turns than its brick-and-mortar competitors (left chart of Figure 2.17). With payment terms, it also created a negative cash conversion cycle that helped fuel Amazon's expansion (right chart of Figure 2.17). Under a negative cash conversion cycle, Amazon could sell suppliers' goods, and then use the money for other purposes before eventually paying for those goods itself.

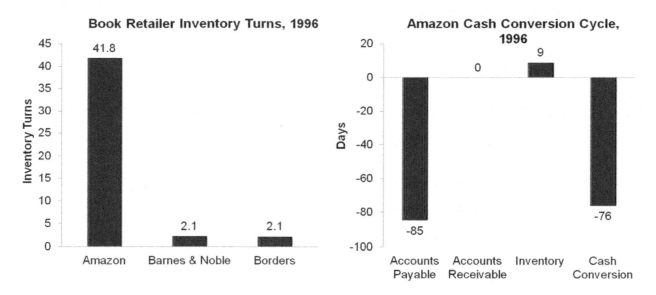

Figure 2.17 Source: Company Statements.

Fast growth and a negative cash conversion cycle enabled Amazon to do two things: grow very rapidly using a minimum of investors' cash investments and create a very high return on invested capital (ROIC) that attracted these investors.

We see by looking at Amazon's cash flows that much of its operating cash was raised by growing its accounts payable. In many years, this was enough to cover the company's negative net income and intensive capital expenditures as it built out its sophisticated distribution system. Aside from the cash Amazon took in from its founding to 2000 from equity and debt investors, Amazon's model allowed it to scale without additional investments; vendors largely financed Amazon's growth for free. Figure 2.18 shows how Amazon grew largely by using its operating cash (driven by accounts payable increases) to cover its capital expenditures, as expressed in the gold line which is over 100% as long as operating cash flow exceeded capital expenditures.

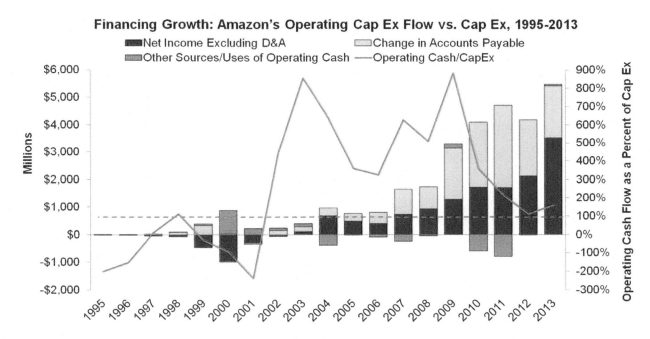

Figure 2.18 Source: Compiled from financial statements available on Cap IQ. Note: When Operating Cash Flow/CapEx is greater than 100%, Amazon funded its CapEx from Operating Cash Flow.

To put it another way, because of Amazon's cash flow from vendors, it was able to grow to a company with over $40 billion in assets, repay shareholders more than it ever raised, and maintain a low level of debt, all while never generating a strong net income. This history is shown in Figure 2.19.

Year (Millions)	Net Income	NOPAT	Free Cash Flow	Equity Issued	Equity Repurchased	Net Debt Raised (Repaid)	Asset Value	Market Capitalization
1994	-$0.1	-$0.1	NA	$0	$0	$0	$0	NA
1995	-$0.3	-$0.2	NA	$1	$0	$0	$1	NA
1996	-$6	-$4	-$1	$9	$0	$0	$8	NA
1997	-$31	-$21	$3	$53	$0	$75	$150	$2,049
1998	-$125	-$69	$39	$14	$0	$248	$648	$19,573
1999	-$720	-$389	-$70	$64	$0	$1,075	$2,466	$22,577
2000	-$1,411	-$314	$274	$45	$0	$665	$2,135	$3,653
2001	-$567	-$151	$72	$116	$0	-$10	$1,638	$5,230
2002	-$149	$69	$221	$122	$0	-$15	$1,990	$8,083
2003	$35	$176	$371	$163	$0	-$495	$2,162	$17,362
2004	$588	$280	$350	$60	$0	-$157	$3,248	$14,267
2005	$359	$307	$411	$59	$0	-$259	$3,696	$16,339
2006	$190	$253	$525	$35	-$252	-$285	$4,363	$16,724
2007	$476	$426	$1,099	$0	-$248	$41	$6,485	$31,341
2008	$645	$513	$1,334	$0	-$100	-$257	$8,314	$25,175
2009	$902	$767	$2,760	$0	$0	-$385	$13,813	$55,751
2010	$1,152	$914	$2,346	$0	$0	-$78	$18,797	$77,185
2011	$631	$560	$1,834	$0	-$277	-$267	$25,278	$81,667
2012	-$39	$439	$1,931	$0	-$960	$2,790	$32,555	$123,985
2013	$274	$484	$2,102	$0	$0	-$617	$40,159	$164,734
Cumulative Total, or Most Recent	$2,203	$4,241	$15,601	$742	-$1,837	$2,069	$40,159	$164,734

Figure 2.19 Source: Company financial statements, Capital IQ, Market Capitalization as of Period Filing Date.

We want to be sure we make this point about Amazon's ability to generate cash from vendors clearly, because there appears to be a broad misconception that Amazon is being funded by its equity holders; it's not. Retail executives marvel over the fact that "Wall Street allows Amazon to get away with nearly nonexistent profit margins" and "spend a billion dollars experimenting" with Amazon Fresh,[58] and one widely quoted description of the company claims that "Amazon ... is a charitable organization being run by elements of the investment community for the benefit of consumers."[59] It's certainly true that Amazon equity holders aren't clamoring for dividends or a share of Amazon's non-existent profits, but much of their leniency can be explained by the fact that they are not being asked to directly fund Amazon's growth nor its experiments.

This is also an important point to grasp as it relates to pricing dynamics between brick-and-mortar retailers and Amazon. Amazon is willing to discount prices in order to gain cash flow, and can do so as long as growth continues. Brick-and-mortar retailers are willing to discount prices and match Amazon in order to retain volume, which is critical to their fixed cost business model. When these two approaches meet, particularly when the goods being contested are undifferentiated, price competition is a natural result.

Amazon's long accounts payable period also drives its high ROIC. Recall that ROIC is a metric that compares a company's operating income after tax to the operating assets for which, either through interest-bearing debt or equity, it has had to pay. While a company's operating assets (e.g. inventory, distribution centers, etc. but not excess cash) are the capital that generate profits, a company doesn't always have to buy these assets with investors' or lenders' money. Instead, a company can use "free" financing provided by customers, vendors and suppliers, and even the government, in the form of unearned revenue, accounts payable, and income taxes payable. While ROIC formulas vary widely, we calculated invested capital for Amazon by subtracting cash and cash equivalents, accounts payable, accrued expenses, and unearned revenue from Amazon's total assets. We calculated NOPAT by taking Amazon's operating income and applying a 35% tax rate. The waterfall chart in Figure 2.20 below will explain our invested capital calculations, and why we made them, for the year 2001.

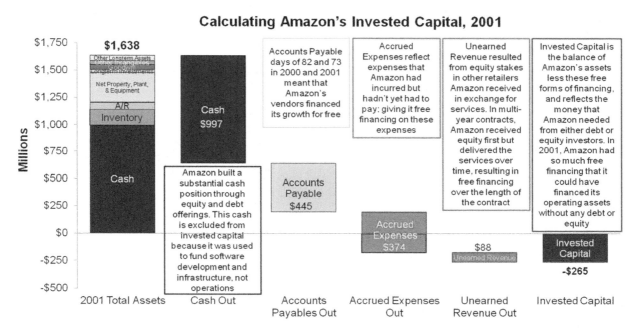

Figure 2.20 Source: Company Statements. Notes: Amazon's financials are reported December 31, when, per Amazon's 10-K, cash and equivalents, as well as accounts payables, reaches its highest levels following the holiday retail season. Amazon reported accounts payable days between 45 and 60 in the quarters between Q4 2000 and Q4 2001.

Note that while most companies will have positive invested capital, Amazon's negative invested capital is a result of its strong cash position and negative cash conversion cycle.

Free financing and a low to negative invested capital balance was, and is, critically important to Amazon and to retailers in general. Because retailers often carry large amounts of assets, from inventory on the shelves and in distribution centers to the stores themselves, investors want to see how productive these assets are. ROIC as a metric reveals how well retailers are managing their operations and finances to pay for these assets and produce a return on them. With neither stores nor substantial inventory, Amazon already had a leg up in the ROIC metric.

We show Amazon's NOPAT and ROIC over time in Figure 2.21. While Amazon's NOPAT margin was negative in its early years, the argument for negative invested capital attracted strong investor interest. Note that in Amazon's earliest years, its strong positive ROIC is misleading as both its NOPAT and its average invested capital was negative. After 2001, when Amazon's NOPAT turned positive, negative ROIC numbers reflect that Amazon's assets were so leveraged against interest free financing that its invested capital was negative. Indeed, with positive NOPAT and negative ROIC, it could be said from an investor standpoint that Amazon was making money out of nothing.

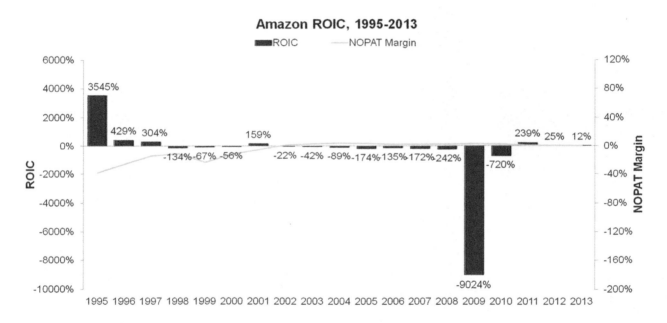

Figure 2.21 Source: Compiled from Financial Statements available at Cap IQ.

No wonder, then, that throughout Amazon's early history, Bezos maintained that it was the wrong time to be profitable, saying, "We were profitable for about an hour in December 1995, but it was probably a mistake. And in December of last year, our book business was profitable. But it's not clear that's in our shareholders' long-term interest."[60] With operating assets financed by vendors, and shareholders satisfied with Amazon's high

ROIC numbers, Amazon could afford to invest heavily in its competitive advantages: software, physical infrastructure, scope, and scale.

With a growth dependent-model and a company that has been growing faster than its industry for many years, one must ask, "What will happen when growth slows?" In the long-term, online retailing will continue to grow, but it will likely do so at a slower rate than during the past decade, and Amazon itself faces several threats to high growth rates in the short-term. If Amazon's growth rate significantly decreases, its ability to create cash flow to cover its operations, expansion, and experiments is severely constrained.

Fueling continued long-term growth in eCommerce is the increased propensity of the digital native, younger generation to shop online. In a September 2012 poll from Ipsos, 18-34 and 35-49 year olds were over 50% more likely to prefer shopping in a non-store environment than 50-64 year olds (Figure 2.22).

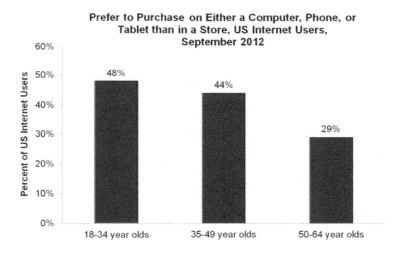

Figure 2.22 Source: eMarketer.

Moreover, smart phone price-check behavior is most evident in the young and affluent, and is also on the rise overall. In Figure 2.23, going clockwise, we present the likelihood of showrooming by generation and then by income level, the last chart shows the growth in smartphone showrooming over just three years.

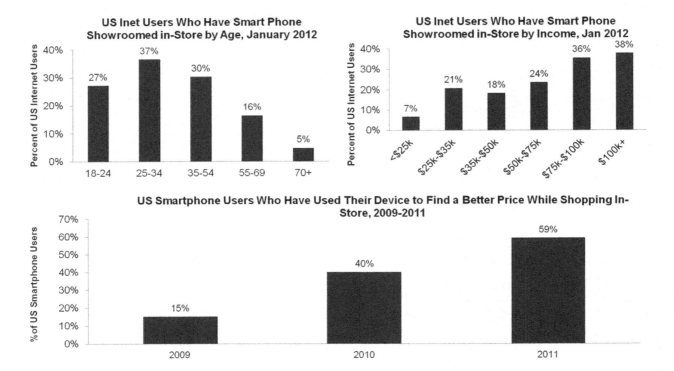

Figure 2.23 Source: eMarketer.

In the long-term, as internet-comfortable younger generations age, displace digital dinosaurs as the economy's consumers, and realize higher incomes, their propensity to purchase online will drive online sales higher. The demographics behind online retailing will drive its continued growth.

However, that does not mean that Amazon will smoothly sail into the future. The rate of eCommerce growth is slowing down, and slowing growth rates are bad for Amazon.

Online sales grow as a result of two inputs: getting more people online and getting those people online to first buy and then buy more. The big gains in getting US shoppers online have already been reaped: online penetration rates for the high-spending cohorts between 18-64 years old are all close to or above 80%, as shown in Figure 2.24.

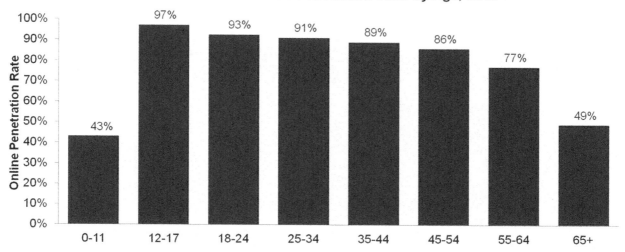

Figure 2.24 Source: eMarketer.

The online penetration rate is even higher for affluent Americans, those who have household income over $100,000. Affluent Americans are both more likely to make a purchase online and on average spend 41% more per purchase than the non-affluent, and so have been important contributors to online sales.[61] Over 98% of them, however, are already online.[62] No wonder that Amazon is focused on driving more sales from existing shoppers through its Prime program.

Prime, Marketplace, and the experimental Fresh may be the few programs Amazon has to drive growth. Amazon has already entered nearly every category that it can, and the categories it has not penetrated are either not suited to online retail, are already served by very strong incumbents, or are too small to make much difference. Figure 2.25 shows the various retail verticals present in the United States in descending order of sales volume. Categories with an Amazon-led, not third-party reliant, presence are highlighted in green.

Category	Percent of Retail Sales	Amazon Active?
Motor Vehicles	17.0%	No
Groceries and Meals	15.1%	Yes
Health & Beauty Care	9.8%	Yes
Fuel	9.7%	No
Apparel	7.9%	Yes
Building and Agriculture Supplies	7.7%	Yes
Electronics	4.7%	Yes
Home Goods	3.2%	Yes
Furniture and Floor	2.8%	Yes
Automotive Supplies	2.8%	Yes
Alcohol	1.8%	No
Sports	1.6%	Yes
Tobacco	1.5%	No
Jewelry	1.3%	Yes
Toys, hobbies, games	1.0%	Yes
Household Fuels and Crude Oil	0.9%	No
Cleaners	0.8%	Yes
Paper	0.7%	Yes
Pets and Pet Supplies	0.7%	Yes
RVs and Mobile Homes	0.7%	No
Books	0.6%	Yes
Glasses	0.3%	No
Crafts	0.1%	No
All Other Merchandise	4.1%	NA
Non-merchandise receipts (i.e. Services)	3.2%	No

Figure 2.25 Source: US Economic Census, 2007, Retail Trade.

Amazon has entered virtually every vertical open to it. Of the categories not being sold by Amazon, Motor Vehicles and RVs, at almost 18% of US retail sales are the largest target. However, new vehicles require a different fulfillment infrastructure than Amazon can currently offer and have entrenched sales networks that manufacturers are unlikely to willingly disrupt. In used vehicles, CarMax has a compelling and competitive omnichannel offering, and eBay maintains a healthy used vehicle auction business – Amazon shut down its auction platform years ago. Due to their flammable and hazardous nature, the 10% of US retail sales composed of fuels can't be fulfilled online. Alcohol and Tobacco, at a little over 3% of total US retail sales have age-based ID requirements and, for wine, special restrictions on interstate transport apply. In fact, Amazon has launched a wine store, but it leaves fulfillment up to the wineries, and we regard this as more of a Marketplace operation. While a few vendors, such as Dish, offer services like TV installation through Amazon, Amazon itself has not moved significantly into fee-based services, and doing so is different from retailing physical products in that the service delivered is not always of the same quality, training is involved unless partnering with third parties, etc. After these categories are excluded, Amazon has about 4.5% of the US retail market that it hasn't entered, composed of Glasses, Crafts, and Other Merchandise. This is not a lot of white space.

Moreover, in the verticals that it is active in, eCommerce penetration has significantly slowed. Figure 2.26 shows eCommerce penetration of retail verticals by year. In many verticals, penetration has not greatly changed in recent years.

eCommerce Penetration of Category at August	2004	2005	2006	2007	2008	2009	2010	2011
Books and Magazines	12.1%	17.4%	18.9%	24.6%	21.3%	22.9%	29.6%	31.0%
Office Supplies	27.0%	25.2%	47.0%	30.2%	24.8%	27.7%	28.3%	28.9%
Consumer Electronics	4.4%	3.8%	5.0%	8.5%	9.6%	11.9%	12.4%	13.8%
Toys & Hobbies	6.0%	9.7%	8.1%	11.1%	11.8%	11.8%	11.3%	11.1%
Flowers, Greetings, Gifts	7.7%	9.4%	8.5%	6.3%	9.5%	8.1%	8.5%	10.6%
Music, Movies & Videos	13.6%	11.9%	12.8%	19.0%	13.9%	10.6%	11.2%	10.6%
Computer Software	7.4%	8.6%	11.2%	9.0%	5.5%	7.6%	6.8%	8.5%
Home & Garden	4.2%	5.2%	4.5%	5.4%	7.8%	8.4%	8.3%	8.5%
Jewelry & Watches	4.4%	6.8%	5.3%	8.5%	8.0%	8.0%	8.3%	8.5%
Other	4.3%	4.5%	4.6%	6.0%	6.2%	6.1%	6.1%	6.2%
Sports & Fitness	1.9%	3.1%	3.3%	4.1%	4.2%	5.1%	5.1%	5.4%
Apparel & Accessories	1.9%	2.8%	3.5%	4.1%	4.0%	4.2%	4.5%	4.9%
Furniture, Appliances	1.3%	1.7%	1.3%	2.3%	3.6%	3.6%	3.4%	3.5%
Consumer Packaged Goods	0.9%	0.9%	1.0%	1.4%	1.8%	2.0%	2.0%	2.0%
Other	4.3%	4.5%	4.6%	6.0%	6.2%	6.1%	6.1%	6.2%
Total	**3.2%**	**3.6%**	**4.1%**	**4.9%**	**5.1%**	**5.3%**	**5.5%**	**5.7%**

Figure 2.26 Source: Alvarez, José et al, "Terry Lundgren at Macy's," HBS case number 9-412-033, Harvard Business School Publishing: Boston, 2012.

Brick-and-mortar retailers' online offerings are more compelling now, and becoming more so as retailers roll out different omnichannel offerings like "buy online/pick up in store." With 50% of online orders at Best Buy and other retailers picked up in store, there may be a latent, untapped desire for this type of service that goes beyond cost-savings and faster delivery times. Walmart, for instance, has found that 40% of online customers who select pay-with-cash on Walmart.com end up paying with a credit or debit card in-store instead, indicating that they were uncomfortable handing over sensitive information online.

Moreover, many of the categories that showed the greatest share loss to online retailers may have matured as online offerings. In Electronics, for instance, a February, 2011 survey by Complete found that 35.8% of respondents bought something in the category online, while 37.8% bought something offline.[63] Can online retailers capture all of that remaining offline spend? Probably not. In the electronics category specifically, manufacturers are beginning to enforce minimum pricing, and many consumers will still want to see a high-end TV in person before they purchase it.

There are obvious product issues across every retail vertical: heavy, low-priced items do not fit well in the online retail model; and while Amazon Lockers may go some way to mitigate the cost of shipping, they don't, and aren't likely to, fit a pallet of dry wall. Items that need to be touched and seen are harder to sell online, barring a "try-before-you-buy" program. And while a try-before-you-buy program may help customers experimenting with mobile phones, it likely won't do much for those buying fresh produce. Due to Amazon's low-price focus which commoditizes products, luxury goods have avoided the platform. This is all to say that there is very likely a ceiling for online channel share in each category, and while that ceiling will vary based on the category, it does exist. For some categories, like consumer electronics, we may already be approaching that ceiling.

For a company reliant on growing accounts payable, slowing growth is bad. Even worse, however, are falling sales. While a remote chance, this is not necessarily an outlandish possibility. Though incredibly sophisticated and efficient, Amazon's fulfillment system faces a critical risk in that it relies on third parties for last mile delivery (e.g. USPS, FedEx, UPS, and smaller regional courier services). One of those third parties, the United States Postal Service, is the vital last step in the delivery system for many customers, and it faces the possibility of dramatic changes. The USPS has lost tens of billions of dollars cumulatively over the past few years, surviving on infusions from the federal government. However, the USPS is intended to survive as a stand-alone entity, and pressure is mounting to reform the service. There are two, quick, operational changes that could help return the USPS to profitability, and both are being considered.

One option is shifting home and curb-side delivery of mail and packages to cluster-box delivery. Under this system, rather than picking up packages outside their doors or at the curb, residents would instead travel to a keyed cluster-box or USPS post office to pick up their mail and packages, affecting about 80 million Americans (residents of newer construction developments and apartment buildings largely already use cluster boxes).[64] This would certainly diminish the convenience of online ordering.

The other option is to charge more for deliveries that cost private carriers more. While the USPS does charge differently based on the distance a package has to travel, the USPS does not charge based on the market price of last-mile delivery. UPS and FedEx, on the other hand, both have surcharges for areas that are more costly to deliver to, such as rural areas where low population density increases costs, and urban areas with special characteristics such as college campuses. These surcharges cover about 25% of the US population.[65] Currently, if a customer is willing to accept a wider delivery window, they can choose to use FedEx's SmartPost or UPS's SurePost programs. Under these programs, FedEx and UPS carry parcels to a USPS center, and then let USPS take the package the rest of the way. One estimate states that without such a service, on average, rural businesses would pay $3.00 more per parcel, and rural residents $5.45 more per parcel.[66] Since this estimate was published, FedEx and UPS have both increased their surcharges, so this older estimate is likely conservative. Were the USPS to increase the rates it charges to FedEx and UPS for last-mile delivery, the 25% of the US population covered by surcharges may find store visits a less expensive choice than online retailing.

There are many reasons to expect slower growth for Amazon, and Amazon's own slowing growth rates (Figure 2.3) provide evidence that this is indeed occurring. There is also the possibility that accounts payables themselves may have reached a breaking point. Amazon's payables period is significantly longer than other general merchandise retailers and most category killers as compared in Figure 2.27.

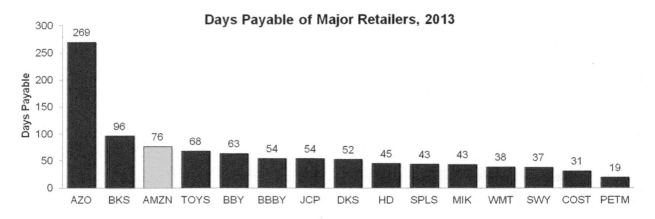

Figure 2.27 Source: Capital IQ.

Were Amazon vendors ever to enforce a payable period closer to Walmart, this would be a large use of cash for Amazon. For instance, in 2012, if Amazon's vendors enforced the same payables period on Walmart as Amazon, Amazon would have seen a reduced average payables amount throughout the year of over $7 billion, sucking up over 60% of its available cash and short-term investments at the end of 2012.

The greatest constraint facing Amazon is continuing its growth. As long as the company continues to grow, it can continue to grow its account payables. This growth in accounts payables has constituted a very important part of Amazon's operating cash flow. If growth peters out, Amazon will be forced to look to its profits (as well as investors and debt issuers) as a source of growth capital. However, a common criticism of Amazon is that its net income line has always been negative or close to zero. Can the company ever be profitable?

Can Amazon Ever Be Profitable?

Amazon's history makes clear that Amazon has grown through low prices, a constantly expanding assortment, and a continuing investment in more fulfillment centers to support that assortment and improve service for customers, all of which have supported its economies of scale and scope. The constant discounting, expansion, and reinvestment have, however, driven the company's margins to near or below zero. This leads many in the investment community to wonder if Amazon can ever be profitable. There is strong evidence to believe that the answer is yes – either through raising prices, or transitioning to a total or nearly total platform rather than a retailer.

We believe there's room for Amazon to raise prices, though the company is unlikely to do so. Estimates of Amazon's price competitiveness against brick-and-mortar retailers are all over the map, and any price gap will vary significantly across retail verticals. For the purposes of discussion, however, William Blair has conducted a fairly comprehensive study incorporating many retail verticals, and estimates an average Amazon discount to brick-and-mortar retailers of between 5% and 8% (after adding estimated sales tax to Amazon purchases) depending on whether customers qualify for free shipping due to basket size or being Prime members.[67] Of course, customers use Amazon for more than just low prices – there's also the ease of use and convenience of delivery. Bezos himself has stated, on more than one occasion, that the company's own elasticity studies suggest that it should raise prices.[68] Amazon doesn't, because, as Bezos says, it wants to do what's best for the customer, and don't want to alienate customers or lose their trust.

To evaluate whether Amazon can become profitable by raising prices, though, we'll look at whether the company's price elasticity and price gap allow it the room to do so. In a recent National Bureau of Economic Research paper, researchers used the implementation of sales taxes on Amazon in five states during 2012 and 2013 to measure the effect these taxes had on customers' Amazon purchases. They calculated a -1.3 elasticity, or in other words, for every 1% increase in price at Amazon, customers' dollar volume of purchases (excluding sales tax) fall 1.3%.[69] If we assume this elasticity holds constant, a 5% increase in Amazon's prices (a significant raise, no doubt, but one that still gives many customers prices 3% lower than they would find in brick-and-mortar stores) would lead to a 6.5% reduction in the volume of purchases bought at Amazon, but only a 1.8% reduction in top-line sales. Working off of Amazon's global numbers and making some allowances for third-party and non-retail costs; the effect of this price increase would be to increase Amazon's EBIT substantially, to a 3.7% EBIT margin as shown in Figure 2.28.

	Amazon 2013	Change	5% Price Increase	Explanation
Sales (Owned and Operated)	$60,903	-$1,111	$59,792	After accounting for lower volume, price increased by 5%
Operating Expenses				
Cost of Sales	$54,182	-$3,522	$50,660	Decreased by 6.5% to reflect lower volume
Fulfillment	$3,317	-$216	$3,101	Decreased by 6.5% to reflect lower volume
Marketing	$1,439	$0	$1,439	No change
Technology and Content	$1,946	$0	$1,946	No change
General and Admin	$462	$0	$462	No change
EBIT	-$443		$2,183	

Figure 2.28 Source: Amazon 2013 Annual Report. Notes: Fulfillment and G&A were allocated by percent of GMV/Sales, Technology and Content, after estimated AWS cost, was allocated by percent of GMV to Owned and Operated, and Owned & Operated was assumed to generate 40% of Fulfillment cost.

While Amazon likely has room to increase prices, it's also possible that as growth at Amazon slows, the company would rely more on the Marketplace model we described earlier. Under this model, Amazon acts as an aggregator of customer demand, a fulfillment and third-party logistics provider, and an advertising and marketing agency rolled into one. Currently, Marketplace referral fees range between 6% and 20% of an item's value. Using the 2013 numbers as above, Amazon's owned and operated sales were $60.9 billion, with associated non-COGs costs of $7.2 billion and net shipping costs of $3.5 billion (assuming no net shipping cost from FBA). Under the marketplace model, the cost of purchasing goods disappears so we exclude COGS, apart from net shipping costs, from this analysis. As a pure-play platform, Amazon needs to set a fee that covers $10.7 billion of non-COGs expenses, or in this case about 17.5% of sales. This fee would include access to customers, fulfillment and shipping, and marketing. Brands could easily pay this fee and be better off than selling to retail outlets, which typically have gross margins between 23% and 50%, with Walmart at 25%. When one takes into account the fact that many of these retailers include the costs of delivering products to stores in their COGS – a cost that is less in the Amazon model because goods are delivered to large fulfillment centers – and that Amazon is priced lower than these retailers on average, there's significant room to increase EBIT, similar to the example above.

Interestingly, if Amazon does transform into a pure marketplace, the cash conversion cycle that fueled its growth may dry up. Under the current retail model, Amazon buys about half of the inventory sold on its site, and then just doesn't pay for it for a very long time. It uses the cash generated in this process to fund its expansion. Under the FBA and marketplace model, sellers instead pay Amazon to hold their inventory and are paid on a

14-day cycle. Under this model, with Amazon no longer buying inventory, it is unable to leverage its accounts payable, and its cash conversion cycle swings positive. The differences in Amazon's current cash conversion cycle and its new cash conversion cycle under a Marketplace model are shown in Figure 2.29.

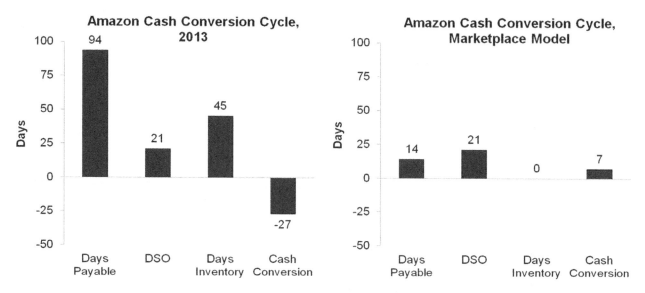

Figure 2.29 Sources: Capital IQ and author calculations. Note: Doesn't account for AWS and other service businesses.

This possible future, however, is probably a long way off. According to one of the major brands we have spoken with, different operating groups run Marketplace and the traditional retailing side of Amazon's business. Furthermore, this brand was denied access to Amazon's Marketplace as a direct seller, with Amazon choosing to instead continue the traditional practice of buying inventory directly and acting as the reseller. By transforming into a marketplace, Amazon would also surrender control of retail pricing to brands and third-party sellers, who may not opt into Amazon's low-price ethos. However, this will be an interesting model to revisit as Amazon's growth slows, and it is no longer able to fund itself through growing accounts payables. In that situation, it may very well turn to being a services-based business for brands, relying on the larger margins this generates.[70]

What is this Book About?

While Amazon certainly faces hurdles in its future, we hope we have made the case that both Amazon and eCommerce are significant threats to brick-and-mortar retailers' physical stores, despite the recent success many brick-and-mortar retailers have reported with store-based and omnichannel online sales. The rest of this book explores the threats and challenges facing different retailers and the strategies they are (or should be) using, depending on their histories, merchandise mix, and particular situations. These range from focused efforts to improve cash flow, to augmenting the primacy of the physical store with additional information and services online, to shrinking and transforming brick-and-mortar stores into operations highly focused on providing key value-adds to customers and brands, such as service or showrooms. This last strategy includes a store-supported general merchandise battle against Amazon which only one retailer, Walmart, really has the potential to pull off.

Even for retailers with a strategy however, implementation can be too late, and delay, deadly. We point to the case of Blockbuster. Blockbuster suffered from a merchandise assortment that was eminently suited for online fulfillment. DVDs and games were standard commodities that were small, light, and could be shipped through low-cost mail options. Based on average customer behavior at both Blockbuster and Netflix in 2004, Blockbuster stores' cost disadvantage per movie rental was about $1.25 compared to Netflix when evaluating just the cost of distributing DVDs by mail and fulfilling them in store.[71] However, after many half-steps and false starts, Blockbuster created an offering that matched consumer needs, retail store abilities, and web possibilities very well. While Netflix users suffered from a lack of available new releases to rent and, before Netflix's fulfillment center buildout, had to wait for their rentals to make a long journey through the mail before being credited with their return, and then wait again for their new orders to come to them, Blockbuster subscription members could borrow new releases in-store and both return their online DVDs and pick up new ones right away at brick-and-mortar locations. Users of Redbox, which rented DVDs out of automated kiosks, had access to a number of new releases, but no more than 70-200 titles per location. Blockbuster, by contrast, supplemented its 2,500 title in-store assortment with its online operation, and had rolled out similar kiosks.

But it was too late. When Blockbuster launched its DVD-by-mail service, Netflix already had almost three million members.[72] When Blockbuster went bankrupt, Redbox had over 24,000 kiosks, three times the amount of Blockbuster and eight times the number of Blockbuster's remaining stores.[73] While Blockbuster's final strategy would likely not have saved its stores from the shift to streaming video, if it had been implemented earlier it may have helped set the company up to make the transition itself, or salvaged something for investors. As it was, by the time Blockbuster finally rolled out its new strategy, it probably would have been better off aggressively closing stores and beginning the wind down process.

Today, Blockbuster's story serves as a warning sign to other retailers: take the threat of eCommerce seriously, have a real strategy for dealing with it, and understand where and how your offering fits customers' needs in the overall retail ecosystem. Our next chapter deals with retailers whose best strategy may be to wind down their business, and the difficulties these retailers face in making this decision.

Chapter 3
Wind Down or Reinvent?

The first threat occurs when there is a digitization of or disappearance of demand for the core category within a store that eliminates the need for physical distribution. Such is the case when physical categories shift to digital consumption, as happened with Blockbuster's movies and games and Barnes & Noble's books. In other cases, demand for a retailer's core product evaporates, as is ongoing with the office supply superstores as offices digitize and both businesses and consumers simply use less paper. Digitization is also affecting the toy vertical as children rely more on digital games and videos than physical toys. Retailers specializing in these categories can expect to see continuous same-store sales declines in these core areas and face a difficult choice: to either wind down their stores or reinvent them in a manner that overcomes the loss of physical products. Office supply retailers are currently facing this decision. These retailers and their choices between the "Wind Down" and "Shrink and Transform the Format" strategies are the subject of this chapter.

Office supply superstores (OSS) face two challenges: eCommerce competition in their technology departments and declining paper consumption worldwide. Much like Best Buy, their technology category is becoming a 'showroom' for customers who are going to hunt for the best deal on the internet later. Even if, through their well-developed online presence and extensive fulfillment infrastructure, the OSS eventually win these sales, sales through the superstores' own online portals decrease sales per square foot at the stores, and make it less appealing to operate large real estate footprints. While somewhat protected by private labeling, the furniture category is also subject to sales fluctuations, particularly during recessions, that make holding inventory in disaggregated stores undesirable. The solutions for these categories will likely mirror those proposed for retailers like Best Buy (which we introduce later in this book), and prototype OSS stores show this evolution unfolding. More broadly, the OSS face competition across their merchandise mix from both online retailers and mass merchandisers who run more efficient operations, as seen in Amazon's and Walmart's lower SG&A expense ratios in Figure 3.1.

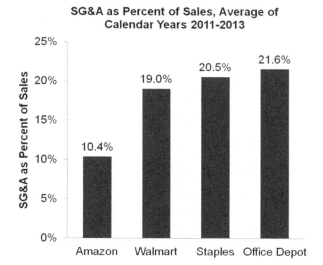

Figure 3.1 Sources: Company Reports. Notes: Impairment, store closure, and merger costs excluded from SG&A; for Amazon, technology and content costs excluded, and total first and estimated third party GMV used rather than sales.

The larger challenge and the greater question for the OSS is what to do with a category that is disappearing? Office paper, stationery, and other paper-related office supplies account for over half of office supply superstore sales, but, as businesses around the world replace paper processes with electronic ones, this core of the OSS industry is being gradually eliminated. This is an existential threat for these companies: if small businesses and consumers no longer use office supplies, what is an office supply superstore for? Through all the recessions this industry has experienced, sales in capital goods like technology and furniture have fluctuated widely, but demand for the stores' main draw— well-priced paper goods and their attendant accessories like staplers, folders, inks, and binders—has remained relatively steady. Recently, however, US office paper consumption has almost continually declined and US production has continued to fall into 2014 as seen in Figure 3.2. This drop-off in consumption has led to follow-on declines in other paper-related materials, such as ink and toner usage (proxied in Figure 3.2 by Hewlett Packard's Printing segment). In light of these declines, we have to believe that these core office supply categories are not experiencing the same pick-up as the overall economy.[74]

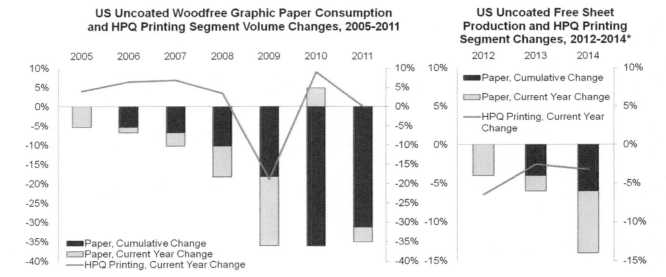

Figure 3.2 Sources: United Nations Economic Commission for Europe, Food and Agriculture Organization of the United Nations; Hewlett-Packard Financial Statements, accessed via *ThomsonOne*; American Forest and Paper Association; Binder, Daniel et. al, Jefferies, 'Office Depot', report dated February 20, 2013; Notes: Paper in 2014 reflects AF&PA YTD numbers as of June, 2014 and HPQ Printing reflects the first half of its fiscal year.

While in the past, the OSS have recovered with the economy following recessions, because of this evolution in the workplace, the OSS industry appears to be decoupling from the broader economy. Figure 3.3 shows that Office Depot comp store sales have moved with the change in the inverse of unemployment in the past, but beginning in Q4 of 2009 they split apart.

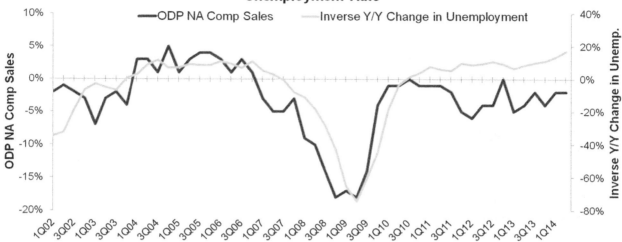

Figure 3.3 Source: Binder, Daniel et. al, Jefferies, 'Office Depot', report dated February 20, 2013.

These issues have caused a falloff in the OSS' operating and return measures, as shown in the latter years of Figure 3.4.

Staples	2005	2006	2007	2011	2012	2013
Same-store sales growth (excluding fuel sales)	3%	3%	-3%	0%	-2%	-4%
ROIC (Op Leases Not Capitalized)	22.6%	23.7%	21.1%	12.3%	12.1%	10.4%
Gross Margin	28.5%	28.6%	28.7%	27.1%	26.6%	26.1%
SG&A as % Sales	20.8%	20.5%	20.7%	20.5%	20.4%	20.7%
Office Depot	**2005**	**2006**	**2007**	**2011**	**2012**	**2013***
Same-store sales growth	3%	2%	-5%	-2%	-5%	-4%
ROIC (Op Leases Not Capitalized)	10.1%	14.6%	8.1%	1.8%	4.0%	8.3%
Gross Margin	30.8%	31.0%	29.0%	29.8%	23.7%	23.7%
SG&A as % Sales	27.4%	26.2%	25.9%	29.4%	22.8%	22.4%
OfficeMax	**2005**	**2006**	**2007**	**2011**	**2012**	**2013**
Same-store sales growth	-1.0%	.1%	-1.2%	-2.8%	-2.5%	
ROIC (Op Leases Not Capitalized)	1.2%	4.4%	4.8%	2.9%	2.2%	4.4%
Gross Margin	24.0%	25.8%	25.4%	25.4%	25.8%	25.4%
SG&A as % Sales	23.1%	22.3%	21.6%	23.7%	24.6%	23.3%

Figure 3.4 Sources: ThomsonOne and Company Reports. Notes: With the exception of same-store sales, data represents total company performance, not just the retail segments; SG&A Expenses do not include impairment and restructuring charges; OfficeMax and Office Depot completed their merger in November, 2013 and Office Depot and OfficeMax 2013 numbers reflect Q42012-Q32013 before the merger date.

Other retailers have experienced this digitization of their core as well. With the advent of digital books, Barnes & Noble faced a similar issue, and Blockbuster experienced rapid change as movies were increasingly streamed or downloaded online. Companies in this situation have two choices: attempt to manage for sustainability by reinventing themselves in a way that maintains their relevance to the consumer, or manage for cash flow by focusing on returning cash to stakeholders through forgoing further investment, shutting stores, selling pieces of the company, etc. The first strategy is risky, consumes precious resources, and may ultimately destroy all shareholder value, while the latter is difficult to accept and comes with its own set of tricky challenges. We will discuss both of these strategies in-depth, their challenges, and potential tactics to mitigate these challenges, as we examine their application in the context of the office supplies industry and how, in many ways, tactics for both of these strategies are already being rolled out by the two players that are left: Staples and Office Depot. Understanding what office supply superstores offered their customers at the creation of the industry just two decades ago, and the circumstances the OSS fall into during recessions, will inform our discussion of these issues.

Before we begin this discussion, however, we should note that the OSS' medium to large accounts services groups are not a focus of this chapter. While an important part of the office supply superstores' businesses, the services operations began as and have remained separate from the retail operations. Rather than being revolutionary as the office supply superstores were, these businesses are mostly the result of acquisitions of medium to large contract stationers. Instead of serving the home-office and small business customers for whom the stores and consumer internet sites were designed, customers of contract supply services are typically medium to large businesses. Instead of retail store-fronts and uniform pricing, the contract supply side of the OSS industry uses sales representatives and negotiated pricing per client. While there are sure to be buying synergies with the added volume of contract supply, and while the logistics of the two sides of the OSS companies have gradually become more intertwined (very tightly so in the case of Office Depot), contract supply is a fundamentally different business than home-office and small business retail, with a different customer and a different business model. Consequently, we will focus our attention on the retail side of the business throughout the rest of this chapter.

Advent of the Industry, Customer Promise, and Operating Model

In 1985, before the advent of big-box office supply stores, small businesses were served very poorly by the prevailing industry structure. Four principal office supply wholesalers in the industry sold to a variety of dealers, who ranged from small, corner stationery stores to regional or national stationers operating delivery contracts out of central warehouses. Businesses with more than 100 employees purchased from large stationers and negotiated discounts for themselves of as much as 80% off list.[75] But these large stationers would often not bother with small businesses, which instead paid high prices at a fragmented mix of independent stationers, drug stores, and whatever small space supermarkets and department stores allocated to office supplies. Invariably, these retail locations were small-format, narrowly merchandised areas, and finding exactly what you were looking for could be a hassle, if the store even stocked it in the first place.

It was exactly this customer problem that spurred the creation of the office supply superstore industry. In 1985, unable to find a new printer ribbon[76] for his home office, Thomas Stemberg, the founder of Staples, realized there had to be a better way for small businesses to buy office supplies. Separately, the founders of Office Depot—Staples' largest competitor then and now—were attempting to start a marine supply warehouse store, but, when they experienced how hard it was to get office supplies and furniture for the new business, they switched their focus to office supplies.[77] With Stemberg's history in warehouse grocery retailing, and the Office Depot team's history running a Home Depot clone, both companies decided this style of retailing had a high potential to succeed in the office supplies category. Both founding teams envisioned stores much larger than anything else currently in business, with a wide and deep assortment of goods, and absent costly frills such as cosmetic decorations, display work, etc. These warehouse stores would provide better pricing, better product selection, and better product availability than the independent stores they replaced.

Office Supply superstores saved small businesses 35-50% on products ranging from paper to office furniture over the independent stationers from which small businesses used to buy.[78] For example, in 1989, small businesses could buy a 12-pack of yellow writing pads for $3.99 at Staples that would normally have cost $11.55 for a dozen at a stationery store or supermarket.[79] Small stationers charged $60 for a case of paper, but Office Depot "[blew] them away at $25."[80] Post-It notes were sold for $11.55 at other office products dealers, but were only \$3.99 at Staples.[81] The OSS achieved these price savings through a mix of volume selling, cost cutting, and self-service.

Volume was critically important to the OSS, as every office supply superstore accepted a lower gross margin on their sales in return for the greater volume they could gain through lower prices. By 1992, when the office supply superstore revolution was already underway, the average stationery store in the industry sold a little under \$400,000 worth of merchandise per year. [82] In comparison, Staples' first store—which had a rocky start and was smaller and more limited in assortment than Staples' future stores—sold almost \$6 million worth of merchandise in its first year.[83] Conservatively estimating that prices at Staples were 35% less than the average stationery store that would be over \$9 million of goods at traditional store pricing, or over 23 times the unit volume of a traditional mom-and-pop store! With that kind of volume, lower gross margins were an acceptable sacrifice.

Office supply superstore chains leveraged their volume to negotiate better pricing than their mom-and-pop peers. Whereas neighborhood stationers bought in limited quantities, office supply superstores bought in bulk, and cut out middlemen. They passed these savings to their customers. Office Depot further emphasized this point by actually operating its stores as warehouses for its first few years, with customers selecting their purchases from the same shelf spots that Office Depot's delivery crews used to pick orders.[84]

Cost-cutting was also a major component of the OSS' pricing advantage, and the OSS achieved this through the warehouse model and through customer self-service. Office supply superstores abandoned the cosmetic frills found in traditional stationers to cut down on the costs of opening and maintaining stores. Floors were concrete, merchandise was stored on steel racks, and, in the case of Office Depot's first stores at least, merchandise was put up in the same containers it came in. Customers at these first Office Depot stores were responsible for opening the packaging and breaking bulk.[85] Office supply superstores also located in "areas that were high density for businesses but were not historically good retail locations."[86] In one instance, Staples even built a store in the parking lot of a furniture store.[87] Per square foot, these locations had lower rental costs than neighborhood stores in the same cities, and the OSS relied on superior pricing and proximity to their target small business markets to draw customers.

Office supply superstores also were the first to introduce private label office products into the stationery market, further lowering prices. While BizMart and OfficeMax introduced private label programs first, Staples and Office Depot followed quickly, and all four companies had private label programs by 1993.[88] The OSS were aided in this by "office supply consumers," who, according to the Wharton Center for Applied Research, had "limited brand awareness and preference" when it came to supplies such as "rubber bands and paper clips."[89]

Self-service, such as that displayed by early Office Depot customers who opened bulk packaging themselves, was a crucial component in the price savings formula found at office supply superstores. In the 1980s, even small businesses could set up delivery contracts with local, small-format stationery stores, and many small businesses enjoyed the convenience of having supplies delivered. The small stationery stores covered the cost of this delivery by simply baking it into their retail prices. For office supply superstores to work, in Stemberg's words, "those businesses that" had "their office supplies delivered" had to "be convinced to send someone out to pick them up." [90] Staples accomplished this through a direct mail campaign that brought office managers and owners into its stores. Once there, they realized how much they could save by picking orders themselves, and frequently became dedicated customers. By providing shoppers with grocery carts and having them self-select their own office supplies, the OSS were able to shave off labor costs that existed in the old stationery store model.

In addition to low prices, office supply superstores also offered greater selection and availability. The OSS strove to be one-stop shops in their vertical. Small businesses used to have to go to multiple, limited-range stores to fill a shopping list, but at these new big box stores they could find everything in one place. The size of these stores and the wide-range of products available became even more important with the adoption of personal computers—and their attendant peripherals and specialized consumables—by small businesses. The neighborhood stationery store just didn't have space to handle the increased product range needed to support this category, further solidifying the superstores' selection advantage.

Beyond greater selection, the OSS also offered better availability: defined as having the product in assortment and having it in stock. This was crucial for many small businesses as it was important not to have a shortage of a critical product in the office. In fact, the stores that Stemberg visited to find his printer ribbon carried the product, but were either closed or didn't have it in store inventory. Both Staples and Office Depot placed considerable emphasis on making sure stockouts were rare, with Staples designing its automatic reordering system to ensure availability[91] and Office Depot focusing on keeping "merchandise in stock and the freight flowing because it would fly off the shelves."[92] The OSS' greater volume aided them in this endeavor as they could economically receive more frequent warehouse deliveries and store more product than smaller, independent stores. Contributing to availability, the OSS could also afford to be open longer than their small neighborhood competitors because, due to their warehouse and self-service model, they operated with fewer staff per square foot.

Together, these price, selection, and availability attributes made office supply superstores the destinations that best fulfilled the purchasing criteria of their target small business customers: getting what they needed, when they needed it, at the best price. Staples' initial, troubled foray into Germany with MAXI-Papier shows how critical these above attributes were to the OSS' success in America. With smaller footprints (14,000 square feet) and less selection (4,000 items) than Staples' US stores, the one-stop-shop availability model was hurt. Even worse, German retailers at the time were not allowed to be open after 6 PM except on Thursdays—so the availability advantage over mom-and-pops was severely constrained. Finally, German law prohibited a company from offering a coupon worth more than 25 cents and it was illegal for a retailer to say that it had guaranteed low prices, making it hard to promote the value small businesses could find at MAXI-Papier. All together, these constraints on the German business seriously impaired the office superstore model and made it difficult to create a profitable chain in Germany, at the same time highlighting how important these superstore advantages were to the American success story.[93]

Looking back on the industry he helped create, Thomas Stemberg of Staples elucidated the superstore's cost and convenience advantage over its predecessors. "There [was] a reason why nobody had low prices in office supplies. If you sold the stuff the way the old guys did it—which is to buy in small lots and try to deliver it by your own trucks and so forth—it's obvious why stationers needed high prices to support those costs ... my aim was to ... satisfy customers with lower prices."[94] "Before Staples showed up, you got your pens and papers at a stationery store at high prices and at inconvenient hours, you had to go to an equally inconvenient machine dealer to buy whatever technology you had then—it was a lot of work and everything was full price, and putting it all under one roof and at a significant discount over what people used to pay ... I think we've made things better for people."[95]

Staples and Office Depot were clearly on to something, and their success did not go unnoticed. Staples opened its first store in May of 1986, and Office Depot opened its first store just a few months later in October of 1986 in Lauderdale Lakes, FL. Office superstores rapidly began sprouting up all over the country. From two stores by two companies in 1986, the industry grew to over 100 stores by the end of 1988,[96] and to over 450 stores by at least 17 companies in 1990.[97]

This unprecedentedly rapid growth was the result of abundant venture capital financing, a consolidated wholesale structure (4 companies supplied the entire OSS industry), an easily duplicated business model, a need to grow quickly in the face of competition, and two major shifts in the American economy. The first of these shifts was the transition of the American economy from manufacturing to service. While this initiated a recession in the early 1990s as large numbers of Americans were laid off in favor of offshoring, it was a boon for office supply superstores. Many laid off workers became self-employed or started businesses,[98] and this huge increase in home-based and small businesses fueled strong demand for home offices and office supplies, creating an explosion in the OSS' customer base. This sudden increase in home-based and small businesses is seen in the numbers and growth rates of non-employer firms and firms with less than 100 employees, shown in Figure 3.5.

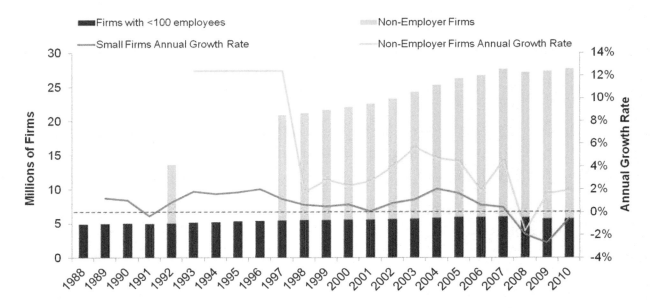

Figure 3.5 Source: US Economic Census.

The rapid adoption of IT was the second major shift in the US economy that supported the rise of the OSS. Office supply superstores launched just at the time when office technology was beginning to be widely embraced by small businesses. The wide adoption of this new technology created a surging category that grew from $11 BN to $57 BN in just five years, as shown in Figure 3.6.

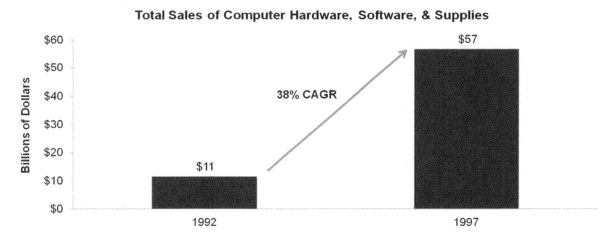

Figure 3.6 Source: US Economic Census.

While office supply superstores all began by targeting small and home-based businesses, they soon found that they were developing a following among ordinary consumers who shopped at office superstores for savings on school and home supplies. Jack Bingleman, formerly Staples' President of North American Stores and later President of International Stores, recalled that, "for the longest time, Staples resisted the fact that consumers, not just small businesses, came to the stores ... While we were born to look after people who were running a business, over time it became clear that we were just the perfect place for students and teachers and consumers and others to come to ... It isn't very long before you realize that there are more consumer computer-and-software buyers than there are business buyers ... You could have sat there and said that the business customer is the only one we're interested in. But we evolved."[99]

To pursue this new customer segment, Office Depot upgraded its new store model and remodeled its existing stores to better appeal to casual consumers. Stores "received a facelift as they transitioned away from the warehouse look with brighter lighting, colorful, easy-to-read signs, and tile floors instead of concrete."[100] Stores also became larger in order to stock more consumer-friendly products, particularly PCs and computer accessories. All the OSS tried to reinvigorate their customer service training to appeal to consumers. The loading of consumer volume into the superstores changed the growth outlook for the entire industry, teaching "each major OPS [Office Products and Supplies] operator that the trade radius required to support one store [was] smaller than previously suspected."[101] With smaller trading radii, it was possible to build more stores in current areas, as well as to expand to areas that previously were thought to be too small to support a store.

These growth drivers led Staples, Office Depot, and the clones they inspired, acquired, and consolidated to change the face of an entire industry, eliminating thousands of independent, small-format stationers. Drawn by the product selection, availability, and value-pricing at these office supply category-killers, small businesses rapidly abandoned their old mom-and-pop suppliers. In fact, the number of these small mom-and-pops more than halved between 1984 and 1993, falling from over 13,500 outlets in 1984 to fewer than 6,000 outlets in 1993.[102] Between 1986 and the early 2000s, the success of Staples and Office Depot was record-breaking—with Staples only the sixth company in history to achieve $3 billion in sales within ten years of start-up[103] and Office Depot even further ahead with $6 billion in sales in 1996 generated in part through a series of acquisitions.[104] Sales at the industry's founders, Staples and Office Depot, grew at a 45% CAGR and a 34% CAGR respectively between 1989 and 2000 (Figure 3.7).

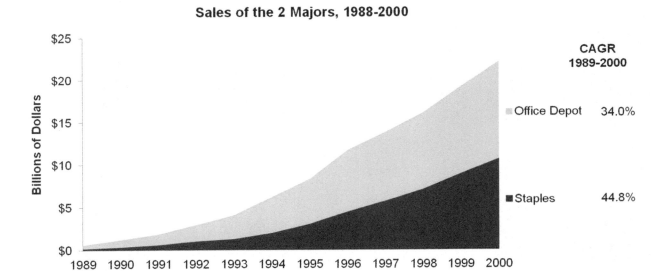

Figure 3.7 Source: Company Reports, accessed via Thomson One.

In 1993, only eight years after Staples was founded, office supply superstores accounted for 14.6% of the office supply market—largely at the expense of small mom-and-pops and the wholesalers who supplied them. This changing channel share is shown in Figure 3.8.

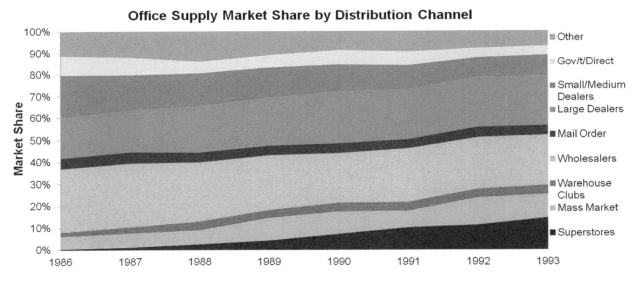

Figure 3.8 Source: L Keith Mullins and James P. Stoeffel, *Smith Barney*, 'Office Depot', report dated January 30, 1995.

Amongst the horde of clones inspired by Staples and Office Depot, there were some initial differences in how the office supply superstore companies operated. However, these differences largely disappeared through the rapid adoption by competitors of successful innovations and due to the consolidation of the various OSS companies into the three majors: Staples, Office Depot, and OfficeMax. The OSS chains became so homogenous, in fact, that Bruce Nelson, CEO of Office Depot, declared in 2001 that "Customers can't tell the difference between Office Depot, OfficeMax, and Staples."[105] Even today, the OSS have not substantially differentiated themselves from each other. Consequently, we feel that our recommendations for the office supply industry are broadly applicable to both of the remaining OSS chains.

Real estate strategies were principally where the office supply superstores differentiated themselves. While most of the clones stayed in a relatively limited geographic range, Office Depot, Staples, and OfficeMax pursued national growth heavily, both through organic store openings and acquisitions. OSS chains that didn't go national were put out of business or subsumed by those that did go national. Though they shared a national focus, the majors pursued very different real estate strategies. Staples, for its part, pursued a 'fortress' strategy, going after big, expensive markets like Boston, New York City, and Los Angeles in a defensive manner. Todd Krasnow, part of Stemberg's original team and Staples' former Chief Marketing Officer, explained that "by building these networks in these big markets like New York and Boston we have been able to make it difficult for the competition to thrive ... we have a very, very good network, and it's really tough to steal customers from a direct competitor when you don't have the economies of advertising leverage."[106]

Office Depot, on the other hand, followed a different real estate strategy and by 1989 achieved double the store count and revenue of its closest competitors. The company stayed in the sunbelt, where rent, taxes, and advertising were much cheaper, and consequently was able to grow much faster. Stemberg reflected on Office Depot's advantages and believed they did so well "because they could afford to advertise heavily. They were in cheap markets. I couldn't buy the New York Times or New York Newsday. Those guys could go to Orlando and buy newspaper advertisements dirt cheap, and bang—open three stores."[107] Not only were opening costs less at Office Depot, lower ongoing advertising and rental costs enabled Office Depot to bring "its stores to profitability more quickly [usually within four months] than its competitors" and with "margins generally [exceeding] competitors'".[108] Higher margins with a shorter time to profitability[109] generated cash for

Office Depot to open even more stores. Office Depot's stronger store growth was also enabled by a markedly different logistics model than Staples. Whereas Staples built distribution centers to break bulk and serve its smaller, high-rent constrained stores, Office Depot built its stores larger with a greater percentage of non-selling space to store the bulk orders suppliers shipped directly to its stores. Without the need to first build a distribution center and then build scale around the distribution center to make a region profitable, Office Depot could penetrate a region in less time and at lower upfront costs than Staples, and was free to rapidly extend its reach without focusing overly much on saturation. As time went on and Office Depot experienced higher inventory levels and operating costs than Staples, the company backfilled in existing markets and implemented a partnership with United Stationers to move towards more centralized distribution before building its own distribution centers.

The effects of these original real estate differences have carried into the present. Office Depot's stores are larger than Staples', and, before the 2013 merger with OfficeMax, experienced more competition in their markets (41.3% of Staples stores were in Staples-only markets, whereas only 17.5% and 21.8% of Office Depot and OfficeMax stores, respectively, had markets to themselves pre-merger).[110] Staples, for its part, continues to have a lock on many metropolitan markets.

The OSS in Recessions: Problems with Technology and Furniture, and Store-Level Reactions

It is our belief, which we will explain later, that the OSS can be considered to be in a permanent recession. Because of this, we think it is informative to look at OSS behavior in the last two recessions, and later examine if that behavior is appropriate today. In both of the last recessions, the OSS have faced issues with their big-ticket categories. They have also responded each time with a coordinated set of store-level decisions that ultimately resulted in fewer, smaller, more efficient stores.

From their birth, office supply superstore retailers focused on staking out new territories and then saturating these markets, moving into large organizations, and entering international markets. These boom times continued into the 1990s, when, as current CEO Ron Sargent recalled, "The economy was booming, so it made sense to continue adding stores and continue growing the business."[111] And, as Basil Anderson, vice chairman added, "We were pulling the sales model, focusing on value and volume."[112] This approach came to a halt, however, as the office supply industry confronted the recession of the late 1990s and early 2000s. While the economic pullback of the late 1980s and early 1990s fueled the explosive growth of the office supply superstore industry, this recession was quite different. Personal computers were barely a category in 1990, but they were about 18% of OSS sales by 1998. [113] These changes in the OSS' merchandise mix are shown in Figure 3.9. Whereas superstores in 1990 were few and far between, in 2000 the three majors had significant overlap in competitive regions and, fueled by sales to consumers, had more densely located stores. Finally, the office supply competitive landscape had changed as well. While "the retail superstore oligopoly — Office Depot, Staples, and OfficeMax — [had] developed and maintained a reasonably rational pricing environment,"[114] mass merchant discount channels began "increasingly flexing their square footage to sell office products at peak selling seasons (e.g. Jan. Feb. when small businesses get new budgets and back to school purchasing is done),"[115] and electronics discount stores (Best Buy and Circuit City) and direct sellers (Gateway and Dell) were driving PC prices down.[116]

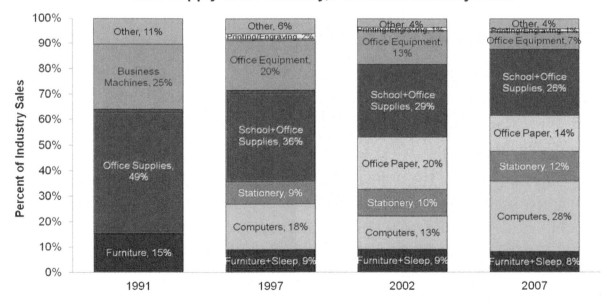

Office Supply Store Industry, Percent of Industry Sales

Figure 3.9 Source: US Economic Census.

The recession hit the computer, business equipment, and furniture categories particularly hard as consumers and small businesses delayed large capital expenditures during the recession. In the third quarter of 1999, Office Depot reported a loss and stated that their earnings would be below analysts' forecasts for the rest of the year, and in response Office Depot's stock price plummeted 30% in a day. The loss was due to incurred expenses for closing underperforming stores and writing down the value of slow-moving inventory, especially outdated technology products.[117] These categories showed similar behavior in the extended economic pullback that began in 2006. This recession again pulled volume out of the stores as seen in the double-digit comp store sales declines of 2008 and 2009, largely a result of declining sales for big ticket items. These categories are problematic in a recession as high-priced capital goods swing the most dramatically and their high prices influence same-store sales to a large degree. Because each store retains inventory, in a downturn brick-and-mortar retailers are left with more unsalable inventory than online retailers. Even when times are good, because the inventory burden is higher, brick-and-mortar retailers suffer more from markdowns brought on by technology obsolescence and fashion. In today's world, technology is also the most heavily showroomed category.

In both recessions, this volume pullback, in addition to pressure from new competitors, created a new economic reality that made OSS trading areas begin to look over-stored. This forced the OSS to take a hard look at their operations and strategy. After the late 90s recession, Staples launched the "Back to Brighton" strategy, designed to refocus the chain on business customers, with the campaign slogan "That was easy." Staples dropped low-priced, consumer-oriented computers and printers from its stores and slimmed down school supplies to refocus on business customers. Staples also redid store layouts to make high-volume items like paper easy to find at the front of the store, and installed clearer signage to help business customers get in and out quickly. Rather than open in new markets, Staples furthered its fortress strategy by focusing on its current markets and "penetrating areas with clusters of stores that were smaller than its traditional stores."[118] Office Depot also refocused on its core business customers, reducing or eliminating "underperforming inventory such as DVD players and computer software for children," which cut the stock-keeping units (SKUs) in its stores by 20% and in its warehouses by 30%.[119] Similarly to Staples, Office Depot redid its store layout to help busy customers find what they needed quickly and aggressively rolled out renovations that made stores smaller and less expensive to operate.[120] The company withdrew from five metropolitan markets and ultimately closed 73 underperforming North American stores in 2001.[121]

The OSS industry also ramped up their private label efforts. For example, Office Depot's private brand penetration was 13% in 2003, 15% in 2004 (increasing private label SKUs from 600 to 3,000 in the process)[122], in the mid-20% range by 2006 and was closing on 30% in 2007.[123] Other efforts at improving gross margin included "leveraging global purchasing power, partnering with vendors, and expanding [the] category management approach."[124] The elimination of low-price, low-margin technology products also contributed to rising gross margins. The office superstores had taken a hard look at improving the operating metrics of their businesses, and the results were evident. The OSS increased their gross margins, decreased their inventory per store, and increased their turns. These changes are shown in Figure 3.10.

Staples Operating Metrics			Office Depot Operating Metrics		
	1998	2006		1998	2006
Gross Margin	23.6%	28.5%	Gross Margin	28.0%	31.0%
Inventory Turns	5.1	9.4	Inventory Turns*	7.2	9.7
GMROI	3.9	6.7	GMROI*	5.2	6.7
Inventory/Store	$1.6 MM	$1.2 MM	Inventory/Store	$1.8 MM	$1.3 MM

Figure 3.10 Sources: Reuters and Company Reports. Notes: *Office Depot's 1997 Inventory Turns were 5.8 and GMROI was 4.3.

In the most recent recession, OfficeMax and Office Depot responded by again addressing excess SKUs, particularly in technology and furniture, and closing unprofitable stores.[125]

Office Supply Superstores and the Internet

The advent of the internet helped the office supply superstores through the slow-down beginning in 1998. The OSS were among the pioneers of online retailing. Office Depot, in fact, set up desk-top ordering with MIT in 1995. At that time, Monica Luechtefeld (EVP of eCommerce and Direct Marketing at Office Depot) recalled, "We saw the vision of what the Internet could mean for businesses."[126] Office Depot, Staples, and OfficeMax all launched internet portals as another leg of their multi-channel strategy, and sales from the eCommerce channel increased substantially. As shown in Figure 3.11, eCommerce rapidly became the preferred method of buying office supplies for Office Depot's Business Services Group (BSG) customers. The eCommerce channel rapidly cannibalized Office Depot's telecenters, and accounted for 88% of Office Depot's BSG sales by 2005. This was a boon for the pressured OSS industry, as the internet was "growing robustly ... [and] given the low cost of transaction,"[127] helped reduce fulfillment costs for delivery orders.

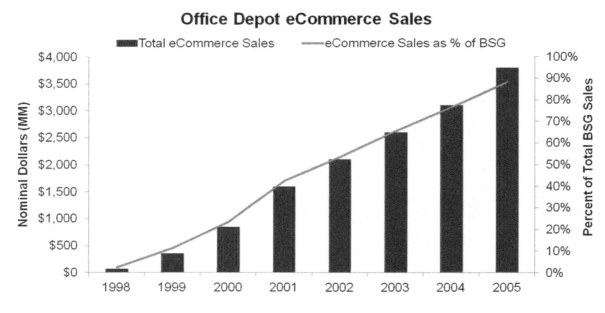

Figure 3.11 Source: Office Depot annual reports. Note: eCommerce sales were reported worldwide starting in 2002.

While numerous internet start-ups popped up to sell office supplies in the dot-com boom, analysts thought that the OSS industry had very strong advantages over these new-comers. Office supply superstores could leverage their in-store advertising to support their online efforts. For example, Office Depot linked their online portal to in-store kiosks in order to target customers with multi-channel options. The OSS were also already in the business of serving delivery customers. Because online orders were similar in profile to the delivery orders the OSS industry was already fulfilling, the OSS could instantly support their online efforts with their existing infrastructure. New start-ups, on the other hand, had to scale up. Finally, given their scale, Staples, Office Depot, and OfficeMax all had stronger purchasing power than the new online entrants.[128] Describing Office Depot, analysts wrote, "management has also indicated that it expects to be profitable in the Internet business in 1999. This is certainly bucking the trend in this sector, since Office Depot should have solid sales growth and profit, the latter of which many Internet retailers are not expected to see for years to come."[129] To compound these advantages, the big three also acquired or partnered with some of these new internet start-ups. In 2002, Office Depot partnered with Amazon to run Amazon's office supplies category with 50,000 office products from Office Depot. Given these advantages and the OSS industry's fast entry into online retailing, it appeared that the OSS were well-equipped to deal with the challenges eCommerce posed to retailers everywhere. Staples and Office Depot even traded between themselves the title of second-largest eCommerce retailer (after Amazon) in later years.[130]

Despite the fact that the OSS are still the top retailers of office supplies in every channel, including online, the introduction of eCommerce to office supplies was a sea change for the industry of the same magnitude as the first Staples superstore. The eCommerce divisions of the OSS not only took channel share from their telecenter-based large accounts operations, they also took channel share from the retail stores. Over the years, office supply superstores have added a number of new categories, such as personal computers, school supplies, and printing services. However, office paper, stationery, and office supplies have continued to form the core of the superstore offering, still accounting for over 50% of sales in 2007. These core categories, however, have made large moves online as shown by the growth in the "Electronic and Mail" channel across these categories in Figure 3.12.

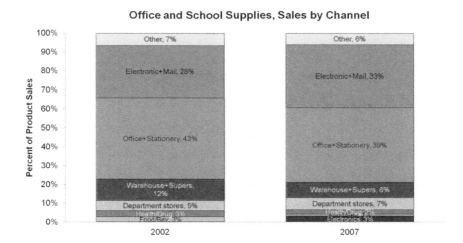

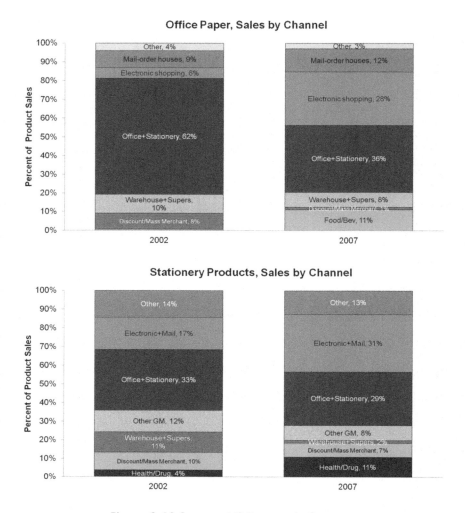

Figure 3.12 Source: US Economic Census.

The OSS have many advantages over other online retailers, including Amazon, such as free same-day delivery and the ease of dealing with one vendor rather than a collection of third-party sellers, both made possible due to the OSS' product concentration. From a perspective of scale, Amazon is estimated to sell only about $400 million of office supplies,[131] less than 4% of the $11.8 billion of office supplies that Staples sold in North American in 2012. It's unlikely, then, that Amazon is buying better, at least in office supplies, than any of the OSS. Even if Amazon was doing so, in the low-priced, commodity consumables the OSS carry, customers are less likely to shop multiple venues to save a few cents. Amazon achieves pricing comparability through buying only the highest volume SKUs itself and then using its extensive vendor network to supply the rest.[132] The OSS, on the other hand, maintain forward inventory, which results in having the fastest delivery times of any online retailer.[133] Buying through an OSS online portal is also easier for the average office manager. Because of Amazon's reliance on third party vendors, multi-item orders can be spaced out over days in multiple deliveries (though this is changing with many vendors' increasing adoption of Fulfillment by Amazon). For the office manager who wants to put away an order all at once, this is an inconvenience.[134] The result is that much of the online migration shown above has been to the superstores' own eCommerce arms. However, this doesn't lessen the damage done to the OSS' physical stores. As the three majors rode casual consumer sales in the late 90s, they extended their locations and trade radii into areas they originally wouldn't have considered. With less solid foundations, these stores are likely most at risk from this channel shift.

The Final Chapter? (2007-Present)

Figure 3.13 highlights many of the changes that have taken place in the North American OSS retail chains over the past three decades: the explosion in store counts, the expansion of average square feet per store, rising SKU counts, and trends in sales per square foot.

North American Retail Only		1987	1992	1997	2002	2007	2008	2009	2010	2011	2012	2013
Office Depot	Store Count	10	284	612	867	1,222	1,267	1,152	1,147	1,131	1,112	1,104
Office Depot	Revenue	$33,683	$1,732,965	$4,714,000	$5,804,449	$6,813,600	$6,112,300	$5,113,600	$4,962,800	$4,870,200	$4,457,800	$4,281,800
Office Depot	Total Square Footage	186,261	5,424,000	N/A	23,620,343	29,790,082	30,672,862	28,109,844	27,559,184	26,556,126	25,518,027	25,001,724
Office Depot	YOY Comp Store Sales Growth	45%	15%	1%	-2%	-5%	-13%	-14%	-1%	-2%	-5%	-4%
Office Depot	Average Square Feet per Store	18,626	23,789	27,500	27,000	24,378	24,209	24,401	24,027	23,480	22,948	22,646
Office Depot	SKU Count	6,500	5,100	6,000	8,200	8,500	8,500	8,500	8,500	8,500	8,500	8,500
Office Depot	Sales per Square Foot	$181	$271	N/A	$246	$229	$199	$182	$180	$183	$175	$171
Staples	Store Count	16	174	685	1,300	1,738	1,835	1,871	1,900	1,917	1,886	1,846
Staples	Revenue	$39,666	$883,088	$4,029,480	$7,166,105	$10,020,941	$9,489,510	$9,364,190	$9,529,757	$9,660,847	$11,827,906	$11,103,160
Staples	Square Feet of Selling Space	220,796	2,559,169	11,193,000	30,109,000	38,319,000	38,713,000	39,188,000	39,538,000	37,365,000	N/A	N/A
Staples	YOY Comp Store Sales Growth	41%	18%	10%	1%	-3%	-9%	-2%	-1%	0%	-2%	-4%
Staples	Average Square Feet per Store	13,800	14,708	15,085	23,161	22,048	21,097	20,945	20,809	19,491	22,000	22,000
Staples	SKU Count	5,000	5,000+	8,000	8,000	8,000	8,000	8,000	8,000	8,000	8,000	8,000
Staples	Sales per Square Foot	$180	$345	$360	$238	$262	$245	$239	$241	$259	N/A	N/A

Figure 3.13 Sources: Consolidated from annual reports, news articles, and analyst reports. Notes: OfficeMax was not founded until 1988 and its corporate history results in periods where information was not available. Due to the lack of information in the public record, we've excluded them from this table. Staples stopped reporting precise square footage estimates in 2012. 2013 year for Office Depot shows the fourth quarter of 2012 and the first three quarters of 2013 to eliminate the effect of the Office Depot/Office Max merger.

Sales per square foot have not significantly recovered since the most recent recession, and strong headwinds face the industry. Comp store sales are consistently down, and are likely to remain so due to the declining demand for paper as well as increased competition from "pure play online retailers, such as Amazon," from traditional competitors, like

Walmart and Costco, who are "enabled by wholesalers to sell more items across multiple categories," and even from independent retailers, who, enabled by the web, have started to make a comeback. Low expectations are also due to the broader macroeconomic environment, which, while regaining momentum, has been deemed a "jobless recovery." For all intents and purposes, the OSS' core category could be considered to be operating in a permanent recession.

Paired with the competition faced in the technology category, this likely means that vast amounts of the OSS' floor space will become unproductive. In the store layouts pictured in Figure 3.14 and Figure 3.15, the color red highlights the challenges that the OSS face. It shows categories that are paper-related, like notebooks, paperclips, and office paper, that face declining demand as both small businesses and consumers digitize their processes. Red also depicts categories where online retailers have excelled, such as technology products. Red also highlights categories, like office furniture, that are likely better fulfilled online due to the volatility in their demand, their slow turnover even in good times, and the amount of space the merchandise physically occupies.

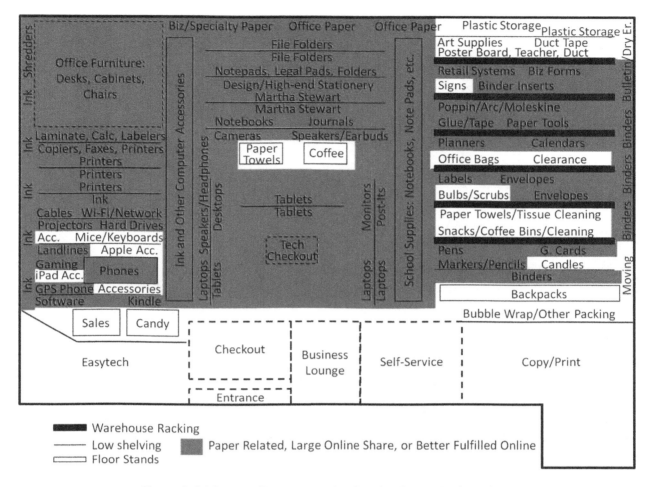

Figure 3.14 Source: Representative Staples Store, Author visit.

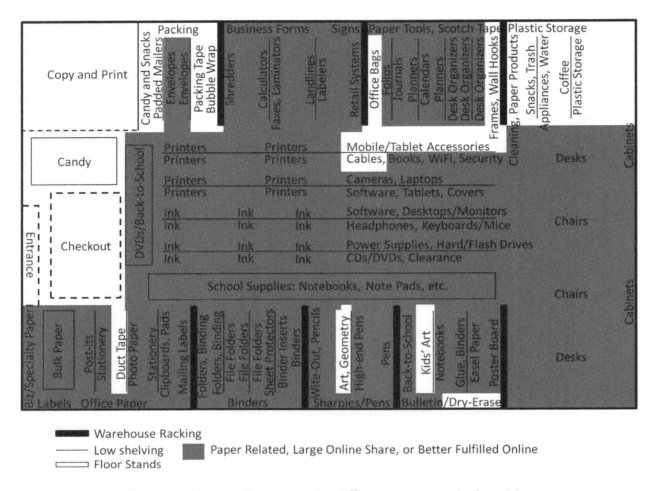

Figure 3.15 Source: Representative Office Depot store, Author visit.

At the same time, the merchandise mix at the OSS has only recently begun to change to reflect these dynamics, as demonstrated by the declining role played by computers and computer products in Staples' merchandise mix, shown in Figure 3.16.

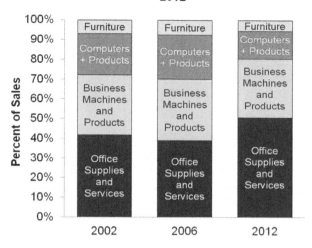

Figure 3.16 Source: Company Reports.

Facing comp sale declines in perpetuity and an excess of real estate, the OSS will need to choose one of two paths: managing for sustainability (through attempts at a "Shrink and Transform the Box" or a "Enhance the Value of the Box" strategy) or managing for cash flow (by adopting the "Wind Down" strategy). To manage for sustainability, the OSS would need to reinvent themselves as destination stores, and introduce new categories, services, and/or business models to generate renewed customer trips, create new profit sources, and ultimately keep stores productive.

In the OSS' case, with their varied departments, any effort to manage for sustainability will most likely resemble a patchwork of these options. Following the new categories tactic, Staples has introduced break room and janitorial supplies in order to make up for lost sales in paper-related categories. Staples' stated aim is to "ramp up" these new categories "faster than the [paper categories] decline."[135]

In the OSS' technology departments, the companies could follow the showroom model being introduced by Best Buy. Under this model, Best Buy provides space within its stores for brands to install exclusive sales areas staffed by brand-provided salespeople. Office and stationery stores accounted for 8% of US computer hardware, software, and supplies sales in 2007[136] (though the OSS have been deemphasizing technology sales for some time) and the OSS have a concentrated small and home-business audience. The opportunity for an electronics brand to address such an audience at scale, and present the business benefits of their products, could be the base for a potential store-within-a-store (SWAS) relationship. Just like Best Buy's Geek Squad, the OSS' Geek Squad-like offerings (Staples' EasyTech and Office Depot's Tech Depot) could support this strategy.

The OSS could also, like Home Depot and PetSmart, adopt a more service-oriented bent. However, unlike home supply and pet customers, office supply customers likely don't need or want help picking commodity products; they just want them quickly. In Staples for Success, Tom Stemberg discusses how hard it is to get people to care about office supplies. Ron Sargent points out that "brands are not as important in the office-products industry"[137] and that "the great thing about office products is that you don't have to taste them [or] try them on."[138] Customer-focused, in-aisle help from associates well-versed in the nuances of the product like that provided by Home Depot and PetSmart is unlikely to be relevant in this vertical outside of the technology category.

That leaves fee-based services as the tool to coalesce the advantages of physical stores into a sustainable strategy against online retailers. In-store, fee-based services have largely meant copy/print shops for the OSS, but this has been changing as the OSS recognized the success of Geek Squad and felt the pressure to combat sales declines. Office Depot and Staples have both rolled out their Tech Depot and EasyTech services to their stores, offering PC setup, installations, virus removal, and other computer-related services. Before its merger with Office Depot, OfficeMax was experimenting with smaller stores it called Business Solutions Centers, complete with Business Solutions Advisers that could act as the customer's account executive. Business Solutions Advisers offered customized product pricing and served as agents for OfficeMax's print, copy and marketing collateral centers; could provide technical services like virus removal, software installation, data recovery, and (through partner GoDaddy) domain name registration and other website building services.

To introduce additional services, the OSS could use a Home Depot tactic, and enable independent service providers to market themselves in its stores. Under this arrangement, the OSS would lease out the surplus space in their existing stores to relevant small business service professionals: lawyers, accountants and payroll professionals, tax experts, human resource consultants, travel and hospitality agents, technologists, marketers, etc. These professionals get space close to their customers, and benefit from walk-in traffic that it may be difficult to identify and market to otherwise. Small businesses currently can't find professional advice beyond stock legal forms and CD-ROMs in the aisles of the OSS, yet it is uncommon for them to use many of these service professionals. Bringing small businesses access to these professionals could fulfill an unmet need. The OSS benefit from being able to offer a diverse array of services without incurring significant training expenses and higher operating costs. By creating a small business support cluster, they strengthen their position as destination stores. Staples' new omnichannel stores feature a softer version of this idea, providing a free business lounge with "informal meeting spaces shoppers can use." One use-case for these spaces is a real estate agent who uses the lounge to sign contracts with clients.[139]

One can envisage three store formats that would incorporate some or many of the tactics described above. These three formats are shown in scale relative to each other in Figure 3.17. The first, a small-format store, would focus exclusively on copy and print services and non-technology product sales. The second, a mid-sized store, would add other services and SKUs provided by the retailer, and the third, using the extra space in the OSS' current large-format stores, would provide space for third-party services.

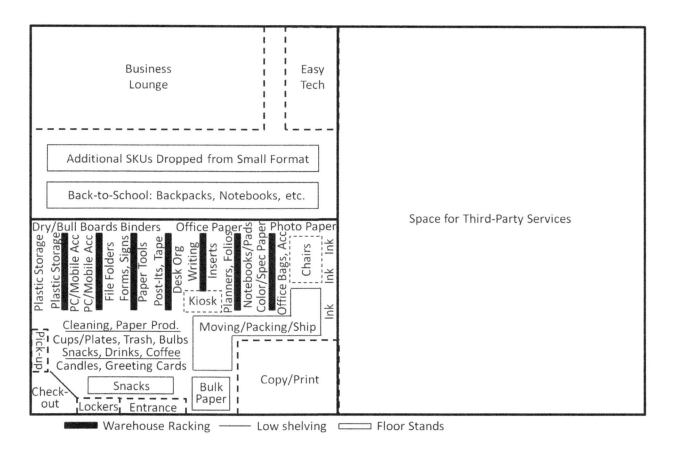

Figure 3.17

This manage for sustainability pathway is not without costs, risks, and challenges, however. Delaying the implementation of the "Wind Down," manage for cash flow strategy in the hopes that bad stores can be rescued consumes people, cash, and time. If the rescue strategy ultimately fails, it will have destroyed value for shareholders. And with the benefit of hindsight, companies fighting to survive don't always make the best decisions. Barnes & Noble tried to combat the Amazon Kindle through the launch of their own eReader, the Nook. The Nook segment of Barnes & Noble has incurred cumulative losses of almost $1.3 billion since 2010.[140] While at one point the business unit was valued at $1.8 billion by Microsoft and Pearson in 2012, that value has certainly fallen substantially after five straight quarters of device and content sales declines and no reversal in sight as of September 9, 2014. Blockbuster quickly went out of business after investing heavily in its own Redbox- and Netflix-like offerings. While to their credit, the OSS are using tactics that, if successful, will reposition their stores, rather than, like Barnes & Noble and Blockbuster, building products and services that by their very nature take sales out of stores, there are many reasons to think that a manage for sustainability strategy using tactics such as those described above will ultimately be unsuccessful.

The showroom strategy being implemented by Best Buy may not work for the OSS. In the OSS, the store space dedicated to technology products has always been smaller than at consumer electronics stores, with fewer categories and less SKUs. Despite the volume that flows through the channel, there may not be enough consolidated demand to justify SWAS or other arrangements. The purchasing criteria for business users are also likely different than those for consumers; consumers are evaluating electronics for entertainment purchases rather than for their applicability to business needs. Consumers want to see their new high-definition television before purchase, whereas small business owners may not care particularly about the resolution on a computer they intend to use for word processing and spreadsheets. Finally, while Best Buy is the only national consumer electronics retailer left, the OSS' grasp on the technology vertical is not as firm. There are still two large players left, and many competitors in other channels sell the paper shredders, computers, and printers that chiefly make up the OSS' narrow technology departments.

Nor is it clear that services will save the OSS. In general, the OSS have struggled to offer a diverse set of services. Office Depot originally piloted a relationship with Best Buy's Geek Squad to offer technology services before committing to launching Tech Depot, its

Geek Squad clone. Both Staples' EasyTech and Tech Depot are more recent entrants to the service market than Geek Squad, and may need time to fully train their technicians. While the OSS have placed these Geek Squad-like services in stores, they've also reduced the technology category in new stores to a handful of internet-connected tablets. It's not clear that, in the long-term, customers will come to a retailer for service when they bought the product somewhere else. In addition, it's not clear that these services will endure. Over one-third of Geek Squad's tech support subscribers are aged 55 to 64, compared to 12% of the general population. Younger customer segments, the digital natives, aren't likely to need the same support when they age due to their greater comfort with technology and the increasing user-friendliness of technology.[141] As the average selling price of technology continues to fall, the OSS will likely experience a similar transition as did Circuit City, where consumers opted to buy new devices instead of paying the costs of repairs and service. This will only get easier as storage, media, and music move to the Cloud, making it easy for anyone to comfortably use a new computer simply by logging into an online account.

Outside of technology services, the picture is not much better. Staples.com was originally intended to deliver business services like accounting and payroll to Staples customers, but the site is still mostly a product, rather than a service, portal. Relying on third-parties to provide these services from dedicated space within an office supply store also means that the OSS must take responsibility for merchandising the area: selecting the right mix of providers, testing them for quality, etc. Home Depot has had trouble relying on third party service contractors, and it's unclear if the OSS would be able to do better.

Most importantly, however, is the belief that both the showrooming approach and the services-based approach promise counterparties some other product (namely paper and related products) to drive traffic. Presumably, business electronics brands would compensate the OSS for providing a showroom in order to take advantage of the foot traffic that the superstores controlled. Similarly, small business professionals would wish to locate their offices and market their services within the OSS because their target clients regularly pass through the store. However, due to the declining use of paper, the OSS's customers don't shop for it as often, and same-store sales traffic growth at the OSS has been mostly negative since the second half of 2007, and consistently declining since 2012. The annual and cumulative impact of these traffic declines is shown in Figure 3.18. While Staples hopes that its new facilities and breakroom categories will replace paper and related categories over time, it's unclear that these new categories can support a store on their own, and it's an open question whether their current strong growth is merely the result of incremental sales on paper-driven trips, or whether these categories, in light of the large amount of competition for them, are traffic-drivers in themselves. Without these routine trips from their target small business audience, it will likely make little sense for either brands or small business professionals to partner with the OSS.

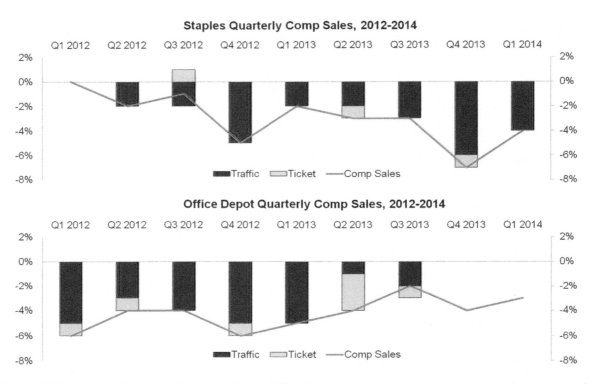

Figure 3.18 Source: Company Reports. Note: OfficeMax also experienced severe negative comp sales, largely because of declining traffic, but did not break out comp sale components between traffic and ticket. Office Depot ceased breaking out these comp sale numbers in Q4 of 2013.

Wind Down and Manage for Cash Flow

Under any strategy, it's likely that an office supply superstore designed for today would look substantially different than the current store base of the OSS. Whether or not the OSS, weighed down by existing store assets and legacy operations can get there, and what 'there' exactly is, are valid questions. Given the challenges described above, it's difficult for us to believe that these tactics, individually or collectively, will be enough to ensure a sustainable future. Rather than spend cash, time, and attention on transforming the chain, it may be more valuable to shareholders if the OSS instead focus on winding down their brick-and-mortar assets, and managing for cash flow. This is a difficult strategy to accept, and there are many challenges to this approach, but shareholders may ultimately end up better off.

As discussed earlier, due to the continuing decline in paper sales and the related decline in comp store sales and traffic, it is our belief that the OSS can be conceived of as being in a permanent recession. The tactics of a "Wind Down" strategy where the retailer is managing for cash flow do not look very different from what the OSS have usually done during recessions: close underperforming stores, eliminate non-productive SKUs, and slim down stores to make them more cost-effective and easier-to-navigate. Additional initiatives that generate cash and support this strategy aren't necessarily bad, but there is an added caveat: in order to avoid destroying shareholder value, new projects should be limited to ones with short payback periods and massive, 'bet-the-farm' Hail Mary plans should be avoided. Even routine store investments, like redoing the carpeting in a store, may be canceled if that store is expected to close soon.

While not explicitly adopting the Wind Down strategy, many recent decisions by the OSS closely parallel the tactics described above. The combined Office Depot/OfficeMax entity plans to close 400 US stores, over 20% of its US store base, by the end of 2016. Staples intends to close 225 North American stores, or 12% of its North American store base, by the middle of 2015. These closures both eliminate unprofitable stores that have been dragging down the retailers' overall profits and funnel the closed stores' sales to their healthier siblings, significantly improving the returns and comp sales of stores that remain open and better leveraging the assets of the healthy stores.

As the OSS close stores, the cash-flow negative ones are obvious targets. Other stores will likely require a more nuanced decision process. A store that is unprofitable could become even more so when shut down if continuing lease costs exceed the expected income of the store. In considering each office supply superstore company's total network of stores, even marginally profitable ones may make sense to close if their sales are expected to be redistributed to neighboring stores of the same chain, as volume continues to be important to the OSS. On the other hand, unprofitable ones may need to remain open if their contributions to distribution center volume and administrative overhead prevent a step function change that would damage profitable stores. As the demand for paper continues to decline, the OSS will need to maintain flexible lease arrangements so that their store closures can keep pace with an unpredictable market.

The OSS have also begun to reduce store sizes. This is particularly important, as this is another way to increase cost leverage by reducing occupancy, inventory, and staff expenses. After years of having some of the largest store formats, including the now-closed megastores in New York City, Office Depot is leading this charge. Office Depot recently unveiled a 5,000 square foot prototype store, and declared that it "intends to use 5,000 and 15,000 square foot prototypes almost exclusively going forward," using its "operating lease expirations (60% of its store base in the next 3 years) to re-size its footprints."[142] Staples is halving its store size to 12,000 square feet in its omnichannel stores.

Colin McGranahan of Bernstein Research describes Office Depot's new 5,000 square foot stores as stressing convenience and ease, offering "roughly half the SKUs of a full-sized store (4500 vs. 8500), with the broadest assortment in immediate need categories (e.g. writing instruments), with a much narrower assortment in furniture and PCs."[143] In the troublesome PC and furniture categories, Office Depot has substituted digital showrooms and online delivery for actual products. It has replaced the furniture pad in its 5K square foot stores with fabric and wood swatches and miniature models of the larger furniture sets, and installed kiosk ordering stations for customers to purchase furniture and technology products through Office Depot's online assortment. The only furniture pieces actually stocked in the store are a few SKUs of carry-with furniture like office chairs. To support this omnichannel model, the small stores are tightly integrated with Office Depot's delivery warehouses and its larger stores so that customers can pick-up online orders on the same day they purchase them. This structure preserves availability and selection and enhances price competitiveness relative to other channels, while making the stores easier to shop for the routine, paper-based items customers buy most often. Office supply superstore customers are, in former CEO of Office Depot Bruce Nelson's words, still looking for "convenience, including help in getting oriented, the ability to find everything on a shopping list, and fast checkout [for basic office supplies]." This new format meets these needs well.

With a mix shift toward services and private label, and away from low-margin technology products, store-level gross margins are higher. Because the 5K square foot stores retain 90% of the sales of the low-performing stores they replace, occupancy is leveraged significantly in these stores, while labor expenses are in-line with sales. The 15K square foot stores have very similar sales profiles to current stores. These new formats boost underperforming stores' gross and operating margins significantly, and Bernstein Research has estimated the new formats' P&L relative to the underperforming stores they replace. We show these calculations in Figure 3.19.

5,000 Square Foot Stores	$ per Store		$s per Square Foot		% of Sales	
	5K	26K	5K	26K	5K	26K
Sales/Store	2,550	2,860	510	110	100.0%	100.0%
COGS ex-rent	1,683	1,916	337	74	66.0%	67.0%
Rent	60	312	12	12	2.4%	10.9%
Gross Profit	807	632	161	24	31.6%	22.1%
Variable SG&A	434	486	87	19	17.0%	17.0%
Fixed SG&A	208	260	42	10	8.2%	9.1%
EBIT	166	-114	33	-4	6.5%	-4.0%

15,000 Square Foot Stores	$ per Store		$s per Square Foot		% of Sales	
	15K	26K	15K	26K	15K	26K
Sales/Store	4,500	4,500	300	173	100.0%	100.0%
COGS ex-rent	3,015	3,015	201	116	67.0%	67.0%
Rent	180	312	12	12	4.0%	6.9%
Gross Profit	1,305	1,173	261	45	51.2%	26.1%
Variable SG&A	765	765	51	29	17.0%	17.0%
Fixed SG&A	327	363	22	14	7.3%	8.1%
EBIT	213	45	188	2	4.7%	1.0%

Figure 3.19 Source: McGranahan, Colin et al, 'Office Depot: Leading the Office Supply Sector Towards a Small Store Strategy?' *Bernstein Research*, report dated January 23, 2012. Note: Includes impact of allocating corporate overhead.

Relative to other channels, these smaller formats have many advantages in the basic commodities they are designed to carry. In these categories, the OSS and their brick-and-mortar and online competitors price nearly equally and convenience is the largest purchasing criteria. The OSS' smaller formats can be located closer to the core small-business customer than can the much larger Walmart and Costco stores. For small business customers looking to find everything on their list in one store, the limited selections at Walmart and Costco are not sufficient, and even the pared-down selection at these small-format OSS stores is much better than that found in other brick-and-mortar channels. For customers looking to get in and out quickly, the large footprints and various other merchandise categories at Walmart and Costco are a hindrance. Against both brick-and-mortar and online competitors, the OSS' stores represent the quickest way to fulfill orders for small businesses that need critical office supplies right away. With smaller, easier-to-navigate stores, this advantage will grow.

Office Depot believes so strongly in these smaller formats that they have updated their entire supply chain to be capable of serving them. Because the smaller formats have limited holding capacity and can't accommodate bulk, they are supplied instead by the Business Services Group, the same division that handles all online and contract orders. Deliveries occur 5 days per week and consist of smaller volumes and each-picks (in some cases), vs. the bulk and pallet-level deliveries of Office Depot's larger stores. With more frequent deliveries, the supply chain for these smaller stores is being driven by demand (pull), rather than to stock (push).[144]

While a massive store renovation and relocation campaign may seem like a direct contradiction of the rule to make no large changes in a Wind Down strategy, and is reminiscent of Circuit City's expensive, last-ditch, fainthearted, and ultimately unsuccessful effort to look more like Best Buy, the logistics system described above makes this transformation possible without violating this precept. Because the smaller formats are replenished almost daily in smaller quantities, the 5K square foot format can reduce store inventory by as much as 50%, which effectively offsets the cash cost of downsizing and relocating existing stores.[145] With a supply chain upgraded to better serve these new formats, and inventory reductions that pay for the opening costs of the smaller format stores, Office Depot appears poised to return to sustained profitability.

Similarly, many other tactics presented as part of the managing for sustainability strategies discussed earlier can be implemented in a way that makes them cheap to test and investment-light to roll out. For instance, Staples' effort to offer new, routinely purchased, low value density office supply categories like janitorial products and break room items fills empty space on the shelves. As paper sales fall off, adding new categories to the store takes advantage of lower-utilized warehouse, delivery, and store infrastructure, and, assuming strong inventory turns, is a relatively cash-light investment. The company takes an even lower investment approach in other categories that it is introducing solely on its website. For these categories, Staples uses a drop-ship model with outside wholesalers. This tactic involves picking up purely incremental sales through Staples' website, receiving the order from a wholesaler, and bundling it at Staples' distribution centers with the rest of the customer's order for next-day shipment. Other tactics, such as SWAS, are also investment-light as long as the brand pays for it, and using a third-party services provider model means that the OSS don't have to invest in training professionals themselves. When implemented in an investment-light manner, these tactics can be low-risk ways to generate additional cash while the company continues to wind down.

The Wind Down and manage for cash flow strategy is really a mindset shift, transforming an organization from a steward of the future to a guardian of cash. It does not preclude trying new things to generate incremental cash, but it does limit the investments that can be made in people, stores, inventory, and technology; unlike a "manage for sustainability" strategy, where retailers would be expected to make significant investments up front and remodel stores every few years. Managing for cash focuses the organization on going out of business successfully. Without this mindset shift, retailers may, on the surface and in the short term, adopt the same tactics, but with many differences at the margin. For instance, in a recession, many retailers will close unprofitable stores and slim down in an effort to maintain profitability. However, retailers hoping for a turn-around, for the market to improve, or simply to prolong the life of the organization and be the last man standing will likely keep their bad stores open too long, or invest in stores that should be closed in order to protect the brand and customer relationships in the hope that business will eventually come flooding back. They may also strive to retain talent, paying compensation that is outsized when compared to the company's future prospects. They may continually overbuy inventory, hoping to be in a well-stocked position for the increase in demand that they believe is right around the corner. The company managing for cash flow, on the other hand, will have accepted that these efforts are futile, and will take the cash saved by avoiding these actions and return it to shareholders.

Importantly, the Wind Down strategy is intended to harvest as much cash as possible for shareholders, not to independently or collectively save the OSS' brick-and-mortar stores. If we believe that paper will continue to be eliminated from America's offices, and so the demand for paper and paper-dependent office supplies will continue to fall, these new formats will not remain profitable indefinitely. Using Bernstein Research's estimates, and assuming a 1% decline in comp store sales every year as the core category declines, we estimate a nine year lifespan for the 5K square foot stores and a six year lifespan for the 15K square foot stores. These scenarios are shown in Figure 3.20.

5K SQFT Store	Year 0	Year 1	Year 2	Year 3	Year 4	Year 5	Year 6	Year 7	Year 8	Year 9
Sales/Store	2550	2525	2499	2474	2450	2425	2401	2377	2353	2329
COGS ex-rent	1683	1683	1683	1683	1683	1683	1683	1683	1683	1683
Rent	60	60	60	60	60	60	60	60	60	60
Gross Profit	807	782	756	731	707	682	658	634	610	586
Variable SG&A	434	430	425	421	417	413	409	405	400	396
Fixed SG&A	208	208	208	208	208	208	208	208	208	208
EBIT	165	144	123	102	82	61	41	21	2	-18

15K SQFT Store	Year 0	Year 1	Year 2	Year 3	Year 4	Year 5	Year 6
Sales/Store	4500	4455	4410	4366	4323	4279	4237
COGS ex-rent	3015	3015	3015	3015	3015	3015	3015
Rent	180	180	180	180	180	180	180
Gross Profit	1305	1260	1215	1171	1128	1084	1042
Variable SG&A	765	757	750	742	735	728	720
Fixed SG&A	327	327	327	327	327	327	327
EBIT	213	176	139	102	66	30	-6

Figure 3.20

To put this in context of an actual small-format store, one can see that even in Staples' new, small-format omnichannel stores, shown in Figure 3.21, substantial floor space is dedicated to products in decline or better fulfilled online.

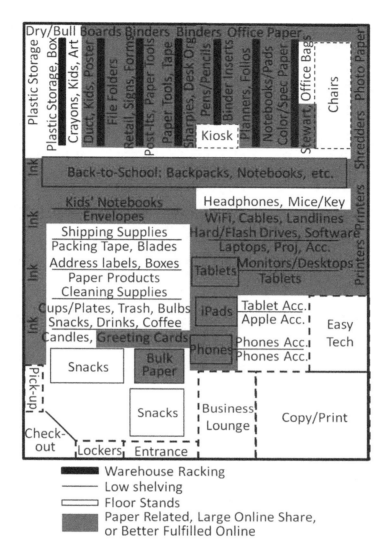

Figure 3.21 Sources: Representative Staples Omnichannel Store, Author visit.

Retailers who adopt the "manage for cash flow" strategy accept the reality that store assets will eventually outlive their usefulness, and, through flexible store leases, are prepared to shed them. While the timeframe presented above may seem short, the above numbers reflect an average, and within the store portfolio, winding down is a process of constant trimming to maintain profitable cash-generating operations for as long as possible.

Obviously, the Wind Down strategy is one that any retailer would have difficulty implementing. Finding a management team that is willing to govern a shrinking company without growth prospects, where, if they do their jobs right, they will eventually be unemployed, is a difficult task. Even more difficult may be convincing store associates to stick with a company that has an explicit intention of going out of business. Fortunately, small formats focused on a few, easily-understood commodity SKUs will be easier to run than large, legacy stores with significant store space dedicated to difficult-to-understand technology products, and high associate turnover may not be a significant cost. Shareholders may also revolt at such a strategy. Private equity ownership, which would treat these companies as a declining annuity rather than a growth asset, may be the only way to effectively implement such a strategy.

Despite these challenges, however, the Wind Down strategy is being employed by other retailers. Eddie Lampert, chairman of Sears, has been routinely spinning out smaller Sears' businesses (e.g. Orchard Supply Hardware, Sears Hometown and Outlet Stores, Lands' End) and borrowing against its Kenmore, Craftsmen, and DieHard brands. Sears then returns the cash to shareholders through holdings in the spun-out companies (the equivalent of special dividends) and share repurchases. Through these share repurchases, Sears' shares outstanding have fallen from 160 million in 2006 following the Kmart and Sears merger to 106 million today. To make this process easier, Lampert has even adopted an organizational structure that breaks up each business unit into its own autonomous organization. This has resulted in an internally competitive and divisive company when other retailers are focusing on how to get departments to collaborate, but, according to CEO and largest shareholder Lampert, it also makes the business units easier to divest.[146] While Lampert is investing in and exploring an internet model, he has embraced store closures and foregone store investments in efforts to make the company profitable again and preserve cash for shareholders.

Netflix is using the Wind Down strategy to milk cash from its expiring DVD-by-mail business. In the heyday of Netflix's DVD service, the company built small, focused distribution centers across the US in order to cut delivery times to customers and maximize inventory utilization. However, believing that the future will be streaming, and seeing DVD subscriber numbers beginning to decline, Netflix turned the DVD business into a cash cow. New inventory is still bought for the service, but little investment appears to be put into growing or sustaining the DVD-by-mail business; it's not even featured on the Netflix home page. To keep the profitability of the business up and maintain its cash generation, Netflix simply closes additional distribution centers as subscriber numbers decline. Eventually, this will probably reach the point where so many distribution centers have been closed that service suffers, at which point subscriber declines will probably accelerate, and Netflix will have milked the DVD-by-mail business for all it was worth.

Between Office Depot and Staples, which retailer succeeds best at the Wind Down strategy (assuming both already have accepted or will at some point be forced to accept this strategy) will likely depend on their legacy real estate locations. Staples has a greater presence in urban markets, and to the extent that acceptably-priced same-day delivery becomes a reality, it will most likely be limited to metropolitan areas. Such a service from other retailers would make Staples' smaller stores a less compelling channel compared to others. On the other hand, Office Depot's exurban stores have larger trading areas. To the extent that customers want to avoid the time and expense of a trip, they may prefer fulfillment by delivery, and be more vigilant about ordering online with enough lead-time to avoid having to go to a store for the immediate need products the new smaller stores are designed to stock.

Given the product dynamics in this space, we feel that both OSS retailers would do well to consider the Wind Down strategy for their brick-and-mortar assets. Going smaller, and reacting to market shifts by closing underperforming stores, are necessary tactics to maintain the profitability of their store-based assets. With shorter leases, less leasehold improvements due to reductions in the furniture and technology categories, and evolving store prototypes, the OSS can position themselves well to maintain the flexible and adaptive real estate model necessary for this strategy. Office Depot's integration of its delivery infrastructure with its new, smaller formats has resulted in huge inventory improvements within these stores, reducing the risk of massive format shifts by paying for the transition through inventory reductions. While many chapters in this book have focused on improving the people assets within stores, smaller office supply stores focused on getting commodity products into the hands of customers would permit the OSS to get by with a lesser-trained, high turnover labor force. This would mitigate the challenge of retaining highly-skilled store employees in a retail chain intentionally headed for a shutdown. The framework we believe the OSS should follow is summarized in Figure 3.22.

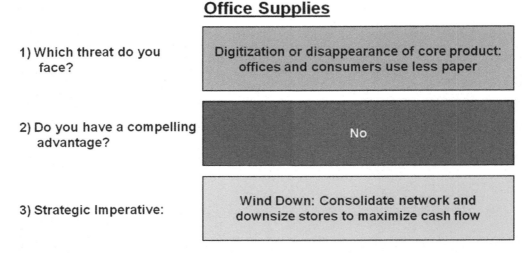

T   Bolster cash flow with incremental online sales

I   Concentrate on basic items and jettison uncompetitive/unprofitable categories; combine store and services group logistics systems

P   As an order taker, can survive with a bare bones, low-skilled, low-paid workforce whose chief jobs are to stock shelves and checkout customers

S   Shrink store formats to reflect fewer product categories, maintain flexible leases, create store network consolidation strategy

Figure 3.22

If the OSS choose this path, they must emphasize the selection, availability, immediate fulfillment, convenience, and 'under one roof' benefits they bring to the table. With customers that value convenience and ease, the office supply superstores must be wary of improvements in online competitors' retail experiences, and be ready to rapidly adapt to changes in customer preference. As OSS stores downsize, they become less destination stores and more emergency/fill-up stores. The OSS may need to be wary of going too far in this transformation. If they downsize to the point where they serve only emergency needs, they begin to look like FedEx Office, which already occupies this space with 1,800 stores serving travelling business professionals. Introducing vendor-sponsored technology showrooms and external service providers would help prevent this, but neither is a solution in and of themselves. Adopting a Wind Down strategy is a difficult choice for any company, but in the case of disappearing core categories, is likely the only way to maximize shareholder value.

Conclusion

Just like many other category-killers, from books to consumer electronics, office supply superstores rapidly took over American retailing in the 80s and 90s through their superior pricing, assortment, and availability. Entering the 21st century, these same businesses have begun to be pushed aside by more efficient online competitors. Office supply superstores have responded with their own, very successful, online portals, and, uniquely among big box retailers, have distribution systems approaching the scale of Amazon. If office supply retailing does transfer to a predominantly online world, the OSS are well-positioned to compete.

However, the question for their brick-and-mortar operations is whether these are five to ten year businesses, or ones that will be around for a lifetime. This is a question that any retailer with brick-and-mortar stores should ask themselves. Brick-and-mortar stores may, like the OSS, be facing digital substitution effects and the impact of online retailers. Or, like Crumbs Bake Shop, simply be waking up to a reality where fickle customer tastes have moved on and cupcakes are no longer en vogue. The answer to this question will help the retailer define their timeframe, and the timeframe can create a mindset that makes decisions on subjects such as lease terms, remodeling, and hiring, among others, much clearer. For brick-and-mortar operations that face a long-term decline in store productivity that will ultimately result in cash flow negative stores, managing for cash flow through store closures is likely in the interests of shareholders. Maintaining short-term, flexible leases, restricting store investments, and keeping store tasks simple will aid this process. To begin this phase of a retailer's lifecycle, however, the company must first accept the reality that its brick-and-mortar stores are on their way out.

Our next chapter looks at Best Buy, a retailer that is trying to reinvent itself to focus on the value it can offer brand partners that online-only retailers cannot.

Chapter 4
Is Showrooming a Problem or a Solution?

In many product verticals, online retailers have tremendous cost, inventory, and selection advantages over their brick-and-mortar counterparts. This brick-and-mortar problem is widely understood. It is well covered in the financial press and it is shared by many category killers in product verticals like consumer electronics, physical toys, home goods, and apparel. Best Buy typifies retailers facing this threat. Despite this threat, Best Buy continues to provide tremendous value to brands and consumers as a showroom for the vertical's latest products. Consequently, rather than wind down its store base, Best Buy is a candidate for the "Shrink and Transform the Format" strategy.

The products Best Buy carries are eminently suitable for online retail. Consumer electronics like digital cameras, computers, and TVs have high value density—that is, they have high average selling prices (ASP), low weight, and (relatively) small sizes. These attributes make shipping cost a very small part of the overall price, especially when compared to the large savings online retailers gain by eschewing store-based real estate and labor. The speed of obsolescence in the consumer electronics category also works to online retailers' advantage. Centralized inventories mean that they are able to satisfy demand with far less inventory on their balance sheets than brick-and-mortar store networks, thus incurring fewer mark-downs and other obsolescence-related costs. Brick-and-mortar stores' greater need for inventory, especially in a category with a high average selling price, like consumer electronics, also means that these retailers require more capital to fund their inventory buys.

This all means that online retailers incur fewer costs to sell items like consumer electronics relative to brick-and-mortar retailers, and therefore can offer lower prices. Compounding the issue, the selection online is appreciably better than that found in-store, which is particularly relevant for some merchandise categories within Best Buy like video games, music, and movies. The brand strength of many consumer electronics plus the multiple, third-party expert reviews of their products found on online retailing sites makes a large and growing proportion of shoppers happy to buy consumer electronics sight unseen. Other shoppers read about products online and also check them out in-store—a practice known as showrooming—but make their final purchase over the internet. Online retailers in consumer electronics are formidable competitors, and their rise has affected electronics retailers like Best Buy greatly. Best Buy has attempted to compete with Amazon directly by offering deep promotions and price-matching. This aggressive pricing has resulted in falling gross margins, while sales lost to online retailers has caused a deleveraging of Best Buy's store base, leading to a higher expense ratio. Deteriorating margins and expanding inventory and store assets have resulted in a lower ROIC. These trends are shown in Figure 4.1.

	FY 2006	FY 2007	FY 2008	FY 2012	FY 2013	FY 2014
Same-store sales growth (domestic)	5.1%	4.1%	1.9%	-2.1%	-1.7%	-0.4%
ROIC (Op Leases Not Capitalized)	47.5%	43.5%	34.2%	17.8%	13.9%	16.4%
Gross Margin	25.0%	24.4%	23.9%	24.2%	23.3%	22.2%
SG&A Expense Ratio	19.7%	18.8%	18.5%	19.4%	20.4%	19.5%

Figure 4.1 Source: Company reports. Note: Best Buy had a fiscal year change in FY 2012. This affects the ROIC metrics for FY 2012 and FY 2013.

The shift in consumer electronics toward online retail appears set to continue. While Best Buy's 2012 sales growth was 0.9%, Amazon's sales in Best Buy categories grew more than 50%.[147] Amazon's "price-check" mobile phone application, which allows users to compare prices in-store to Amazon's website, has increased pressure on brick-and-mortar gross margins. Because Amazon, according to a Wells Fargo study, "beats bricks-and-mortar retailers across the board on average electronics prices,"[148] this price-check app encourages showrooming behavior where customers use "Best Buy as a showroom and information center for purchases that they ... later make on Amazon."[149] In 2012, Best Buy itself estimated that 20% of the people entering its stores intended to make their purchase online.[150] Moreover, as smartphones become more prevalent, data plans become cheaper, and the price gap between superstores and online retailers widens (as superstores must make up in price what they lose in volume), the percentage of shoppers showrooming is likely to grow.

Online retailers are not Best Buy's only competition: mass merchandisers and warehouse clubs have continued their consumer electronics onslaught, increasing their market shares by up to 200 bps in some product categories between 2007 and 2012.[151] New competitors have also entered the arena. Where big box consumer electronics stores once offered "vendors a showcase for value-added, prestige products,"[152] today's most revolutionary manufacturers such as Apple and Microsoft are opening their very own showrooms. Mobile phone carriers, such as AT&T and Verizon, operate their own networks of mobile phone stores even as Best Buy sells their subscription plans to its customers.

Two trends in Best Buy's merchandise mix also affect the productivity of its stores: convergence, or the ability of one device to handle multiple functions once spread over a number of devices, and digitization, or the ability of a service once delivered through a physical product to instead be delivered online. Both trends result in same-store sales declines at Best Buy as customers either buy one item instead of many, or buy digital goods online rather than physical ones in-store.

Across Best Buy's merchandise portfolio, examples of these two trends are everywhere. In 2011, in computers and peripherals, sales of stand-alone monitors declined 6% as all-in-one desktops and laptops replace the old component system of a tower and a monitor and computer users increasingly use televisions as screens. Sales were down in the automotive category by 9%, making for three years of sales declines, as smartphone apps with turn-by-turn direction capability and live traffic updating (as well as newer cars' built-in navigation options) replace stand-alone GPSs. Imaging devices declined 11% in sales in 2011 due to weak performance in cameras and camcorders as smartphones increasingly capture and record images, and add important features such as instantaneous sharing and editing. Portable media players, such as iPods, portable DVD players, e-Readers, etc. have been crowded out by smartphones and tablets as well, with sales of portable MP3 players down 37% in 2011. Printer sales declined 2% as files and photos are shared online rather than being printed. The ability to back up a PC through services like Carbonite or Google Drive is eliminating the need for separate external hard drives. In home audio and video, the shift to digital memory, streaming services, and smart TVs eliminates the need for CDs, DVDs, and physical video game discs; as well as dedicated players, receivers, and game consoles. While sales of Blu-Ray players rose 9% in 2011, this was against a backdrop of an overall decline of 24% in video players. Convergence is present in Blu-Ray as well since game consoles like Sony's PlayStation incorporate Blu-Ray (as well as streaming video, music, internet connectivity, etc.).[153]

Even appliances are seeing examples of convergence. One-drum washer/dryers are gradually moving out of the niche category. In small appliances, "due to urban renewal, counter space is the new kitchen currency" and multi-purpose food preparation appliances are in demand.[154] High-end blenders are popular as are all-in-one juicers, food processors, soup makers, stand-mixers, etc. Walmart, for example, recently introduced its own multi-functional beverage system that uses one standard pack to make everything from coffee to tea to juice.

However, Best Buy's store footprints don't reflect these trends. Substantial amounts of Best Buy's stores are still dedicated to long-tailed games, movies, and music—categories very similar to books, where, even before the digital progression, Amazon made its bones out-pricing and out-stocking retailers like Borders and Barnes & Noble. With the digital transition underway, this category is rapidly evaporating. Much of the rest of the store is dedicated to categories that may, in the near future, consolidate into smaller packages or even into other, multi-featured devices. While tablets have been a bright spot for Best Buy, it's possible they will take share away from PCs and laptops, while in many cases offering lower price points. Even in the event of a resurgence in the core TV and computer categories, customers increasingly look comfortable buying these categories online. In Figure 4.2 and Figure 4.3, we show two sample Best Buy store layouts (an urban and a suburban store) colored according to the degree of online penetration in the category. Categories with between 10%-15% eCommerce penetration are colored yellow, and those with greater than 15% penetration are colored red. The product evolutions discussed above are reflected in the large amount of yellow and red displayed in Figure 4.2 and Figure 4.3.

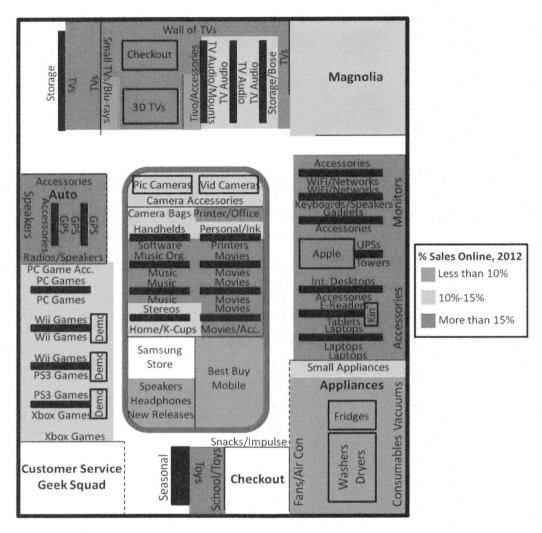

Figure 4.2 Sources: Author Visit to an Urban Store Location; Euromonitor International, 2013, Passport GMID.

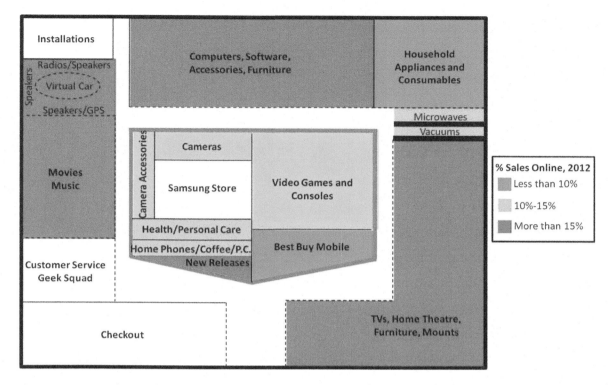

Figure 4.3 Sources: Author Visit to a Suburban Store Location; Euromonitor International, 2013, Passport GMID.

The traditional arguments often used for the staying power of brick-and-mortar retailers, serving the unbanked and providing purchase security, either do not apply to Best Buy or are losing power. Eighty percent of the unbanked belong to households with under $30,000 in income.[155] For these customers, Walmart offers cash-based transactions, secure delivery, and enough breadth and depth to satisfy their demands. Amazon can cater to a spectrum of low-end through high-end customers with a wide selection of merchandise, and, through its new (though limited) locker program, can guarantee secure delivery to customers. Mass merchandisers and online retailers continue to beat Best Buy on shelf price, a major draw for customers despite Best Buy's promise to price match physical and online retailers upon request. With more efficient competitors present, and Best Buy clearly in trouble, is there a reason for Best Buy to keep going?

In answering this question, we believe there are a few enduring truths in consumer electronics retailing that must be understood: (1) In consumer electronics, low price is the ultimate competitive advantage, (2) services are often showroomed, and (3) technology trends demand flexibility. We'll discuss key aspects of Best Buy's history in order to flesh these issues out. Then, using these truths as context, we'll explore online and discount retailers' impact on Best Buy. Finally, we'll suggest a model that will align Best Buy with these truths.

Consumer Electronics Customer Price Sensitivity

From the very beginning of the industry, every shift in consumers' preferred channels for buying consumer electronics has been driven by superior pricing. Consumer electronics is a high-ticket category, and consumers have been and are willing to shop around to save on the purchase price.

Before the widespread growth of electronics superstores in the 1980s, televisions, radios, speakers and other consumer electronics and appliances were largely sold through small specialty stores and mail order catalogs, or, in the case of appliances, private labeled and sold in department stores like Sears. Early adopters, principally young men, came to these small specialty stores to learn more about new, sophisticated audio products, and expert salespeople introduced them to the products that best fit their needs. The product category had high gross margins, which supported the personalized and high quality service offered as well as the salespeople's commissions.

In the early 1970s, Circuit City, then called Ward's, began experimenting with 40,000 square foot showrooms called "The Loading Dock," which sold audio, video, and major appliances. By 1981, Ward's found this large format so compelling that it rebranded the format to "Circuit City Superstores," listed on the New York Stock Exchange, raised $30 million, and rapidly began to close down its other operations to focus on building a chain of superstores.

The primary benefit of these superstores over the small outlets they displaced was their superior pricing. With almost every product carried in these first superstores being a high-ticket, major purchase, and with customers carefully researching their home electronics and appliance purchases, the opportunity to save significant money on these items was compelling. As Circuit City put it at the time, "Confronting costs of $300, $600, to $1,000, the vast majority of buyers are determined to save as much money as possible. They understand that a 5% savings on the goods we sell is meaningful and are willing to shop for it."[156] The Circuit City superstores achieved lower prices than their small outlet counterparts through both national purchasing power and the high volume-low margin retailing model that they adopted.

Circuit City also benefitted from an explosion of revolutionary consumer electronics products as the category expanded beyond audio to include televisions, cameras, video recorders, and associated media. These were products that future Best Buy CEO Brad Anderson would have called "mythic:" new, poorly understood by customers, and sold best through verbal presentation and demonstration.[157] The large Circuit City superstores were able to present a complete, one-stop assortment that smaller stores simply lacked the floorspace and knowledge to stock. The superstores were also able to provide services, like microwave cooking classes, which introduced customers to new technology.[158]

Circuit City's superstore model was so successful that it was quickly adopted by other consumer electronics retailers, including Best Buy. These chains all displayed strong growth, with the top ten chains growing at a compound annual rate of 35% between 1981 and 1986 versus the industry's 13% growth.[159] These top ten chains, their sales in 1981 and 1986, and their 5-year CAGRs are shown in Figure 4.4. By 1986, those superstore retailers with greater than $200 million in sales cumulatively accounted for 9% of industry sales, even though many had been in operation for less than a decade.[160] Small audio stores couldn't compete on price and many quickly went out of business.

	1986 Sales	1981 Sales	5-Year CAGR
Circuit City Stores	$1,011,000,000	$176,000,000	41.9%
Highland Superstores	$656,000,000	$133,000,000	37.6%
Dixons Group's Silo Holdings	$546,000,000	$211,000,000	20.9%
Federated Group (Macy's)	$430,000,000	$75,000,000	41.8%
Crazy Eddie	$352,000,000	$98,000,000	29.1%
Fretter	$273,000,000	$61,000,000	34.9%
Lechmere (est.)	$240,000,000	$90,000,000	21.7%
Best Buy	$240,000,000	$9,000,000	92.8%
Audio/Video Affiliates (AVA) (Rex)	$228,000,000	$15,000,000	72.3%
Newmark and Lewis	$214,000,000	$49,000,000	34.3%

Figure 4.4 Source: Circuit City 1987 Annual Report. Note: Table shows fiscal years most corresponding to calendar years.

The consumer electronics superstores of the 1980s generally all looked like the original Circuit City superstores. According to Best Buy CEO and founder Richard

Schulze, "the average customer recognized little difference among superstores, with their discount prices, multiple-step purchase processes, commissioned salespeople, and ubiquitous service plan and extended warranty packages."[161] The stores were large, anywhere from 30,000 to 40,000 square feet in size, and focused on consumer electronics and appliances. Selling space was only about half the store, with the rest of the space dedicated to a large stockroom and an in-store service area. The sales floor was principally used for display models. In order to buy something, a shopper would alert a sales counselor of their needs, receive individualized advice and usually some aggressive upselling, buy the chosen product on the floor, and then the sales counselor would pick it up for them from the stockroom. This system maximized customer interactions with sales counselors. Even if customers already knew what they wanted, they couldn't actually pick up anything to buy without first having a sales counselor retrieve it from the stockroom.

Sales counselors at these superstores were well-trained. At Circuit City, every new sales counselor received two weeks of training, some of it at company headquarters in Richmond, VA, and Los Angeles, CA. Each Circuit City superstore was also equipped with a large sales training room to facilitate ongoing training, which happened up to two times per week, and included visits by manufacturers' representatives to explain new products.[162] Further, Circuit City counselors specialized in one of the store's five product categories to ensure a high level of expertise; a commission system aligned individual incentives with the company's goal for counselors to go the extra mile to provide service and information to customers.[163] The high degree of training and the commission structure meant that, while less expensive than the small stores they replaced, these early superstores still required fairly fat gross margins.

The next retail innovation to reshape the consumer electronics retail industry attacked these gross margins and won customers over with even lower prices. The rapid expansion of superstores and the steamrolling of smaller competitors had given way to fierce price competition between the superstore majors in the 1980s. In 1987, Highland Superstores, then a much larger company than Best Buy, began to open stores within Best Buy's selling area. Overwhelmed by Highland's greater scale, Best Buy searched for a way to win the price war at any cost, and found it.

Acting on negative customer feedback regarding aggressive salespeople, Best Buy broke with standard practice in the industry and began eliminating commissioned sales representatives from the selling floor.[164] This approach eventually culminated in the Concept II store, unveiled in 1989, which took as its core belief that "the traditional superstore format was out of sync, in large part, with the needs or preferences of most shoppers ... [who had] only a limited need for sales help and a desire for hassle-free buying (no service plan contracts, no waiting for merchandise from the back room, no switching from counter to counter)."[165] The key preferences found in Best Buy's consumer research included:

- No-pressure selling
- An enjoyable shopping process
- Having the ability to see, touch and feel the merchandise
- Having access to trusted brands
- Having service available, but only when needed
- Convenience—to be able to shop near where they lived
- Broad assortment—one stop shopping
- Guaranteed low price—did not like to shop around[166]

Best Buy's Concept II stores were built around enabling customers to make the purchases they wanted, and driving down costs so that savings could be passed on to customers in the form of lower prices. The Concept II stores eliminated many expensive luxury features, and looked and felt like warehouses, with cement floors, industrial racking and lighting, and inventory stocked directly on the selling floor.[167] Other features delivered both convenience for shoppers and, through customer self-service, lower labor costs for stores. Self-help product information and Answer Centers replaced cadres of roaming, trained salespeople, and purchasing was streamlined.[168] Now that available inventory was stored in the selling area, customers could buy a product without ever talking to a salesperson except at checkout—and rather than try to push warranties on customers, Best Buy associates staffing the registers aimed just to get them on their way. Best Buy replaced the shirt and tie outfits of commissioned sales counselors with the khakis and blue polo shirts of sales associates. Rather than career men, these new sales associates were often part-time workers in high school or college, and were considerably less well-trained. They were paid salaries rather than commissions, with lower overall pay.

Concept II stores were thus able to operate at two-thirds of their previous labor force, and the lower staffing costs compensated for the lost revenue from sacrificing service plans.[169] The impact of this new labor model was virtually immediate and is shown in Figure 4.5. Following Concept II's introduction in 1989, Best Buy's operating expense ratio plummeted and the company passed the savings on to its customers in lower prices, causing its gross margin to decline. Also contributing to Best Buy's declining gross margins were the actions of some of its vendors. High-end appliance vendors, shocked at the minimal support their products received on the sales floor and the stark atmosphere of the warehouse store, pulled their brands from Best Buy. Many of Best Buy's consumer electronics vendors, while they remained in the store, denied access to their intermediate and upscale products with higher price points and margins.

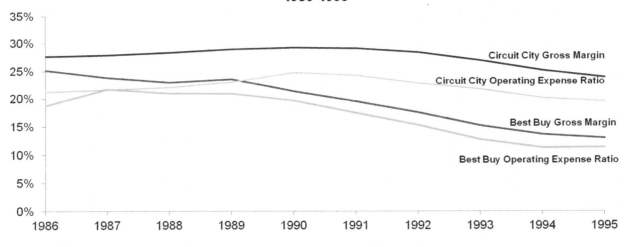

Figure 4.5 Sources: Company Reports, compiled from Thomson One and Reuters. Note: Operating Expenses exclude one-time fees such as restructuring charges, appliance exits, etc.

Despite being one of the smaller consumer electronics retailers, Best Buy was now able to price more competitively than any other retailer. These low prices drove Highland out of the Twin Cities in 1990, and Best Buy then aggressively entered

Highland's markets and outcompeted the company on price. At the insistence of its non-trade creditors, Highland was forced to liquidate in 1992.

Customer acceptance of Best Buy's new format was very strong. Due to the ease of opening Concept II stores (they required little investment, cost little, had little need for highly-trained store personnel, and turned inventory rapidly), Best Buy was able to take advantage of customers' receptiveness and grow rapidly. By 1995, Best Buy's buildout of its highly productive stores had rocketed its sales ahead of archrival Circuit City's. Best Buy's square footage and sales over this time period are shown in Figure 4.6.

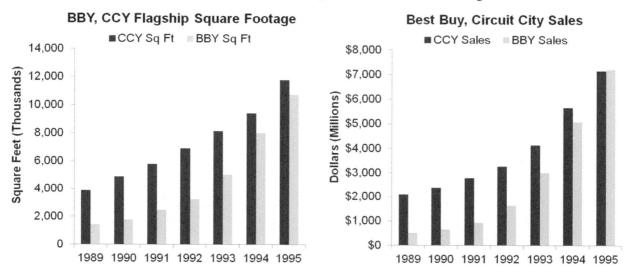

Figure 4.6 Source: Wells, John R. and Danskin, Galen, "The Rise of Circuit City Stores, Inc.," HBS case number 9-713-401 Boston: Harvard Business School Publishing, 2012.

By the early to mid-1990s, Best Buy and Circuit City were the dominant players in a fragmented electronics marketplace that included mass merchandisers like Walmart at the very low end, department stores that remained strong in appliances despite pressure from retailers like Home Depot, and super specialty players like CompUSA and Musicland competing in individual categories within Best Buy's merchandise mix.[170]

Circuit City had survived the early- and mid-90s volatility that wiped out many of its lookalikes simply by being the largest player in consumer electronics, bar none. In 1986, Circuit City was almost two times the size of its next largest competitor, Highland Superstores. By 1991, before Highland went out of business, Circuit City was almost three times as large as Highland. While its scale helped with buying, Circuit City leveraged its size in a number of other ways. When American credit markets contracted during the recession of the late 80s and early 90s, superstores faced difficulty in getting credit for their customers from the superstores' third-party partners. In response, Circuit City created its own credit department. The importance of access to credit can't be understated. By the mid-1980s, 40% of customer purchases were typically made on credit, rising to 50% by 1989, so accessing credit was a key part of the purchase process for many shoppers.[171] While overleveraged superstores like Highland, Newmark and Lewis, and countless others were being decimated by hugely negative comps, Circuit City's credit department preserved the company's comp sales (Figure 4.7).

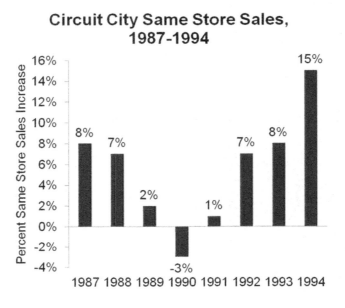

Figure 4.7 Source: Wells, John R. and Danskin, Galen, "The Rise of Circuit City Stores, Inc.," HBS case number 9-713-401 Boston: Harvard Business School Publishing, 2012.

Likely, this is very much because Circuit City was able to independently finance customers who, due to a lack of credit, couldn't buy from anybody else.

Compared even to a 1992 Best Buy, Circuit City was something of a laggard in terms of operating metrics like inventory turns. However, Circuit City did use its scale to create a logistics chain that was sophisticated for its time. Comparing Circuit City to recently bankrupt number two Highland, Sheldon Miller, president of United Audio Centers said, "Highland had marketshare, but that didn't mean anything ... Its margins were thin and getting thinner. A chain like Circuit City has one of the finest automated warehouse systems in the U.S., which allows them to keep tight control over their costs. Highland never had that."[172]

While Circuit City had benefitted from scale, its superstores hadn't changed much since "The Loading Dock" was first introduced. Circuit City had always stood by its belief that "price, while essential, is not enough ... Today's consumer wants full value—including sales floor and product service."[173] Circuit City's stores still used well-trained, commissioned salespeople and its inventory was still kept in a separate stock room. Even into the 2000s, Circuit City continued to have only 60% of its floorspace dedicated to sales. Circuit City's square footage, divided between selling space and non-selling space, is shown in Figure 4.8. Rather than pursue a low-cost, low-price model like Best Buy, Circuit City had instead chosen to locate its stores close together, in a self-cannibalizing fortress strategy that the company believed would erect impenetrable barriers to entry due to the regional density benefits of advertising and distribution.

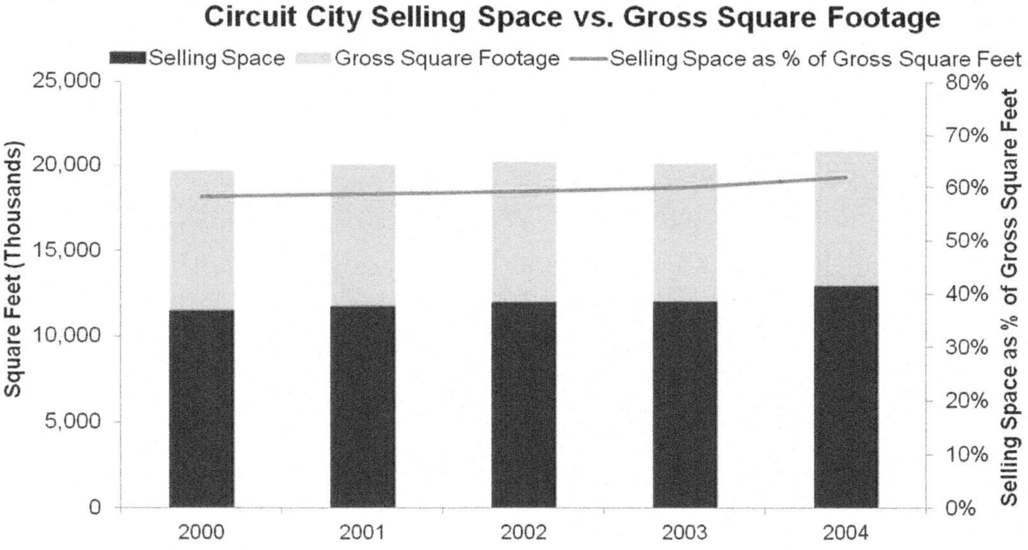

Circuit City Selling Space vs. Gross Square Footage

Figure 4.8 Sources: Company Reports.

Taking advantage of Circuit City's quiescence, by 1996 Best Buy had built its labor, inventory, and real estate model into an operating cost advantage over Circuit City of 780 basis points on a common-size income statement. Between 1996 and 2003, this operating advantage would fluctuate between 777 bps at its high, and 491 bps at its low—leaving Best Buy plenty of pricing room to overcome Circuit City's density-based advantages. Best Buy's and Circuit City's gross margins, operating expense ratios and net margins during this period are presented in Figure 4.9, and of note is the gap between the two companies' operating expense ratios.

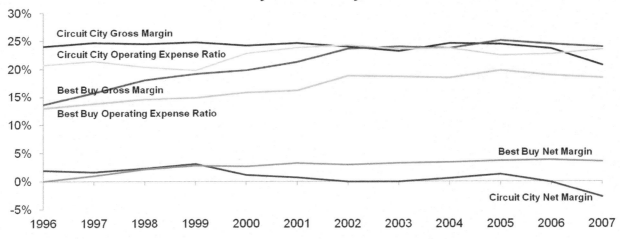

Figure 4.9 Sources: Company Reports. Note: Net Income Excludes Extraordinary Items (such as the discontinued operations of DivX and CarMax of Circuit City).

It could be said that throughout the 1980s and early 1990s, Best Buy out-operated its competition while Circuit City was content to merely out-size theirs. By 1996, other superstore competitors were either bankrupt or about to become so. Best Buy and Circuit City were evenly matched in scale.

While the lack of high-end merchandise previously served to distinguish the two retailers, Best Buy's Concept III store, launched in 1995, began to bring this "mythic" merchandise back into its superstores. Even with this step, Best Buy maintained its commitment to a low operating cost model. Rather than use sales associates to sell these goods, the company instead relied on automated high-end demonstration areas like television surround sound systems so that customers could experiment with different configurations, a life-size virtual car where customers could play with different speaker choices, a speaker room with a diverse array of music so that customers could choose the speakers that best matched the music they liked, additional listening and demonstration areas for music CDs and video games, and a revamped appliance pad. These remodeled stores, together with Best Buy's increased scale and importance, coaxed back the brands that had abandoned Best Buy during its Concept II phase, such as Sony, while new high-end brands were added, such as Waring and DeLonghi.[174] By the mid-1990s, Best Buy's and Circuit City's merchandise mix looked similar.

Best Buy began to challenge Circuit City directly in many of its core markets, and Circuit City felt it deeply. Between 1990 and 1994, Circuit City's share in markets served dropped from 25% to 20%, although national market share had increased.[175] Circuit City's high-service model, with extensively trained salespeople and much unproductive store space, was simply too expensive. As Best Buy attacked Circuit City with price, it turned out that Circuit City's dense network of stores was actually quite fragile. When Circuit City began its strategy of densely clustering its markets with superstores, stores cannibalized each other and sales per square foot remained low while Best Buy's sales per square foot expanded significantly over the period. This pattern is shown in Figure 4.10.

Figure 4.10 Sources: Wells, John R. and Danskin, Galen, "The Rise of Circuit City Stores, Inc.," HBS case number 9-713-401 Boston: Harvard Business School Publishing, 2012; and Wells, John R. and Danskin, Galen, "The Fall of Circuit City Stores, Inc.," HBS case number 9-713-402 Boston: Harvard Business School Publishing, 2012.

Consequently, when Best Buy used its operating advantage to break Circuit City's stranglehold on its markets, Circuit City did not have much margin room or same-store sales runway to react to the new entrant. In addition, Sears, Walmart and Home Depot introduced aggressive price-cutting and discounting in the appliance market, shrinking

Circuit City margins there as well.[176] As a result, Circuit City consistently underperformed in comparable sales and many times faced negative comps, save for a brief resurgence in its comp store sales due to dramatically increased flat screen television demand as viewers shifted from analog to digital and demanded larger screens in the mid-2000s. Circuit City's and Best Buy's comp store sales are compared in Figure 4.11.

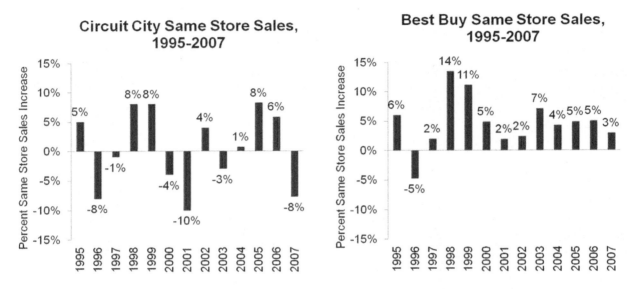

Figure 4.11 Sources: Wells, John R. and Danskin, Galen, "The Rise of Circuit City Stores, Inc.," HBS case number 9-713-401 Boston: Harvard Business School Publishing, 2012; and Wells, John R. and Danskin, Galen, "The Fall of Circuit City Stores, Inc.," HBS case number 9-713-402 Boston: Harvard Business School Publishing, 2012.

Without sustained increases in comp sales, Circuit City lost sales leverage and its operating expense ratio climbed as its net margin fell.

Circuit City tried to respond, but Best Buy proved year after year that price mattered most. Finally, the recession that began in 2007 finished the company off for good. Same-store sales declined below the level needed to support Circuit City's operating costs and on November 4, 2008, Circuit City filed for Chapter 11 bankruptcy protection. Best Buy, by focusing on a low price operating model, had proved over the two decades since the Concept II store was first introduced that, in consumer electronics, low price is the ultimate competitive advantage.

To Best Buy's misfortune, the advantage of a lowest price offering extended beyond just specialty stores, however. By 2008, Best Buy had beaten Circuit City and was the sole remaining national consumer electronics retailer. But during the intervening years, warehouse clubs, supercenters, and online retailers had swooped in and taken a large chunk of the category at Best Buy's very core, the television, as shown in Figure 4.12.

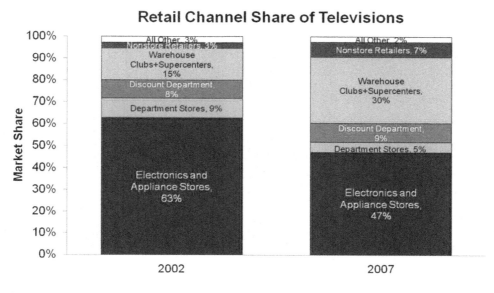

Figure 4.12 Source: *Merchandise by Kind of Business,* US Census.

While Best Buy had defeated its specialty electronics competitors with low prices; now, warehouse clubs, superstores, and online retailers turned this tactic against Best Buy, with Best Buy becoming a showroom for other retail channels. In the past, these competitors had "targeted mainly price-conscious customers, without providing extra support or services; however, in 2003, Walmart began to push into the higher-end consumer electronics that had been Best Buy's most lucrative domain, and Dell was bringing its highly successful direct-sales model to bear, selling everything from MP3 players to flat-panel TVs along with its portfolio of own-brand computers."[177] Supercenters and warehouse clubs were able to price-compete in these areas by leveraging their scale and density advantages and by focusing on a few, key, high volume items rather than a broad electronics assortment. Particularly in the winter quarter, where Best Buy earned a third of its sales and consumers actively shopped consumer electronics for holiday gifts and home purchases, mass merchandisers were able to flex their square footage and promotional mailings to move into Best Buy's categories and undercut its prices.

These new competitors would increasingly make the pricing environment more promotional. The holiday season of 2006, for example, was a "blood bath" for consumer electronics retailers as Walmart and Lowe's forced down prices of popular flat-screen televisions.[178] As soon as the new year began, Circuit City and Best Buy entered discussions with manufacturers in the effort to prevent a repeat holiday season, but this negotiation was ultimately unsuccessful.[179]

The recent success of supercenters, warehouse clubs, and nonstore retailers, as well as Best Buy's current aggressive price-matching policies and shrinking gross margins, are testament to the fact that price remains the major competitive advantage in consumer electronics retailing, and reinforces the importance of looking outside one's specific retail channel for other threats that may be on the horizon.

Showrooming is Nothing New

In consumer electronics, price competition and showrooming have always gone hand-in-hand. Showrooming behavior is not a new mechanism of the electronic age, but, as Circuit City noted in 1987, is created when customers face the purchase of a high ticket item.

Tweeter provides one example of early, documented showrooming behavior. Tweeter was a high-end, high-service retailer of premium audio and video equipment competing against Lechmere and Circuit City. Tweeter's high opening price points resulted in a high-price reputation, and the company was losing sales in the hyper-competitive 1990s. Tweeter's focus groups revealed that consumer electronics shoppers thought about purchasing a product one to two months before physically making the purchase, which gave them time to shop around at two to three retailers. Eighty percent of these shoppers checked newspaper advertisements for product availability and price information, and "virtually all of these consumers delayed purchase until they saw the desired product or class of product advertised in a newspaper circular."[180] Consumers were well-informed, price-aware, and waited for the best deal.

In a situation eerily analogous to modern consumer electronics stores' battle against internet retailers, Tweeter and other high-end retailers were providing high service to many customers for free. One-third of the shoppers entering Tweeter's doors specifically came to Tweeter to decide what to buy with the help of Tweeter's highly trained sales professionals. They then went to Lechmere, Circuit City, or Fretter in the belief that they could get a better price there, effectively treating Tweeter as these other companies' showroom.

To overcome this showrooming, Tweeter introduced Automatic Price Protection (APP). Under APP, Tweeter would mail a customer a rebate check if the company saw a lower price for an item that the customer had bought in the past 30 days. The innovation was widely lauded in the press, and Tweeter believed it played a part in its short-lived survival.[181] APP is a stronger form of Best Buy's current policy of price-matching other retailers upon a customer's request, but in Tweeter's case, APP was aided greatly by the relatively narrow overlap in inventory between Tweeter and its competitors.

It appears that Best Buy took advantage of this showrooming behavior in its battle against Circuit City. Out of the 1,329 stores operated by Circuit City and Best Buy in 2006, 1,138 had a rival store within ten miles, and 609 were in a market with a competitor's collocated store (e.g. a Circuit City store competing with a Best Buy store less than one mile away).[182] This high degree of collocation would have reduced customer friction with regards to showrooming, as customers could often walk across the street to compare prices between the two chains. This location strategy merely presaged the transparency of online retailing, where a hurdle to price-checking items online is almost non-existent.

Technology and Economic Trends Demand Flexibility

The consumer electronics industry is subject to wild fluctuations in sales due to technology revolutions, product cycles, and macroeconomic conditions. Retailers who have been unable to respond to changes in these factors and competitive pressures have gone bankrupt, or have failed to realize optimal returns. We'll provide a few examples of just some of the radical changes in the consumer electronics industry over the last four decades that have made the fortunes of those retailers that were flexible enough to adapt, and forced those that weren't out of business.

The small, specialty audio stores of the pre-superstore era suffered heavily as the audio market matured throughout the 1980s. More retailers began to carry the audio category, and the products themselves began to become more widely understood by consumers, which decreased the need for professional sales help. Audio retailers that weren't able to change quickly enough went out of business: "victims of a declining customer base, intense competition, and their own ineptitude."[183]

The consumer electronics industry as a whole experienced a technology revolution throughout the 1980s when nearly every product was rapidly evolving or a revolutionary concept. Circuit City's 1984 annual report hyped a huge stream of new product innovations. In TVs, component televisions that could be configured for optimum customer desires were replacing packaged systems, and other innovations in development or initial release included digital television with stop-action replay and screen-in-screen, direct broadcast satellite, and flat color TVs with depth of just a few inches. The VCR was itself a revolutionary product and it was evolving rapidly with the introduction of camcorders and then programmable VCRs that would allow consumers to watch a show even if they missed its airing. Compact discs for HiFi sound had just hit the market and cellular telephones and car phones were changing the definition of connected.[184]

VCRs provide a good example of what the revolution in these products looked like. This "must have" item drove growth in the whole consumer electronics category in the 1980s.[185] Factory sales of VCRs more than doubled over two years, rising from $1.5 billion in 1982 to over $3.7 billion in 1984, and despite this explosive growth, the penetration rate of VCRs in American households was still less than 20%. Fast-forward to 1990, and six years later the penetration rate of VCRs in American households was 72%.[186] Over half of American households bought their first item in this product category during just six years! For Circuit City, this was a windfall as same-store sales and sales per selling square foot marched upward, as seen in Figure 4.13.

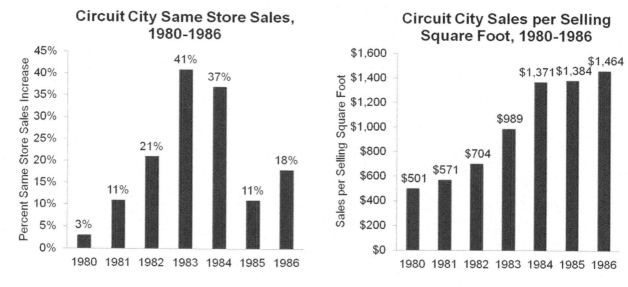

Figure 4.13 Sources: Company Annual Reports. Note: Chart on right shows sales per selling square foot, rather than sales per square foot shown in Figure 4.10 'Sales per Square Foot, 1987-2007.'

The growth in VCRs also manifested itself in a markedly different sales mix at Circuit City, with VCRs occupying a much greater percent of sales (Figure 4.14).

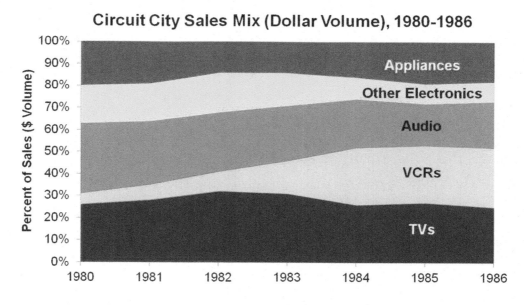

Figure 4.14 Source: Circuit City Annual Reports.

VCRs as a percent of Circuit City's sales grew from 5% in 1980 to 27% in 1986! This is a startling growth pattern for an individual product category. To respond to sudden surges in a category like this, retailers must remain flexible with regards to store layouts, operations, inventory policies, etc.

While VCRs were clearly a standout category, they were not alone. Concurrent with the overall technology revolution of the 1980s, the rise in two-earner incomes provided greater discretionary income and the move to the suburbs provided dens that needed to be filled. These factors combined to fuel a booming consumer electronics industry that grew at a 20% CAGR from 1980 to 1984, as measured by factory shipments of consumer electronics, shown in Figure 4.15.

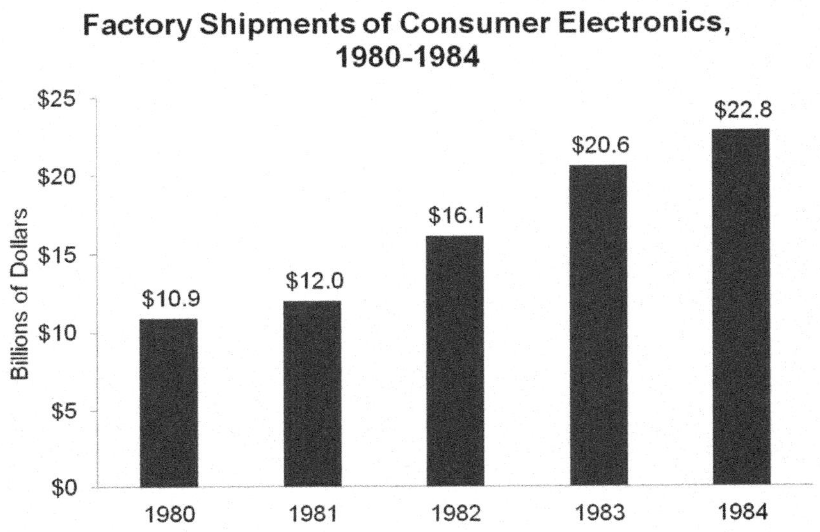

Factory Shipments of Consumer Electronics, 1980-1984

Figure 4.15 Source: Circuit City 1985 Annual Report.

However, this rapid expansion came to a halt in the economic pullback of the late 1980s and early 1990s. Due to this recession and the First Gulf War, Americans curtailed their purchases of big-ticket entertainment items. At the same time, many of the revolutionary products that led to surging growth in consumer electronics were now undergoing only incremental improvements, and same-store sales flattened and declined. Because retailers had bet on continued booming growth, most major markets were over-stored, with 1.8 more competitors than the trading areas could support.[187] Additionally, to achieve this rapid expansion, according to Robert Heiblim, President of Denon America, retailers had "leveraged to the max [and were] borrowed-out with no provision for a downturn."[188] The overly-levered retailers with no flexibility suffered greatly, and, of the top 10 consumer electronics retailers in 1986, very few were left by 1997, with those colored red in Figure 4.16 having declared bankruptcy or been acquired by 1997:

	1986 Sales	Status in 1997
Circuit City Stores	$1,011,000,000	Going Concern
Highland Superstores	$656,000,000	Bankruptcy: August, 1992
Dixons Group's Silo Holdings	$546,000,000	Merged with Fretters: September, 1993
Federated Group (Macy's)	$430,000,000	Going Concern
Crazy Eddie	$352,000,000	Bankruptcy: June, 1989
Fretter	$273,000,000	Bankruptcy: September, 1996
Lechmere (est.)	$240,000,000	Sold to Montgomery Ward, closed in their bankruptcy: August, 1997
Best Buy	$240,000,000	Going Concern
Audio/Video Affiliates (AVA) (Rex)	$228,000,000	Going Concern
Newmark and Lewis	$214,000,000	Bankruptcy: August, 1991

Figure 4.16

Best Buy was almost among these failed retailers. The industry price war and the flight of high-end vendors and product lines following the launch of the bare-bones Concept II store had driven Best Buy's gross margins to their lowest point in 1995. Best Buy's net income margin was vanishingly thin, to the point where a single large misstep could significantly damage the company. Best Buy's falling margins, compared to Circuit City's, are shown in Figure 4.17.

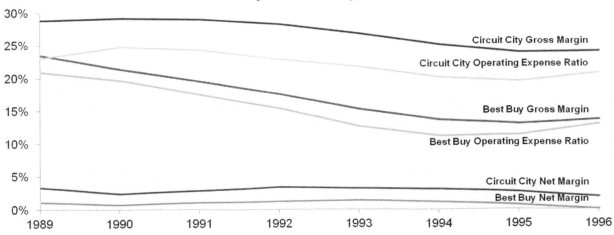

Figure 4.17 Source: Consolidated from *ThomsonOne*.

In preparation for the 1996 holiday season, Best Buy had borrowed heavily to stock up on computers. Shortly afterwards, however, Intel Corporation unveiled its latest chip and demand for existing computers running earlier generation processors fell sharply. Early in the new year, burdened with mountains of unsold and almost unsellable PCs, Best Buy's stock tanked as the company was forced to request an extra 60 days to pay its bills.[189] Best Buy's Net Income margin for fiscal 1997 (calendar 1996) ended at 0.02%.

With so many actual and near-bankruptcies driven by large debt loads, it's clear that financial flexibility is required to survive in this category. Even Circuit City may have survived if it had made better capital allocation decisions. As Best Buy, warehouse clubs, supercenters, online retailers, and other discounters continued to out-price Circuit City, the company did attempt to change course through a remodeling plan that created a more warehouse-like format and shifted inventory from the stockroom to the sales floor. However, the remodels were expensive. Circuit City had already invested hundreds of millions of dollars in failed DIVX technology,ii CarMax, and a share repurchase program. It no longer had the resources to update its behemoth network of tired boxes and, unable to change its operations, its fate was sealed.

---

ii DIVX was a DVD alternative intended to eliminate returns and late fees from the rental market. However, the format never gained widespread consumer acceptance and production and support were halted.

The Future of Best Buy

The persistent truths in consumer electronics retailing are that consumer electronics customers will shop for the lowest price, and that the consumer electronics industry is subject to substantial volatility. Best Buy's initial response to the presence of lower-priced competitors, Customer Centricity, ran smack into these truths.

The goal of Customer Centricity was to transform Best Buy from a retailer selling product to an institution helping customers solve the problems they were facing with their devices. To do this, Best Buy added significant costs to its stores, such as expensive infrastructure renovations like the installation of elaborate home-theater displays. Customer Centricity also adopted an expensive labor model involving higher-trained sales associates engaged in complex, integrated, multiple product and service sales, in contrast to its former self-service model staffed with low-skilled workers. Best Buy hoped this new model would fund itself through sales of bigger ticket items like home theater systems and attachments like peripherals, accessories, and services. However, attachment sales depend on first winning the sale of the big ticket item. In the face of easy price-comparisons with other retailers and a recession that stymied demand for high-end electronics, this new strategy failed.

However, the fundamental idea behind Customer Centricity—that Best Buy could serve as the intermediary between the customer and new, exciting, connected, "mythic" technology—is very sound. Research from Samsung argues that Best Buy still provides a valuable venue for consumer electronics shoppers to familiarize themselves with potential purchases. Tim Brenner, manager of Consumer Insights and Analytics at Samsung Mobile, describes customer purchase behavior that is distinctly "non-linear" and still emphasizes the in-store experience: "Instead of looking at one product review or getting one friend's opinion on a product and then immediately buying the product, consumers now find themselves constantly rotating through product reviews and word-of-mouth opinions and making multiple visits to retail stores before deciding whether to buy." In some cases, shoppers are even conducting a reverse form of showrooming on Amazon's site, with 24% to 30% of consumers reading product reviews there and many then going off to see the product first-hand at a physical store. In Benner's words, "It is somewhat surprising that the retail experience is still king."[190] This behavior echoes the research behind Best Buy's Concept II stores, where customers wanted the ability to personally see, handle, and interact with devices before they purchased them. Even now, Best Buy shows more products than Walmart throughout the year, and provides an opportunity to try multiple products from multiple brands in one place, as well as to ask questions from sales staff if so desired. While Amazon stocks a wider range, it can't provide the opportunity to test out multiple product options in-person at a whim.

There is, then, still a need for retailers like Best Buy that can provide a broad assortment of non-commodity goods easily accessible to consumers. However, in the current environment, Best Buy is unable to capture that value. We believe that retailers like Best Buy that face such strong online and mass merchandiser competition need to focus on the unique values and benefits they offer parties in their ecosystem, and then adapt by pursuing strategies that best create and capture that value; this is the "Shrink and Transform the Format" strategy. Retailers facing a similar threat but that can offer no unique value will find themselves managing for cash flow as they Wind Down their operations.

For Best Buy, success at the "Shrink and Transform the Format" strategy means providing consumers a destination to browse and educate themselves on a range of mythic products from a diverse array of manufacturers: experiencing how they can all fit together and learning about what solution best fits their needs. Best Buy must become an agent for its brand partners—and be paid for it—and not just another distribution channel. To do this, the consumer electronics superstore will have to die, but the consumer electronics showroom will be brought to life.

In a world where consumer electronics customers always have and will continue to shop for the lowest prices on big ticket items, and are now aided by online and mobile technology, offering free product showrooms and hoping to make those expenses back through in-store sales of those same products will eventually cease to be a tenable business model. Instead, the processes of shopping and fulfillment for these products must be separated so that Best Buy can deliver and be credited with its maximum value to all stakeholders: brands, consumers, employees, and shareholders. It's likely that Best Buy's future store won't directly stock or deliver many of the goods it displays, in most cases that is a task best left to online fulfillment—either from Best Buy or another retailer. Best Buy's stores will simply provide a showroom and service base for consumer electronics brands, and rather than be compensated for these services through inflated prices paid by customers, will be paid directly by brands.

Brands could fund Best Buy's operations and achieve this future through three options: vendor allowances, Minimum Advertised Pricing/Unilateral Pricing Policies (MAPP/UPP), and store-within-a-store (SWAS) formats. With vendor allowances, Best Buy would be paid by brands just to keep their most innovative products on the shelf. MAPP policies attempt to institute price controls so that, no matter the distribution channel, the product costs the same everywhere. The SWAS model organizes merchandise by brand and brands can support this tactic by renting dedicated space in the store for their products and/or supplying their own sales staff.

These different options will likely have different levels of efficacy. Of these three strategies, we believe that SWAS will be much better for all stakeholders. Especially today, with third-party sellers having access to a range of platforms through which they can take advantage of supply chain leaks, MAPP is difficult to enforce. It is also more likely to work well for products that create instant gratification and where transporting the item from the store to customers' homes is not a burden, so as to overcome the convenience of home delivery. With same-day delivery on the horizon, the protection afforded by MAPP may be overstated. In addition, MAPP only constructs price supports for what, in consumer electronics retailing, is a more expensive method of order fulfillment. Likewise, vendor allowances simply subsidize what is possibly a sub-optimal operation. Both vendor allowances and MAPP pricing would keep Best Buy solvent, and as such may be useful interim steps, but will not deliver the highest value to the brand or consumer. Unless they are applied in ways that force a change, neither option absolutely demands that Best Buy change its current operation, and under these two regimes Best Buy would likely remain a retailer, rather than becoming a showroom.

Particularly in consumer electronics, where families of products are designed to work together, SWAS would be a more compelling way to introduce customers to new technology, brand families, and device interconnectivity. SWAS also enables the processes of shopping for a product and actually buying it to be divorced. Separating the two means that online fulfillment, with its efficiencies over in-store fulfillment, can be given the green light without reserve. By reducing costs in the supply chain, prices to the customer can be lowered, and with lower prices, manufacturers will likely be able to sell more product, which will help manufacturers leverage their fixed costs better. In addition, because of short technology cycles in consumer electronics, brands make the most margin at a product's introduction before its eventual obsolescence forces markdowns. SWAS will help brands actively push these new products during the time of their peak profitability.

It's also important to note that the showroom concept goes beyond the SWAS model where brands directly employ sales associates. The brand-supported SWAS model described above helps large brands present high-margin, new, premium products. A good example of this model is the Samsung SWAS within most Best Buys. Yet premium brands that don't have the product range and volume to directly employ their own sales force within Best Buy stores also need a showroom in order to sell customers on the advantages of their products. These customers rely on Best Buy to group similar, premium brands together into a compelling experience, and on Best Buy associates to be knowledgeable on the details of each product line. Best Buy currently serves these smaller brands through Best Buy-run showrooms like Magnolia Audio-Video and Pacific Sales.

Outside of the premium segment, customers still often want to test more commodity products, like lower-end mobile phones or point-and-shoot cameras, in-person. For the most part, these customers know the details of what they're buying and don't require expert sales help; they just want to hold the products in their hands before purchase. They don't need to go to a destination store; instead they'll choose the place that's most convenient for them. Best Buy serves this customer need through its Best Buy mobile stores. These small-format locations can stock a wide variety of small items in locations convenient to customers.

These latter two showroom concepts are an important part of serving the diverse needs of both customers and brands today. The brand-supported SWAS model won't work for brands too small or products too commoditized to support the costs of their own SWAS, but Best Buy-run SWAS could be supported by vendor allowances geared towards creating this model, or MAPP/UPP could support the current retail model until Best Buy transitions into a future business model. For instance, one brand that we spoke with uses vendor allowances to spur specific actions on the part of retailers. Under this system, retailers are rewarded for activities like creating specific displays, ensuring that the products are turned on and presented correctly, carrying a broad range of the retailer's merchandise, etc. This brand, like many brands, cares primarily about making sure their products are bought, and wants to support retailers not so much through direct product sales, but by incentivizing actions that ensure the sale happens somewhere.[191]

For shareholders of Best Buy, any of these options (vendor allowances, MAPP/UPP, and showrooms) is likely better than the current precarious state. Brands supporting SWAS with their own sales associates removes SG&A costs from Best Buy's income statement, and being able to charge for rent adds an important new source of revenue. Higher average prices in the marketplace due to MAPP would mean that Best Buy could convert more of the customers that showroom in its stores, allowing the company to continue to adequately cover its cost base. Vendor allowances would directly pay for store operations.

These three approaches shift at least some cost onto brands, and their acceptance of this new paradigm will be the largest hurdle to Best Buy's transformation. It is in brands' best interest to get on board. In office supply superstores, the technology department has already begun to be trimmed in order to make it competitive in today's environment, demonstrating that the threat at Best Buy is real. At this point, Best Buy essentially has a monopoly on brick-and-mortar specialty consumer electronics retailing. Without Best Buy, consumer electronics brands would have to rely on mass merchandisers and online retailers to help consumers understand new technology and drive its adoption; an extraordinarily unlikely scenario. Brands that join Best Buy's SWAS platform will have a competitive advantage over brands that don't—as demonstrated by the many brands that are strategically building their own stores. Building these stores within Best Buy will likely prove a more cost-effective and more customer-convenient way of pursuing this strategy.

Brands have also already demonstrated their loyalty to Best Buy. David Strasser, of Janney Capital Markets, believes Best Buy's strong brand relationships show up in its three consecutive years of gross margin improvements despite being in an industry that has shown an overall gross margin decline. Best Buy performs essential services for vendors—showcasing and explaining new products and new technologies—that justifies offering them better pricing and exclusive products.[192] Backing this assessment is Scot

Ciccarelli of RBC Capital Markets, who reminds us that "vendors helped Circuit City and even Tweeter stick around for years after they probably should have shut their doors" in order to not be solely reliant on Best Buy as a distribution partner. Now, "Best Buy is simply too big and too important to the vendor community," who are reluctant to find themselves left with just Amazon and Walmart. [193] It's likely that brand partners will continue to be very supportive of Best Buy.

Best Buy's services offering is also a valuable complement to the brands and customers who will be using Best Buy's SWAS-based showrooms. The individual SWAS are not likely to invest in their own home theater, high-end audio, or appliance installation teams, and Best Buy can help its customers integrate these items into their homes, clearing a customer hurdle to purchase. Geek Squad members can continue to serve as focal points for customers seeking solutions to their home network or PC problems, and can help customers implement new connected home technology. As Best Buy well knows, the Geek Squad can also serve as small businesses' outsourced IT function. While other competitors, such as Staples and Dell, have attempted to replicate Best Buy's Geek Squad offering through acquisitions or partnerships, only Best Buy has grown its services business to such a large scale. This is certainly an area that is important for Best Buy to continue to grow, given its high margins and the clear cross-selling opportunities that exist for the brick-and-mortar and online stores.

Best Buy will need to maintain flexibility across all areas of the company, from store operations to corporate structure. As fulfillment functions are taken out of the stores and changes in Best Buy's product categories continue to play out, Best Buy will likely occupy a smaller format. Predicting when or how this transformation may occur is difficult, and so the company should look for shorter leases, or find retail partners that may be willing to sublease parts of their stores on short-term contracts. The company's focus on part-time, hourly store associates has served it well when it has needed to lay off labor. However, its move into services (e.g. Geek Squad), while necessary, may reduce some of this operating flexibility through its use of higher-trained, more permanent employees. Best Buy may need to find ways to mitigate this through cross-training or similar programs. Adopting a showroom model rather than a strictly retail one will help Best Buy overcome the inventory challenges that almost bankrupted it in 1997 and continue to hold it back today relative to online retailers.

From a corporate perspective, Best Buy should watch out for excessive amounts of long-term debt. Trade creditors, in general, have been supportive of troubled consumer electronics retailers—and Best Buy's large accounts payable balance and its status as the last electronics superstore mean that they probably will be again—but outside creditors have often forced bankruptcies, as in the case of Newmark & Lewis. One consumer electronics manufacturer, Apple, is infamous for hoarding cash; and, given the need to renovate and shift store locations, remerchandise, refixture, etc., Best Buy should consider pursuing this approach as well.

The history of consumer electronics is one in which the lowest-priced retailer is the one that ends up winning. For Best Buy to survive into the future, it must change this paradigm by transforming itself from a retailer into a brand partner and showroom. Under the "Shrink and Transform the Format" strategy, the future Best Buy will likely not directly sell goods (save possibly through its own online channel), but will instead help others sell goods by working with brands to introduce customers to new, mythic goods, providing a destination where customers can interact with devices before they purchase them, and creating the service infrastructure that helps customers use their purchases. This transformation will also create a more flexible Best Buy.

Current Best Buy Approach

With this picture of what we think the future of consumer electronics retailing will look like, we must ask how far along Best Buy is on the road towards becoming this future store with regards to corporate flexibility, omnichannel strategy, and store tactics.

From a corporate flexibility standpoint, the company continues to pay a dividend. For the last five years (ending January 2, 2014, February 2, 2013, March 3, 2012, February 26, 2011, and February 27, 2010) cash dividends paid as a percent of free cash flow ranged between 9% and 53%. Best Buy's days cash on hand has ranged from nine to twenty-six days. For a company facing a rapidly changing competitive landscape, and with a need to substantially alter its retail formats and operating principles, the extra flexibility gained from halting its dividend payments and using its increased cash reserves to invest in the future is substantial. While any company would worry that canceling its dividend could signal a weakness or lack of confidence in its cash flows, the substantial decline in Best Buy's stock price in 2012, and the subsequent dramatic increase following news of the Samsung SWAS, indicate that investors are likely holding this stock as a turnaround story (i.e. for capital appreciation, and not as a dividend play) and would welcome a cohesive strategy for the future. It's encouraging that the upper end of the days cash on hand range, twenty-six days, occurred in Best Buy's most recent fiscal year. From a debt perspective, too much of which has often bankrupted retailers, accounts payable have been a majority or close to a majority of Best Buy's total liabilities. Its long-term debt as a percent of total assets has stayed low, between 4% and 12% over this time period. Indeed, until recent earnings problems, Best Buy has maintained very conservative debt coverage ratios (operating income divided by interest expense), often in excess of 10x, since its almost fatal debt crisis in 1996. From a corporate debt perspective, Best Buy has wisely maintained flexibility.

Over the short term, there are many efficiency efforts underway at Best Buy to cut expenses and increase profitability, which one would expect to see in a turnaround effort, such as headquarter headcount reductions and supply chain optimization, among others. Looking at the long term, among the three major initiatives of (1) transforming its superstores, (2) shifting cost responsibility onto brands, and (3) better leveraging its online channel, substantial progress has been made, but there is a long way to go before the future store is realized.

In his "Renew Blue" strategy, CEO Hubert Joly (installed in 2012) aims to "reinvigorate and rejuvenate the customer experience," develop a "leading edge, multichannel shopping experience," "work with vendor partners to innovate and drive value," and continue to cut unproductive costs.[194] To date, the major transformations at Best Buy include stronger partnerships with brands (including attracting Samsung and other brands into a store-within-a-store arrangement), emphasis being placed on Best Buy Mobile, a lukewarm promise to reduce square footage by 10% over the next ten years, investing heavily in the online experience, and growing Geek Squad as a brand and a service.

On the front of shifting some cost responsibility to brands, Best Buy appears to be doing some of everything. A kind of indirect vendor allowance shows up on Best Buy's balance sheet, with accounts payables offsetting almost 40% of Best Buy's invested capital compared to 10% to 20% for most other brick-and-mortar retailers. Many brands have implemented minimum advertised pricing and/or unilateral pricing policies (MAPP and/or UPP) on their high-end products, threatening to halt shipments to any dealer who breaks their set price. Daniel Binder, with Jefferies, believes that manufacturers implemented this policy in response to Amazon's disregard for minimum advertised pricing, which has devalued products in the eyes of consumers, driving down prices and Consumer Electronics manufacturers' profitability.[195] So far, Samsung, Sony, LG, Panasonic, and Sharp have all set MAPP or UPP, primarily on high-end TVs but potentially with other products to follow, as shown in Figure 4.18.

Manufacturer	Affected Products	Other Comments
LG	2012 5700 series and higher TVs	Will not allow higher-end TVs to be sold on third-party marketplace websites and will enforce UPP on online retailers
Panasonic	Specific products not disclosed	Will not allow higher-end TVs to be sold on third-party marketplace websites; reduced number of direct dealers
Samsung	2012 ES6100 series LED and E550 series plasma and higher TVs; ES6000 and E6500 series Blu-ray players	Will halt shipments to dealers caught selling below UPP prices
Sharp	90" Aquos LED TV	Currently does not plan to expand UPP to additional models
Sony	2011 XBR and KDL series TVs; 2012 EX and HX Bravia series TVs; all tablet PCs; selected headphones, receivers, and projectors	Will utilize third-party organization to monitor pricing

Figure 4.18 Source: Binder, Daniel et. al, 'Best Buy: BBY Protects Share With Price, FCF Miss On WC Timing,' *Jefferies*, report dated January 11, 2013.

UPP has had immediate effects, nearly equalizing prices on UPP models at Best Buy and Amazon throughout 2012, including during the promotion-prone holiday season.[196] This is exactly the type of support that Best Buy and Circuit City both requested (with little success) from their brand partners after the 2006 holiday season, and it looks as if the brands are now willing to provide it.

Another example of this vendor support is Best Buy's Samsung store-within-a-store partnership. While details on the partnership are scarce, it appears to be the case that Samsung supplies its own, Samsung shirt-wearing sales associates to sell Samsung's high-end, new products in a Samsung-branded area of the store. Apple also has been granted its own branded store section, but doesn't supply its own sales associates. While it is believed that neither Samsung nor Apple share in the occupancy costs for these areas, the addition of a Samsung-sponsored sales associate should relieve some SG&A pressure from Best Buy, and also should contribute to lift on Samsung products (where Best Buy makes better than average gross margin), as shoppers are able to learn more about the products from well-trained Samsung sales associates.[197] This is in contrast to Best Buy's previous reputation as a store with a lot of products but not much product knowledge. Samsung's new SWAS, in contrast, look more like Apple's stores, with only a handful of products on display.[198]

More telling are the motivations behind this relationship. As Samsung continues to position its Galaxy line of smartphones and tablets against Apple's iPhones and iPads, it needs a channel to feature key innovations. Rather than build its own retail space like Apple, Samsung took advantage of Best Buy's already existing traffic and space. It paired its SWAS move with an advertising campaign featuring the stores in Best Buy, further moving Best Buy along a path towards a "wow" destination store. With Samsung's physical presence inside brick-and-mortar stores, their commitment to a unilateral pricing policy is likely also strengthened. It is our belief that for the Galaxy line to succeed, it needs an avenue to directly connect to customers. If Best Buy becomes the arbiter of customer decisions and the enabler of its brand partners, Best Buy will grow in importance.

As Best Buy continues to leverage its access to customers and its ability to disseminate the latest innovations to a wide population, it should be able to attract more brand partners for SWAS. This would strengthen Best Buy's position as a destination store where customers can compare the best of a multitude of retailers, and further reduce pressure on Best Buy's selling expenses through increased use of brand-sponsored sales associates. There are signs this is happening, as Microsoft recently introduced its own Windows SWAS within Best Buy stores to feature Windows-based smartphones, laptops, ultrabooks, tablets, and Xboxes, staffed by dedicated Microsoft sales associates as well as Best Buy associates.[199] As this progression continues, and the concept of SWAS becomes more valuable, Best Buy may also be able to begin charging rents for the SWAS space, improving its income statement.

Even in the absence of a full contingent of SWAS partners, the new "Connected" store format that Best Buy is slowly rolling out features many showroom qualities. Similar to its work with Magnolia, Best Buy has created Pacific Sales SWAS (a high-end home appliance retailer Best Buy acquired) within these formats that feature a fully functional living room, outdoor patio, and home theater. These high-end, immersive experiences both leverage Best Buy's ability to provide hands-on testing, and demonstrate the service offerings that Best Buy can offer to customers desiring "connected homes." As the list of innovative, national brands with the resources and product variety to support a self-staffed SWAS is relatively small (Apple, LG, Panasonic, Philips, Samsung, Sony), it's encouraging to see Best Buy create these experiences for smaller brands.

In addition, the rest of the Connected Store benefits from a more showroom-type approach as well. It is much more hands-on, as one analyst observes "most departments feature working display models of the hottest new merchandise, giving visitors a chance to get some first-hand experience with smartphones, music accessories, home theater systems and more."[200] The Connected stores also have lower shelves and better signage, so that customers can help themselves more easily. Best Buy has also made significant labor improvements in these stores through in-store Geek Squad-provided customer support. When shoppers walk in, they are greeted by a Solutions Center, a large service desk where Geek Squad members help customers in getting their iPads to connect with their laptops, iPhones, and TVs, "so they leave the store with working gear instead of 'a box of problems.'"[201] With these labor investments, Best Buy's in-store service model could be the glue that combines the various future brand SWAS into a unified showroom, and provides yet another customer service that brands may not have been able to provide on their own.

Of course these investments in in-store service raise questions as to how Best Buy will support the increased labor cost. The Geek Squad model in the past has been a high gross-margin business, with agents travelling to customer locations to perform their operations. Now, however, Geek Squad agents are also permanently in the stores in order to ensure customers have no problems with their purchases (which increases satisfaction and avoids costly returns), as well as to cross-sell to small business customers. As Geek Squad moves into complementary store service and sales, it's unclear if product, versus service, gross margin is enough to support them. And, while other parts of Best Buy are trimming down in order to compete with online retailers, the investment in more Geek Squad agents will add substantially to SG&A and reduce the company's part-time labor model flexibility. To us, this speaks even more clearly to the need for a switch to a showroom model, where brands directly support this added service expense as a competitive differentiator rather than asking Best Buy to try to cover it out of product sales.

Best Buy Mobile, the convenient smartphone and tablet showroom, has met with tremendous success. From a 2% market share in phones in 2007,[202] Best Buy has grown its share to 6% in 2011.[203] Both Best Buy Mobile and Best Buy superstores were quick to remodel, remerchandise, and realign sales incentives for tablets as competing models to the iPad were released. Tablets and smartphones come with the ability to sell attachments and connections, increasing the potential revenue and gross margin on each sale. Best Buy is continuing to work with the format, and recently began opening in strip malls as well as mall locations to take advantage of lower rents with similar traffic patterns. Best Buy Mobile is also present within Best Buy's superstores themselves, and is placed at the front of the store. These independent locations and in-store placements enable customers to test product in a manner convenient to them.

Best Buy has also demonstrated flexibility in its merchandising abilities at its superstores. In an effort to compete with Game Stop, by 2011, Best Buy had added the ability to buy and sell pre-owned games in 90% of its stores. Best Buy supported the category with online and in-store pre-ordering and additional digital content. While we don't see a future in games as physical items, Best Buy's ability to move quickly—and hopefully move out quickly if conditions warrant—is heartening. While its "shiny disc" movies and music business will eventually disappear, Best Buy did introduce flexibility into the product category in the short term, entering into an agreement in 2011 with a third party distributor that will be responsible for assortment, distribution, inventory, and in-store presentation. Since 2011, Best Buy has twice reduced the space devoted to music and movie discs by up to 50% to create space for mobile, tablets, gaming, and appliances in its stores.[204] In the most recent remerchandising, Best Buy is reducing the CD/DVD square foot allocation from about 12 to 13% of the store to 6 to 7%.[205] Beyond games and other media, Best Buy acted quickly to get on top of a firming market in home sales when the company began to focus on appliances after the Great Recession.[206]

In addition to its work on Best Buy Mobile and its superstores, Best Buy is also rethinking its omnichannel experience. Starting in 2011, the company began increasing its online-only assortment, and added "Ship-to-Store" and "Friends & Family guest pickup" functionalities. In the beginning of 2011, over 40% of online buyers picked up in-store.[207] To accommodate both the greater number and greater share of online orders being shipped to store, the connected store features a larger in-store pick-up section,[208] making it easier for BestBuy.com shoppers to quickly get their deliveries. One example of how Best Buy's omnichannel strategy can cater to the strengths of both its retail stores and its online channel is in televisions, where, in 2011, the company increased its total stock-keeping unit (SKU) count by 25%. To do this, however, Best Buy selectively decreased the models in the stores by 20% and increased the models available as online-only.[209] By making commoditized televisions online-only products, Best Buy can price-compete with online retailers without causing price confusion in the stores and can reduce its inventory by aggregating these models' inventory one level up in the supply chain. Best Buy is also expanding its online fulfillment program into all of its existing distribution centers and improving inventory allocation in the distribution centers closest to customers—all of which results in a more efficient supply chain and quicker time to customer.[210]

Best Buy is also investing heavily in its online experience. The company has insourced the management of its eCommerce operation from Accenture and is also working on beefing up its online search functionality, speed, assortment, product information, and attachment selling capabilities (including services). Best Buy is also integrating its Reward Zone, Best Buy, and Geek Squad online platforms to provide a more seamless experience. [211] This investment should help drive up Best Buy's below-average online conversion rate of 1.3%, where about 9% of customers do not buy due to poor product availability, assortment, and product information—issues management thinks can be fixed.[212] These efforts are paying off: Best Buy's domestic online sales grew 20% in FY 2014, with domestic online growth accelerating to over 25% in the fourth quarter of FY 2014, 29% in the first quarter of FY 2015, and 22% in the second quarter of FY 2015. With online sales constituting 13% of Best Buy's domestic revenue in the fourth quarter of FY 2014 (whereas other brick-and-mortar retailers don't consider their online sales material enough to break out), it appears the transition to online fulfillment and a showroom-based store is underway.[213]

While there is lots of good news, one caution is that Best Buy's stores are still very large. The average Best Buy superstore is approximately 40,000 square feet, which, though down from over 45,000 square feet in 2001, still leaves a lot of unproductive space. Even the Connected Store described earlier replaced a 58,000 square foot store with a still large 45,000 square foot store. Given the categories disappearing and converging inside Best Buy's stores, Best Buy may want to consider moving into a much smaller box. Especially with the cost of extra leasehold improvements from adding higher-end Magnolia, Pacific Sales, and SWAS set-ups, Best Buy should be sure it's investing in stores that can survive its disappearing categories. So far, however, Best buy has indicated it plans to reduce square footage through store closures, rather than through smaller formats.

Given Best Buy's long store leases and its inability to rapidly close underperforming stores, Best Buy may want to reconsider this approach. At Best Buy's Q3 analyst day conference in late 2012, Best Buy management reported that only 59 "underperforming" superstores (or about 6% of Best Buy's total domestic superstore base) would come off lease over the next four years. Overall, Best Buy only sees 12% of its superstore leases end each year.[214] These long leases reduce Best Buy's flexibility to respond quickly to shifts in consumer categories, and mean that underperforming stores stick around as a drag on company profitability. Anything Best Buy can do to increase its lease flexibility, such as subleasing space or signing shorter leases in future, will be beneficial to a retailer at the mercy of rapid product cycle shifts. As more big box retailers downsize their space or even exit the market, Best Buy's power over landlords may increase, and it would be in Best Buy's interest to leverage this into more flexible leases.

While online competitors and mass merchandisers have taken a lot of share in best Buy's categories, using Best Buy's historic low-cost offering against it, recent changes in Best Buy's external environment appear positive. As of the beginning of 2014, sales tax is automatically collected in 19 states on Amazon purchases, and many states are seeking to address the online sales tax issue themselves in the face of stalled federal legislation.[215]

Vendor pricing support is becoming increasingly commonplace. Best Buy is also largely making the right moves to deal with the online threat: matching channels and formats to customer desires by migrating low-priced commodity products from the store to the internet, expanding the Best Buy Mobile format, and creating destination stores supported by vendors that are focused on upscale, innovative products.

The continuing channel and format evolution unfolding at Best Buy utilizes the company's assets in the best ways. Customers want informed opinions and curated selections, convenience in handling items before they buy them, the lowest prices, and service that can help them overcome their knowledge gaps. It is becoming clear that the superstore is no longer the single best way to address customer needs in consumer electronics, and by shrinking and transforming this outdated format, Best Buy is using a multi-format and multi-channel model to best serve customer needs. Best Buy superstores are gradually evolving into destination showrooms staffed by hyper-informed, brand-trained sales associates supported by Best Buy's own Geek Squad. These showrooms introduce customers to the newest and most innovative technology. Best Buy Mobile stores serve as convenient areas for shoppers to handle and experiment with strong velocity, high ASP, compact products like tablets and smartphones. Best Buy's online site price-competes with mass merchandisers and online retailers across a range of commoditized products.

In these formats, we see the prototype of what we believe to be the future Best Buy store following a "Shrink and Transform the Format" strategy: convenient, destination showrooms relying on online order fulfillment. Best Buy is no stranger to inventory issues, having come close to bankruptcy by over-ordering outdated computers. Holding high-ASP, cutting-edge goods with fast product cycles in-store simply doesn't make sense when fulfilling orders online is much more efficient, customers often go through multi-day purchase cycles and voluntarily delay purchase, and revolutionary product introductions like VCRs and digital TVs can change a physical store's merchandise mix in a very short time. Holding commoditized products in-store also doesn't make sense when online retailers can offer lower prices, unless there's a market for immediacy. Best Buy's investments in its online channel will help it bridge the gap between being a retailer and becoming a showroom that relies predominantly on online fulfillment. As Best Buy becomes a showroom, it will have to upgrade its labor model. When Best Buy was competing to be the lowest-cost channel of distribution, part-time labor made sense. However, those days are over. Best Buy's Connected Store format and SWAS have made great strides in improving salesmanship and incorporating Geek Squad. This better-trained labor is what's needed to position Best Buy as an agent for its brands, the disseminator of technology improvements to the masses, and the bridge that helps connect shoppers to "mythic" products. As a backdrop to these changes, observers should remember that consumer electronics retailers in the past have died (and lived, in Best Buy's case), by being flexible enough to accommodate changing consumer tastes, competitive environments, and product cycles. Looking ahead, experimenting constantly, and creating a more flexible organization overall will be crucial to Best Buy's success long-term. Best Buy's decision framework and the changes it will need to make to its TIPS assets are summarized in Figure 4.19.

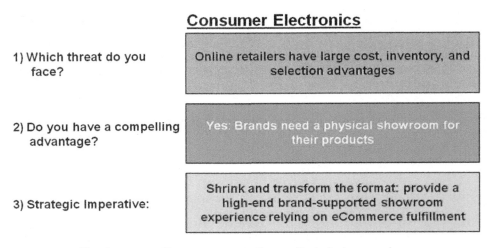

Consumer Electronics

1) Which threat do you face?
> Online retailers have large cost, inventory, and selection advantages

2) Do you have a compelling advantage?
> Yes: Brands need a physical showroom for their products

3) Strategic Imperative:
> Shrink and transform the format: provide a high-end brand-supported showroom experience relying on eCommerce fulfillment

T   Improve eCommerce operation so that chain can rely predominantly on online fulfillment.

I   Stock commodity products online and display high-end electronics in-store; few, if any, items sold in-store.

P   Brands provide hyper-informed sales associates for their products; where brands are too small to support a SWAS, Best Buy provides high-end experience with knowledgeable associates. Best Buy Geek Squad functions as cross-brand support network.

S   Shrink store formats to reflect fewer product categories and renovate stores to feature high-end SWAS and product displays.

Figure 4.19

Perhaps no retail operators have been as flexible as supermarkets over the years. So we will address this retail vertical next. Supermarkets rapidly adopted a one-stop-shop format in the 1930s, found ways to compete against Walmart in the 90s, and have proved adept at continuously remerchandising their boxes to respond to changing consumer tastes and demands. Supermarkets have faced down a number of threats over the past 80 years, and, as broad-assortment retailers, face the same threats as office supply stores and Best Buy, and also face challenges from dollar stores, supercenters, and a customer base that is changing in tastes, behavior, and economic ability. However, the rise of online grocers may be the competitors that push grocery retailers over the edge, unless they can formulate a response that addresses the many challenges they face.

Chapter 5

Will the Internet Push Grocery Retailers Over the Edge?

Supermarkets, much like department stores, mass merchandisers, supercenters, and other broad-assortment retailers are facing impacts across almost every category in their stores. Reading the commentary of equity analysts, one is impressed by the extent to which supercenters like Walmart and warehouse clubs like Costco have stolen supermarket customers and taken over categories that were previously the sole domain of supermarkets. But the assault on supermarkets is actually much more widespread, and comes not just from traditional competitors like supercenters and warehouse clubs, but also from new entrants like dollar stores and online retailers, and from shifts in consumer habits. We believe that there are several key issues that will effect a dramatic change in the supermarket industry over the next five years.

First, eCommerce will shift significant dollars out of the industry. Although home delivery does not seem to be a viable alternative in the supermarket space today, a combination of fragmentation in consumer shopping behavior and emerging alternatives to home delivery will change how Americans buy consumables. The inexorable march of internet technology will create significant changes in the expectations and behavior of supermarket shoppers that will open up opportunities for new and creative concepts. Related to this, the consumer need for convenience will continue to explode and retailers will need to find solutions that solve problems for time-starved customers. While online retail of groceries doesn't generally have cost advantages, some segments of consumers are more than willing to pay for convenience.

Second, the bifurcation of income in the US will accelerate and lead to an even greater need for supermarkets to provide value. Supermarkets have long relied on a high-volume, low-margin model, and the large, vibrant middle class that characterized mid-twentieth-century America was essential to supermarket success. However, the supermarket sweet spot in the middle of the income distribution has been shrinking for decades. As income inequality accelerates, the ability of supermarkets to remain competitive will diminish as volume flees for Walmart or migrates to higher-end retailers like Whole Foods. Supermarkets have already reduced costs dramatically in order to compete with much more efficient competitors, and they can no longer generate price savings by cutting heads. Now too they lack the residual store-level talent to shift strategy and provide service. Consequently, these downward trends create an unstable situation for supermarket retailers.

Third, the bifurcation of consumer shopping trips will continue unabated with consumers looking for meal solutions on an almost nightly basis (trips that have been going disproportionately to Quick Serve Restaurants [QSRs]) and filling in their non-perishable needs (household items, canned goods, health and beauty care) on separate store-based trips. These non-perishable trips are a place where eCommerce and other non-traditional competitors like dollar stores will shine, and the winners of the past two decades, supercenters, will fail. This trend will continue to shrink the freedom supermarkets have to manage pricing, service, and product assortment. While beautiful perishables departments have been a cornerstone of many supermarkets' strategies and formats, Americans have greatly simplified their meals over the past three decades, and many have either forgotten or never learned how to pull these raw ingredients into a meal. Because of this, demand for the core perishables category is declining.

This will lead to a fourth significant issue: the amount of excess space that supermarkets will have on hand. This will manifest itself not just in the number of excess stores in a chain's network that will need to close but, more importantly, the excess space in every individual location that a chain operates. As we will show, supermarket store size has risen dramatically over the last 30 years yet consumer behavior indicates a need for this space to shrink dramatically. Space will become an albatross around the necks of most supermarket chains as they struggle to figure out how to productively deploy or shrink the space in what has become a very inflexible format.

Finally, the wave of human health concerns (especially relative to obesity) will cause supermarkets to rethink some of their core strategies.

We are currently in the midst of many of these changes, and because of them, the past two decades have been challenging for supermarket companies. The recent recession has made things worse. Store closures have become increasingly common, household names like A&P and Winn-Dixie (now part of Lone Star owned Bi-Lo) have entered (and emerged from) bankruptcy, and supermarket giant Supervalu is laying off workers, closing stores and selling assets to Cerberus Capital Management in a bid to stay afloat. Even large chains, like Safeway, have struggled with generating high returns on invested capital, and Safeway has also been purchased by Cerberus Capital Management. Kroger, for its part, has done very well and improved its operations significantly, as seen in its falling SG&A Expense Ratio in Figure 5.1. However, it is focused on improving a box and a style of retailing that, as we will see later in the chapter, may face an existential crisis if European-style, purpose-built Drive stores (small warehouse formats where customers order online and pick up orders) come to America. These Drive stores are apt examples of the "Shrink and Transform the Format" strategy.

Kroger	2005	2006	2007	2011	2012	2013
Same-store sales growth (excluding fuel sales)	3.9%	5.7%	5.5%	4.9%	3.5%	3.6%
ROIC (Op Leases Not Capitalized)	8.6%	9.4%	9.3%	4.9%	10.1%	8.9%
Gross Margin	25.6%	25.0%	24.4%	21.5%	21.2%	21.2%
SG&A as % Sales	22.1%	21.5%	21.0%	20.0%	18.3%	18.4%
Safeway	2005	2006	2007	2011	2012	2013
Same-store sales growth	5.9%	4.4%	4.4%	1.1%	0.8%	1.7%
ROIC (Op Leases Not Capitalized)	7.3%	8.6%	9.0%	4.5%	4.2%	5.0%
Gross Margin	30.3%	30.3%	30.0%	27.9%	27.4%	27.3%
SG&A as % Sales	26.8%	26.2%	25.8%	25.9%	25.6%	25.5%

Figure 5.1 Sources: Company Reports. Note: Fiscal Years Chosen to Most Reflect Calendar Years.

Over the next few pages we'll present a treasure trove of data on the industry. The data show what may appear to be small but are, over time, inexorable changes in the consumer and retail landscape; changes that continue to play out and damage supermarkets' positioning. While it's easy to disregard these changes due to their current size and limited impact, bear in mind that net margins at supermarkets are already exceedingly thin. With costs such as rent and labor largely fixed and gross margins low, supermarkets need to attract a broad audience to be profitable. Much like in the airline industry, high volumes are crucial to good financial performance, and even small declines in sales can be deleterious to a supermarket's profitability. Given the sheer volume of dollars flowing through the grocery category, even slight movements in channel share can have enormous impacts on supermarket companies' bottom lines—impacts that can mean the difference between survival and death. Supermarkets' challenges will be amplified over the next several years and will lead to either significant internal changes in the supermarket industry or a disruption of this industry by outside forces.

What will the future look like? And what strategies can supermarket companies deploy to remain relevant? Over the course of this chapter, we'll look at historical consumer behavior and how it has recently evolved to fit our modern lifestyle, examine the evolution of supermarkets since their inception in the 1930s—both where they have succeeded and where they have failed—and place all this information in the context of an increasingly competitive food and meal environment. With this background, we'll be able to make some bold predictions for the future.

The Current Category/Occasion Structure of the Supermarket Industry and Changing Consumer Behavior

Today's supermarket is largely made up of four product groupings, each targeting a different shopping trip motivation. Three of these trip motivations are under pressure and are often better served by non-supermarkets. The fourth is being reduced in importance by consumer behavior shifts. Figure 5.2 presents these product groupings and the pressures they face.

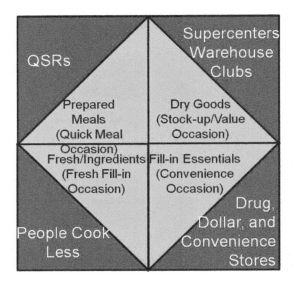

Figure 5.2

We believe one of the root causes of supermarkets' poor positioning is that the business model of the traditional supermarket company has caused them to lose focus on serving customers. Supermarkets have generally been focused internally on cost reduction and management of manufacturers over the last twenty years. In pursuit of vendor fees and cost competitiveness, supermarkets have made strategic missteps that have taken them further away from the quick, easy, and convenient shopping model that today's mass consumer is looking for and have given rise to mounting customer dissatisfaction. This dissatisfaction has left the door open for new players—e.g. supercenters, dollar stores, upmarket food stores like Whole Foods and Trader Joe's, and internet retailers—to successfully enter the market. These alternatives are now widespread enough and of sufficient quality that in 2006, for the first time, a measurable percentage (1%) of American consumers did not set foot in a traditional supermarket.[216] While that number may seem miniscule, for decades supermarkets have been a weekly ritual for every American household, and the fact that some households no longer need supermarkets at all is telling. Once shopping rituals are broken, it is very difficult to re-establish them.

To understand the strong headwinds facing supermarkets, one needs to place the industry in the context of the significant developments in how Americans choose what and where to eat and how time starved consumers think about shopping in general. Across the American meal landscape, the consumer has increasingly been asking: "Who can give me the easiest, most convenient meal at the best price?" (And lately that question often also includes an important unmet need, "Can you make it healthy?") For our purposes, we will define convenient as fitting in well with a person's needs, activities, and plans, involving little travel. We will use "easy" to mean requiring little effort or endeavor, undemanding. For example, a grocery store that is within steps of your domicile is convenient but that store may be organized in a way that is difficult to shop and requires a great deal of effort to navigate. It is not an easy store to shop. On the other hand, a store that is far from home may be inconvenient but it may be well laid out and provide the ability to create customer specific smart shopping lists from your loyalty card data that reduces the amount of effort required to shop there, i.e. it is easy.

In the supermarket business one manifestation of this desire to make food easy has been a surge in the level of frozen prepared food consumed. In fact, Americans have doubled the share of their food expenditures spent on frozen prepared food from 3.25% in 1995 to a high of 6.51% in 2007.[217] (The Great Recession appears to have attenuated some of these gains, with the most recent data from 2010 pegging the real dollar share of frozen food for the average consumer unit at 6.14 %.)[218]

Even more telling is how Americans are actually preparing meals in their homes. The NPD Group has tracked both consumers' purchases as well as their at-home activities since 1984. Data from their consumer panel points to dramatic changes in Americans' home behavior. Americans have steadily desired more convenient meals and this has meant some or all meal preparation being done outside the home. Supporting this, the top chart in Figure 5.3 shows that since 1984, the percent of main dishes served at main meals described as "fresh" or "homemade" has dropped steadily, from 62.6% in 1984 to a low of 48.8% in 2009, as shown in the top chart of Figure 5.3.[219] In line with this convenience trend, Americans also desire increasingly simpler and easier meals, and, as the bottom chart in Figure 5.3 shows supper, our largest meal, is steadily consisting of fewer dishes.

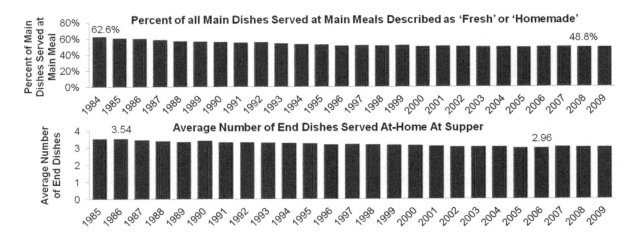

Figure 5.3 Source: The NPD Group, Eating Patterns in America (25th edition), September 2009.

Concurrent with our decisions of what we eat and how we eat, our ways of preparing meals at home have also shifted dramatically to reflect an increased focus on ease of cooking. The saturation rate of microwave ovens remained steady in the mid-80s through much of the 1990s and early 2000s, but had rocketed up to 96% by 2009.[220] Unsurprisingly, there was a corresponding increase in the percentage of main meals prepared with microwaves, rising from 10.5% in 1985 to 22.5% in 2009; while the percent of main meals where a stovetop was used decreased from 51.6% to 33.2% over the same time period.[221] But even looking at the "what" and the "how" doesn't tell the whole story of Americans' continued at-home shift towards ease, convenience, and value. It is instructive to also look at the "why" across meal parts, which are presented in Figure 5.4, the NPD Group's Top 5 Motivations for Selecting Meal Foods.

Percent of Meal Occasions – Top 5 Motivations for Selecting Meal Foods					
Breakfast		Lunch		Supper	
It's my favorite/what I like	48%	Easy to prepare or get	37%	Really tasted good	45%
Part of my morning routine	48%	Quick and easy to cleanup	32%	Easy to prepare or get	42%
Could get it/eat it fast	43%	Could make/get it quickly	32%	Fill up/satisfy hunger	40%
Easy to prepare	43%	Didn't cost a lot	24%	Serve something everyone would like	34%
Quick and easy to clean up	30%	Could eat/drink quickly	23%	Something that took little/no planning/thought	34%

Figure 5.4 Source: The NPD Group, Eating Patterns in America (25th edition), September 2009.

The ease and convenience motivations are easy to see for Breakfast. In fact, after "It's my favorite" and "Part of my morning routine," ease and convenience motivations round out the entire top five. These ease and convenience breakfast motivations are also reflected in the fact that the average annual restaurant breakfasts eaten in the car per American have increased from 2.2 in 1984 to 8.6 in 2009![222] For lunch, ease, convenience, and value motivations take all five of the top slots. Ease, convenience, and value are less prevalent at Supper, with only "Easy to prepare or get" and "Something that took little/no planning/thought" in the top five. But, after expanding motivations to the top ten for supper, "Quick and easy to clean up," "Didn't cost a lot," and "Could be made or gotten quickly" all make the list.

Americans are motivated to make their at-home meals easier, simpler, and more convenient through their choices of what to eat and how to prepare it. We also see very similar trends in another side of Americans' eating habits: the meals we eat away from home.

Americans' history with meals eaten away from home (e.g. in restaurants or diners, at café carts, bought from a drive-through and eaten on the way to work, etc.) has been 'If I can have more of it at the same price, I want it.' If we conceive of price as a percent of disposable income rather than as a fixed number, the most striking trend in Figure 5.5 is how stable the percent of disposable income spent on food away from home has been: varying between 3.0% and 4.4%.[223] As Americans' disposable income grew, they increasingly favored eating out-of-home as the twentieth century progressed, however, there appears to be a relatively stable amount of the household budget that Americans are willing to spend on this pursuit.

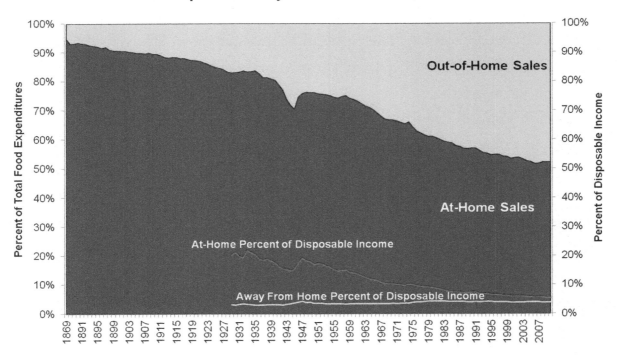

Food Expenditures by At-Home vs. Out-of-Home

Figure 5.5 Sources: Compiled from Table 1 and Table 7, Food Expenditure Series, Economic Research Service, United States Department of Agriculture.

In the latter years shown in Figure 5.5, it appears that a rough equilibrium was reached between out-of-home and at-home food expenditures. This is deceptive. In a time of stagnant disposable income, Americans have found ways to eat more food out-of-home in a way that's faster and more convenient—while still only spending the same roughly 4% of their disposable income on out-of-home food and keeping the 50/50 out-of-home/at-home expenditure split. In effect, Americans have increased the value they derive from out-of-home food.

How are Americans doing this? Largely by beginning to treat out-of-home meals as they have been treating at-home meals—buying them ready-to-eat! As a share of meals purchased at restaurants, Americans have completely flipped positions on eat-in vs. take-out over the past two decades. In 1984, Americans ate 57% of meals bought at restaurants inside the restaurant and 43% away from it; whereas in 2009 they ate just 39% of restaurant meals inside the restaurant and 61% outside of it![224] Why the switch? It's both less expensive and more convenient to show up at a restaurant and have your takeout meal waiting for you, and Americans are eating less often at middle-tier restaurants in favor of casual and fast-casual restaurants. Over three-quarters of Americans' restaurant meals are now eaten at Quick Service Restaurants (QSRs) like McDonald's and Subway; with 77.4% of U.S. annual restaurant meals consisting of QSR visits in 2009 vs. 73.3% in 1994.[225] Consumers increasingly want meals fast and cheap, and every meal eaten outside of the home is lost volume for supermarkets. Supermarkets need to answer the consumer demand for quick, convenient, inexpensive meal solutions in order to survive. Value and convenience are not new to the supermarket industry, and played a defining role in the industry's evolution from the 1930s to today. What those terms mean and how they are delivered, however, have shifted in a way that demands a new supermarket response.

The History of US Supermarkets: A Highly Flexible, Adaptive Format

The blueprint for today's supermarket was created in 1930 when Michael Cullen opened his first large-format, self-service supermarket offering customers both value and convenience. By consolidating the previously separate businesses of dry goods, green grocery, and butchery into one location, King Kullen provided a one-stop shop for food needs. With locations near major population centers and ample parking, this one-stop-shopping was a revolution that redefined convenience.

More importantly, Michael Cullen also promised tremendous value, running ads with copy like "You Wall Street Chain Stores have been making millions from the public for years with your outrageous prices. Chain Stores, drop your prices, give the poor buying public a chance."[226] Cullen's value innovations defined the strategy that would be followed by supermarket companies, and later big box category killers, for the next several decades. By relying on customer self-service Cullen, eliminated the need for behind-the-counter labor that used to personally pick customers' orders for them. Rather than locate in expensive main street districts, Cullen kept his overhead low by locating in lower-rent areas (while still being close to major population centers and with large amounts of parking). Finally, Cullen recognized the importance of volume and that if he could sell large enough quantities of products rapidly, he could set lower prices than competitors and still end up ahead. All together, these attributes created a store that provided customers with both convenience and value. The concept was very successful. So successful, in fact, that Cullen's innovation was rapidly replicated by major grocery chains. Four years after Michael Cullen founded his first store, a survey counted 94 supermarkets. Two years later that number had ballooned to 1,200 in 85 cities.[227]

As consumers continued to leave urban areas and migrate to the suburbs, supermarket chains followed and Cullen's model became the standard supermarket format throughout the US. By 1950, 15,000 American supermarkets were in business.[228] Freed from the size constraints of their first urban locations, supermarkets progressively expanded in both size and scope to accommodate new products, brands, and customer demand. Michael Cullen's original one-stop-shop promise moved beyond food to include health and beauty products, home goods, and a variety of other categories.

The rise of supercenters like K-Mart, Walmart, and Target throughout the 1980s and 1990s dramatically changed the nature of competition within the supermarket industry. While not necessarily conveniently-located, supercenters, and even more so warehouse clubs, were the epitome of cost-cutting, volume, and one-stop shopping. These competitors tore through many core supermarket categories and quickly gained market share. The following eight categories in Figure 5.6 represent about 95%[iii] of supermarket dollar volume and the impact of supercenters and warehouse clubs in some categories is staggering:

[iii] Based on dollar volume recorded in the 1997 Economic Census.

Grocery (Produce, Meats, Cereals, etc.)

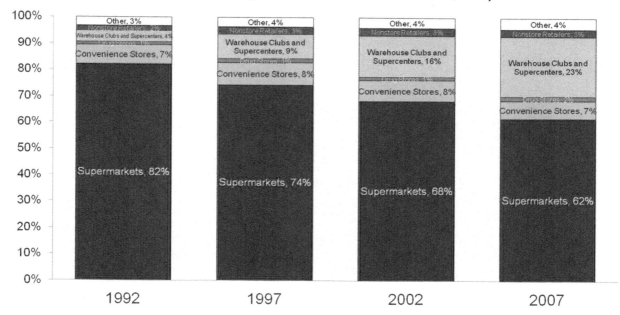

Paper Products

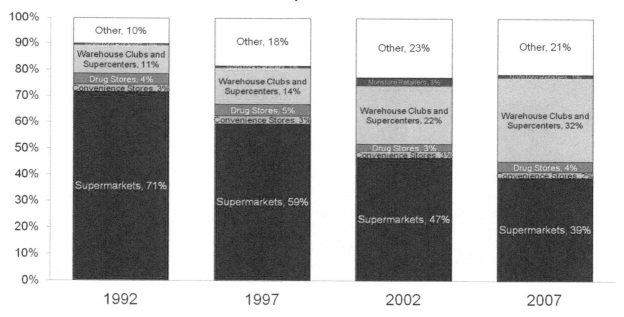

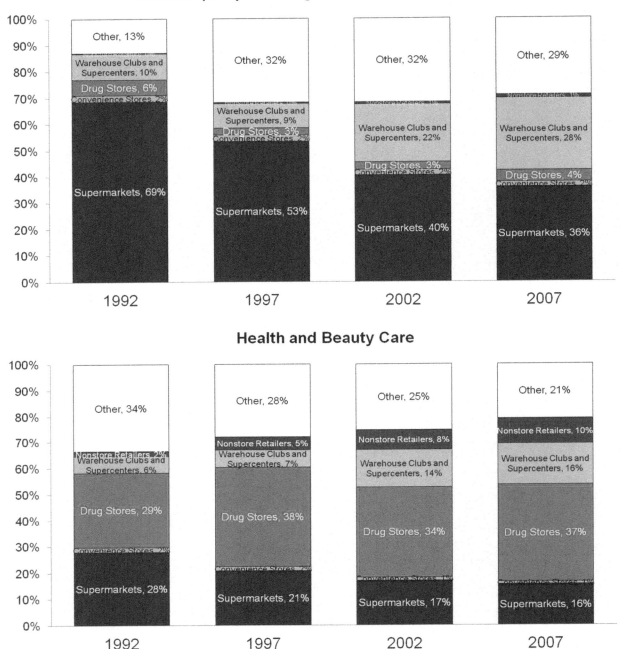

RX

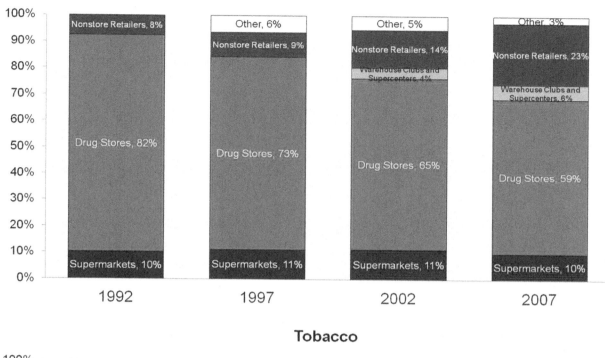

Tobacco

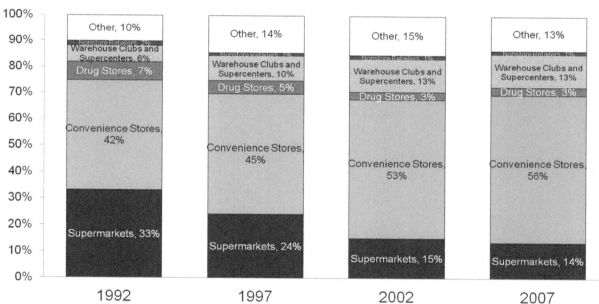

Alcohol

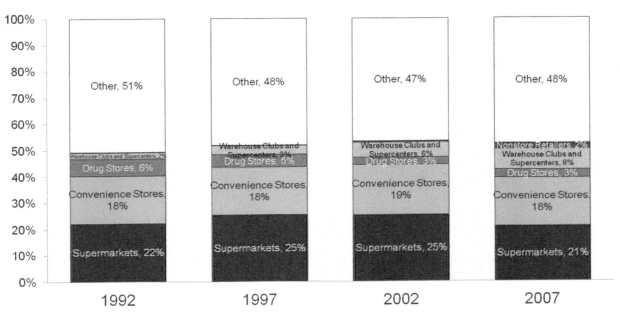

Meals (Meals, snacks, sandwiches and non-alcs for immediate consumption, no frozen meals)

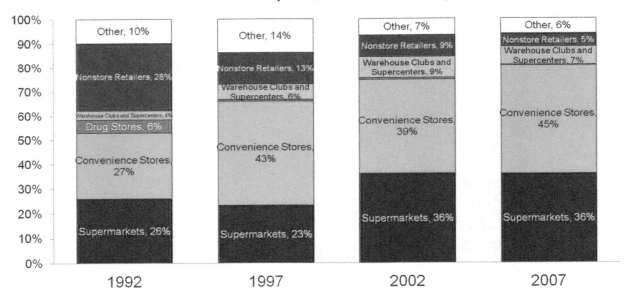

Figure 5.6 Sources: Compiled from 'Merchandise by Kind of Business' and 'Kinds of Business by Broad Merchandise Line' in Merchandise Line Sales, Retail Trade Subject Series, Economic Census, for years 1992, 1997, 2002, and 2007 and author's calculations. Specialty Stores excluded. Note: Due to category reclassifications, 1992 and 1997 numbers are not always comparable. For instance, packaged snacks were moved from "meals" to "grocery" between 1992 and 1997.

In regulated categories like tobacco, alcohol, and pharmacy products, the impacts of warehouse clubs and supercenters were not as severe. But warehouse clubs and supercenters have run away with the market in categories like paper products and cleaners. These latter categories are ones where the products sold are largely standard, national brands with long shelf-lives. With the quality of the product being uniform across channels, consumers are happy to shop in large quantities at warehouse clubs and supercenters where they get the best prices, or in drug and dollar stores as a convenience. The largest single category in a supermarket is, of course, the grocery category, and even in this supermarket stalwart, warehouse clubs and supercenters gained tremendous market share over the past two decades. Overall, across these categories, supermarkets have gone from a real share of 60% in 1992 to just 38% in 2007.[229]

The intense competitive threat from supercenters and warehouse clubs spurred further attempts by supermarkets to enhance their position on Cullen's original strategic trio of cost-cutting, convenience, and volume. With mass merchandisers and warehouse clubs—Walmart in particular—entering the grocery business and leveraging their scale and purchasing volume to out-price supermarkets, consolidation of regional and independent supermarket operators became widespread in the 1990s and 2000s. The scale and efficiency advantages of regional consolidation in terms of purchasing power, shared distribution volume, and consolidated market demand led to fewer, but stronger, competitors to Walmart. As a result of this consolidation and the new economics imposed by Walmart and Costco, a regionally-consolidated supermarket retail landscape remains today, one that has no true national players save Walmart and, increasingly, Kroger and Cerberus-owned Albertsons.

Supermarkets also focused on offering better prices to customers by introducing a wide variety of high-value store brand products. These store brands were a major coup for supermarkets, contributing higher gross margins as well as providing customers with increased value, which has been especially important during the recent recession. Customers have received these store brands well, and today, 97% of American households consume store brand foods on a regular basis:[230] nearly one of every four products bought in supermarkets, drug stores, and discount stores (24% of unit volume) is now a store brand, and almost 20% of supermarket dollar volume is in store brands.[231]

The bright spot for supermarkets in the fight for shopper trips has been prepared meals, where supermarkets (and convenience stores) have actually increased share relative to other retail channels (of course, QSRs are a strong player in the food-service vertical). In the latest evolution of a trend that started in the late 90s, supermarkets have aggressively remerchandised to feature an "a la carte" area of fresh, prepared meals to reflect consumers' increased focus on buying finished meals. Placing this category at the front of the store is a way in which supermarkets have made meals easy for customers. Supermarkets have also emphasized fresh produce at the front of the store. These are areas where supermarkets' biggest competitive threats, supercenters, dollar stores, and warehouse stores, have not been as effective at competing based on their trip dynamics. Consumers usually stock up over a relatively limited number of trips at supercenters and warehouse stores. These channels have thus had a harder time selling large volumes of limited shelf-life perishables (e.g. produce) and fresh prepared foods. Dollar and convenience stores are not currently well equipped to sell significant perishables volumes due to their smaller formats, limited selections, and discount atmosphere. Alongside QSRs and convenience stores, supermarkets can offer enough variety and location convenience to make these ready-to-eat and ready-to-heat meals work for consumers.

Outside of consolidation and store brands, however, supermarkets have gone too far in furthering Michael Cullen's strategies of cost-cutting, one-stop-shopping, and volume, and have damaged their offer to consumers. Supermarkets have aggressively tried to compete on price with Walmart and deeply cut and shifted their labor pools over the past two decades to do so. Self-checkout stations have eliminated cashiers. Shifting from processing food in-store to outsourcing much of the preparation work has eliminated skilled positions. A shift to more use of part-time labor has allowed better allocation of employee hours but has also resulted in less-trained, less knowledgeable, and less engaged employees. All of these activities decreased supermarkets' operating costs—savings which supermarkets passed on to consumers in the form of lower prices—but also detracted from the store experience and have caused a stagnation in customer satisfaction at major chains up until around 2008 as shown in Figure 5.7.

Supermarket Company Satisfaction Scores

Figure 5.7 Source: "Benchmarks by Industry, Supermarkets", American Customer Satisfaction Index, 2012, http://www.theacsi.org.

Supermarkets have also made strategic decisions that undermine the ease and convenience motivations of their shoppers, such as the decision to build progressively larger stores. As supercenters entered the grocery space, supermarkets expanded the size of their prototypical stores in an effort to compete with supercenters on assortment. The rise of store-brand products also contributed to increasing store size. As supermarkets introduced store brands in a product category, existing items, or stock-keeping units (SKUs), were often left on the shelf in order to ensure that supermarkets could fulfill whichever product demand customers had. (It is important to note that supermarkets also receive manufacturer fees to keep national brand products on the shelf and promote them regularly.) The magnitude of this store size growth is seen in Figure 5.8 based on data from the Food Marketing Institute.

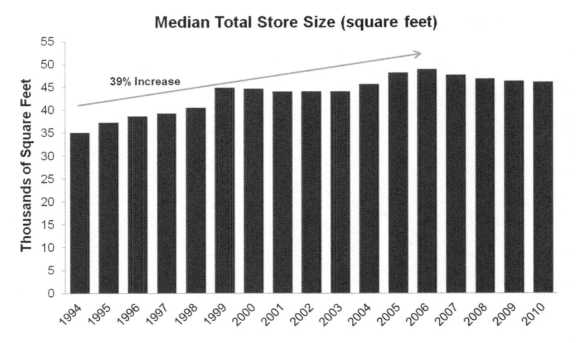

Figure 5.8 Sources: Compiled from Food Marketing Institute, *Food Marketing Industry Speaks*, Years 1994-2010.

Unfortunately, supermarkets have not been able to compete on either selection or price with supercenters. By expanding store footprints and stocking stores with even more products while eliminating skilled labor, they have gained all the negatives of supercenters—crowded checkouts, cluttered aisles, consumer difficulty in finding product efficiently, and difficulty getting help—while reaping few of the benefits. Supermarket pricing has continued to be significantly higher than their low price competition with fewer and fewer capabilities to differentiate them.

These larger store footprints also made it harder for supermarkets to operate profitably as they require more staff, generate higher occupancy expenses, and generally just cost more. In the case of supermarkets, these higher costs weren't compensated for with higher volume as supercenters and warehouse clubs continued to take market share. The continued competition with alternative channels and the larger store formats of supermarkets have resulted in lower real productivity per square foot as seen in Figure 5.9.

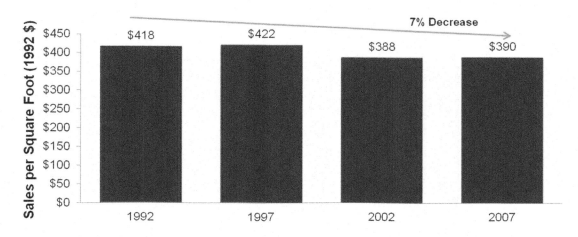

Figure 5.9 Source: Floor Space by Selected Kind of Business, Miscellaneous Subjects, Census of Retail Trade, U.S. Census Bureau, from Years 1992, 1997, 2002, 2007. Indexed to weighted CPI based on supermarket volume.

Data from the Food Marketing Institute's annual survey (presented in Figure 5.10) confirms this decline, and shows that this downward trend continued through the recession and has so far failed to turn around.

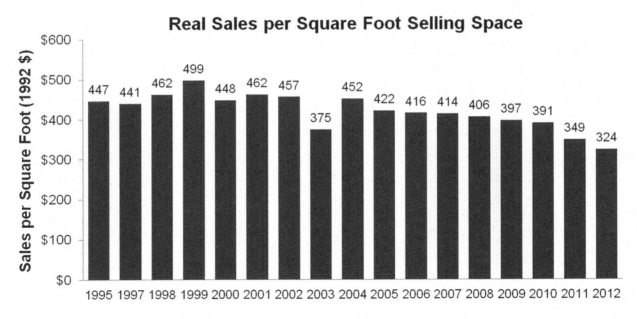

Figure 5.10 Sources: *Food Marketing/Retailing Industry Speaks*, Food Marketing Institute, various years; nominal sales per square foot converted to real sales per square foot using a weighted CPI of supermarket categories. Note: The US Census draws on a broader set of respondents than does FMI, and so its results are more likely to accurately reflect changes over time. FMI states that "Since the sample and mix of respondents vary somewhat from year to year, direct year-to-year comparisons should be made with caution. However, FMI believes that the conclusions drawn from these surveys provide an accurate picture of general trends in the food retail industry." While extreme outliers such as years 1999 and 2003 are likely the result of data inaccuracy rather than changes in the industry, the overall downward trend is believable.

Given the already low margins in the supermarket business, this decline in real sales productivity of approximately 7% between 1992 and 2007 (according to the Census, and even more if one uses the FMI data) is a very significant problem. (Mercadona, in contrast, has been able to compete against hypermarkets by making polar opposite decisions to US supermarkets, with highly paid store associates working in limited-SKU, smaller footprint stores. See the sidebar on Mercadona for a description of the company.)

Mercadona and the "Good Jobs Strategy"

As a counterpoint to US supermarket retailers who have focused relentlessly on cost reductions through labor cuts, we look to Zeynep Ton's analysis of Mercadona, a Spanish supermarket chain, and the "Good Jobs Strategy" that it follows. While US retailers suffer from shelf-level stockouts, data inaccuracy, promotion non-compliance, and shrink—largely due to underinvestment in training, wage levels, and staffing levels—Mercadona has turned this labor paradigm on its head.

Mercadona generates double the sales per square foot and over 50% more sales per employee than the average US supermarket, and between 1998 and 2008 grew revenue and profits at 10-year CAGRs of 22% and 26%, respectively.[232] The company accomplished all this while investing twenty times more in training for its employees than US retailers and while maintaining a workforce that has consistent, scheduled work hours, is 85% full-time and salaried, and where a new employee's wage is two times the Spanish minimum.[233] Mercadona's associates work within a store that limits selection to the "highest-quality, most affordable products" (9,000 SKUs per store vs. over 40,000 at US supermarkets), employs more labor than strictly necessary, and where they are empowered to help customers choose between products and cross-trained to perform a variety of store tasks.

While many retailers talk about being customer-first, Mercadona executes on it, and uses its employees to do so successfully. Due to the limited assortment in Mercadona stores, associates can competently talk to customers (or "bosses" as the company refers to customers) about items within their departments, educate customers on how to cook the products they're buying, and sell them any additional items they need to make the meal they're planning. Rather than losing a sale if a customer can't find what they are seeking, Mercadona associates can redirect them to a different item within the store assortment. The abundance of labor and high levels of cross-training mean that Mercadona is better able to deal with both periods of high traffic, when more associates shift to working the registers and answering customer questions, and low traffic, when associates spend time restocking, cleaning the store, ordering additional inventory, and effecting store changes.

It also means that store labor is not constantly shifting from barely-completed task to task, and Mercadona employees have time to consider what they are doing, and whether there is a way to do it better. If they can think of such a way, management listens. This collaborative process improvement has resulted in a number of laboratories throughout Mercadona stores where Mercadona employees experiment with ways to improve "stock, services, and processes."[234] Of course, the massive investment in training and cross-training only makes sense if employees stay at Mercadona to use it; of course, Mercadona's well-paid, fulfilled associates rarely leave. The company has an employee turnover rate of just 3.8%.[235] Similarly, because Mercadona associates are so happy, the company's shrink level is much lower than that of other retailers'.

These strategic missteps are exacerbated by what is a very real disconnect between supermarkets and their end-customers. Like IBM and mainframes, vendor allowances may be what hold supermarkets back from evolving with their own industry. The ultra-competitive environment that developed as supercenters and warehouse clubs expanded forced supermarket margins lower and lower. As a result, supermarkets became progressively more dependent on allowances received from branded food marketers for services like promotions, slotting, and contracted shelf space. In their 2011 financial statements, both Kroger and Safeway reported vendor allowance offsets to cost of goods sold that were larger than their actual EBITDAs.[236] Traditional supermarkets today make more money from their vendors than they do from their customers! It's easy to imagine that supermarkets would rather create bigger stores that are less convenient for end-customers in order to host more products and build more display spaces for vendor-fee-paying national labels. The availability of vendor fees insulated supermarkets from their deteriorating position with end-customers and postponed the sense of urgency needed to make significant change. Supermarkets have been more focused on short term financials than long-term customer needs.

As supermarkets took their eye off the customer, many other retailers have stepped in to push grocery retailing forward. In some cases, shoppers themselves have led the change. New shopping methods adapted by consumers may have made warehouse clubs more convenient than supermarkets in categories where consumers tend to stock-up. Trip data from Nielsen's Consumer Panel shows a decrease in trips to grocery stores and a corresponding increase in trips to warehouse stores, presented in Figure 5.11.

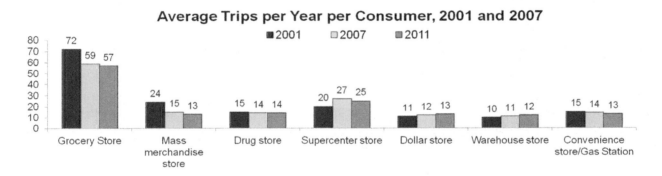

. Figure 5.11 Source: "Nielsen: U.S. Consumers Making Fewer Shopping Trips," Nielsen press release, March 17, 2008, on Nielsen website.

While the rise in gas prices has certainly played a part in this trend as consumers have consolidated trips, it's also possible that, with new eating habits, Americans just find shopping at other outlets easier. These changing trip profiles, in combination with ticket and grocery-led comp store gains at supercenters and warehouse clubs relative to supermarkets,[237] suggest that consumers have been substituting multiple trips to supermarkets with more frequent and larger trips to warehouse stores. Aiding this shift is Americans' increased consumption of frozen prepared food. Because of frozen food's long shelf life, warehouse clubs and supercenters have been able to remerchandise around this category and offer great value. Consumers have responded by shifting their trip patterns and buying behavior to take advantage of this. They have even made changes in their homes to accommodate this new pattern. Figure 5.12, based on data from the Department of Energy's Residential Energy Consumption Survey, shows the percent of households with a second freezer and/or refrigerator.

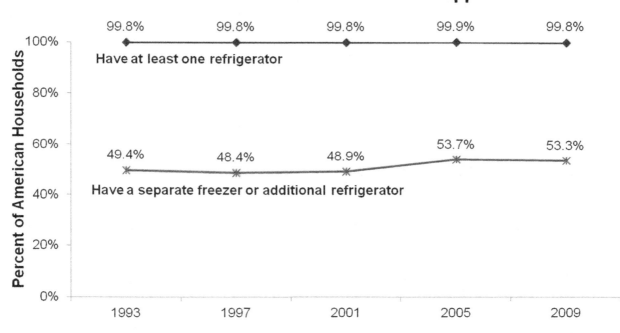

Figure 5.12 Compiled from 'Appliances', Housing Characteristics Tables, Residential Energy Consumption Survey Data, US Energy Information Administration, Years 1993, 1997, 2001, 2005, 2009 and author's calculations.

The percentage of households with separate freezers or additional refrigerators increased between 2001 and 2009; at the same time, we saw growth in warehouse club trips and increases in the amount of frozen prepared meals consumed. In addition, refrigerators and freezers have also been expanding in capacity over this time period.[238] Put it all together and it looks as if Americans are loading frozen food into basements and garages and consequently don't have to visit the supermarket as often. These stock-up trips to warehouse clubs don't just save consumers money. By replacing multiple trips to supermarkets, they also save time. With Americans' increasingly busy lives, saved time means more convenience.

The recent recession has also brought to light the increasing success of dollar stores in the US. This success is encapsulated in a few headline numbers: the combined store count of the four largest dollar-store banners (Dollar General, Dollar Tree, Family Dollar, 99 Cents Only) outnumber that of the three largest drug store banners (CVS, Rite Aid, Walgreen's).[239] Dollar General's over 11,000 locations make it the largest retailer by store count in the US.[240] Since 2006 the four main dollar store chains have experienced nearly uninterrupted quarterly year over year same-store sales growth.[241] But dollar stores were growing even before the recession and it's worth asking why.

The dollar store format has a unique strategic focus and business model. While dollar stores follow the warehouse club model of limited SKUs, they carry a high proportion of store brand products, sell products in much smaller sizes, and occupy a fraction of the space of a warehouse club (approximately 7,000 square feet). Dollar stores' small footprint gives them two distinct advantages; they are able to locate much closer to population centers than supermarkets or supercenters (ideal for urban areas), but they also require less foot traffic to remain profitable making them ideal for rural areas that lack the population density to support a big box store. Additionally, their model of keeping prices low through a limited assortment of high velocity SKUs, tight labor budgets, private labeling, and low overhead mean that their prices can be lower than both supermarkets and supercenters.[242] When one reviews the earnings calls from both Family Dollar and Dollar General, these quotes from their CEOs stand out: "Our strategy of value and convenience continues to resonate well"[243] (Howard Levine, Family Dollar) and "we continue for customers [sic] both value and convenience."[244] (Rick Dreiling, Dollar General). These are companies that focus on exactly what their customers, not manufacturers, are looking for. While their limited product offering means that dollar stores can't wholly replace supermarkets, their high convenience and value offering help dollar stores continue to steal volume from both supermarkets and supercenters. Read the profiles on this page to learn about how Dollar General has become the Walmart of rural America and how Family Dollar is effectively competing with supermarkets in urban America.

Family Dollar—Urban Ability	Dollar General—Rural Ability
Walk into your typical Family Dollar and you'll find yourself in about 7,150 square feet of selling space choosing between 6,500 SKUs.[245] It will be well-lit and attractive, not your deep discount store stereotype of yesteryear. You also could be in an area generally described as a food desert, off-limits to traditional supermarkets but open to Family Dollar's small footprint and low operating cost model.[246] This close-to-you, easy-to-shop small format offers a lot of convenience. ITG Investment Research analyst John Tomlinson captures this in a Smart Money column: "Folks are so broke and so busy that they can't afford the gas and time required to shop big-box discounters on the edge of town. Your typical dollar store, meanwhile, is close to home and a tenth the size of your average Walmart. Most shoppers spend just 10 minutes and 10 bucks in the store. In 2012, this is how we prefer to shop."[247]	Like Family Dollar, Dollar General operates as a general merchandiser following an EDLP model. In contrast to Family Dollar, however, Dollar General has explicitly targeted sparsely-populated locations, with more than 70% of its stores serving communities with less than 20,000 residents.[248] These communities are often too small to support a grocery store, much less a Walmart, but Dollar General's low-cost model of limited product selection (approximately 10,000 SKUs) and small footprint (7,200 square feet) fits in well.[249] Often the only food store in close proximity, shoppers at Dollar General have a much different experience than their equivalents at supermarkets or supercenters. Whereas supermarket and supercenter customers often plan their trips in advance and spend hours in the store, Dollar General's limited selection, condensed layout, and site-selection focusing on convenience and high traffic routes lead to customers making frequent trips and staying less than ten minutes.[250] While not a one-stop shop, this is a much simpler and more convenient food shopping experience than most US consumers experience, and Dollar General's strategy has paid off. Dollar General experienced uninterrupted quarterly year-on-year same-store sales growth since 2006,[251] and at 11,000+ stores, Dollar General's growth has made it the largest US retailer by store count.[252]

Worryingly, brick-and-mortar competitors aren't the only elephants in the room. The earlier channel share figures depict a strong gain in prescription medicine and health and beauty care products for non-store retailers, chiefly electronic and mail-order drug stores and pharmacies. Part of the explanation for this is that many non-store drugstores/pharmacies are heavily pushed by their brick-and-mortar drugstore owners, and these non-store retailers can offer very competitive prices. Many medical plans also require mail order fulfillment of maintenance medication (e.g. Lipitor). But another facet is the convenience of having prescriptions arrive in the mail, right on time, every time, without adding another trip to a store or waiting at a drugstore pharmacy counter for your prescription to be filled. The relatively high value density of prescription medicines and health and beauty care products also make direct-to-home shipping cost effective. Prescriptions are a trip driver for supermarkets, and their migration online will likely mean less trips. This is worrying in itself, but will online retailers be able to cater to customer needs in other supermarket product categories as warehouse clubs and supercenters have done?

Despite Webvan's early failure in this area, there are signs that online grocery shopping may be a force to contend with in the future. Amazon is rolling out its AmazonFresh program in Seattle, FreshDirect is operating profitably in New York City, and Peapod has had a long operating history in Chicago, Washington, D.C., and New England. These programs and others are actively expanding into new cities. Both online grocery retailers like FreshDirect and Peapod and brick-and-mortar supermarkets like Tesco in the UK and Auchan in France are also finding ways to increase penetration by experimenting with online ordering paired with customer pickup. Internet Retail as an industry scores significantly higher in customer satisfaction than do traditional supermarkets—a worrying difference as it leaves the door open for internet retailers to significantly disrupt the supermarket industry.

There are, of course, a number of reasons to believe that these direct-to-home operations will remain limited. FreshDirect takes advantage of New York City's high population density to achieve operating efficiency; and Peapod[253] and AmazonFresh[254] both increase the average consumer's total grocery bill once delivery charges and generally higher per-unit prices are taken into account, which may limit these services to a wealthier population segment (we've presented a sample of Peapod prices compared to a Stop & Shop store to illustrate some of these price differences in Figure 5.13). All online grocery operations in the US are relatively small, with sales volume of just a handful of traditional supermarkets: Peapod sold just half a billion dollars in 2012 (0.9% penetration of its markets in New England, the Mid-Atlantic, and Midwest),[255] FreshDirect claimed $400 million of sales in 2012 (1.9% penetration of its market of greater New York City),[256] and AmazonFresh was estimated to have $60 million of sales in 2012 (1.1% penetration of its greater Seattle market).[257][258] But even in a limited role, a service like AmazonFresh is bad news for supermarkets. Non-store supermarkets can probably get by as niche services for the wealthy given their more variable, non-store cost structure. However, traditional supermarkets, with high and largely fixed operating expenses and low gross margins, rely on incremental sales beyond their operating expenses to generate gross profit. Any consumer movement to online-only retailers will make it increasingly difficult for traditional retailers to operate in this very competitive space. And, if the example of Ocado in the UK (see sidebar) is any kind of predictor for the future of grocery in the US, the impact of online retailers may not be so limited.

Price	Stop & Shop	Peapod	Peapod/Stop & Shop
Milk	$3.69	$3.79	103%
Cereal	$3.99	$3.99	100%
Eggs	$3.09	$2.59	84%
Orange Juice	$3.00	$3.00	100%
Bread	$0.99	$0.99	100%
Peanut Butter	$4.49	$5.59	124%
Jam	$2.79	$2.79	100%
Carrots	$2.49	$3.29	132%
Veggie Dip	$3.99	$2.19	55%
Frozen Entrees	$2.50	$2.50	100%
Ice Cream	$4.99	$4.99	100%
Paper Towels	$6.99	$6.99	100%
Hot Dog Buns	$1.50	$1.50	100%
Hot Dogs	$4.19	$5.99	143%
Steaks	$8.99	$12.49	139%
Bell Peppers	$9.95	$9.95	100%
Pasta	$1.49	$1.49	100%
Pasta Sauce	$3.99	$3.99	100%
Item Total	**$73.11**	**$78.11**	**107%**
Delivery Fee	N/A	$9.95	
Order Total	**$73.11**	**$88.06**	**120%**

Figure 5.13 Sources: Author visits. Note: Not all promotions in Stop & Shop sample store were present on Peapod.

Ocado: Online Groceries in the UK

While online penetration of grocery retail remains low in the United States, in the UK, driven by both brick-and-mortar retailers and their online-only counterparts, it has expanded significantly (Figure 5.14), far greater than US online retailers' limited market shares.

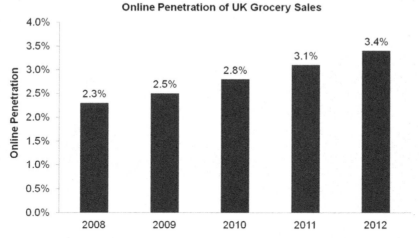

Figure 5.14 Source: Tracey, James and de Speville, Marc, "Ocado: Coming of Age," *Redburn*, May 13, 2013.

On the back of these higher penetration rates, and aided by the UK's relatively greater population density, Ocado achieved over $1.1 billion in sales in 2012 compared to leading US online grocer Peapod's 2012 sales of $500 million.

Ocado has used this scale and growing density to become significantly more efficient in its fulfillment operations, with employees picking over 20% more units per labor hour in 2012 than in 2007, and delivering 50% more orders per van. This progression in Ocado productivity is exhibited in Figure 5.15.

Figure 5.15 Source: Tracey, James and de Speville, Marc, "Ocado: Coming of Age," *Redburn*, May 13, 2013.

These efficiency gains yield large savings, which Ocado is committed to passing on in the form of price cuts to its customers.

As Americans increasingly re-urbanize and US online grocery retailers gain some of the same technology, scale, and density benefits as their UK counterpart, Ocado, it's entirely possible that the United States will see similar levels of online retail penetration.

An Inflection Point for Supermarkets

Supermarkets, perhaps more than any other category of retailer, have been extraordinarily flexible over the past 80 years of their existence. They've continually expanded to accommodate divergent customer tastes, remerchandised to suit evolving consumer demand, and changed whole aspects of their business model in order to stay ahead. And, while supermarkets have taken some wounds from supercenter and warehouse club competition over the past two decades, they have survived. So why do we think supermarkets have to make drastic changes now in order to remain relevant?

We believe that supermarkets have taken their current model as far as it can go, and it's not working. If supermarkets were to add more space (as they continually did up until 2006), that space will be less productive. Customers are seeking smaller stores that are easier to shop and make better use of their limited time. Even with supermarkets' intense focus on cost-cutting over the past two decades, Walmart can still offer consistently cheaper prices on traditional supermarket products than can supermarkets. In order to be price competitive, supermarkets could take additional costs out of their operations. However, supermarkets have already cut significant labor (the largest cost other than the cost of goods sold) from their budgets, and in most cases are left with a poor service offering as a consequence. Cutting more labor in its current form will make customers even less satisfied with the supermarket experience!

From an assortment perspective, consumers are of two minds. They want to be able to find any item they want (driven by the enormous selection available on Amazon) but they also want an easy shopping experience that curates the assortment for them, like that delivered by Trader Joe's and Costco. Supermarkets do poorly in both of these aspects of assortment as their selection can't compete with the internet and their dependence on vendor fees keeps them from curating their assortment.

Supermarket retailers have also relied on having dense networks of conveniently located stores where customers didn't have much choice over which brand they frequented. This has been a distinct advantage over the years but the emergence of dollar stores and others who sell grocery products have significantly diminished this advantage. While supercenters, dollar stores, and online retail are the most threatening competing channels, the increasing fragmentation of food retailers is greater now than ever before. As supermarkets have expanded their offering, they've engaged new competition. Supermarket categories are being carried by an increasingly diverse set of retailers. Drugstores are increasingly serving in a supermarket-convenience capacity along with convenience stores themselves. Building material dealers like Home Depot have taken a big chunk out of the Cleaners category (an 11% share in 2007). Even discounters like TJ Maxx and Marshall's offer food products. As US consumers increasingly desire convenience, they are picking up food products wherever they happen to be shopping. While the impact of each competitor varies, the cumulative impact is to cut significant amounts of desperately needed volume from supermarkets.

Supermarkets have also marginalized many end-customers due to their focus and over-dependence on vendor allowances rather than customer needs. This focus on financials over customers is ultimately fatal in a world with so many food-store alternatives. As different grocery channels (like dollar stores and warehouse clubs) continue to grow and take customers away from supermarkets, national brand manufacturers will reduce the allowances they pay to supermarkets. Eventually, the crutch supermarkets have leaned on may buckle. (To see a business model that puts customers front and center, see the sidebar on Costco.)

Costco—Customer Focused

Costco essentially acts as a value-curating agent for its customers, offering only products they believe to be the best value—defined as a combination of quality and price. This customer agent role is emphasized when one examines Costco's net income: it is roughly equivalent to the membership fees its customers pay. Costco relies on its membership fees as practically its sole source of profit. This focuses Costco on serving its customers. By limiting its mark-ups to 14% on branded products and 15% on private label products, Costco makes just enough on selling products to cover its expenses, and passes vendor allowances and other surpluses on to customers.[259]

Costco's labor policies also contrast significantly with supermarkets. While supermarkets have been trapped in the vicious cycle of cutting labor to stay profitable; by paying good wages, providing health insurance, offering paths to advancement, and providing a great place to work Costco has created a virtuous cycle that creates skilled, motivated employees that better serve Costco customers. This focus on the customer adds up, with Costco's dedicated customers making it the largest warehouse club in the world. Costco's success is marked by both its high customer satisfaction scores compared to the average supermarket chain (Figure 5.16) as well as by its high employee satisfaction reflected in Costco's inclusion on the Glassdoor "Best Places to Work" list—the only food retailer to be listed other than Trader Joe's.[260]

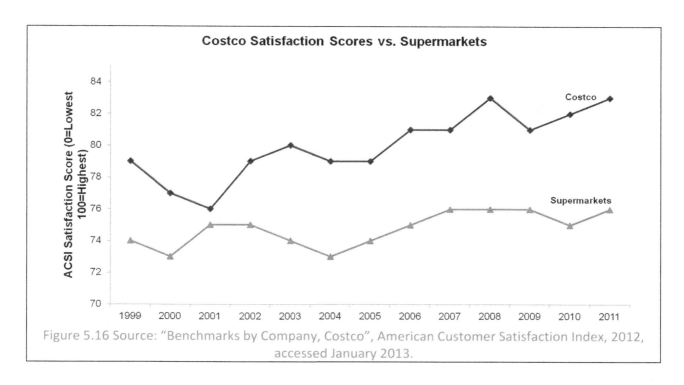

Figure 5.16 Source: "Benchmarks by Company, Costco", American Customer Satisfaction Index, 2012, accessed January 2013.

Supermarkets' historical strengths are arguably better delivered by other retailers. This creates an interesting positioning predicament for supermarkets. Supercenters and warehouse clubs continue to cater to those customers looking for high value, dollar stores are growing stronger with customers looking for both convenience and great prices on staple items, and online retail is the ultimate in convenience and assortment, especially for routinely purchased, non-perishable items. With warehouse clubs and supercenters occupying the value segment in consumers' minds, and online grocery delivery offering greater convenience, traditional supermarkets are left in an odd middle ground of being not as cheap as supercenters but not as convenient as online retailers.

Pair this unstable positioning with a middle class that continues to shrink, and it is unlikely supermarkets' positioning will continue to work. Lower income shoppers are more motivated by value, and higher income shoppers are more likely to value the convenience of online shopping or the higher-priced but higher-quality produce of Whole Foods. Traditional supermarkets' base of middle class customers is itself disappearing, which can be seen in the shrinking percent of middle income adults depicted in Figure 5.17.

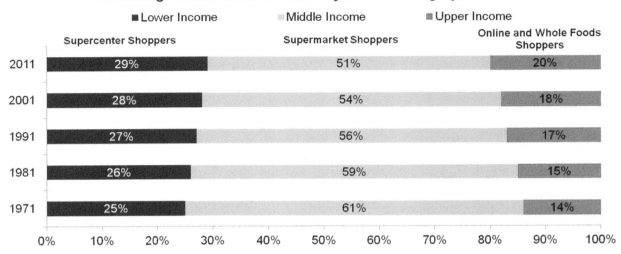

Figure 5.17 Source: Pew Research Center, "Chapter One: Overview" in *The Lost Decade of the Middle Class*, August 22, 2012, www.pewsocialtrends.org/2012/08/22/the-lost-decade-of-the-middle-class/#chapter-1-overview, accessed October, 2012. Notes: Lower Income defined as household income below 67% of the national median, Middle Income as household income between 67% and 200% of the national median, and Upper Income as over 200% of the national median; adults assigned to income categories based on their size-adjusted household income.

In an increasingly polarized income environment, traditional supermarkets find themselves offering a product that people either can't afford to buy, or don't want to.

In addition to disappearing, the middle-class customer that supermarkets have served for so long is also changing, and in ways that supermarkets will have a difficult time catering to. Americans are cooking less, and in some cases have forgotten how. Supermarkets' positioning as a place to buy raw ingredients is becoming less powerful given this trend. But supermarkets don't seem to see this in the long-term. The Food Marketing Institute has conducted a poll on supermarket companies' strategies each year since 2006. Almost unanimously in the industry, supermarkets respond that their highest strategic direction is a perishables emphasis. But if everyone's doing it, and it doesn't appear to be working, is it really a strategy? And in prepared meals, where supermarkets have shown the greatest strength, the nature of the supermarket format is holding them back. While supermarkets are heavily saturated and convenient to most Americans, they are not necessarily easy to shop for prepared meals. With the exception of a few chains such as Wegman's (which has dedicated checkout lines for its massive prepared meals spaces), the prepared meals sections of many supermarkets isn't large enough to support dedicated checkout, ingress, and egress. Customers buying a quick, fresh meal must wait in the same long checkout lanes as customers shopping other areas of the supermarket; an obstacle which they do not face when they choose to eat at QSRs.

Compounding these issues, many of the innovations that supermarkets have used to survive over the past few years aren't proprietary to supermarkets—and the advantages they confer dissipate as they are widely implemented. Store brand products, for instance, deliver a lot of value to the consumer, and have consequently become increasingly popular. In fact, the largest food brand in the country is a store brand known as "Great Value." Unfortunately for supermarkets, this is Walmart's store brand. Other channels that have entered traditional supermarket categories, such as drugstores and dollar stores, also have store-branded products. The core promise of store brands, getting a cheaper price for an equivalent or better good, is now widespread, and so low- to medium-quality store brands used as pricing tools are not generally a unique strategic advantage. If everyone can (and does) do it, how unique can it be? The exception here is high quality store brands, which do create differentiation. For example, Trader Joe's private labels 80% of its products and maintains high SKU turnover because the company focuses on providing high quality at a great price and creating constantly new experiences.[261] While Costco has built trust in its consumers that it will deliver the best overall value (defined as a balance of quality and price) in the field, Trader Joe's has built trust in its consumers that its private label *is* the best overall value in the field. Both approaches have allowed these retailers to reduce the SKUs they need to carry in a category and so make the in-store shopping experience much easier.

All of this matters in the battle for trips between these different channels. Supermarkets are losing, thanks in large part to their positioning and eroding customer base. The consulting firm Oliver Wyman has done very interesting research on how traditional supermarkets' positioning is affecting their ability to generate trips. To get the most trips, a supermarket must be conveniently located to the customer and highly satisfy their most important needs. Oliver Wyman has found that customer satisfaction is dependent on these four elements (with proportional weight for each).[262]

- Value (28%): prices of products, value for money, etc.

- Quality and Differentiated Choice (36%): quality of products, freshness, selection of fresh, premium, specialty, and uncommon items
- Service (27%): level of service from staff, friendliness and helpfulness of staff, checkout time, ease of shopping, cleanliness, in-stock rates of sale items
- Basic Choice (9%): basic staple and everyday items in stock

Oliver Wyman believes that these four elements can be further condensed into two: "Value," the first element, and "Offer," which consolidates all the rest. Comparing today's grocery retailers across these elements, Oliver Wyman believes that those retailers above the line of best fit (the "Fair Trade Line") in Figure 5.18 are providing extreme value, a fantastic offer, or a workable combination of the two and are therefore "winning the satisfaction battle ... and reaping the sales benefits."[263] Note that to win the satisfaction battle, a retailer does not need to excel in both value *and* offer, but can also succeed by performing well on either side of the spectrum.

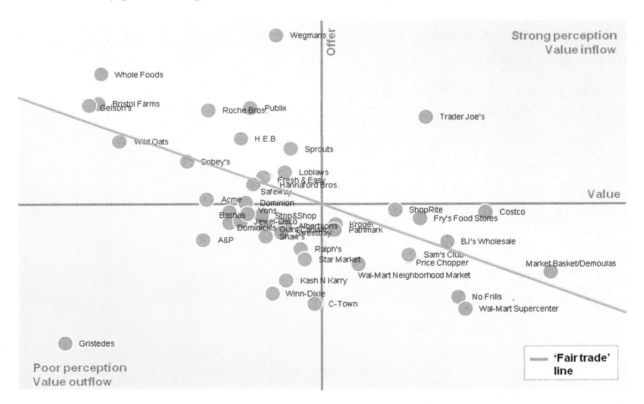

Figure 5.18 Source: Beswick, Paul, et. al., "Winning at Home: How retailers can win a greater share of their natural customers," *Oliver Wyman*, 2008.

Those supermarkets below the Fair Trade Line are what we would characterize as traditional supermarkets, while those above largely offer something different either in terms of business model (and Price), such as Costco and BJ's, or in terms of their service or product offering (and Offer), as in the cases of Trader Joe's, Whole Foods, and Wegman's.

In the battle over trips, this differentiated positioning matters. Oliver Wyman segments trips as coming from two types of customers, those who make up inside draw for whom the retailer's location is the most convenient,[iv] and those who come from outside a supermarket's draw area. Unsurprisingly, high inside draw rates are also linked to high customer satisfaction. When Oliver Wyman looks at grocery retailers, they find that traditional supermarkets' "undifferentiated offers" result in significantly lower inside and outside draw rates, leaving them in the bottom left quadrant of Figure 5.19.[264] In other words, supermarkets are losing the trips battle.

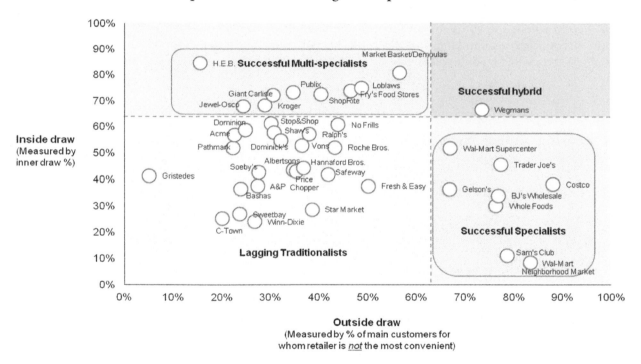

Figure 5.19 Source: Beswick, Paul, et. al., "Winning at Home: How retailers can win a greater share of their natural customers," *Oliver Wyman*, 2008.

[iv] Oliver Wyman defines inside draw as "the percentage of customers for whom a retailer is the closest option that chooses that retailer as their primary store." The customers who make up the denominator of the inside draw statistic are the total pool customers who are closest to a retailer. They would naturally shop at that retailer out of convenience, everything else being equal. For them to shop elsewhere requires a decision to shop somewhere more inconvenient, often in pursuit of other criteria, such as value or offer.

To see how one chain successfully marries together the components of Oliver Wyman's Value/Offer model, read the sidebar on Denmark's Netto.

Netto

Similar to Family Dollar in the United States, Netto of Denmark has shown that the hard-discount approach is a solid fit in many urban and suburban markets. The company describes its formula as "act like a hard discounter, but place our stores in neighborhood areas."[265] The small format allows Netto to locate conveniently in its target customers' neighborhoods. The hard-discount model delivers the value part of Oliver Wyman's equation, but Netto undertakes many activities that run contrary to the typical hard-discount model. Contrary to most hard-discounters, Netto's own-label share of sales constitutes only 35% of total sales, leaving a lot of room for national label, premium products, thus satisfying Oliver Wyman's Quality criteria.[266] The company further encourages Quality by investing in high quality own-label product and merchandises the store for each region it serves.[267] Netto also infuses a lot of Service into the hard-discount model, investing in pleasing store environments, employee training, and superior customer service.[268] Like all hard-discounters, Netto suffers from limited range with small footprint stores carrying 1,000 SKUs on an EDLP basis and 200 "spot lines" on special offer.[269] However, with range being the least important input to satisfaction as measured by Oliver Wyman, the chain has not been overly penalized by this. Netto has successfully expanded the concept to Germany, Poland, and Sweden where the company localizes its merchandising to each market. In Germany, the share of hybrid discount stores Kaufland and Netto Marken-Discount expanded from 7% to 17% in the decade ending in 2010, while traditional hard and soft discounters' share remained relatively flat.[270]

Traditional supermarkets' relatively higher prices, undifferentiated offerings, disappearing and/or changing customers, and expanded competitive environment all lead to the most troubling fact of all: supermarkets' customers don't like them. In a 2012 Consumer Reports survey, more than half of the consumer panel had something to complain about regarding their regular supermarket.[271] In addition, a study conducted for Bosch found that 66% of respondents believed that shopping for groceries takes the greatest amount of time of all household chores—a marked area for improvement when Americans are looking for ease and convenience.[272] And in a stack-up against other industries (Figure 5.20), supermarkets look more like the US Postal service in terms of customer satisfaction and less like ultra-convenient internet retailers.

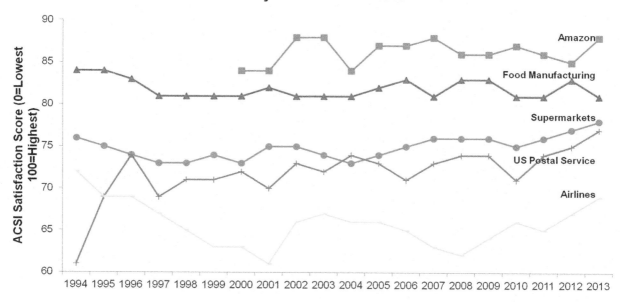

Figure 5.20 Source: "Scores by Industry", *American Customer Satisfaction Index*, 2012, http://www.theacsi.org/acsi-results/scores-by-industry-popup-all.

In their current incarnation of undifferentiated large footprint formats catering to an eroding customer base, supermarkets' lower productivity numbers and the continued competitive threat from alternative formats may mean that modern supermarkets are just too big—in terms of store sizes and other assets—to succeed. Their economic performance certainly appears to bear this out, as, compared to all the primary outlets that deal in supermarket categories, traditional supermarkets have the lowest returns on assets, and their ROAs are still declining, as seen in Figure 5.21.

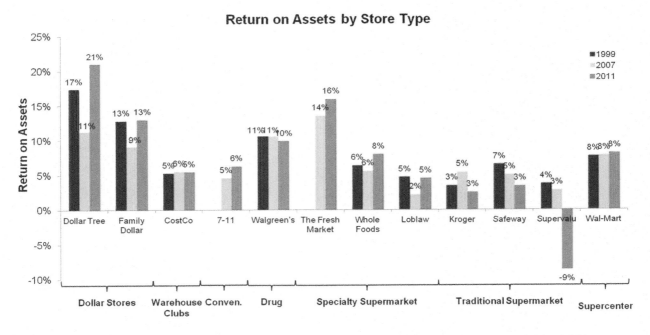

Figure 5.21 Source: Company Financial Statements, via Thomson One, accessed July, 2012.

Over the past two decades, consumers have been looking for cheap, easy, convenient access to supermarket products. Supermarkets have done a poor job of providing this relative to their competition and have struggled to differentiate themselves. Other channels have taken over supermarkets' key historical strengths—assortment, low prices, ease of shopping, and proximity to the customer. When combined with the other issues facing supermarkets, this has left supermarkets in a very vulnerable position. In a market typically characterized by slow, gradual shifts over time (such as the market share gains of Quick Service Restaurants—400 basis points over 15 years—and Frozen Prepared Meals—326 basis points over 12 years), the effect that alternative channels have had on the supermarket channel is enormous. It appears that while consumers may only change what they eat slowly, they'll change where they buy it very rapidly! And so supermarkets should be very worried. Their current incarnations are not working, and we believe we are at an inflection point for significant change in the industry. What can supermarkets do in the future to stay relevant?

The Future

The current supermarket shopping environment is filled with contradictions and challenges. The dominant supermarket format has gotten much larger over the last two decades yet it seems to have done little to solve the key problem consumers face: the need for convenient, easy, inexpensive, and healthy meal solutions. The many attempts by supermarkets to answer the age-old question of "What's for dinner?" (or breakfast, or lunch), have generally been unsatisfactory. Shopping trips through these large stores also take too long for time-compressed shoppers. Consumers see grocery shopping as a terrible, time-consuming chore. Supermarkets boast significant variety, often carrying 50,000 or more SKUs,[273] but consumers have trouble finding what they want and have become used to finding items easily on Amazon, which carries over two million SKUs in supermarket categories alone.[274] The supermarket industry has worked hard to improve its cost structure in order to compete with big box stores yet their pricing is still significantly higher than Walmart. Because of these cost reductions, very little labor has been left in stores to help with services customers require for meal planning, nutrition advice, and event planning. The employees that are left are usually harried and ill-equipped to deal with customers. Many of them have been trained as machine operators to get the greatest efficiency out of the system; they have not been trained to be salespeople or service providers. Supermarkets have also moved away from urban locations, following their customer base and seeking the land required for their large format stores, yet now the US is becoming re-urbanized with many large urban cores growing in population. Supermarkets are seemingly in the wrong places, at the wrong time, solving the wrong problems. The product-based approach that supermarkets have taken in the past has been commoditized by the competition. Supermarkets need to create experiences and services that distinguish them from their competition.

Supermarkets however, have a long history of being flexible and adaptable. When Michael Cullen proved that his large format, self-service store worked better, store sizes across the industry grew rapidly. When supermarkets thought they needed to grow to compete with Walmart, another round of store expansions occurred. As consumer tastes changed, supermarket operators found new products to stock in their stores. However, today, with long lease terms and permanent fixtures inside many stores, supermarkets may be hampered in their ability to adapt. Therefore, the time to begin responding is now (if not years ago).

Consumer grocery shopping behavior has begun to bifurcate between perishable shopping trips that revolve around meal solutions and non-perishable trips that revolve around value priced consumables (purchases that can be done online). In the retail environment of the future, it's possible to imagine a situation where supermarkets are cut out completely. Non-perishable needs could be easily fulfilled by an online retailer, while small format stores and QSRs meet the need for meals and other perishables. Supermarkets can only be competitive in this future by adapting to these shifts in consumer behavior.

We believe an idealized future supermarket will have all the products that consumers like to personally see and handle on display (e.g. produce, prepared meals), but that the majority of the store's product display and inventory space (e.g. canned goods, household items) will be eliminated by automated selection of orders fed in from consumers' smartphones and online accounts. As we will show, the "Shrink and Transform the Format" strategy is a very compelling proposition in the supermarket vertical. It builds a format around supermarket's strengths in fresh and prepared meals, the "periphery" items shown in the representative current supermarket floor layout in Figure 5.22 where supermarket areas of strength are highlighted in green, while still providing an affordable one-stop shop for all the products where shopping is a chore.

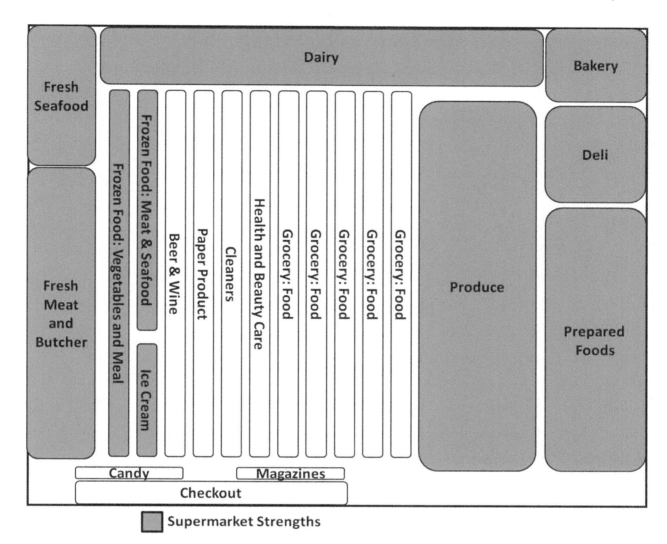

Figure 5.22

However, supermarkets currently own or have long leases on enormous amounts of retail space with significant leasehold improvements—refrigeration, plumbing, HVAC, etc.—that make it difficult (if not cost-prohibitive) to repurpose stores for a wholly different use. Abandoning all this space and moving to a completely new format would take time and significant capital. Therefore, a short term option is for supermarkets to lease significant portions of their current store space to specialty stores or category killer chains that are on the hunt for convenient, smaller footprints for their current offerings (think office supplies, consumer electronics, cell phones, banks, toy stores). Supermarkets could become more like miniature malls, focused on food with side concessions for other products.

Leasing Fallow Space to Improve Customer Satisfaction

It is likely that 30-50% of supermarket square footage is underutilized and creating a significant drain on supermarket returns. Of course, not all supermarkets can shut down old locations and move to new stores closer to population centers. Given the current difficulties faced by retailers in areas such as office supply, consumer electronics, and toys it would seem counterintuitive that these categories of trade would be seeking out additional space that supermarkets could make available to them. However, category killers suffer from two problems that the supermarket may be able to solve: one, the lack of convenience of their locations and two, the related inability to drive impulse purchases. Supermarkets have very dense networks that are geared toward customer proximity and generate on average 11,500 customer transactions per store per week.[275] These other categories of retail trade are destination retailers with far fewer stores per inhabitant. Many, like Best Buy, need to adapt their formats to a new strategy. Others, like Office Depot, are in the midst of a long-term campaign to close stores and transition to smaller formats. If space in a supermarket were to be made available for lease to these other categories, all retailers could benefit. The supermarket could receive a higher return on their space than they currently earn and other retailers could be assured of significant traffic to their now right-sized locations. Supermarkets could help to make the transition to different store formats and store networks easier for these category killers.

This is not an entirely new concept. Historically, supermarkets even anchored mall locations before the increasing size of shopping malls and the limited entry points of larger shopping centers detracted too much from the supermarket convenience proposition.[276] Today, supermarkets, and in some cases dollar stores, are still sought-after anchors in smaller shopping centers as the higher trip profiles of supermarkets benefit surrounding merchants. Walmart's introduction of grocery products in effect anchored the entire rest of the store around the value grocery proposition to create significant foot traffic for other departments.

Supermarkets are not newcomers to the concept of merchandising a shopping center. Kroger's real estate group actively owns and operates many of the shopping centers located adjacent to their supermarkets. Safeway actively develops new shopping centers through its wholly-owned subsidiary Property Development Centers.

Supermarkets are also not strangers to bringing in third parties—like Starbucks and other QSRs, local banks, dry cleaners, and real estate companies—into in-store alcoves. While we believe locating smaller format, easier to shop food stores closer to the customer is the ideal, the method we propose provides a necessary stepping stone as supermarkets live out leases or find new tenants for old stores. However, the real long-term answer lies with a stand-alone automated store of the future, similar to the purpose-built Drive stores that have been built in France.

Automated Future Store

Imagine walking into a store that resembles a European market, with ready-to-eat or ready-to-heat meals on display, alongside fresh produce, meats, deli selections, and bakery products. In a back area not accessible to customers all of the routinely purchased packaged items (e.g. dry grocery, dairy, frozen food, health and beauty care products, paper goods, cleaners, etc.) would be available through mechanized selection that would serve completed orders to customers in the store. The customer would never interact with the many aisles of dry goods that they currently consider to be a chore to shop. These routine items could be pre-ordered through an electronic shopping list (think Peapod or Amazon) and be ready for pick up when the customer arrives or the customer could shop for these items through electronic catalogues in the store with very rapid turnaround of order selection.

The fresh goods and meals departments could be offered at a very high quality with many interesting and perpetually new offerings that would encourage frequent trips. This fresh goods portion of supermarkets' merchandising has not been and will not be easily copied. To see this, look at the differences between warehouse clubs' and supercenters' sales of unpackaged, need-to-see-to-buy, and perishable categories (like fresh produce and meats) and their sales of long-lasting, packaged categories (like Frozen Food) in Figure 5.23. If we imagine a continuum of perishability, with produce and meats expiring quickly, dairy in the middle, and frozen foods as a long-lived category, we see that the percentage of warehouse club sales relative to the combined sales of supermarkets and warehouse clubs follows this perishability gradient. Warehouse club sales are the lowest as a share of supermarket and warehouse club sales in produce and meats, and the highest in the Frozen Food category.

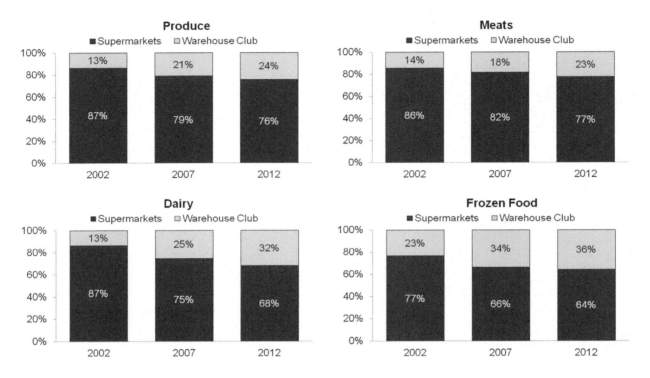

Figure 5.23 Sources: Compiled from 'Merchandise by Kind of Business' and 'Kinds of Business by Broad Merchandise Line' in Merchandise Line Sales, Retail Trade Subject Series, Economic Census, for years 2002 and 2007 and author's calculations. Specialty Stores Excluded.

With consumer trips to supercenters infrequent and focused on stocking-up, limited shelf-life products like fresh goods are better served by supermarkets. Making it easy to buy perishables and finished or near-finished meals will enhance the already large convenience advantage that supermarkets enjoy vis-à-vis warehouse clubs and supercenters and take back ground in the battle against QSRs.

The mechanized selection in this new format would cut routine labor, but in a way that will increase customer satisfaction as shopping and checkout become much faster. Supermarkets can reinvest the large amounts of labor saved through this change in format and technology into value added services such as nutritionists, meal planners, cooking advisers, sommeliers, and event planners. These services would encourage interaction with store employees. As Trader Joe's, Whole Foods, and Wegman's have shown,[277] positive experiences with supermarket staff lead to increased loyalty on the part of consumers. Interaction with real-life employees during the shopping process is also something online retailers can't duplicate. The focus of supermarkets would move away from pure operating efficiency and vendor allowance generation to innovation in food products, hospitality, and services. The mechanization used in this future store is a significant departure from current practice and carries significant risk. Clarence Saunders, founder of Piggly-Wiggly, tried a similar idea twice, once in 1936 and again in 1948, with Keedoozle and failed (see the sidebar on Keedoozle). However, the mechanization creates a smaller store footprint that will allow supermarkets to locate more conveniently to customers, it enables a redeployment of labor to more customer-centric skilled roles, and it increases customer satisfaction for routine purchases.

This is a blend of the online and brick-and-mortar supermarket models. This new format attempts to marry the best of online ordering—convenience, ease, uniform and rapid processes, database power, and the ability to communicate real-time and automatically with customers—with the best of brick-and-mortar retailing—the cost benefit of not having to solve the "last mile" of delivery to the customer's door, the tactile shopping experience in key categories, and human interaction where it counts. However, critics will likely point to three reasons online supermarkets don't work: 1) consumers desire a tactile experience for food purchases, 2) negative impacts on basket expansion, among them impacts on impulse buying, and 3) negative impacts on promotion and slotting fees. This blended model attempts to overcome, wholly or in part, all of these criticisms.

Keedoozle—An Idea Before Its Time

Before Michael Cullen, many claim there was Clarence Saunders. Saunders is credited with introducing the concept of self-service to supermarkets, launching the self-service Piggly Wiggly chain in 1916. Like Michael Cullen's supermarket innovations, Saunders' self-service innovation was quickly cloned as well, but that didn't stop Piggly Wiggly from growing to 2,660 stores by 1932.

After a Wall Street debacle took Saunders' Piggly Wiggly shares from him, he came up with a store concept to extend the principle of self-service even further: Keedoozle ("Key Does All"). In the Keedoozle system, each dry goods product was displayed behind a glass window. When a shopper wanted to select something, she dialed in her quantity and inserted her key into a slot below the window. This triggered a tickertape on her key to be marked accordingly. Behind the scenes, shop employees removed the selected product from bins, placed it on a conveyor belt, and at check-out the customer presented her tickertape, with the charge already tallied, and picked up her groceries. Photos of this process are shown in Figure 5.24.

The concept is remarkably similar to how supermarkets like Tesco currently fulfill click-and-pick-up orders. Saunders saw it principally as a way to save labor and cost. Unfortunately for Saunders, the concept was ahead of its time: machinery breakdowns happened often and the system couldn't handle peak loads.[278] This is not to say though, that with the right technology the idea couldn't make a comeback!

Figure 5.24 Source: Miller, Francis, "Keedoozle, We Hardly Knew Ye," *Life Magazine*, 1948, available at http://life.time.com/culture/keedoozle-americas-first-automated-grocery.

The tactile experience doesn't much matter when customers are buying packaged goods, as shown by shoppers' price-driven defection to warehouse clubs and supercenters for these goods. Packaged goods categories are, for the most part, composed of large national brands easily recognized and uniform across channels as well as their store-brand counterparts. In some categories, such as health and beauty care, customers have shown that they don't really care if they even see these products first, as they are happy to order them online for home delivery. Tactile experiences matter in fresh goods, which is why the perishables section of the store remains as the centerpiece of this new format.

Basket expansion is of course critical to retailers that depend on volume. In this new model, checkout racks, visicoolers at checkout, and promotional end-displays could still exist and encourage impulse-buying, though the time spent in front of them will likely be shorter. But, having customers order through an application program actually has a lot of potential to build out a basket as well. Home delivery company FreshDirect, using the customer histories its users build over multiple orders, builds baskets in two ways: suggesting items a customer has bought frequently in the past but hasn't yet purchased in her current order and cross-selling products that generally accompany items the customer is purchasing. These two methods together contribute 5% of total revenue for the company, and represent valuable, real-time communication with customers to which traditional supermarkets don't currently have access.[279] In addition, better trained associates that suggest products and help customers create meals would expand customers' baskets.

Vendor allowances are the life raft keeping supermarkets afloat, and supermarkets would understandably be hesitant to abandon these fees and charge into an uncertain future. However, in this idealized store, many of these allowances can still exist in ways that do not disadvantage customers. Let's use Safeway as an example. According to Safeway's 2011 10-K, vendor allowances received by supermarkets fall into three categories: promotional, slotting, and contract. Promotional allowances are how vendors get supermarkets to promote their products through any one or a combination of a price reduction, a feature in a circular, a display, or a preferred location in the store. These form the lion's share of the vendor allowances, with Safeway reporting that 95% of its vendor allowances are promotional. Slotting fees make up 3% of Safeway's vendor allowance total, and reimburse the company for the cost of putting new products on the shelves. Contract allowances, at 2% of Safeway's total vendor allowances, pay Safeway to keep a product on the shelf for a minimum period of time or until a volume threshold is reached.[280]

In this idealized model, promotional fees still exist. Display cases are still present (though there may be less of them given the smaller footprint and decreased need for checkout lanes in this new model) and a new product area could be created in the store to both capture promotional revenue and retain the element of discovery. New promotional avenues could even be found, such as app-based circulars that communicate directly and more personally with customers, ads within the ordering platform, or the rank-order of products displayed under a search query. Slotting fees and contract allowances will still exist as well, insofar as supermarkets can still charge for hosting the product on their ordering platform and for loading it into the mechanization. Vendor allowances based on an automated, mechanized, and online system would even solve the compliance issues that have dogged many promotional campaigns. There are precedents for these allowances to online grocery retailers. When Peapod was a public company, its advertising income from suppliers was 5.1% of its sales in 1997. More recently, Ocado's other income, which includes this revenue stream, accounted for 2.3% of its sales.[281] In the future, while some vendor allowances will likely disappear, others may take their place; but more importantly, the benefits to the consumer outweigh the sacrifices to the vendors, and the supermarket overall has the potential to be more profitable.

Let's look at all the advantages of this new format in detail. Shoppers currently spend significant amounts of unproductive time walking aisles looking for the particular product they want. It's sometimes hard to find which aisle the item is slotted in, and the item is often buried in an assortment of similar products. Once customers fill their cart, they spend more time unloading and reloading their cart to checkout and wait in line. In this new model, consumers could either access in-store panels to select their basket when they enter the store, or order from home or via smartphone before they arrive. With past orders tied to their customer accounts, they can easily find the products they routinely buy. Their picked orders will be waiting for them at the checkout when they have completed shopping the fresh section. With the majority of their basket already boxed and registered, throughput through the checkout will be faster than ever before. In fact, checkout could be completely eliminated for those customers who use electronic payment or who can check themselves out with their mobile devices. This format offers consumers exactly what they want: the time-efficient convenience of a small-format green grocer where they can easily choose the products (like produce, meats, and prepared meals) for which they enjoy shopping, without the tedium, inconvenience, and difficulty of large store aisle-walking and clutter, and all at an attractive price!

Removing the big store hurdles would help improve customer satisfaction. Internet Retail tops the American Customer Satisfaction Index. Taking humans out of the consumption and purchase processes for standard, uniform, and known goods where the purchase is driven by the customer removes variability in the retail process and makes it easier to provide a satisfying experience. This is exactly what automated stores can do for the dry goods categories. By shrinking the format, this strategy reduces the size and cost burden of overly large US supermarkets, while at the same time making it easier and more convenient for customers to purchase their groceries through the transformative use of technology. It also opens up new areas for growth and customer satisfaction.

Supermarkets are already experimenting with components of this mechanized model. In Long Island City, the home of FreshDirect's distribution center, FreshDirect customers can opt to pick up their pre-picked orders at the distribution center and avoid the delivery fee usually charged. In Europe, many supermarkets have been implementing this order and pick up idea (in English often referred to as click-and-collect) for years at Drive locations.[282] In the US, Peapod is rolling out pick up stations at Stop & Shop supermarkets. This system is essentially 'pick-up in store' for supermarkets. It enables customers to order their grocery goods (both perishable and non-perishable) online, but instead of the orders being loaded on trucks for delivery to customers' homes, customers choose a store at which their orders will be held. They then pick up their orders at times convenient to them. This provides the ease of online ordering but removes the need to be at home to meet the order, and also saves the delivery fee associated with online grocery orders.

To achieve click-and-collect, retailers have often adopted a hybrid strategy where they use store labor to walk around a traditional supermarket and fill customer orders from the shelves. While certainly the least infrastructure-intensive approach, this method is grossly inefficient compared to the purpose-built Drive model. Much of the added expense in click-and-collect is labor, and in a hybrid store pickers can only pick at an average of 70-80 items per hour, while in a purpose-built Drive location, pickers can work at a rate of 180 items per hour, with the rate being closer to 300 items per hour in the best organizations.[283] Under the purpose-built Drive model, a dedicated warehouse is built for click-and-collect orders. These warehouses stock fewer SKUs, concentrating on just high-volume ones. Products in the warehouse are separated into enclosed temperature zones. From within these zones, workers fill the portions of customer orders specific to their zone. Completed orders wait in the zone or temperature-controlled holding areas until customers are ready to pick them up, at which point the orders are brought to customers' cars. If the customer hasn't ordered ahead, they can do so from kiosks in the parking lot.

While customer orders are still fulfilled manually, filling orders from a dedicated warehouse rather than a store has a number of advantages. Wasted aisle, backroom, and overhead space is removed, which, together with a reduced number of SKUs, creates a smaller and less expensive format. Purpose-built Drives don't share real estate with large hypermarkets, so can locate more conveniently to customers. Labor is more productive within these smaller formats because they are covering less ground, and because of the benefits of a warehouse environment. Rather than searching the shelves for a particular item which might be in a promotional rack or simply hidden away, the warehouse laborer knows exactly which aisle, shelf, and bin holds the product they are looking for. Touch points inside the store are reduced as goods can be stacked by cases rather than placed on shelves individually, and labor hours spent 'fronting' and 'facing' product are eliminated.[v] It's clear when inventory needs to be replaced on a shelf and stockouts are reduced. Because warehouse employees don't share the aisle space with casual shoppers, some level of automation or picking technology is often introduced into these purpose-built Drives. Pickers in a warehouse Drive don't have to compete with store customers who get in the way and mess up inventory counts on the shelf when they select their own items. Though their means of fulfillment are different, both the hybrid and purpose-built Drive options eschew last leg grocery delivery which, due to its cost and

---

[v] Fronting is the practice of bringing merchandise from the rear of the shelf to the front in order to present a uniform line of product, and facing is the practice of rotating fronted merchandise so that the labels face outwards towards the shopper.

the necessity of timing delivery for fresh goods, has proven a barrier to wide-spread adoption of online grocery buying. Either option, however, can be combined with a delivery network.

Unsurprisingly, Drives face many of the same challenges confronting online grocers. While few companies comment on the profitability of their click-and-collect operations or provide much detail on how profitability is calculated, Auchan's purpose-built Drive operation, called Chronodrive, is profitable whereas many hybrid operations are believed to break-even at best. This discrepancy is due to the lower operating costs of the warehouse Drive system, and the lower initial investment to build a warehouse as compared to a full supermarket.[284] In addition, fresh products like fruits, vegetables, meat, and fish don't sell as well in a Drive setting as they do in a hypermarket, with these categories counting for only 8.5% of Drive sales as compared to 20% of hypermarket sales in 2012.[285]

The Drive concepts are, however, still evolving. In a bid for greater profitability, pilot Drives that contain much more automation are being tested. To overcome customers' aversion to buying fresh goods sight unseen, Tesco encourages customers to check their produce before accepting it, and if unsatisfied, they can return it at the collection point with no penalties before they leave.[286] Auchan is also experimenting with formats that may overcome the fresh goods problem. The first, Chronovillage, surrounds a purpose-built Chronodrive with small expertly-staffed stores, such as a green grocer, a sommelier, a florist, etc.[287] Another Chronodrive gives customers the option of selecting their fresh produce personally from a small display area.[288] By utilizing the Chronodrive warehouse for center aisle SKUs and separate customer-accessible areas for fresh goods, these experiments come very close to our idea of what an ideal store would be.

The Drive concept, both hybrid and purpose-built, has recently exploded in France. From a little over 600 Drive stores and hybrid locations in 2010,[289] click-and-collect grew to 2,278 locations by June, 2013, with 20% of the population using click-and-collect to buy groceries.[290] These stores are now the future focus of many French food retailers. Auchan, the originators of the Drive concept, opened 48 food-focused stores in France in 2013, 43 of which were Drive formats. Of the company's 550 food-focused stores in France, 156, or almost 30%, are Drives. Despite its rapid growth in outlets (largely driven by hybrid Drives), however, Drive sales make up a relatively small portion of the French grocery retailing landscape in terms of value. Drive outlets were estimated to account for 3.8 billion Euros of sales in 2013,[291] which accounts for only 1.8% of a 215 billion Euros grocery retailing market in France (though compared to US grocery delivery companies' smaller regional shares, this is large for a new fulfillment channel).[292] However, Drives are exhibiting strong organic growth. Drive sales in 2012 were estimated to be 2.2 billion Euros,[293] yielding a sales growth rate in 2013 of 73%. Meanwhile Drive outlets grew from 1,926 on December 6, 2012 to 2,659 on December 1, 2013,[294] a growth rate of 38%. Assuming Drive outlet openings were evenly spread throughout the year, three-fourths of the channel's growth has come from same-store sales and whatever ramp-up was left in 2012's new Drive openings.[295] With such strong growth trends and a pressure to open stores, the Drive concept puts supermarket and hypermarket retailers in a precarious position as price-competition heats up and Drives cannibalize legacy store sales.

For the first time, in-store grocery prices are becoming publicly available online. Unsurprisingly, this has heightened price competition between Drive operators. Leclerc, for example, has installed price-check terminals in its stores, launched a price-check app, and created a website enabling customers to compare prices between its stores and those of its competitors.[296] This price competitiveness will likely negatively affect gross margins within the industry at a time when supermarkets need to make large investments in eCommerce.

In France, as in most developed countries, supermarkets and hypermarkets are well saturated. Purpose-built Drive stores, while more efficient, cannibalize sales at existing stores, while hybrid stores add another layer of labor cost on top of supermarkets' already thin margins. Leclerc, which has focused on building hybrid Drives and simple pick-up points, rather than purpose-built Drives, estimates that 25% of its Drive sales come from its own hypermarkets, with the balance coming from other retailers.[297] A Nielsen study suggest self-cannibalization may be higher, but also confirms that Drives take sales from other retailers. Nielsen estimates that hypermarkets which added a same-brand Drive in 2013 lost 1.7% of their sales to the Drive. However, the addition of the Drives added 1.3% to the sales of the combined hypermarket/Drive entities. Those hypermarkets that faced competition from another brand's Drive? They lost 0.6% of their sales to the competing Drive, indicating some level of stickiness for retailers (perhaps driven by their private label brands), but also suggesting that building Drives might be a race between retailers to steal each other's share.[298] At the same time that Drive locations cannibalize hypermarkets, they also consolidate the retailer's position in its market area by taking sales from competitors.

French store operators therefore face tremendous pressure to roll out Drives in their market areas before their competitors preempt them. The fastest and easiest way to do this is to tack them on to existing hypermarkets and supermarkets. Additionally, the cannibalization of the hypermarkets in these hybrid Drives doesn't affect the hypermarkets' productivity (the Drive orders are filled from the shelves of the hypermarket), but the additional labor cost from picking goods in a store setting likely impacts profits. Purpose-built Drives, on the other hand, do cannibalize the hypermarket, and the effect is serious. If the purpose-built Drive is ultimately the winning format, retailers will have to carefully manage this rollout over many years in order to manage the pace at which their hypermarkets are cannibalized so as not to innovate themselves into unprofitability. However, a smaller retailer, or an entirely new entrant, does not bear the cost of these legacy stores, and could rapidly roll out Drive locations to the detriment of hypermarkets. While Drive formats do look like the future, grocery retailers face difficult choices: even lower profits in a format that may be disrupted later, gradual self-disruption, or a costly race to self-disruption in an effort to preempt competitors. How this retail evolution continues, and whether or not existing grocery retailers will be the ones on top at the end, is still very much unclear.

The examples of Drive in France and Ocado in the UK show that, at least in these countries, there was a latent demand for some form of time-saving grocery retail that was just waiting to be matched with a supply that was not dramatically more expensive. While America's low population density in most areas precludes the rapid expansion and universal penetration of delivery services, purpose-built click-and-collect formats could be supermarkets' most powerful weapon in their unfolding war with supercenters, warehouse clubs, dollar stores, and non-store retailers. The smaller format of this store allows it to locate closer to population centers, eroding dollar stores' advantage and capitalizing on a convenience aspect supercenters and warehouse clubs can't compete with. Even if they replicate the automation, they will still remain inconvenient formats to shop (unless Walmart adopts this format in its Neighborhood Market and Express store rollout). Supercenters are largely outside of population centers, block the supermarket section with the whole rest of the store, and have check-out aisles clogged with other people shopping for all the other items that these stores offer.

Supermarkets have historically been quick to adopt new technology such as self-checkouts and scan-and-bag systems, and there are real first-mover advantages to an eCommerce-linked supermarket. The use of computerized ordering, either through an online account associated with a loyalty program or through a smartphone builds up a shopping history at a particular chain. The owner of that data can then leverage it to create routinized lists for the shopper that serve as the base for each trip. This results in faster trips and more convenience for the customer, and creates switching costs where the customer's first experiences shopping at any other store will again involve manually selecting items until another shopping history is built. For retailers trying to make margins and create switching costs, this ability to track order history without offering price inducements is an improvement on loyalty card programs, whose across-the-board discounts for members are a significant cost for retailers with such low margins. It's also likely that not every supermarket chain will execute well in launching these new formats, just as many companies sell online, but few do it as well as Amazon. These differing levels of performance will create some level of switching costs due to service expectations.

With these advantages in mind, we'll analyze the financial impact on a per-store basis. Figure 5.25 shows the store-level common-size income statement of a typical large format supermarket doing $30 million in annual revenue.

Net Sales	**100.0%**
Gross COGS	83.0%
Less Vendor Allowances	6.6%
Net COGS	**76.4%**
Gross Profit	**23.6%**
Labor Expense	11.5%
Occupancy Expense	4.8%
Other Operating Expenses (Utilities, Credit Card Fees)	2.9%
Total Operating Expense	**19.2%**
EBITDA	**4.4%**

Figure 5.25 Source: Confidential Store ProForma.

The largest impact from collapsing the center of the store into automation is to cut a lot of labor hours that were used to restock shelves and check out customers in the old model, while making the remaining store labor more efficient through fewer product touch points, simpler processes, and smaller coverage areas. Because the format of this supermarket can be much smaller (20,000 sq. ft. or less), the occupancy costs are also reduced substantially. Figure 5.26 presents a few scenarios working off the typical $30 million/year store's pro-forma presented in Figure 5.25. We vary the labor and occupancy savings; use fixed costs for the capital cost of the mechanization, store opening expenses, depreciation, and maintenance; and include impacts on foot traffic, basket size, and vendor allowances. We haven't made any adjustments for price in these scenarios, even though the pricing levels will likely come down as these more efficient formats are rolled out. However, price competition will have a more damaging impact on traditional format supermarkets, and may hasten the rollout of more efficient models.

Future Store Format on Store EBITDA

■ Typical Store   □ Future Store

	Upside	Expected	Downside
	4.4% / 21.1%	4.4% / 20.7%	4.4% / 20.2%
Square Footage Reduction	60%	50%	40%
Store Labor Reduction	60%	60%	60%
Capital Cost of Auto-Pick	$10,000,000	$10,000,000	$10,000,000
Store Opening Expenses	$1,000,000	$1,000,000	$1,000,000
Life of Auto-Pick Machine and Store (Years)	10	10	10
Maintenance Cost of Auto-Pick (% Purchase Price)	5%	5%	5%
Increased Foot Traffic	10%	10%	10%
Basket Size Impact	0%	0%	0%
Vendor Allowances Impact	-10%	-10%	-10%
IRR	32.7%	31.8%	30.9%

Figure 5.26

While of course it would be nice to sit on these increased profit margins, these profits would be best re-invested into many of the attributes that supermarkets have lost over the past two decades of cost-cutting. Following the Netto example, investments in highly-trained staff, pleasing store environments, customer service, and discounted prices will move supermarkets out of Oliver Wyman's "Lagging Traditionalists" category. It's believable that supermarkets could see the same success as Netto and US dollar stores, but without the handicap of a hard discounter's limited range.

This format, if implemented correctly and adopted by consumers, can have a huge impact on the profitability of current store locations. But it also opens up the door to exciting growth prospects in the last frontier of American supermarkets: urban environments.

Based on population data from 2000, the USDA's ERS states that 47.6 million people, or 17% of the total US population, live both in urban areas (territories that encompass more than 50,000 people) and more than one mile away from a supermarket.[299] Common barriers to supermarkets locating in urban environments include the higher rents required, the lack of suitable space, bureaucratic hurdles, increased shrink costs, and a customer trip profile that features more trips but smaller baskets.[300] However, the features of this ideal store, with its small footprint and emphasis on automation, overcome these challenges. In an industry that has long been considered saturated, the urban market is a large growth opportunity.

In the meal solutions landscape of the future, health will also become increasingly important as the burdens of historically poor food choices catch up with Americans. In the past, supermarkets have been adaptable to shifts in consumer demand, as evidenced by the widespread rise of organic selections and prepared meals. While stores will certainly need to remerchandise to provide healthier alternatives, the overall health problem is a more complex issue that will require a wider variety of responses beyond 100-calorie snack packs. Part of this response will need to involve customer education and product selection systems. Some examples of these are Marsh Supermarkets' Project 18 Approved shelf tags, Delhaize's Guiding Stars program, and the NuVal Nutritional Scoring System, all of which seek to help shoppers make informed choices. Customers themselves will need to be educated not only on how to use these systems, but on the overall components of food health. This is one area where increased investment in supermarkets' employees will help. In a country where up to 28% of people don't know how to cook,[301] store employees could play an important role in teaching customers how to choose and prepare food items, how in-store health selection systems work, and answering their unique questions. For a new take on how a supermarket can help its customers make healthier meal choices, read in the sidebar about how Picard has developed a business model that reflects similar convenience-focused food trends in France as seen in the US and about HEB's efforts in Texas.

Prepared Meals Focus (Picard)

We've seen how Americans are increasingly gravitating towards prepared meals for the convenience factor. It turns out the same thing is happening in other countries as well, and Picard Foods has capitalized on the trend in France. However, unlike many of the prepared meals in the US, Picard has been able to offer frozen, prepared meals at a high value in a convenient format, and keep them healthy.

Picard stores offer a little over 1,000 SKUs, and almost all products are Picard branded and frozen.[302] Picard's 2,600 square feet pedestrian stores easily site within urban centers and are reached mainly through foot-traffic and mass transit.[303] The interiors of the stores consist of aisles of chest freezers laid out in a meal-planning assortment—appetizer, entrée, dessert—in a sterile-seeming atmosphere that emphasizes food safety in the cold chain. While 1,000 SKUs may seem low, the products are largely finished meals and so provide substantial menu options, and Picard's reputation for high-quality means that customers aren't looking for other brands and don't want to see duplication. The stores are easy to shop, and if you can't make it to the store, Picard also offers home delivery. This service and convenience focus extend into the store's employees as well, who are prepared and educated to answer customer questions and are paired with phone support and a medical group that offers personalized advice and answers questions outside the scope of store personnel. The emphasis on convenience at Picard in terms of siting, emphasis on prepared meals, quality, service, and health have paid off; with Picard controlling 17% of the frozen food market in France in 2009, up from 9% in 2000.[304]

Bringing Health to Partners and Customers (HEB)[305]

HEB provides a blueprint for community involvement. The company donates 5% of pretax earnings to local civic and charitable organizations, incorporates employees (Partners) and customers in its community initiatives, and uses its supermarket base to support food banks, recycling efforts, and obesity prevention.

Like many of HEB's programs, its obesity prevention efforts began as a result of the entrepreneurial spirit fostered in the company. A Partner who had successfully lost weight began to talk to co-workers, which led to hosting "Lunch and Learns," which grew into the current program. For partners, HEB conducts in-store education programs around food, body, and life, gets Partners invested in monitoring critical biometric data, asks them to commit to health goals, and hosts a competition modeled after "The Biggest Loser" (the Slimdown Showdown) that promotes and evangelizes a healthy lifestyle amongst the entire Partner community. These partner initiatives are now beginning to extend into initiatives aimed at customers as well, including store tours of healthy items and how to prepare them, biometrics screenings, customer education efforts, making own-brand products healthier, and staging a Slimdown Showdown competition for customers.

Conclusion

Across retail we are seeing a commoditization of product availability and pricing because of the internet. In order to win in this new world, retailers need to provide services that enhance the product (e.g. curation, test driving, nutrition and meal counseling), easily compared prices that beat those online, and/or convenience that trumps online ordering (e.g. an immediately available gallon of milk). The players that can best provide these customer benefits will be the winners over the long haul. While many believe that supermarkets are relatively protected from online retailers, this does not mean there is no room for supermarkets to take advantage of the benefits of eCommerce.

Our own view is that supermarkets face many challenges, online retailers being only one of a host that affect almost every category in the store. The ways that Americans shop for food and other supermarket categories are changing, and supermarkets have yet to change with it. Changing consumer demands, behavior, and knowledge; an eroding of supermarkets' traditional base of customers; and new competition from a host of different retailers as well as QSRs all come together to put the supermarket model in jeopardy at a time when it is already struggling to survive. Quite probably, stores that provide clear, sometimes niche, customer-focused value like Costco, Whole Foods, and Trader Joe's will survive, even prosper, as America's demographic trends widen their customer base. But traditional supermarkets, trying to be everything to all people, will continue to lose share to supercenters and, increasingly, dollar stores and the internet, if they do not change. Because of supermarkets' one-stop promise and the fact that almost every category is affected by these broad changes in consumer behavior, there is no cross-subsidy plan or neat solution to their crisis. Rather, the entire store has to be reinvented.

In their current state, supermarkets' assets do not support the future that is coming. Supermarkets are not solution-oriented at a time when customers are looking for solutions in areas like meal planning, health, and nutrition. Supermarkets have depleted their human assets over the last two decades and are now bereft of skilled service people who can help customers. Supermarket's store assets are composed of stores that are just too big, and shopping trips are difficult and take too long. Supermarkets' large stores in the suburbs prevent them from entering urban areas at a time when the US is re-urbanizing and suburban locations are becoming less interesting.

Supermarkets' inventory strategy is to have lots of variety in-store, but not enough for internet-age customer expectations, and too much to make any of it easily searchable by the in-store customer. They are specialists in commodity items that are nearly omnipresent and provide little additional value to the product. On the technology front, most supermarkets have been slow to adapt to rapid consumer changes in online and mobile use. Supermarkets are labor intensive operations with lots of labor that adds no value to the customer.

Supermarkets need to radically change their assets as part of the "Shrink and Transform the Format" strategy to face their many challenges. Smaller store sizes will eliminate the aisles of wasted space in today's supermarkets, while enabling supermarkets to build out a base of small, conveniently-located stores that create a pleasant, convenient, and easy shopping environment, even in urban locations. Supermarkets can leverage web and mobile access in combination with a radical new store format to remove the drudgery of shopping for groceries. With inventory that is mostly commoditized, such a format would be the most convenient and cost-effective way to deliver supermarket products. Finally, supermarkets can reinvest in their human capital to become solution providers, especially in areas like prepared meals, meal planning, and nutrition counseling. This tactic adds additional value to supermarkets' commoditized product and makes the supermarket a trusted partner for its customers.

It's difficult to predict whether click-and-collect or store pick-up will be the dominant method of grocery shopping in the future. It's quite possible that consumers will have the option of both, with delivery more prevalent in dense urban environments, and click-and-collect more commonly seen in suburban environments. The same automated store format could serve both needs. By a drastic transformation of their assets, supermarkets can create a sustainable, defensible business (these TIPS assets changes are summarized in Figure 5.27). However, the pace of change seen in other countries speaks to the need for US retailers to begin planning what will be a very difficult and perilous transition now. Otherwise, they face a long, painful future of being outcompeted by not only the current host of other channels trying to take away their business, but new entrants as well.

Supermarkets

1) Which threat do you face?	Digitization or disappearance of core product: Americans eating out more and cooking less
2) Do you have a compelling advantage?	Yes: Regional density and distribution networks, good locations, experience selling perishable items and prepared meals
3) Strategic Imperative:	Shrink and transform the format: Technology used to make shopping CPG easier, stores refocused to provide meals and education

T   Introduce automated picking systems and mobile ordering platforms.

I   Fresh goods and prepared meals displayed for customers, CPG goods in warehouse fulfillment.

P   Better trained, higher quality store labor to help customers with selection, meal planning, and preparation.

S   Shrink store formats to locate closer to customers, gain greater leverage on occupancy costs (e.g. lease fallow space), and make grocery shopping easier and more convenient for customers

Figure 5.27

The question over the future of grocery raises another question: What will happen to the largest grocer in the US, Walmart? With 55% of Walmart's sales being grocery sales, changes in this retail vertical as well as the online threats against its general merchandise categories call the giant company's future into question. It may be that Walmart's massive scale holds the key to a strategy that could supplant Amazon.

Chapter 6
Is Anybody Safe?

The history of Walmart is well known, so we will confine ourselves to a brief history of discounting and Walmart, focusing on the key features that we believe are most pertinent to Walmart's future as the company competes with other brick-and-mortar stores and with Amazon.

Discounting as a retail practice, that is, selling large volumes at low margins out of a low-cost store, began in supermarkets in the 1930s. However, it spread to general merchandise in the 1950s and 1960s due to changes in both supply (manufacturers) and demand (consumers), as well as the actions of intermediaries (retailers and state and federal governments). By the conclusions of World War II and the Korean War, technological innovation had dramatically increased the efficiency of manufacturers. At the same time, the end of wartime production and a return to a consumer-led economy left manufacturers with significant overcapacity. Meanwhile, the heyday of the middle class was in full swing: new, progressive tax policies left the middle class with more income, access to consumer credit was ramping up and families were more inclined to turn to household debt to finance purchases, and wages were higher than before the war due to organized labor negotiations, an increase in two-income families, and a better educated and more skilled workforce.[306]

There was both great supply and great demand. However, the intermediaries at the time, namely department stores and variety stores, were more focused on generating high margins than on moving large volumes. Indeed, gross margins at department stores and variety stores had increased significantly through the first half of the 20th century as shown in Figure 6.1.

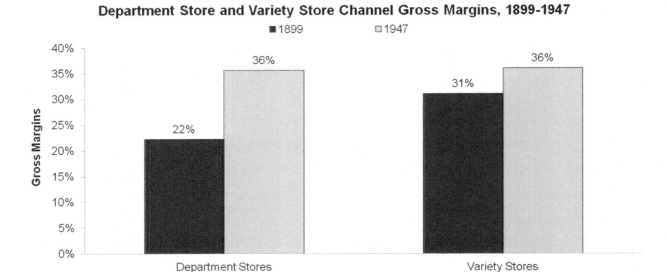

Figure 6.1 Source: Vance, Sandra and Scott, Roy, *Wal-Mart: A History of Sam Walton's Retail Phenomenon.* New York, New York: Twayne Publishers, 1994.

Department stores, especially, had generated higher gross margins partially through an emphasis on private label goods. This, in turn, caused manufacturers to create their own national brands, supported with advertising.

However, manufacturers still needed an outlet for these nationally-branded general merchandise goods. Discounters filled this gap. Early discounters had both low fixed costs—occupying cheap real estate and using bargain fixtures—and also low variable costs, jettisoning many department store services and relying on customer self-service to keep operating costs low. By using nascent national brands rather than private brands, they both drew customers in and saved on advertising. Reflecting these low costs, discounters in this early period had markups as low as 15%.[307] But to make this low margin work, discounters needed to move a lot of volume at a high velocity. They required access to large populations and first situated themselves in cities then, like department stores, followed consumers into the suburbs of urban areas. Many early discounters also relied on membership programs focused on federal employees, teachers, and unions to draw in a large number of customers and, sometimes, to get around laws restricting combined wholesale and retail operations.

Manufacturers wanted a channel that could move their product at high volumes and fill their surplus capacity, and newly-flush consumers wanted reliable name brands at low prices. Discounters satisfied both parties. Many recent entrants into the middle class also felt uncomfortable at department stores, which, aside from Sears, targeted higher-income shoppers. Many in the new middle class felt more at home with discounters.[308]

Department stores, seeing the new breed of discounters undercut their prices significantly, lobbied to create state and federal price-maintenance laws. These laws were intended to set uniform pricing in the retail channel. However, the laws were infrequently enforced, and discount stores routinely violated minimum pricing. The manufacturers, for their part, moved significant volume through the discount channel and had little incentive to crack down on discounters violating minimum pricing (eerily reminiscent of the current minimum pricing battles retailers are waging against Amazon).[309] Compounding the pricing issue, many department stores had moved upscale in the 1960s, perhaps in efforts to further increase their gross margins and distinguish themselves from variety stores and the nascent discounters. While 'bargain basements' had been common in urban department stores, many regional chains did not include these areas in their suburban stores, ceding 20–30% of their former clientele to discounters.[310]

No one chain of stores was more closely associated with this era of discounting than Kmart. Kmart began its life as Kresge, a chain of almost 700 variety stores located in downtown locations. As supermarkets and drugstores expanded their merchandise lines and encroached on Kresge's offering throughout the 50s and 60s, as discounters rose to prominence, and as target consumers moved from urban to suburban lifestyles, executives of the chain realized their historic model was in trouble. Under the leadership of Harry Cunningham, who the company had previously tasked with analyzing the discount store model, Kresge opened its first Kmart discount store in 1962. Like other discounters, Kmart stores featured large store formats (100,000 square feet), located as anchor tenants in small, suburban shopping centers serving medium to large cities, and sold national brands at a discount. By the late 1960s Kmart was the largest discounter in the US in both store count and sales volume. The company's success was attributed to its location strategy of saturating a city by placing several Kmart stores in its surrounding suburbs and then reaping density, and later scale, advantages. Competitors tended to have more scattered operations.[311]

While Kmart was rapidly rising to discount channel dominance, the owner of another chain of variety stores, this one in rural Arkansas, had also correctly perceived the threat that discounters posed to the variety store model. Unlike Kmart, Target, and many other discounters who had roots in downtown variety stores or in city-based department stores, Sam Walton had seen firsthand that rural customers could send significant volume to a discount operation. Sam Walton's view of the rural consumer was that they would 'leak' sales to cities, often driving several hours to make a major purchase in an urban center. Shopping at larger, urban stores saved these rural consumers a few dollars and offered a better selection compared to their home towns' small, 4,000 to 12,000 square foot, variety stores.

Walton thought that by using the Kmart model—offering national-brand merchandise at discount prices—he could aggregate the demand of many small towns and rural farms at a single location closer to these communities than to a large city. By aggregating this demand, he could offer an assortment of competitively-priced merchandise comparable to what rural customers would find in a large city, and so stop the leakage of spending dollars from rural communities to urban centers. Walton's initial experiments proved successful, and he rapidly transitioned his business from a chain of small format rural variety stores to a chain of large format rural discounters, with the business really beginning to take off when Walmart filed for an IPO in 1970. The rapid growth in Walmart's store count is shown in Figure 6.2.

Figure 6.2, Sources: Compiled from company reports and Vance, Sandra and Scott, Roy, *Wal-Mart: A History of Sam Walton's Retail Phenomenon*. New York, New York: Twayne Publishers, 1994.

Rural Operations

Walmart's rural locations played an important role in its history, sheltering it from industry shakeouts and providing scale and cash to fuel the company's advance into more urban locations later. Today, Walmart is still a dominant retailer in rural areas, though it faces new threats in its historical strongholds.

In the 1960s and 1970s, while most discounters focused on urban locations, Sam Walton was busily opening up Walmart discount stores throughout the rural Southeast. At the time, over 40% of Americans lived in areas (on farms, in small towns, or in small cities) with less than 25,000 people,[312] so the potential market was very large. As shown in Figure 6.3, Walmart didn't begin to leave the rural Southeast until after 1985, when the company began to enter the Midwest, New England, and California.

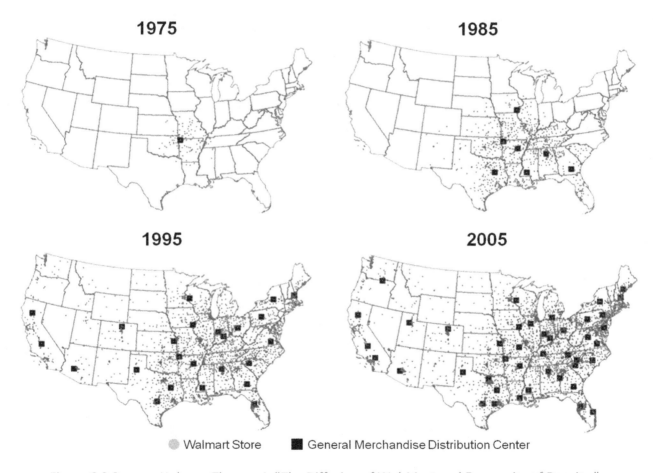

Figure 6.3 Source: Holmes, Thomas J, "*The Diffusion of Wal-Mart and Economics of Density*," Econometrica, Vol 79, No. 1, January, 2011.

Walmart's rural locations had lower start-up and operating costs than more urban areas: land costs were cheaper, wages were lower, and an aversion to organized labor in rural small towns kept unions out of Walmart's stores and distribution centers.[313] Lower costs enabled the company to grow quickly and achieve scale rapidly.

Walmart also frequently had its rural markets to itself. As Gamble-Skogmo, another large format rural discounter, commented, "If you're first, you're apt to be alone ... Most towns ... won't take two stores of that size."[314] In most of Walmart's early locations, small variety and general stores in its market areas were its only competition. These small stores, sometimes independently owned, had higher prices and more limited selection than Walmart, and were easy competition. In all but one of its locations at the end of the 1960s, Walmart was "the largest nonfood retailer in the community" and, proving Sam Walton's thesis, Walmart stores drew in customers from beyond the immediate towns where they were located.[315]

In contrast, by the 1970s, discounters had turned suburban shopping centers into a warzone. Discounters in these locations competed with department stores, variety stores, drugstores, supermarkets, and other discounters. As stagflation hit the US in the 1970s, urban discounters saw their costs increase due to inflation, but couldn't raise prices due to the intense price competition they faced. During this time, many discounters dropped out of the game, or took steps that would later set them up as easy targets for Walmart.

Kmart, for example, adopted private label merchandising to increase margins and become more competitive on price, and, dissatisfied with the returns in its urban discount operation, began opening category killers. Kmart had dropped its focus on discount store operations, and by the late 80s, when Walmart began opening urban locations in competition with Kmart, Kmart's discount operation was significantly outdated. In 1990, only 10% of Kmart stores were less than three years old, while 45% of Walmart stores had been opened within the last three years.[316] Kmart's technology systems were non-existent, and its stores often suffered from stockouts. Walmart by contrast, had invested heavily in computerized inventory and routing systems. Kmart's discount strategy had stagnated, while Walmart innovated with supercenters that combined general merchandise and grocery goods. In 1990, Walmart was a much more formidable opponent than it had been even ten years earlier, and Walmart quickly supplanted Kmart in its urban locations.

As for other rural discounters, the two major players in addition to Walmart were Gibson's and Tempo (a Gamble-Skogmo banner). Gibson's operated as a franchise model, and while it achieved significant scale, some of its franchisees became so large that they defected from Gibson's and began to operate independently. These defections deprived Gibson's of both franchise fees and scale, and created smaller regional chains that Walmart could outmuscle. Gibson's went out of business following a lawsuit. Tempo, like many other retailers, was the victim of an overleveraged buyout. With the fall of these two retailers, Walmart had much of the rural landscape to itself.

Distribution and Operating Model

The low prices on which Walmart built its success were also due to its superior logistics operations. Interestingly, this superiority also grew out of its rural base. When Sam Walton was first starting out, "no major distributors were willing to supply his remote market area ... nor were trucking companies, which gave excellent service to Memphis, Kansas City, and St. Louis, accustomed to providing frequent service to the country towns in which Walton's discount stores were located."[317] While Kmart and Woolco used the same distribution systems that supplied their variety stores, Walton knew that his "only alternative was to build a warehouse so we could buy in volume."[318]

Walton then proceeded to put up stores within a one-day drive of this first warehouse. As Walmart expanded and stores were built further away, Walmart would simply build a new distribution center to service existing stores and the new market area. Rather than expanding by city as other discounters did, which left large gaps between points of distribution, Walmart's focus on rural locations allowed it to expand in a tight-packed, radial formation from northwest Arkansas and saturate its market area, as seen in the maps in Figure 6.3. This density resulted in distribution, marketing, and management efficiencies. Whereas urban discounters would have to enter each new urban market area from scratch, and so endure either high trucking costs from another city's distribution center or low local distribution center volume as stores ramped up, Walmart's new distribution centers were already partially filled from existing stores when they opened. With a dense network, deliveries could be made more frequently, reducing stockouts and inventory needs at stores. In the early 1990s, Walmart often made daily deliveries to stores, whereas Target averaged a delivery every three to four days, and Kmart only delivered once every five days.[319] Because of this ability to rapidly replenish its stores, Walmart could respond more quickly to demand shocks.[320] Regional advertising and even word-of-mouth had greater impact as a result. The dense network of stores permitted Sam Walton to keep a close eye on early stores. Store managers (and later regional executives), could commute back to Bentonville for Saturday morning meetings. Finally, saturation of these rural communities "discouraged competition" and increased awareness.[321]

Aside from density, Walmart also benefitted from its growing scale to both make investments and negotiate with suppliers. The company implemented computer systems as a core component of its operations, launched its own private satellite network, and adopted bar codes, well before Kmart did so. These investments resulted in rapid and up-to-date inventory numbers for Walmart's stores, distribution centers, and suppliers, enabling Walmart's supply chain to further reduce inventory and avoid stockouts. Walmart worked with suppliers to make the supply chain more efficient by, for example, requesting specific packing sizes, helping plan factory locations, and using its own trucks to pick up inbound shipments. It also used its growing scale to negotiate better pricing.[322] In the early 1990s, Walmart furthered its commitment to supply chain technology and supplier cooperation by rolling out RetailLink, a database of SKU and store level sales which gave suppliers real-time product sales data and allowed them to better understand how their products were received in the marketplace. Walmart's densely stored operating areas and partnerships with its vendors resulted in it having lower logistics costs (as well as lower costs overall) than Sears and Kmart. The three companies' logistics expense, SG&A expense ratio, and gross margin are compared in Figure 6.4.

Figure 6.4 Sources: Vance, Sandra and Scott, Roy, *Wal-Mart: A History of Sam Walton's Retail Phenomenon*. New York, New York: Twayne Publishers, 1994 and Company Statements. Note: Sears reported data for SG&A and Gross Margin is for 1993 due to changes in reporting data.

Walmart's logistics superiority was complemented by its 'everyday low prices' (EDLP) policy. Adopted from early discounters, which saw no need to offer limited discounts or sales as they were already priced well below department stores, EDLP "meant that products were displayed at a steady price and not discounted on a regular basis."[323] This was in contrast to the 'high-low' pricing scheme used in the 1970s and 1980s by Walmart's competitors, where short-term discounts "rotated from product to product, necessitating huge inventory stock piles in anticipation of a discount," and resulting in a bullwhip effect throughout the supply chain due to the resulting spikes in demand. The use of EDLP smoothed demand, making the supply chain more efficient. Because EDLP retailers did not have to load up on inventory ahead of a sale, they also didn't have to deal with the residuals left over from a sale and the attendant, further markdowns to move this product. Nor did they need extra backroom and floor space, and their attendant overhead costs, to hold product for these sales events. And on the flip side of this surplus inventory problem, by smoothing demand EDLP also reduced stockouts that occurred during promotional events if enough inventory wasn't ordered.[324] EDLP also eliminated the need to perpetually advertise new discounts, saving Walmart money in advertising costs, which further reduced prices on a permanent basis.[325] Employee time was also saved, as employees no longer had to spend time reticketing items ahead of sales and after them, or dealing with the frustrations of sales events.[326]

Today, Walmart's distribution system is a marvel of a supply chain designed to move product into stores quickly, cheaply, and with a minimum of inventory in the supply chain. To accomplish this, Walmart U.S.'s 158 general merchandise, grocery, fashion, and import distribution centers, each with a 200-mile delivery radius, rely on efficient logistical practices such as full pallet cross-docking and full and split-case picking that minimize warehousing and transfer costs.[327] The result is that there is very little inventory inside Walmart's distribution centers. In the company's leading distribution center, located in Bentonville, products delivered to receiving can be loaded into a store-bound trailer in under 45 minutes. For large volume stores, those trailers will depart every day as they either weigh or cube out, whereas trailers destined for lower volume, smaller stores still manage to deliver three times per week.[328]

Virtuous Cycle—Driving Down Prices

While department stores and variety stores sought to increase their gross margins, Walmart was famous for actively decreasing its gross margin. Walmart started with low prices, limiting markups to no more than 30% in the first stores in order to attract volume. As stores ramped up in volume and number, spreading more sales over the fixed and semi-fixed costs of distribution centers, store assets, and labor, Walmart would take the incremental profit and invest it in lower prices for customers, continually driving down its prices. As Walmart grew in size, it used its scale to negotiate better deals with vendors and invest in its distribution network, all of which generated savings that were passed on to customers. This cycle is depicted graphically in Figure 6.5.

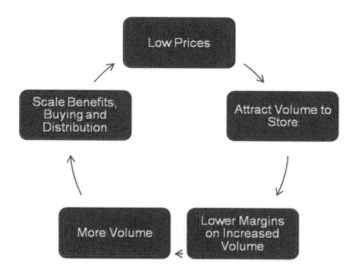

Figure 6.5

This pattern is clearly seen throughout the 1980s as Walmart drove down its operating expenses and gross margins, while still managing to keep a fairly consistent spread between the two, as seen in Figure 6.6.

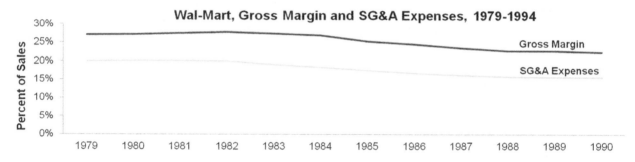

Figure 6.6 Sources: Company Financials from Capital IQ.

Low prices have been a huge part of the Walmart story from the beginning. Competitors, especially department stores targeted towards low to middle income shoppers like Sears and JC Penney, had tremendous difficulty competing. Walmart's business model was unstoppable throughout these years, and its sales grew and grew, reinforcing its virtuous cycle and significantly outdistancing its legacy competitors. Figure 6.7 depicts Walmart's extraordinary growth compared to its discount department store competitors, with the companies' total sales indexed to 1983.

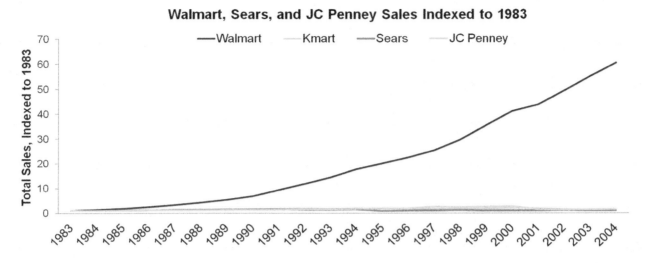

Figure 6.7 Sources: Company Financials, accessed via ThomsonOne. Note: Sales numbers are total company sales, not just US segments.

Amazon has now adapted elements of this model, maintaining low prices to drive online shopping adoption at almost zero net income and continually seeking volume to fill its distribution center network.

Suburban Push, Sam's Club, Supercenters, and Growth

Walmart remained a rural discounter up until the 1990s, with still over half of its stores located in towns with populations between 5,000 and 25,000 in the mid-80s. Walmart had been looking for a way to get into areas with higher population densities, such as the exurbs and suburbs of cities, but hadn't yet found it. The suburban retail environment of the 1980s was not right for Walmart's standard discount format. In 1983, Sears had sales of $32 billion, Kmart of $13 billion, and Walmart of only $5 billion. Suburban areas were saturated with department stores and discounters, and the industry was heavily competitive. The 1980s witnessed a series of consolidations and failures among discounters. Walmart needed a new format to distinguish itself in the crowded field, and thought that warehouse clubs could lead its push into the suburbs.

In 1983, Walmart opened its first Sam's Club. Walmart's warehouse club operated at a 13% gross margin as compared to the typical Walmart store's gross margin of around 20-25%; stocked 3,500 distinct items, or stock-keeping units (SKUs), in 109,000 square feet compared to the 70,000 SKUs in 40,000 to 50,000 square feet typical of Walmart discount stores of the time; and achieved over double the sales per square foot and over three times the inventory turns of a standard Walmart.[329] Since the Sam's Club division hit its stride, it has accounted for between 11% and 18% of the company's total sales, with 12% of Walmart's total sales coming from Sam's Club in 2012. However, membership warehouses, by definition, aren't for everyone, and with Walmart's history of being the dominant retailer in its market areas, it was still looking for a format that was more widely appealing and capable of leading the suburban charge.

Hypermarkets, which combined grocery and general merchandise goods in massive stores, had leapfrogged over the small grocers and shopkeepers they replaced and achieved a considerable market position in France. While US retailers Meijer and Fred Meyer both had chains of 100,000-115,000 square feet stores combining general merchandise and food by the late 1980s, many observers were skeptical that hypermarkets could compete against the disciplined, large, and well-operated regional supermarkets that had continually refined themselves since the 1930s.[330] Kmart and Walmart only jumped into the hypermarket arena after French companies Carrefour and Euromarché began opening stores in the US. However, Walmart's and Kmart's 200,000+ square foot hypermarket prototypes were deemed by customers to be too large, time-consuming, and confusing.[331]

Despite the setback with its hypermarkets experiment, Walmart was convinced by its Sam's Club operations that a joint grocery and general merchandise format was possible, and Walmart continued to iterate on the concept. The supercenter format was introduced in 1989. This new format was considerably smaller than Walmart's hypermarkets, lacked concessions like bank branches and auto-servicing, removed big-ticket items like boats, and featured the deeper general merchandise selection of a Walmart rather than a Sam's Club. Combining higher margin general merchandise goods with groceries enabled Walmart to treat groceries as loss-leaders and trip generators, and Walmart made up the discounts with increased general merchandise sales. From the beginning, the supercenter proved a success, especially against often unionized supermarkets. In the first town to gain a supercenter, one grocery store closed before the new store was even built, and the remaining supermarket experienced a 50% volume drop when the supercenter opened. Even though it had high-margin general merchandise in its mix alongside lower-margin groceries, Walmart was able to achieve a lower overall gross margin (and, unsurprisingly, a higher net margin) than traditional supermarkets (Figure 6.8). Walmart's lower gross margins and higher net margins were greatly aided by the lower rents in its rural locations and its non-union workforce.

	Walmart		Kroger		Dollar General	
	1989	1994	1989	1994	1989	1994
Gross Margin	22.8%	21.4%	22.3%	24.2%	29.4%	29.0%
SG&A % Sales	15.7%	15.4%	19.1%	20.9%	25.2%	20.7%
Net Margin	4.1%	3.2%	-0.1%	1.2%	2.0%	5.0%
Inventory Turns	5.2	5.2	10.6	10.9	2.8	3.3

Figure 6.8 Sources: Company Financial Statements accessed through Capital IQ. Notes: Net Margins exclude extraordinary items. 1989 was the year the first superstore was opened.

Supercenters were initially used to replace and relocate older Walmart discount stores, but Walmart knew it now had a format which it could use to mount its suburban expansion. Walmart rolled supercenters out rapidly across the US, growing from nine supercenters in 1990, to 888 in 2000, and 1,906 in 2005, becoming the leading food retailer in the US in the process. Today, groceries account for 55% of Walmart US sales,[332] and in 2005, Walmart was estimated to have grocery prices up to 15% lower than supermarkets.[333] We believe that today, Walmart considers itself a grocer first and a general merchandise store second. In Walmart's 20th Annual Meeting for the Investment Community, company executives mentioned many types of grocery-oriented trips (stock-up trips at supercenters, routine trips at supermarkets, and quick fill-in trips at dollar stores), but didn't comment on any general merchandise-oriented trip motivations.

As Walmart entered suburban markets, with higher real estate and operating costs, its expenses began to rise and Walmart followed by increasing its gross margin (Figure 6.9). This brought Walmart more into line with traditional grocers like Kroger, though Walmart still maintained a lower SG&A expense ratio (Figure 6.10).

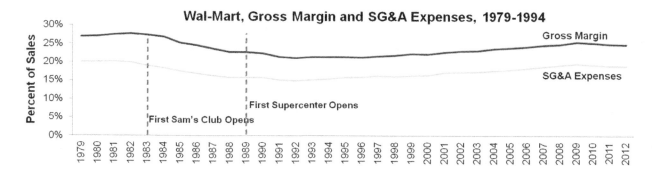

Figure 6.9 Sources: Company Financial Statements accessed through *ThomsonOne.*

	Walmart		Target		Kroger		Dollar General	
	1994	2007	1994	2007	1994	2007	1994	2007
Gross Margin	21.4%	24.6%	26.6%	30.0%	24.2%	24.4%	29.0%	27.8%
SG&A % Sales	15.4%	18.8%	21.3%	21.7%	20.9%	21.0%	20.7%	24.1%
Net Margin	3.2%	3.4%	1.9%	4.5%	1.2%	1.7%	5.0%	-0.1%
Inventory Turns	5.2	8.3	5.9	6.8	10.9	11.3	3.3	5.0

Figure 6.10 Sources: Company Financial Statements accessed through *Capital IQ.* Note: Net Margins exclude extraordinary items.

With Walmart's substantial store openings through the 1990s and 2000s, today, two-thirds of US residents live within five miles of a Walmart store and the company is the only grocer with a national footprint.[334]

Walmart Today

The scale, logistics and technology advantages, store placement strategies, and labor policies that Walmart built during its days as a rural discounter propelled it past Kmart, Sears, and a string of regional grocery chains to become the largest retailer in the world. However, the world has changed since Walmart climbed its throne.

Walmart is clearly no longer just a rural discounter, but with its many store locations outside of metro areas, rural stores are still an important part of its business. Indeed, Walmart's concentric growth from its roots in northwest Arkansas leaves the company with a heavier weighting towards its origins in southern, and presumably rural, areas compared to other discounters (Figure 6.11).

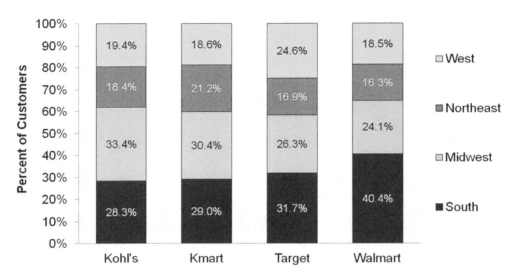

Figure 6.11 Source: Carmichael, Matt, "The Demographics of Retail," *AdAge,* March 19, 2012, available at http://adage.com/article/adagestat/demographics-retail/233399/.

However, the American population has increasingly been shifting to more urban areas, with 72% of Americans living in urbanized areas with populations greater than 50,000 today.[335] Such locations would have been off-limits to the 1970s-era Walmart. Walmart's traditional small towns are no longer as large a part of the overall market, and rural areas with declining populations may no longer be able to support a full-fledged Walmart in future.

In addition, Walmart is also no longer alone in these rural areas. In the past, Walmart largely had rural areas to itself, drawing traffic from not only the towns where the company placed its stores, but from surrounding towns as well. Walmart discount stores and supercenters would capture much of a market area's spending by putting inefficient, independent variety and general stores out of business. Today, however, Walmart no longer controls an effective monopoly over rural areas, and its rural stores face competition from Amazon and a number of large, well-run dollar store companies, most prominent of which is Dollar General. Amazon's general merchandise selection is enormous and is priced competitively, and rural customers may find that waiting two days, or even five, for an online order to arrive is more convenient than driving to a distant Walmart. Dollar stores are also an attractive alternative for certain types of purchases. The major dollar stores now sell groceries, home necessities and a selection of general merchandise goods at prices close to Walmart's. By leveraging an array of tactics including private label brands, an everyday pricing strategy, and compelling messaging, dollar stores achieve low price perception, and in fact, Dollar General has bested Walmart in Kantar Retail's Opening Price Point survey for the last three years.[336] Dollar stores' convenient locations pose a real alternative to a supercenter trip for goods not sold online, like engine oil, or for immediate needs, like milk and eggs. Dollar General is a strong rural competitor, with over 70% of its stores in communities with fewer than 20,000 residents—the same communities in which Walmart originated.[337] The successful penetration of dollar stores in rural areas can be seen by looking at the map of dollar store density in the US in Figure 6.12, which shows a remarkable similarity to Walmart's own pattern of growth in the rural South.

Dollar Stores per 10,000

0.4 0.8 1.2 1.6

Figure 6.12 Source: Martin Prosperity Institute, from Florida, Richard, "What Dollar Store Locations Reveal About America," *The Atlantic Cities*, February 7, 2012.

While dollar stores have gained particular attention in the recession as more and more consumers found themselves on limited budgets and without the cash or credit to buy the value-size purchases most closely associated with Walmart and warehouse clubs, dollar store chains have actually been steadily growing their store bases for much of the last decade, as seen by the three major dollar store chains' constantly expanding store counts presented in Figure 6.13.

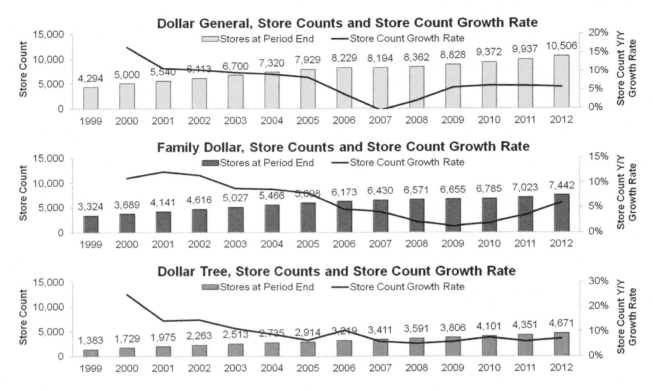

Figure 6.13 Source: Retrieved from Wharton Research Data Service.

All of the top three dollar store chains have more stores than Walmart, with Dollar General having over twice as many. In rural areas, where the closest full-line grocery and general merchandise store is often a Walmart supercenter some distance away, the large number of dollar stores represents a convenient, fast, and easy way to make fill-in or convenience trips at a competitive price. The targeted trips that customers take to dollar stores not only take this direct business away from Walmart, but, much like the targeted purchase behavior seen at online retailers, they deprive Walmart of an opportunity to build a customer's basket through its broader assortment of general merchandise.

As a result of Walmart's discount model and its focus on rural areas, its customers have lower incomes than those of other discounters like Target and Kohl's, and also of Amazon, as shown in Figure 6.14.

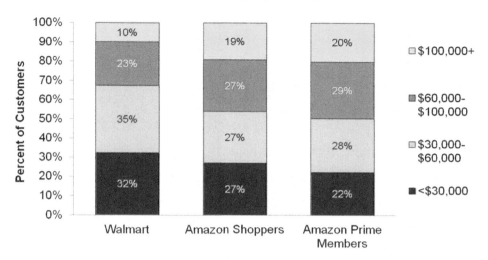

Retailer Customer Demographics by Income, Feb 2012

Figure 6.14 Sources: Carmichael, Matt, "The Demographics of Retail," *AdAge,* March 19, 2012, available at http://adage.com/article/adagestat/demographics-retail/233399/ and Pace, Mark, "Attention Retailers: Amazon Prime members are located in aisle 5," *Compete Pulse*, available at https://blog.compete.com/2013/04/17/attention-retailers-amazon-prime-members-are-located-in-aisle-5/. Note: Due to survey methodology, the results of the AdAge survey were recalculated using population data from the US Census to match the cohorts in the Compete survey.

Walmart's higher proportion of low-income customers has been cited as a defense against Amazon.[338] There are a number of reasons why lower-income customers have not adopted online retail: a lack of access to the internet, a lack of access to credit or debit cards and a reliance on cash, and a lack of a secure place to receive packages, among others. On the other hand, however, there are also reasons why online retail is appealing to lower-income customers, most important of which are the low prices available online and the removal of the need to find transportation to out-of-the-way discount locations like Walmart.

Amazon's Lockers experiment could help alleviate many of the problems low-income customers experience with online retail as Lockers provide a safe place to receive packages, potentially could accept cash in the future, and can be located close to customers who lack access to a car or don't want to or can't spend money on gas or public transportation. As technology drives down the cost of both devices and connections, smartphones, tablets, or netbooks will provide these customers with cheaper access to the internet. Walmart certainly should be worried about an Amazon threat to their low-income customers.

Walmart is preparing for this threat already. Two-thirds of the US population already live within five miles of a Walmart, and Walmart continues to roll out smaller formats closer to customers. These locations' proximity lessens the transportation burden on customers. The company has also rolled out a "buy online-pick up in store" program, and has combined it with "Pay With Cash," a program that lets customers order a product online and pay for it in store.[339] While Amazon Lockers are still a limited experiment and have not yet included any kind of cash-based transaction feature, Pay With Cash allows unbanked, low-income customers to buy any Walmart.com purchases at a Walmart store. These moves are a good defense in general merchandise and big-ticket categories. Walmart doesn't face as much of a threat to its low-income customers from Amazon in grocery, as lower income shoppers are less able to order consumer packaged goods (CPGs) in the bulk quantities that Amazon offers and are unable to pay the higher prices of AmazonFresh. However, it's not as useful to have a category strength against Amazon if dollar stores are picking up sales from Walmart.

Dollar stores have resonated with the low-income customers with which Walmart is most closely identified. While dollar stores now appeal to a wider income profile than in the past, as many upper-income consumers "traded down" in the recession and dollar stores renovated to appeal to these new customers, dollar stores are still heavily weighted towards lower income shoppers. Indeed, while 32% of Walmart shoppers earn less than $30,000 a year, 42% of dollar store customers fall into that category.[340]

For these low income customers, dollar stores' greater number of locations isn't just about convenience. Amongst low-income customers, the costs of car ownership or other transportation to get to a Walmart can be significant, and the cost of a trip to a supercenter has risen substantially since 2005 as gas prices have dramatically increased (Figure 6.15). It is less expensive to travel to dollar stores' closer-to-customer locations.

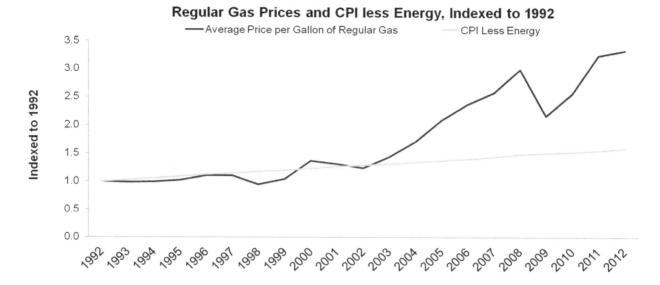

Regular Gas Prices and CPI less Energy, Indexed to 1992

Figure 6.15 Sources: Regular, All Areas, All Formulations data from US DEA, CPI Less Energy data from US BLS.

Dollar store merchandising of low-price, low-volume units has also been appealing to hard-pressed shoppers. While it has adopted "dollar store areas" within its stores, this merchandising is not as effective in Walmart's stores. In order to make its model work, Walmart uses value-packs to both provide great value and capture volume to cover its fixed costs; selling paper towels a roll at a time does not achieve this. In addition, Walmart's large supercenters are inconveniently located for customers; they won't simply drop by for a small fill-in trip. For customers who are living paycheck to paycheck, dollar stores' smaller packages, lower price points, and closer locations are easier to fit within a weekly budget.

While together Dollar General's, Family Dollar's, and Dollar Tree's combined sales are only 12% of Walmart's US sales, they continue to open stores at a rapid pace, and their comp store sales have handily outdistanced Walmart's in the past few years (Figure 6.16).

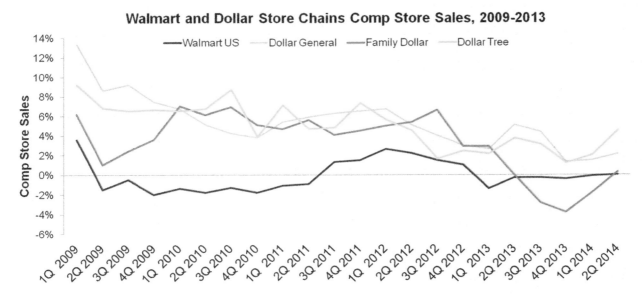

Figure 6.16 Sources: WRDS and Company Documents.

While dollar stores are small now, they are also not the only brick-and-mortar competition that Walmart faces.

In reaction to Walmart's rapid rise to dominance in the grocery industry, supermarkets have consolidated and invested in lower prices. The supermarket chains that remain today are larger and stronger than the relics Walmart drove out of business in the heyday of the supercenter. Kroger, for instance, has duplicated Walmart's strategy of reinvesting profits into price, with the result being that Kroger is now within 8%-15% of Walmart's prices compared to being 20% more expensive previously.[341] Using gross margin as an indicator of shelf price, we see in Figure 6.17 that Kroger and Safeway have been closing the price gap with Walmart. While gross margins between the three retailers aren't comparable given differences in merchandise mixes, location strategies, and employee costs, the trends are reflective of a narrowing price gap.

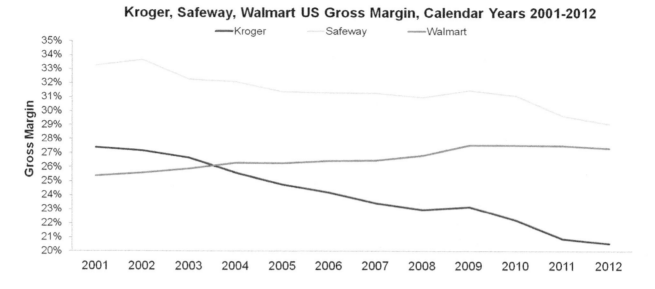

Kroger, Safeway, Walmart US Gross Margin, Calendar Years 2001-2012

Figure 6.17 Source: Company Reports.

Walmart attributes its rising gross margin not to price increases, but to reduced markdowns and shrink, a changing merchandise mix, and supply chain initiatives such as increasing its global sourcing.[342]

The overall price gap is still to Walmart's advantage, but competitors have found ways to compete within it. Kroger's extensive loyalty card program and partnership with dunnhumby[vi] enables it to target promotions selectively; narrowing the price gap further for Kroger's most profitable customers. Combined with its more convenient locations and investments in customer service, Kroger's price investments have been enough to grow the company's market share from 19.1% in 2007 to 21.1% in 2012, without opening many new stores.[343]

There is evidence that newly price-competitive supermarkets and convenience- and price-focused dollar stores are directly impacting Walmart's operating model, especially in a sustained environment of higher gas prices. Walmart has not always provided exact comparable stores traffic and ticket numbers in its earnings calls, but it always at least gives an indication of whether they were positive or negative. In Figure 6.18, where exact numbers were reported, we've included them as a line. Where only an indication of positive or negative comps was given, we've charted these as vertical bars with no representation for magnitude.

[vi] A customer analysis consultancy that grew out of the Tesco club card program

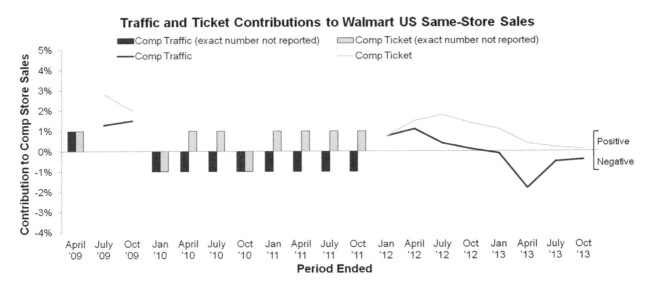

Figure 6.18 Sources: Company Pre-Recorded Earnings Calls, available at Walmart's corporate website, author estimates.

While trade-down customers accounted for the early increases in comparable traffic and ticket, rising gas prices and pressure on lower-income consumers rapidly lead to falling traffic numbers. In 12 of the past 19 quarters, Walmart has experienced negative comparable traffic. While consumers shopping less in general was the most-cited reason for shopping less at Walmart in a May 2014 survey, a desire to shop retailers offering a more pleasant shopping experience and/or retailers more conveniently located to home and work, among them supermarkets and dollar stores, were also top reasons for shopping Walmart less.[344] Even worse for Walmart than customers shopping less, some customers have abandoned the company entirely. Walmart's penetration of total U.S. shoppers has been trending downward since late 2007 as measured by Kantar Retail's ShopperScape survey.[345]

While a general decline in customers is obviously a bad thing, that doesn't paint the whole nature of the problem facing Walmart. Walmart is losing its primacy in the CPG categories, which, since the launch of the supercenter, have been integral to Walmart's store model. The supercenter model relies on low grocery prices drawing customers into the store so that Walmart can sell them higher-margin, general merchandise items as well. However, in recent years the advantages of dollar stores (and similar ones at drug stores) have resulted in the dollar store channel gaining share against supercenters in the CPG category where their merchandise mixes most overlap (Figure 6.19).

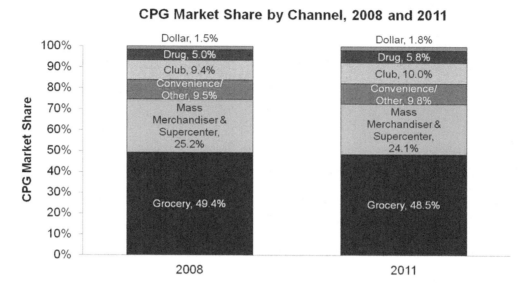

Figure 6.19 Source: Conroy, Pat et al, "Dollar store strategies for national brands," *Deloitte*.

Looking back over Walmart's reported comp sales in its key merchandising categories, one sees that Walmart's poor comp performance has been, unsurprisingly, related to discretionary categories that were most heavily impacted by the recession. In the midst of these categories' recovery, however, Walmart has begun to report negative comp sales in its grocery business. The recent negative comps in the grocery category are attributed to Walmart's consumables and dry grocery business, two grocery sub-categories that are a focus of dollar stores.[346] Walmart reports that these negative comps are attributable to customers trading down, and that the company is gaining market share in consumables overall. We believe that dollar stores are dampening Walmart's progress in these sub-categories given their recent poor performance at Walmart, the large percentage of trade-down private label products at dollar stores, market share gains in these sub-categories at dollar stores, and the belief that Walmart is focusing price investments in these categories going forward to better position itself.[347] Walmart relies on these routine, ongoing purchases to generate trips and give it a chance to sell its higher-margin general merchandise. Losing primacy in the grocery category disrupts the supercenter business model.

Both Kroger and the dollar stores, as well as many other retailers, have benefitted from the technology and logistics innovations that Walmart introduced to retail at a massive scale. While Walmart is still the leading user of these innovations, cross-docking—the practice of unloading materials from an incoming semi-trailer truck or railroad car and loading these materials directly onto outbound trucks, trailers, or rail cars, to minimize storage time and handling—is used by many retailers in at least part of their supply chain. Many of Walmart's competitors also use the Agentrics-developed "Retail Interface" software platform to duplicate Retail Link's functions, and computers are far more ubiquitous now than when Walmart used its IBM mainframes to show up Kmart. The technology battle has shifted to online retail, where, like Walmart, Amazon has developed many of its own proprietary systems and logistics innovations.

Amazon's logistics network has been deliberately built to pick millions of SKUs cheaply and efficiently for delivery to individual customers. Its non-specialty fulfillment centers are giant structures, often over a million square feet in size. In these fulfillment centers, individual items are sorted into bins based on computer algorithms that optimize for space usage and picking. Items sit in these bins until pickers collect them into a tote, which is then delivered to packaging. After an order is consolidated into a package, the package travels via a miles-long conveyor belt network to the appropriate outbound bay.

By contrast, Walmart's logistics network is designed to move items quickly and efficiently to stores, not to individual customers. As a result, each-picking is more expensive in this environment, SKU selection is limited, and the existing distribution centers have limited ability to adjust to new requirements. Walmart's world is one of cases and pallets, rather than each-picks. Inbound cases already allocated to stores are placed on a conveyor system that automatically delivers them to the appropriate outbound door. Pallets that have already been assigned are moved by forklift. Cases and pallets not yet allocated for store delivery are put away in storage racks to be picked later.[348] Pickers can each-pick from these stored cases, but the focus in Walmart's warehouses is moving goods to stores, not directly to customers. The result is distribution centers optimized to move goods in volume, not by single pieces. In addition to faster delivery times and shipping cost savings, this is likely one of the reasons Walmart employs ship-from-store for some online orders.

While Walmart's general merchandise fulfillment centers can be even larger than Amazon's, the fact that they're moving goods to stores in volume means that they can't fit as many SKUs within these large facilities. Rather, Walmart's general merchandise distribution centers deal with the limited amount of SKUs being sent to stores, not the wider eCommerce catalog. To provide the wider Walmart.com assortment, Walmart has constructed purpose-built eCommerce fulfillment centers. Walmart only has three of these fulfillment centers currently, however, compared to Amazon's 60.

Amazon Fresh poses little danger to Walmart's perishables business as it is limited both geographically and to income cohorts higher than Walmart's core customer. However, Amazon itself poses a significant threat to not only Walmart's general merchandise lines but also to its grocery business. In general merchandise, Amazon's low-cost, no-store model enables it to significantly undercut Walmart prices on high-ticket items. In consumer electronics, for instance, Amazon is estimated to enjoy an 11% price advantage over Walmart.[349] While pricing in eCommerce changes often, in at least one study, Amazon's grocery business has managed to achieve something like price-parity on a per item basis with Walmart, largely by merchandising bulk packs in a manner more similar to Costco than to Walmart, and, as detractors will often point out, operating at near or below break-even. This study, which includes only items sold directly by Amazon and excludes shipping costs as these orders generally qualify for free shipping (either through Prime, Subscribe & Save, or on a $35 order minimum), is shown in Figure 6.20. (Of note, in an example of the dynamic pricing in this space, a later study by Kantar Retail found the Amazon first-party Edible Grocery basket to be 14% more expensive and the General Merchandise basket 14% less expensive at Amazon, a reversal of the dynamic presented in Figure 6.20).[350]

Edible Grocery	Walmart SC Price	Amazon Price	AMZN/WMT
Edible Grocery	$151.48	$147.80	98%
Non-Edible Grocery	$141.40	$140.64	99%
Health and Beauty Aids	$78.16	$74.38	95%
General Merchandise	$206.53	$211.48	102%
Total	**$577.57**	**$574.30**	**99%**

Figure 6.20 Source: Zybowski, Anne et al, "Walmart vs. Amazon: Who is the Price Leader?" *Kantar Retail iQ*, July 31, 2013, available at
http://kantarretailiq.com/Digital/ArticleDetails.aspx?viewall=1&id=636622

In newer categories, like grocery, third party merchants fill in much of the assortment on Amazon.com, and in the grocery category (unlike in the consumer electronics category), their prices are often much higher than what one would find at a supercenter. In fact, in the Kantar Retail price study presented in Figure 6.20, if one includes items sold by third-party merchants on Amazon, Amazon is 16% more expensive than a Walmart supercenter. However, we feel that looking only at items sold directly by Amazon is the most accurate way of looking at these prices both as a reflection of Amazon's current state as well as a base for future predictions: third party prices can fluctuate wildly, and as the grocery category matures, Amazon will likely co-opt many items into its first party offering.

Of course, if Amazon were to make the 8% operating margin that Walmart US earns currently, it would have to raise its prices 7%. However, in the long term, Amazon will likely bring its operating expenses lower as it reduces shipping cost by locating closer to customers. In the near term, if Amazon can convert more customers to its Subscribe & Save program, with its 5% and 15% off discounts and presumably lower costs due to flexibility in scheduling fulfillment and delivery time, or its Pantry program, a price increase would be a wash with Subscribe & Save discounts.

The high-quantity bundles, and resulting higher opening price points, sold by Amazon are not accessible to low-income customers, and this is a valid criticism. Higher income customers, however, with credit and storage room to spare—and over 30% of Walmart's customers have household incomes greater than $60,000—may have been shopping at Walmart only due to lack of a better option as Walmart has crowded out other brick-and-mortar retailers in many areas. Amazon's lower prices combined with the convenience of online ordering may keep these customers out of Walmart stores. In fact, 15% of shoppers with household income greater than $60,000 who, in May of 2014, reported shopping less at Walmart, indicated that they were doing so because they were shopping more at online retailers.[351] With less volume from higher-income customers, Walmart may find that it needs to raise its prices to make up for the volume shortfall.

For a company like Walmart, that has always used price and efficiency to attract traffic, the presence of a lower-cost, more efficient general merchandise operator undermines their entire business model. If Amazon can succeed at driving down Walmart's prices and decreasing Walmart's gross margin on its general merchandise goods (regardless of its possible impact on the grocery category), Walmart can no longer use higher-margin general merchandise goods to justify its loss-leader approach to groceries. If it raises its grocery prices, supermarkets are waiting in the wings to swoop in and take their customers back.

Next to the almost $300 billion behemoth that is Walmart US, the threats of an old supermarket, a handful of $5-$15 billion dollar stores, and an online retailer with US sales only 10% of Walmart's may seem minor. While Walmart's rise to general merchandise and later grocery dominance was rapid, disruptive, and surprising to many, its fall, caused by this trio of retail channels, may look more like a slow chipping away of Walmart's position. From a product perspective, Walmart's entire store is up for grabs as depicted in Figure 6.21.

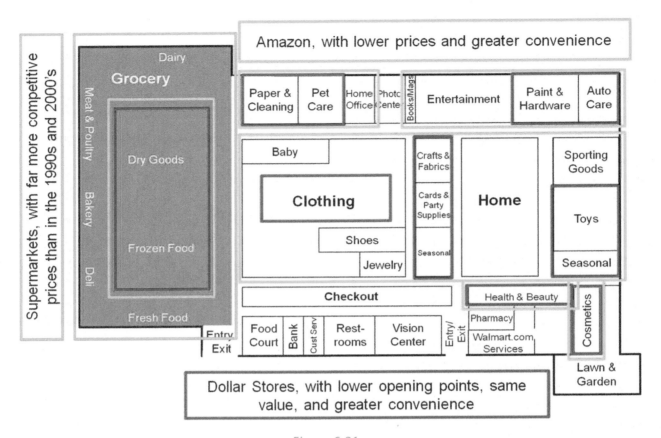

Figure 6.21

In addition to this product competition, Walmart's entire business model is at risk. The supercenter functions by attracting customers through low-priced groceries, and then selling them higher-margin general merchandise goods. Dollar stores and supermarkets capture trips, preventing customers from walking in Walmart's doors in the first place and precluding any sales of higher margin general merchandise items. For those customers that will still come to Walmart for groceries, Amazon's lower prices and mobile price-check app either pre-empt the purchase of general merchandise goods at Walmart, or exert price pressure, lowering Walmart's gross margin on these goods. In either case, if Walmart can no longer sell general merchandise goods to grocery customers, or if it makes less money doing so, it can no longer afford to subsidize grocery prices to attract customers. Without lower grocery prices, there's no reason for customers to make the trek out to Walmart's exurban locations, invalidating the entire concept of the supercenter. These dynamics are depicted in Figure 6.22.

Figure 6.22

After focusing for years on rolling out supercenters, and wrestling most recently with how to compete against Amazon, Walmart has begun to re-envision itself. It's doing so, quite fittingly, by first figuring out a new logistics model, and embracing its status as a grocer first. In this new model, Walmart is following the "Shrink and Transform the Format" strategy by turning its supercenters into distribution nodes, and by opening small format supermarket and dollar store clones that will also function as eCommerce collection points.

Walmart has long located its supercenters on the periphery of towns and cities, and drawn customers out through low prices. As competitors have grown closer in pricing, Walmart's new plan is to take the fight into the city through an array of smaller formats, serviced from its own supercenters. In Walmart's view, customers are now taking three types of brick-and-mortar grocery trips. The trip at the heart of Walmart is the weekly, monthly, or event-driven stock-up trip. In between these stock-up trips, customers are making food trips to dollar and grocery stores that result in reasonably large baskets. If a customer only goes to a supercenter every month, it's reasonable to assume that they have a large perishables spend outside of Walmart given the short shelf life of these products and that they're planning weekly meals outside of Walmart. Walmart calls these occasions the "basic food trip, the traditional grocery trip." There is also the immediate access trip, with a small basket that Walmart once associated with convenience stores but that dollar stores and drug stores are now capturing. As seen in Figure 6.23, the majority of trips are of this small, immediate need and convenience variety. Then, of course, there are online purchases.

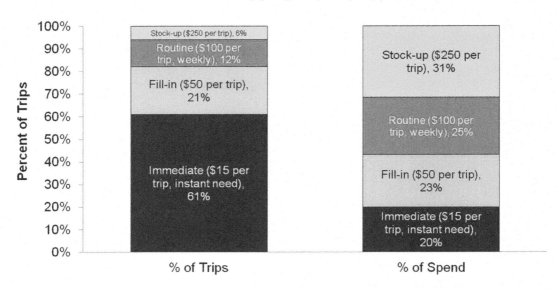

US Shopping Trips by Type, 2011

Figure 6.23 Source: Hale, Todd and Taylor, Stuart, "The Just in Time Consumer: How Shopping Trips Align with Economic Woes," *Nielsen Newswire,* January 31, 2011.

By creating the stock-up trip with the introduction and growth of its supercenter format, Walmart is the source of this trip fragmentation. The company provided an example of one of its markets, which we republish in Figure 6.24, showing its supercenters on the periphery, and highlighting the grocery, dollar, and drug stores that have sprung up since 2003 to serve customers' food, convenience, and immediate needs. As shown in the last map in the sequence of Figure 6.24, Walmart believes it has the opportunity to locate smaller formats inside this metro region.

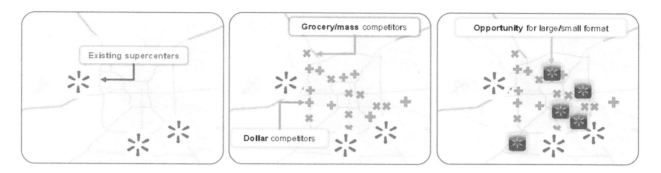

Figure 6.24 Source: Company Reports.

While Walmart feels confident in its ability to capture stock-up trips with its traditional supercenters, making it fast and easy for customers to buy everything they need at once, they are experimenting with a smaller 70,000 square foot supercenter to get closer to customers. For its market saturation strategy, however, Walmart is relying on its Neighborhood Market and Express formats. With 300 stores in 2013, Walmart has been experimenting with Neighborhood Markets to fulfill the basic food trip since 1999. At 40,000 square feet, Neighborhood Markets are smaller and have a narrower assortment than many supermarkets. Neighborhood Markets are heavily oriented towards fresh perishables and grocery products, with fuel recently introduced. The company plans to open 400 more Neighborhood Markets over the next three years. Walmart's much newer Express format is designed to compete for immediate access trips with dollar stores, with similar merchandising but also including fresh goods and a pharmacy. Walmart has 20 units in this format now. In addition to penetrating urban areas, Neighborhood Markets and Express stores are also intended to stand alone in rural areas.

The smaller stores will share overhead and back-office tasks, such as hiring, with supercenters, but more importantly, Walmart intends to service these smaller formats using the existing backrooms of its supercenters. Walmart's supercenters have more warehouse square footage and inventory than the company's distribution system.[352] Under Walmart's scheme, its standard 53-foot trailers would make the trip from its distribution centers to its supercenters, carrying pallets intended for both the supercenter and the smaller formats. In the supercenter backrooms, pallets destined for Neighborhood Markets and Express stores would be cross-docked into smaller trucks. These smaller trucks, would, in turn, make the trip to Neighborhood Markets and

Express stores, and could, potentially, also drop packages at USPS Destination Delivery Unit (DDU) locations, taking advantage of the lowest cost method of shipping goods to consumer's homes.

While Walmart's new plans may risk cannibalization of supercenter sales, in many cases, as Walmart states, they've already been impacted by competitors and the additional impact of Walmart's own small stores has been lower than expected in test geographies. In an important reframing of the situation, Walmart has boldly declared that, in effect, it believes any sales taken from a supercenter by its smaller formats are sales that would have been lost anyways as alternative channels mature. Additionally, the potential to capture more online sales and sales from competing channels may outweigh the impact to the supercenters, as depicted in Figure 6.25.

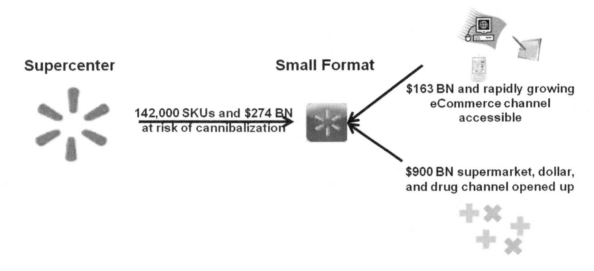

Figure 6.25

Walmart also believes that its Neighborhood Market and Express formats target different trip motivations than supercenters, and will more directly compete with supermarkets, dollar, and drug stores than with supercenters. The company has demonstrated in its Walmart.com and Walmart supercenter pricing that it is not averse to pricing and merchandising differences between its channels. Maintaining the cheapest, most value-pack-oriented pricing at its supercenters and introducing differently sized and priced merchandise at its smaller formats may cement these trip characterizations.

Greater small store sales can also benefit supercenters from a logistics perspective. Walmart's lowest performing 10% of supercenters have an on-shelf availability score of 92%, while Walmart's average on-shelf availability is 95%. Increasing on-shelf availability would result in higher sales, and could compensate for cannibalization from small formats. The new logistics structure could help in two ways. Moving more volume through the supercenters would enable more frequent deliveries. This creates a more responsive supply chain, which can respond more quickly to stockouts. With 99% in-store availability of products, however, the real issue for Walmart is getting products from its backrooms onto its store shelves efficiently.[353] Using supercenters as distribution centers will require more associate hours in-store, and this may give store management more flexibility around scheduling and greater ability to boost on-shelf availability. Additionally, if more backroom space is needed to cross-dock orders for Neighborhood Markets and Express stores, this may be a more productive use for parts of the entertainment category than in-store offerings—and these categories' shift online may enable Walmart to better compete with Amazon.

The small formats also reap a number of benefits. In addition to cost advantages from sharing major parts of the supply chain and back office tasks, due to their tether to Walmart's supercenters, Walmart's smaller formats can carry fresh categories like deli and prepared foods (e.g. a la carte meals, rotisserie chickens, etc.) that would otherwise not have been open to them. These categories are generally difficult to carry in small formats due to the lack of space for preparation and service, but in Walmart's ecosystem, supercenters can prepare these meals and then transport them to the smaller stores. Walmart also plans to individually merchandise these small, 10,000 SKU formats based on current data in its point-of-sale system and from its eCommerce platform, and drawing on the broad 140,000 SKU assortment of its supercenters. This tailors each small store to its immediate community. Because of these benefits, Walmart believes an Express store can generate sales of as much as the combined sales of three to five dollar stores, and a Neighborhood Market more than ten dollar stores combined.

These small stores will also serve as eCommerce points for Walmart's web business, bringing package pick-up much closer to Walmart.com customers. For a customer ordering online, anything in the standard supercenter assortment can be delivered from the supercenter to the small format within the same day provided the order is received early enough. SKUs outside of the supercenter assortment will continue to be fulfilled out of eCommerce only distribution centers, and delivery to a small format could take place within a day or two. Of course, eCommerce orders can also be delivered directly to a customer's home.

Bringing these various fulfillment capabilities together, Walmart envisions its future supply chain will look like Figure 6.26.

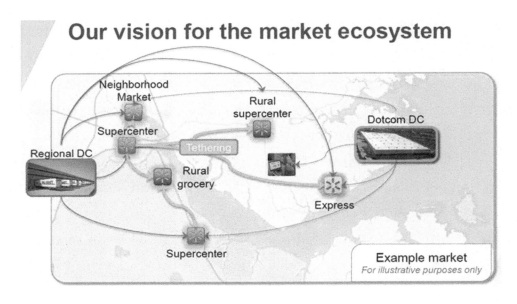

Our vision for the market ecosystem

Figure 6.26 Source: Company Reports.

This vision of the future of retailing is very different from Amazon's. Both retailers are unquestionably seeking to dominate multiple categories in the retail industry, offering everything from groceries to dishwashers, and leveraging the internet to offer assortments unavailable in brick-and-mortar stores. But their visions differ substantially when it comes to how customers' orders actually get into their hands. In Amazon's model, its network of fulfillment centers, strategically placed around population centers, take customer orders all the way until last mile fulfillment.[vii] Packages from Amazon are delivered either through third parties, or, if Amazon Fresh really takes off, through Amazon's own trucks, directly to customers' doors. In Walmart's vision of the future (despite its Walmart To Go service) it abdicates the last mile to its customers. Instead, Walmart plans to own retail stores that are so much a part of its customers' lives that

---

[vii] Last mile fulfillment refers to the distance between an order's last distribution point in the logistics chain and its final destination (for example, a home or office).

picking up orders at the corner store is no less convenient than having packages delivered to their homes. Imagine in some cases why this might be so.

For example, in the morning before work, you've discovered that you've run out of milk. You don't want to leave your groceries in the communal office, no online grocery delivery service will deliver an order that small, and you don't want to go out of your way to a supercenter on the way home. Luckily, there's a Walmart Express right on your path home from work. At work, you also decide to finally buy the fishing rod you'll need for the weekend. You log on to Walmart.com, buy a rod, and choose for it to be delivered to that same Express store. It arrives that day from the supercenter five miles away. On your way home from work, you pick up both your milk and a package containing your fishing rod at the Express store, at no additional cost.

Or, assume you habitually stop at the closest Neighborhood Market every week to replenish your household supply of produce and other fresh items without the inconvenience of walking around a 180,000 square foot supercenter. For the past week, you've also been shopping online at Walmart.com, saving to your basket books you want to read, shoes you want to wear, and some new high-end cookware you've been saving for. You usually do your grocery shopping on Sunday, so you set your pick-up date at the Neighborhood Market for Sunday. A Walmart.com eCommerce fulfillment center picks your order, funnels it into the Walmart distribution system, and it arrives at the Neighborhood Market for Sunday delivery at no extra cost. You pick it up then, along with the groceries you were already coming to get, with no time added to your trip.

Or, imagine you're making an immediate purchase online. You're having dinner guests the day after tomorrow and you want some unique glassware. You're used to buying these sorts of things online because of the huge selection available, and you find the glasses you want on Amazon. Because they're over $30, you luckily also qualify for super-saver shipping. Unfortunately, you need them a lot sooner than 5-7 days out, and, like most Americans, you're not a member of Amazon Prime, so two day shipping will set you back a bit. You begin to explore other options. You search online for the glasses, and you find them at Walmart.com. They're marginally cheaper, because Walmart doesn't have to pay for last-mile delivery, and even better they can be at your local Express store in two days, at no extra cost. You pick them up on your way to work the morning of your dinner party, leave them in your trunk all day, and have them at home with you well before your guests arrive.

Of course, to make this work, Walmart needs formats that are more convenient than supercenters. Out of all retail channels, grocery (excluding Walmart), dollar, and drug stores accounted for 65% of total trips in the US in 2013, as compared to mass merchandisers' and supercenters' combined share of 22%. The average consumer is taking three trips in one of Walmart's new channels for every one trip in the company's traditional channel.[354] With the mass merchandiser, supercenter, grocery, dollar, and drug channels combined, the average shopper is taking over two trips per week. Even for trips outside of the normal routine, like in our last example, stopping at an Express store solely for picking up an online order is far more convenient than driving to a supercenter. For Walmart to succeed in its vision of out-competing Amazon in online retail through physical stores, it clearly needs to densely penetrate these more convenient formats.

The selection of the dollar and grocery channels is important for other reasons as well. Walmart, leveraging its position as the only national grocer, has chosen two formats that are ubiquitous and densely populated. They are also two channels that Amazon, as much as it tries, will likely never significantly penetrate as it has parts of the supercenter. Amazon Fresh, to date, has been a more expensive choice for many consumers, limiting its appeal to the broad stretch of society that most frequents traditional supermarkets. Instead, traditional, large format supermarkets have experienced more share loss from the many new types of retailers now offering grocery goods, the most effective of which has been Walmart supercenters.

On the surface, it may seem puzzling for Walmart to introduce a format that supercenters have spent much of the past two decades bankrupting. However, among the mixed set of retailers offering grocery items today, Walmart's Neighborhood Markets should be a strong competitor. Neighborhood Markets have a smaller, more cost-effective format than large-chain supermarkets. Compared to the dollar/drug emphasis on packaged and frozen goods, they have a greater emphasis on fresh products. Compared to a Dollar General Market, Dollar General's larger store format, a Neighborhood Market has a greater proportion of space dedicated to grocery goods.

Essentially, starting with a clean slate, Neighborhood Markets appear to have reduced the space given to the most heavily contested grocery categories, and emphasized the fresh category where purchases often involve in-person tests for ripeness and freshness, something which Amazon can't compete with.

Dollar stores are also a channel that Amazon is unlikely to impact. Lower income customers account for an even greater part of their customer base than Walmart's, and Amazon's bulk quantities are unlikely to gain traction among customers living paycheck to paycheck. Amazon can't deliver the low-priced, small measure products that dollar stores carry because the costs of each-picking and delivery are significant compared to the products' $1-$10 price points. Online retail is unlikely to impact the dollar stores. While still evolving, the Walmart Express format, larger than traditional dollar stores at 10,000-12,000 square feet, offers produce items that traditional dollar store formats struggle to provide. As such, Express stores look more like the stores of 99 Cents Only, Dollar General Market, or even the private label focused Aldi, and have the potential to fit neatly into this market.

Neighborhood Market and Express stores can also succeed in rural locations, a geography where, due to low population density, Amazon Fresh is likely dead on arrival. These new channels position Walmart well against both its current brick-and-mortar and online competitors. Against Amazon, lower prices and faster delivery times are made possible through Walmart's already extensive distribution system and by relying on customers for last mile delivery. For online customers motivated by price and service, this is a compelling offering. Against supermarkets, Neighborhood Markets' tailored assortment and ready access to a much greater array of CPG and general merchandise items through the supercenter tether is important. By moving center store categories online via the tether, the concept is in some ways similar to the robotized center store we believe is the future for supermarkets. In time, Walmart may even adopt the Drive format as well. Against dollar stores, convenient package pickup and creating access to an online assortment for low-income customers are important differentiators.

Capital Investment Required is Enormous

But what will it take to make this happen? What does Walmart need to build in order to have a store-based eCommerce fulfillment model accomplish what Amazon's delivery model has already achieved? As Walmart wants to duplicate the grocery retail landscape that surrounds its supercenters, exploring this landscape is a good place to start. Figure 6.27 details the existing grocery retail landscape and the key per-store inputs in each channel: employees, capital expenditures, and inventory.

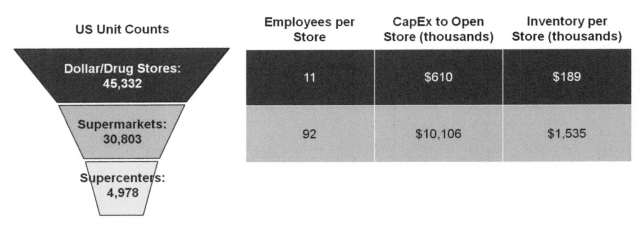

US Unit Counts	Employees per Store	CapEx to Open Store (thousands)	Inventory per Store (thousands)
Dollar/Drug Stores: 45,332	11	$610	$189
Supermarkets: 30,803	92	$10,106	$1,535
Supercenters: 4,978			

Figure 6.27 Sources: WRDS, *Food Retailing Industry Speaks*, by Food Marketing Institute, various years; Company Reports. Notes: Independents are included in supermarkets, but not included in Dollar/Drug as being less likely to carry a competitive grocery selection. Instead, Dollar General, Dollar Tree, Family Dollar, Fred's, and Ninety-Nine Cents Only were included in dollar store counts, and Walgreen's, Rite-Aid, and CVS were included in drug store counts. Employees per store, CapEx, and Inventory numbers based on average amounts for past years for publicly available comparables.

Ignoring Walmart's low penetration rates in California and New England, and assuming that owning a national supermarket and dollar store chain will get Walmart most of the way to full eCommerce coverage in its store pickup model, we estimate that Walmart would need to operate 5,000 Neighborhood Markets and 15,000 Express stores. Taking into account the ratios in Figure 6.27, and Walmart's 2013 count of Neighborhood Markets and Express stores, Walmart would need to hire 600 thousand additional employees—almost half again as many as the 1.4 million employees that currently work in its supercenters. It would also have to build or acquire almost all of the 15,000 Express stores it needs and over 4,600 Neighborhood Markets. This amounts to a capital expenditure of over $55 billion, and a net working capital investment of $6 billion, using average channel inventory, receivables, and payables per store numbers (summarized in Figure 6.28).

(millions)	CapEx/Store	Inventory/ Store	Receivables / Store	Payables/ Store	Total Cap Ex	Net Working Capital
Express Stores	$0.61	$0.36	$0.03	$0.12	$9,207	$4,052
Neighborhood Markets	$10.11	$1.44	$0.45	$1.47	$47,031	$1,963

Figure 6.28

This $60 billion asset investment amounts to almost two-thirds again as much as Walmart US' $98.7 billion in total assets in 2013, and doesn't include any additional expenses such as new distribution centers to serve the incremental volume or pre-opening expenses. Amazon, by contrast, served all of North America very well in 2013 with only $26 billion in total assets. Without a doubt, Walmart's proposed model is asset intensive.

Operationally, Walmart's plan may also pose challenges. Walmart's US operations have always centered on large-format stores, and the move to smaller stores raises questions about Walmart's ability to fit them into its existing structure when the definition of a store manager goes from managing hundreds of associates to managing a handful. It appears that Walmart will fold these smaller stores into the operating structure of the supercenters. Headquarters will merchandise the Express stores based on POS and zip code data collected by the supercenters and similar data collected by Walmart.com. Hiring and other administrative tasks will be performed by the supercenter. Is this the best structure for smaller stores, though? Could they respond better to local market characteristics with more autonomy? Unlike a supercenter that sees a huge number of customers a week, and where customers will go a month between store visits, Walmart Express stores may see the same local customers every day, and associates will likely get to know them very well. Will small stores be able to respond to these customers' needs if they are tightly controlled? While new to the US, small stores aren't necessarily new to Walmart. Walmart de Mexico Bodega stores are built in 4,000 square feet, 16,000 square feet, and 40,000 square feet formats. While still too early to draw any comparisons, it will be interesting to see how much these stores share with Walmart's US small formats.

As far as creating the new fulfillment infrastructure, Walmart already has many pieces of it in operation, though at a much smaller scale. A sizable portion of eCommerce orders are already picked and packed in Walmart supercenters and then shipped directly to customers' homes. Site-to-store orders are also picked in the store, and all Neighborhood Markets already have Site-to-store capabilities.[355] Walmart already has three broad-assortment eCommerce-only fulfillment centers. The company will have to make those programs more efficient and expand them to more stores, but the only really new part of the proposed system will be using smaller trucks to take cross-docked pallets and supercenter picked-and-prepared items from supercenters to smaller formats. Given Walmart's ownership of its transportation fleet, it has the expertise in-house to accomplish this.

Can Walmart's Current Store Models Handle eCommerce?

Walmart's current share of online retail is small, and eCommerce makes up less than 2% of the company's total sales. If Walmart achieves its expanding eCommerce goals, and its customers begin to look like Amazon customers, could its stores handle that kind of online volume? While current stores have Walmart.com service desks, the business is still small. What would a Neighborhood Market or an Express store look like as an eCommerce distribution hub? And how would it compare to Amazon's shipping model?

For this analysis, we have assumed that Walmart and Amazon are, or in the near future will be, equally efficient at getting product within a few miles of their intended customers. For Amazon, this is generally a UPS or FedEx distribution center, though, in the future, will be Amazon's own fulfillment centers or possibly even a USPS destination delivery unit (DDU), or, in other words, a local post office. For Walmart, this is any of its supercenters or proposed Neighborhood Market and Express stores. While site-to-store orders today reach the store both on Walmart's own trailers and through third-party carriers, we believe that in the future online orders will travel to these stores not through third-party carriers, but through Walmart's own supply chain. Dot-com distribution centers could be co-located with general merchandise or grocery distribution centers, or less-than-truckload loads could be consolidated at Walmart's Center Point facilities. We think this is a fair assumption as Amazon is extending its fulfillment network closer to major cities, and Walmart is building more eCommerce-specific fulfillment centers to layer on top of its massive existing distribution network. This means that the difference in cost and convenience will really come down to the last mile delivery of customers' orders.

With new fulfillment centers, rapidly growing Prime membership, and competitive pressure from Walmart's new distribution model, we believe that all online orders will look like Prime orders. In other words, two-day Prime-type shipping is the new normal for Amazon, and every other online general merchandise retailer. As detailed in a Deutsche Bank report, Prime shipping costs are driven by the need to use Air and Premium 2-day shipping options, resulting in an average shipping cost per item in 2012 of $5.50.[356] If Amazon already had a far flung, optimally balanced fulfillment network and used only Premium 2-day shipping with no Air shipping, the major cost lever under its control, Amazon's shipping cost per item would still be $4.41. In the event that Amazon controls more of its outbound supply chain, and begins delivering every order directly to a USPS DDU, its last mile fulfillment cost per item could be as low as $1.20 cents considering current Parcel Select rates, estimated Amazon volume discounts, and Prime bundling rates. Because this possibility, as well as the possibility of delivering Amazon packages nationwide via Fresh vans, is so far out in the future, will likely remain an urban-centered initiative, and depends to a large extent on Amazon first successfully out-competing Walmart's proposed new fulfillment system, we don't consider it in any of our estimates.

By contrast, Walmart's Express and Neighborhood Market anchored delivery model is much more cost effective, and may be able to provide package pick-up for between forty and fifty cents per item—a cost 90% less than Amazon's. We've looked at two states of the world in Figure 6.29, one in which Walmart customers look like regular Amazon shoppers, and one in which they resemble Prime customers, with the difference being in the number of items ordered online and the bundle rate. Of the two, however, we feel that, given free store pick-up and fast delivery in Walmart's proposed distribution network, its customers' online purchase behavior will more closely resemble current Amazon Prime behavior.

Walmart eCommerce, In-store Pick-up Model	Express Format		Neighborhood Market Format	
Online-Ordered Items per Store per Year	Non-Prime Behavior	Prime Behavior	Non-Prime Behavior	Prime Behavior
Trade Area, population	10,000	10,000	35,000	35,000
Percentage of population under 18	23.5%	23.5%	23.5%	23.5%
Trade Area, population over 18	7,650	7,650	26,775	26,775
Online-ordered items per customer per year	3.6	26.7	3.6	26.7
Online-ordered items per store per year	27,540	204,255	96,390	714,893
Space Required In Store	Non-Prime Behavior	Prime Behavior	Non-Prime Behavior	Prime Behavior
Online-ordered items per store per year	27,540	204,255	96,390	714,893
Average Days packages wait in-store for pick-up	2	2	2	2
Average items waiting for pick-up in store on any day	151	1,119	528	3,917
Average packed item volume, cubic feet	0.8	0.8	0.8	0.8
Package Space required in-Store, cubic feet	119	886	418	3,099
Storage Rack maximum height, feet	6	6	6	6
Square Feet Required in Store for Packages	20	148	70	517
2:1 overhead space required for package space	40	295	139	1,033
Total Square Feet	60	443	209	1,550
Rent per square foot per year	$ 7.4	$ 7.4	$ 14.0	$ 14.0
Annual Rent Expense per store for online-ordered items	$ 444	$ 3,293	$ 2,925	$ 21,695
Employee Time Required to Service Online-Ordered Items	Non-Prime Behavior	Prime Behavior	Non-Prime Behavior	Prime Behavior
Online-ordered items per store per year	27,540	204,255	96,390	714,893
Bundle Rate	15%	25%	15%	25%
Online orders per store per year	23,409	153,191	81,932	536,169
Associate Time Required to service customer (minutes)	3	3	3	3
Associate Time Required to service customers (hours)	1,170	7,660	$ 4,097	$ 26,808
Average Hourly Associate Wage, no fringe	$ 10.76	$ 10.76	$ 10.76	$ 10.76
Associate Wages to service online order pick-up per store	$ 12,594	$ 82,417	$ 44,079	$ 288,459
Cost per Item	Non-Prime Behavior	Prime Behavior	Non-Prime Behavior	Prime Behavior
Rent Expense	$ 444	$ 3,293	$ 2,925	$ 21,695
Associate Wages	$ 12,594	$ 82,417	$ 44,079	$ 288,459
Total Cost	$ 13,038	$ 85,710	$ 47,004	$ 310,154
Items	27,540	204,255	96,390	714,893
Orders	23,409	153,191	81,932	536,169
Cost per Item	$ 0.47	$ 0.42	$ 0.49	0.43
Cost per Order	$ 0.56	$ 0.56	$ 0.57	0.58
Operational Metrics	Non-Prime Behavior	Prime Behavior	Non-Prime Behavior	Prime Behavior
Package Pick-up hours per day	12	12	12	12
Package Pick-up days per year	365	365	365	365
Average Packages Picked-up per hour	5	35	19	122
Store Square Feet	12,000	12,000	40,000	40,000
Percent of Store Required for Online Pick-up	0.5%	3.7%	0.5%	3.9%

Figure 6.29 Sources: Trade Area Population based on stated 4,500 and 8,000 Trade Area populations for Dollar General and Family Dollar respectively, and reflects Express' larger store size. Prime and non-Prime items ordered per year based on numbers from Sandler, Ross et. al, "Moving Closer to Customers—The Good, Bad, & Not At All Ugly," *Deutsche Bank,* March 22, 2013. Average package size estimated from category unit shares of Amazon.com as estimated by eDataSource and reported by Internet Retailer, and from observed package sizes delivered. Rent Expense reflects Dollar General's rent per square foot assuming a 90% selling square foot ratio. Walmart average hourly associate wage from Walmart Sustainability: http://www.walmartstores.com/sites/sustainabilityreport/2007/associatesWages.html.

Of course, there are limits to this model. The biggest assumptions are that everyone over the age of 18 in a trade area shops at Walmart.com exactly as they currently do at Amazon today, and opts to pick up all of their online orders at a Walmart store rather than have them delivered to their homes. Given the penetration rates of supermarkets, dollar, and drug stores in North America today (99%, 51%, and 65% respectively),[357] and Amazon's penetration rate of 45% of Americans over 18, this is ambitious, but may not be too far off.

Given the scalability of Walmart's model—both up and down—it doesn't really matter, though. The major cost in the model is associate time, which is variable. If customer behavior looks more like that of a regular Amazon customer, or if a Walmart Express or Neighborhood Market's online order penetration is only a fraction of their trade areas; Walmart could use the same locker system that Amazon is experimenting with. At the lowest service level, customers could be asked to find their own packages among the pick-up racks and checkout using the standard lanes. If not a locker or self-service model, the service desk could be staffed with an associate call button rather than a dedicated employee. As a sensitivity check on the possibility of low volumes, if customer order pick-up took six minutes rather than the three we've modeled, the cost per item is eighty cents to a dollar—still significantly less than Amazon. If scale benefits, such as a constantly staffed service desk, or technology benefits enable Walmart to bring pick-up time down to two minutes, the cost per item would be around thirty cents.

We also assume that Walmart and Amazon will have the same cost to get an item to the customer fulfillment stage: store pick-up for Walmart and a hand-off to a third-party carrier for Amazon. In reality, Walmart's online orders will likely travel more miles before the customer fulfillment stage begins, but we don't expect this to have much of a cost impact. Because Walmart is delivering online orders to a large number of stores inside an urban area, rather than to a comparatively small amount of carefully located fulfillment centers outside of a city like Amazon, Walmart online orders will have to travel a few extra miles to reach the fulfillment stage. However, Walmart's online orders are traveling these miles on already established delivery routes, and depending on how full Walmart's trailers and small-store trucks currently are, may not necessitate extra trips. If they do add enough volume to require more trips, the cost of their delivery may be partly covered by the creation of a more responsive supply chain as discussed earlier. Assuming Walmart doesn't catch up to Amazon's 52 US fulfillment centers (as of the end of 2013), online orders will also likely have to travel farther to get into Walmart's supply chain. However, as mentioned previously, less than truckload online orders could be consolidated at Center Point facilities, and since Walmart controls its own inbound freight, online orders could be backhauled into Walmart's store delivery network, again reducing the cost of delivery. We also have not attributed any capital costs to Walmart's in-store online fulfillment service areas, but don't expect the costs to be large enough to materially influence the outcome.

Walmart may need to worry about the program becoming too successful. Amazon is famous for its logistics flexibility, using headquarters workers in the past and RV campers today to satisfy holiday daily order volume that at peak can be as much as 9x Amazon's average order volume.[358] Fulfillment centers are more flexible than stores, and can respond to holiday demand with just-in-time deliveries from vendors and by increasing the workforce to keep items moving out of the storage bins. Walmart doesn't control its customers' order pick-up however, and its retail stores have less ability to adjust to demand. We have modeled for average order volume, and during the holidays, Walmart may have to respond with the holiday tactics it has always used, like trailers in the parking lot, to accommodate extra order volume. We have accounted for neither the reduction in customer service nor any added cost such a solution entails.

With eCommerce still growing much faster than brick-and-mortar commerce, average order volume is likely to increase. At what point this becomes onerous on the store and disruptive to the customer is difficult to predict. Retailers like AutoZone have been running sizable, staffed warehouses akin to package pickup locations inside their stores for years. In any case, penetration rates and average customer behavior have some time to go before they look like the model detailed above. Of course, shipping savings of almost $4 per item may help them get there faster.

The bottom line is that online orders are additive: they will fit on the trucks, associates will stow them, and customers will come to the stores to pick them up. Despite being excited by the possibilities opened up by these smaller stores, however, Walmart is approaching growth cautiously, with only 150 small format stores planned for 2014. In fact, Walmart has always been slow to expand its smaller formats. The Neighborhood Market format has been around since 1999, yet over the past 14 years,

Walmart has only built 300 units. This is likely because the returns profile for a Neighborhood Market look like those of a supermarket, rather than the far more profitable supercenters.

Commenting on Neighborhood Markets' slow expansion, Jay Fitzsimmons, a Walmart SVP, said "It takes the same number of food managers to run a Neighborhood Market as it does a Supercenter, and of the two, we'd rather open Supercenters. We are also constrained by space in the distribution centers, and Supercenters are the best use of that scarce resource."[359] Even so, in recent years, Walmart has grown its Neighborhood Market store base while major supermarket chains have shrunk theirs (Figure 6.30). Compared to the total number of Walmart supercenters, however, the number of Neighborhood Markets is still small.

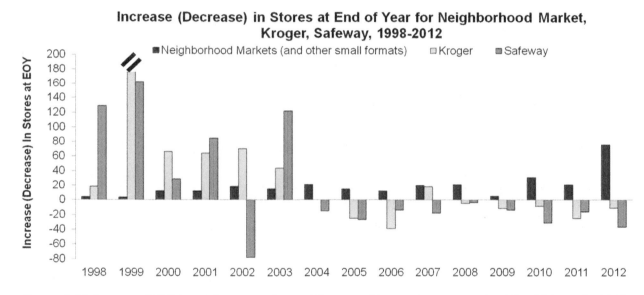

Figure 6.30 Sources: WRDS and Company Annual Reports. Notes: Kroger acquired Fred Meyer in 1999, Safeway acquired Dominick's in 1998, Carr-Gottstein and Randall's in 1999, and Genuardi's in 2001.

With Neighborhood Markets now tethered to supercenters, the possibility of selling additional general merchandise items and online orders through Neighborhood Markets raises their returns profile considerably, just as the supercenters' combined grocery and general merchandise operations were so compelling. Using a mix of Safeway's, Walmart's, and Amazon's financials focused on the retail business, we modeled what kind of online volume it would take per store to give a supermarket the same ROIC as a Walmart supercenter under three states of the world: one where

Walmart keeps the entire fulfillment cost advantage over Amazon, one in which it shares it equally with customers, and one in which the company is very price competitive and gives it all to the customer. For each scenario respectively, a Neighborhood Market would have to fulfill 170,000, 215,000, and 295,000 online-ordered items per year. These numbers fit within the bounds we would expect to see from a Neighborhood Market as defined by our in-store eCommerce model, and we believe them to be achievable. Dollar stores already have a higher ROIC than a Walmart supercenter, and online order fulfillment would only improve their returns.

Fulfilling online orders through stores significantly changes the returns of the supermarket-like Neighborhood Markets, and Walmart does report that it's willing and able to ramp its store openings up considerably if the 2014 buildout confirms their assumptions. Still, Walmart doesn't have much time to make up its mind. Pre-merger and at their peak, Dollar General, Family Dollar, and Dollar Tree opened about 1,300 stores per year between the three chains; with Dollar General estimating that only 14,000 potential locations remain for dollar stores. Walmart will either need to get started quickly to achieve its vision, or be ready to acquire one of the dollar store chains whose smaller store formats may not be ideal for what Walmart has in mind.

The risk to acting quickly is that Walmart could be left holding a large operation that the customer just doesn't want. The big bet is that, to save a few dollars, customers will give up delivery to their door and pick up their packages somewhere else. This is not so outlandish a proposition as it may first appear. Amazon has found throughout its history that lowering delivery cost drives increased purchases, and free shipping has been the company's best marketing tool. By reducing the cost of shipping through store-based fulfillment, Walmart is really just borrowing a page from Amazon's book. In addition, changes to the United States Postal Service may mean that customers have to pick up their packages from non-home locations anyways. One can also draw a comparison to the rise of big box office supplies retailers. By relying on self-service to fuel lower prices, these retailers attracted customers in droves and put the older, personal service stationery shops out of business. Finally, there's the fact that 50% or more of the online orders at Walmart and many other brick-and-mortar retailers are fulfilled in-store. The future might already be here.

Conclusion: A Walmart or an Amazon Retail Future?

Walmart's strategy epitomizes the framework we believe retailers should adopt. The company has identified the threats it faces, both from eCommerce and from brick-and-mortar retailers. In responding to these threats, it has drawn on the unique advantages it has relative to other retailers: its enormous footprint and sophisticated logistics systems. Walmart's implementation of the "Shrink and Transform the Format" strategy includes major changes to its TIPS assets to create a more value-oriented method of delivering eCommerce orders to customers. These TIPS assets changes are summarized in Figure 6.31.

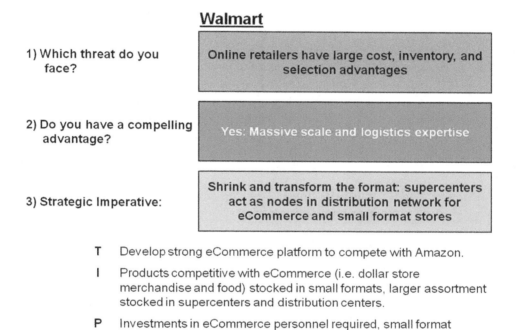

Figure 6.31

The transformation that Walmart must undergo highlights the risks and costs of a "Shrink and Transform the Format" strategy. Unlike the other strategies we discuss in this book, this strategy requires retailers to make large investments in further store assets and take bets on new operating models that often include competencies that brick-and-mortar retailers may not possess to a great degree, such as the technology and management expertise to run an Amazon-like eCommerce operation. While Walmart's plan looks great on paper, there are many reasons to doubt that Walmart will be able to execute against this plan. Currently, Walmart lacks the TIPS assets to fulfill this strategy. It doesn't have a significant number of small stores and hasn't embraced the wide assortment provided by numerous third party sellers. The user experience on Walmart.com is nothing to rave about after several years of heavy investment. Even if Walmart deploys the right TIPS assets, customer acceptance is not guaranteed, and Walmart will have to work hard to make the package pickup process easy for customers, unlike the current checkout experience at its supercenters. While Amazon scores highly in customer satisfaction, Walmart is one of the lowest-rated retailers in America. Walmart has only recently committed to this strategy and its implementation has been conservatively-paced; success may take years to evaluate. Meanwhile, the company is certainly a sick patient; its historic strength in rural locations has eroded and its cost advantages have evaporated. The cure suggested by this plan may not only be too late, but it may be impossible for Walmart to execute given its culture and traditions.

If Walmart does successfully implement the "Shrink and Transform the Format" strategy, Walmart's and Amazon's visions of the future of retail are not necessarily in direct conflict, at least in the near future. Supermarkets and dollar stores today are already at least marginally profitable, and that's not likely to change soon. Walmart's customer base, especially as it moves into dollar stores, will continue to be lower-income, while Amazon's leans towards higher income customers—especially in its Prime and Fresh programs. It's entirely possible that these two demographics will prefer, either for cost, safety, security, or convenience reasons, to shop differently.

This is not to say that both retailers aren't trying to move into each other's markets. Amazon's Lockers have the potential to bring its services to lower-income communities, while Walmart's To Go grocery service is clearly after the same market as Amazon Fresh. In that pursuit, Walmart continues to grow its online assortment and its online tools. Today, Walmart has five million SKUs available online compared to 2 million SKUs a year ago. 80% of these SKUs are from third-party partners like Wayfair. By comparison, Amazon has over 230 million items—consisting partly of large third-party sellers like Wayfair, but also of small, independent sellers' offerings, a vendor group Walmart has not yet indicated its interest in pursuing. Walmart remains heavily focused on price online, and it states that over 70% of the time, Walmart will have the lowest price on any item in its assortment online—effectively bringing EDLP to online retail. This price focus may be where Walmart wants to remain, for now at least.

Instead of building out expensive distribution centers to replicate Amazon's extraordinary selection, Walmart, and its deal-oriented customers, may be better served by a focus on price within a narrower assortment. The story of Levi's jeans coming to Walmart, where Levi's created a Signature line with a lower price point and lower quality exclusively for the massive retailer is illuminating.[360] Walmart has an unrivalled ability to negotiate with suppliers for deals that are valuable to its customers. By expanding assortment online beyond the supercenter, but keeping it much smaller than Amazon's, Walmart would reap the advantages of an *almost*-endless aisle, such as entering new categories that can't be supported in-store, but also manage to funnel volume into a more limited set of SKUs. Limiting the online assortment means that Walmart could build smaller, cheaper eCommerce distribution centers than Amazon, and build them more quickly. Limiting assortment also means that Walmart could concentrate its vendors and better predict demand, and so cut better deals with suppliers who, in turn, could set up more efficient, predictable production. The end result would be that for products sold by both Walmart and Amazon, Walmart.com would have the cheaper base price in addition to any fulfillment advantages, but consumers would lack the enormous option set found at Amazon. For a low-income customer base that will be increasingly price-focused, and likely cares more about getting the best deal on a needed item rather than being offered a wide variety of choices, this is a win.

Along this same line, rather than continuing its fight to enter major urban environments, Walmart could cede these areas to Amazon and instead concentrate on its more rural and exurban populations. With their lower population density, these areas are most costly for Amazon and its third-party carriers to service, and Amazon Fresh will have a difficult time ever taking root. At the same time, Walmart's new formats give it a strong challenge to Dollar General.

Starting in this way certainly doesn't mean ending here. Walmart's bottom-of-the-pyramid, rurally focused approach bested Kmart, and refining its eCommerce abilities in its low income and/or rural demographic, at a more cost-effective scale, could lay the foundation for a bigger push against Amazon later. For Walmart to compete against Amazon in urban and higher-income markets, it will need a format that can enter these cities and that appeals to these shoppers. Neighborhood Markets may be part of the answer, and visits to Walmart's new supercenters in Washington, DC certainly feel like higher-end experiences, but outside of Chicago and DC Walmart has had trouble penetrating urban environments. The still-nascent Express stores could be part of the answer as well, but if, like dollar stores, they focus on frozen meals, they will have trouble winning over public health advocates. Instead, we believe Walmart should bring back its now-closed Marketside format, which focused on providing a quick stop to pick up fresh and prepared items, and consider how Marketside could fit into its new fulfillment model. Bringing fresh produce to urban food deserts is hard to criticize, and easy access to healthy prepared meals is something that upper income customers value as well. Coupled with the supercenter tether, this is the closest format to what we consider to be the future of grocery.

Whatever path Walmart chooses in its execution of this strategy, if it is successful, Amazon's positioning in the market is at considerable risk. To date, Amazon has been the online retailer with the best prices, broadest assortment, and superior service. Amazon has been able to be all three because there has been no online retailer capable of competing with it. With a new Walmart becoming more price-competitive, and beginning to offer a service level that fits neatly into its customers' everyweek lives, Amazon's advantage could be whittled down to just its assortment.

Chapter 7

Skating to Where the Puck is Going to Be

In the previous chapter, we wondered whether anyone was safe from the online threat. In the next two chapters, we'll examine two retailers, who, for a variety of reasons, occupy very defensible positions that provide generalizable lessons for other retailers. PetSmart is one of the fortunate companies that we believe are mostly protected from an online threat. The pet product vertical (by which we mean pet food, supplies, accessories, and services) does not lend itself to online retail. For one thing, pet food, the largest category in the industry, is bulky, heavy, and expensive to ship. The premium brands of pet food that PetSmart specializes in have largely refused to enter distribution channels outside of the pet superstores, veterinarians, and independent pet stores. While the industry suffers from supply chain leaks like any other industry, pet food's expensive shipping costs blunt the impact. Meanwhile, the second largest category in the industry, services, requires in-person, physical fulfillment. PetSmart has created an unrivaled service organization in its industry, encompassing an array of offerings delivered in-store. Finally, non-food products, like pet toys, are often the result of impulse buys arising from a store visit. Because of a mix of product characteristics, consumer buying behavior, and forward-looking TIPS investments, PetSmart is relatively insulated from an online competitive threat, barring an unlikely massive shift to online purchases of pet food. PetSmart serves as a fantastic example of how a retailer capitalized on the nature of its product vertical to create stores that are largely safe from the online threat, a prerequisite for the ability to adopt the "Enhancing the Value of the Box" strategy. This chapter will focus on the actions that went into creating this defensible store base.

Given PetSmart's defensible stores, it's not surprising that the company has performed well in recent years, with high same-store sales growth and returns on invested capital, and expanding margins, as shown in Figure 7.1.

	FY 2005	FY 2006	FY 2007	FY 2011	FY 2012	FY 2013
Same-store sales growth	4.2%	5.0%	2.4%	5.4%	6.3%	2.7%
ROIC (Op Leases Not Capitalized)	17.9%	15.1%	13.9%	19.3%	25.8%	27.4%
Gross Margin	31.2%	30.9%	30.7%	29.7%	30.7%	30.8%
Operating Expense Ratio	22.9%	23.3%	23.2%	21.4%	21.0%	20.7%

Figure 7.1 Sources: Company reports. Note: Other revenue from Banfield operation left out from Gross Margin and Operating Expense Ratio.

PetSmart has been able to achieve these results through a well-executed strategy that simultaneously built and rode an industry wave. PetSmart's story is one of diagnosing industry changes and competitive concerns, and then creating brilliant solutions to stay ahead of the curve. We believe other retailers seeking to defend their brick-and-mortar assets can learn much from PetSmart's creation of its service organization, though we acknowledge that PetSmart was able to accomplish its service-based approach in special circumstances.

The Humanization of Pets and Its Effect on the Pet Industry

The pet industry has greatly benefitted from an overall increase in the level of pet ownership in the US. The percentage of households with at least one pet has grown over the last two decades, while at the same time the number of pets owned per household has also expanded (Figure 7.2). Simultaneously, there has been an increase in the amount households spend on their pets in total and likely per pet as well.

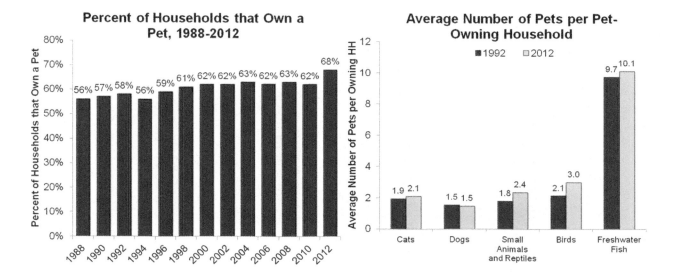

Figure 7.2 Sources: Compiled from Ryan, Amy, 'PetSmart Inc, Initiating Coverage with a Pawsitive Rating,' *Oppenheimer & Co. Inc.,* November 8, 2005, accessed via *Thomson One*, August 30, 2013 and APPA press releases.

This first trend has seen the level of pet ownership expand from 56% of US households in 1988 to 62% in 2010, and, as the effects of the most recent recession wore off, 68% of US households in 2012. The reasons behind these increasing levels of pet ownership center on the changing demographics of the United States. As baby boomers formed households, they often included pets as part of their plans. Then, as the boomers' children grew up and moved out, boomers often continued to keep pets, or bought pets for the first time, for the companionship they provided. The boomers' children, meanwhile, "delaying marriage and putting their careers first," bought pets for the same reason.[361] Pets have become a replacement and a substitute for children. Scientific research continues to validate the health benefits of animal companionship.[362] And, indeed, both the number of cats and the number of dogs now exceeds the number of children in the United States (Figure 7.3).

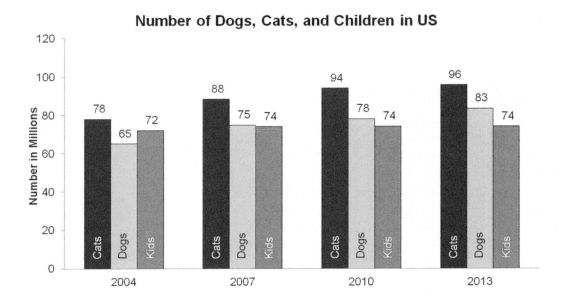

Figure 7.3 Sources: Ryan, Amy, 'PetSmart Inc, Initiating Coverage with a Pawsitive Rating,' *Oppenheimer & Co. Inc.,* November 8, 2005, accessed via *Thomson One*, August 30, 2013 and Mandel, Mark, 'Initiate Coverage with a Buy Rating and $53 Price Target,' *ThinkEquity,* October 17, 2011, accessed via *Thomson One*, August 30, 2013 and Ciccarelli, Scot, 'PetSmart, Inc.—Compelling Long-Term Growth Potential with Some Downside Protection,' *RBC Capital Markets*, July 25, 2011, accessed via *Thomson One*, August 30, 2013 and "Pet Industry Market Size & Ownership Statistics," *American Pet Products Association,* accessed on September 1, 2013 and available at http://www.americanpetproducts.org/press_industrytrends.asp and US Census population numbers.

As pets replaced children in the household lives of many Americans, pets were increasingly humanized. Figure 7.4 displays many examples of this humanization, such as the increasing number of dogs who now sleep inside as opposed to the backyard, the number of animals who receive treats throughout the day or gifts at some point during the year, even the number of pets dressed up for Halloween (15.1% in 2012 compared to 11% in 2007).[363] Pet owners are even putting thought into what to do after their pet dies (and so creating new opportunities for the pet industry), with 17% of dog owners and 8% of cat owners considering cremation and an urn, amid other burial options such as caskets and headstones.[364]

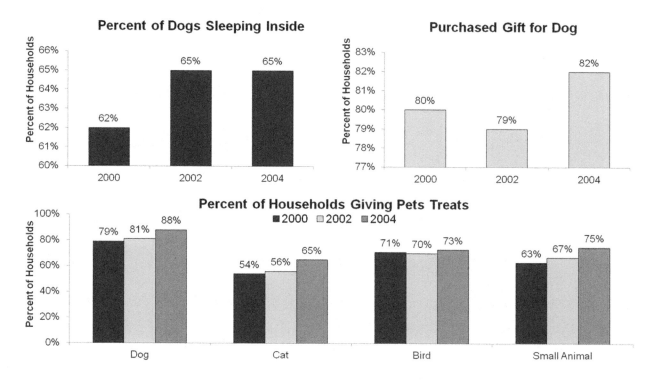

Figure 7.4 Source: Ryan, Amy, 'PetSmart Inc, Initiating Coverage with a Pawsitive Rating,' *Oppenheimer & Co. Inc.,* November 8, 2005, accessed via *Thomson One*, August 30, 2013.

This substitution of pets for children has resulted in an increasing amount of household spend on pets, even through recessions. From 1984 to 2008, the amount US households have spent on pets has increased at a 7.2% CAGR. Even during recessions, households continued to increase spending on pet necessities such as food, while decreasing spending on more elective products and services such as supplies (e.g. toys, accessories) and veterinarian visits (Figure 7.5).

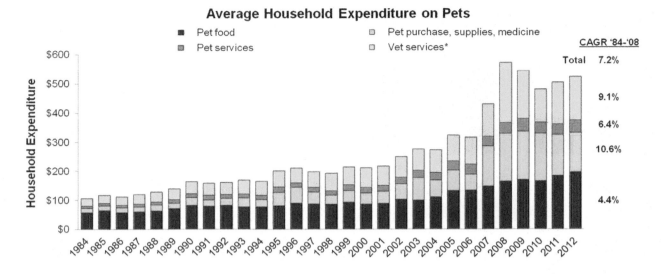

Figure 7.5 Sources: US Bureau of Labor Statistics, 'Pets' for All Consumer Units for time series 1984-2012 and Henderson, Steven, 'Spending on Pets: "Tails" from the Consumer Expenditure Survey,' *Beyond the Numbers,* Bureau of Labor Statistics, May 2013. Note: *Data includes surgical services at veterinarians, which is not included in the APPA industry total numbers above; *Veterinary spending highly uncertain due to the low percentage of households reporting expenses, as evidenced by the highly variable amount in this category between 2007 and 2008.

To add relevance to these numbers, consider that in 2011, food expenses for the average American were $3,785 per capita. In comparison, for 2012, total reported expenses for the average dog were $1,122, and total reported expenses for the average cat were $602.[365] Pet expenditures in total have gone from only one-half of a percent of a household's total expenditures in 1984 to a full one percent of total expenditures in 2012.

For the pet products industry, this has meant both an increase in the number and variety of products sold (e.g. dog beds, pet costumes, etc.) as well as an increase in the quality and price points of items sold (e.g. organic dog food and treats). This has translated into strong and consistent growth over the last two decades (Figure 7.6). Since 1994, the pet industry has grown at a 6% CAGR, and annual growth has never dipped below 4%.

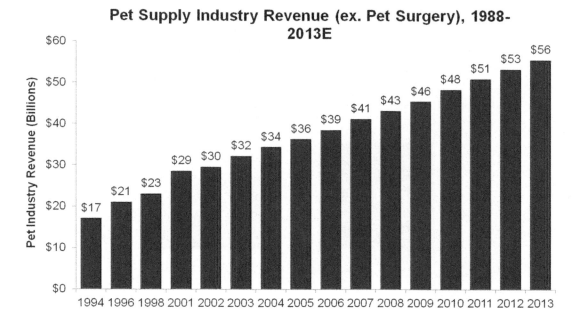

Pet Supply Industry Revenue (ex. Pet Surgery), 1988-2013E

Figure 7.6 Source: "Pet Industry Market Size & Ownership Statistics," *American Pet Products Association,* accessed on September 1, 2013 and available at http://www.americanpetproducts.org/press_industrytrends.asp

The humanization trend has also resulted in the growth of services purchased, as time-starved, traveling, or older pet owners turn to service providers not only for grooming or veterinary care, but also for services such as boarding, day care, and pet-walking. The changing attitudes towards pets and the expansion of pet products and services has led to a shift in the industry from being merely a supply chain for food and litter, to one where products and services have been gaining wallet share. This is apparent in the 10.6% 1984-2008 CAGR for household expenditures on pet products compared to the 4.4% CAGR on pet food shown in Figure 7.5, as well as in the shifting share of industry sales for each category shown in Figure 7.7 where services has gained solidly.

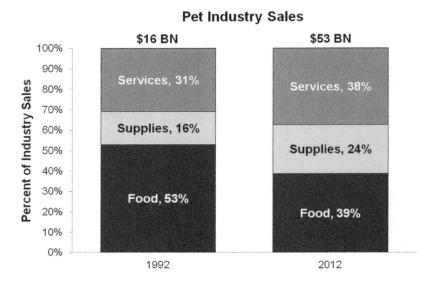

Figure 7.7 Sources: Vroom, Christopher E. and Miller, Barbara E., "PETsMART, Inc.," Alex, Brown & Sons, September 8, 1993, accessed via Thomson One, August 30, 2013 and PetSmart 2012 10K. Note: Excludes surgical veterinary care. Live animal sales (4% of industry sales) included in the 2012 Services category to match adoption costs included in the 1992 Services category, but not broken out separately.

PetSmart, the pioneer of pet supply superstores, has benefitted tremendously from this growth, growing its own sales at a 22% CAGR between 1991 and 2012 (Figure 7.8).

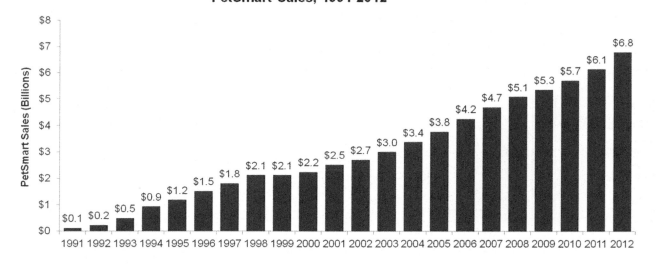

Figure 7.8 Sources: PetSmart Company Reports, accessed via Thomson One, August 30, 2013. Note: Years represent the most closely matched calendar years to fiscal years reported.

The Importance of Premium Pet Food

While food no longer represents a majority of sales in the industry, it has continued to grow as well. The trend towards increasing quality, price points, and selection in the industry began in the food category. In the 1980s and 1990s, high-quality food drew on science-based diets targeted to the breed, overall health, and life-stage of pets; as well as premium ingredients such as lamb or pure chicken meat versus mixed bone and meat meal. Reflecting human trends in food, high-quality pet food began to move towards organics in the 2000s, and today, the highest-quality food offerings include fresh products with limited shelf lives sold out of refrigerators. These trends are shown in the continuing trend of the value growth of pet food outpacing its volume growth (Figure 7.9).

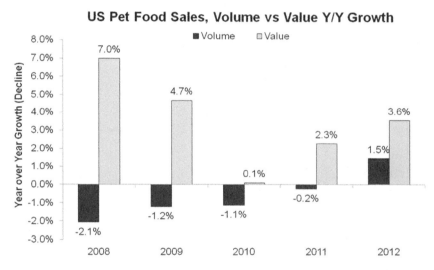

Figure 7.9 Source: "Pet Care in the US," *Euromonitor International,* October 2012.

This evolution in the food category is what originally distinguished pet superstores from other channels like independent pet stores and supermarkets. Premium pet food conveyed a number of advantages for both pets and pet owners when compared to supermarket brands. For the pet, premium food offered "higher caloric density; improved ingredient quality (pure chicken meal versus bone and meat meal); fixed formulation versus varied formulation based on the cost of raw materials; ... improved palatability ... and [improved] skin tone and coat."[366] For the pet owner, "smaller portions are needed, stool volume is reduced because of better digestion [making for easier clean-up] ... and the higher unit price is largely neutralized by the smaller required portions; thus the cost per serving can be less than that of supermarket brands."[367] As pet owners grew to treat their pets more and more like humans (especially dog and cat owners), and became more attentive to their pets' dietary needs and comfort, the premium pet food category became increasingly important to consumers.

Despite the increased customer demand, premium pet food manufacturers chose not to supply grocery stores or mass merchandisers, and restricted sales to specialist pet supply stores and veterinarians. They did so because they thought the premium prices charged for their food lines required a high level of category-specific, knowledgeable service that could convince customers premium food was the right choice for their pet. This level of service was unavailable in the grocery and mass merchandiser channels. Premium pet food manufacturers were confirmed in this belief when Kal-Kan (owned by Mars), attempted to sell its premium *Expert* line in the grocery channel. Despite a $75 million marketing campaign, without in-store service to educate customers on the benefits of the product, Kal-Kan couldn't convince customers to pay twice as much for *Expert* as grocery brands.[368]

Premium pet food was also very important to PetSmart, accounting for 25–30% of its 1992 sales, in addition to driving trips.[369] Indeed, pet food was actually the primary focus of the company's first two stores, which were called *Pet Food Warehouse,* and were completely price-focused. These first stores adopted the warehouse-style design of the era, complete with steel racking, poured concrete floors, and full-case merchandising, offering deep discounts on just food and supplies.

Despite PetSmart's food focus, high-end vendors initially resisted selling to the company. PetSmart overcame this resistance by opening its first stores in Phoenix, where the local distributor was weak, in order to prove that it could both effectively increase sales for premium pet food manufacturers and maintain in-store service levels comparable to specialty pet retailers. PetSmart trained its associates in the differences among premium food brands and lines within a particular brand.[370] Associates maintained and expanded their product knowledge through the "rigorous" PACE (PETsMART Associate Continuing Education) training program. Merchandising and marketing were centralized so that store managers could focus on training associates and delivering a high level of customer service.[371]

These efforts paid off for specialty pet manufacturers. PetSmart offered full lines of premium pet food, with an assortment broader and deeper than traditional small-format pet specialty stores or non-pet-focused supermarkets and warehouse stores. PetSmart's associates introduced their customers to new items they would never have come across elsewhere. This effectively expanded the market for premium and specialty pet products in America. The PetSmart impact is captured in "statistics from the Hills Company, a premium food manufacturer," which "suggested that the market for premium products grew by 40% following the entry of PETsMART into the Atlanta market."[372] Because premium brands didn't invest in advertising, but instead relied on retail distribution to introduce customers to products, PetSmart's education model greatly benefitted premium pet product manufacturers.[373]

PetSmart's success created strong bonds with vendors, leading pet food brands to collaborate with the retailer on marketing strategies for their products.[374] PetSmart's ties to premium pet food manufacturers were also an important defense. Because pets often react adversely to changes to the types and brands of food, once a pet-owner switched up to a premium pet food diet, they could virtually no longer shop in the grocery or mass merchandiser channels, which did not carry these lines.[375] And, with lower prices than the specialty channel, these pet owners were likely to continue to buy their specialty food at PetSmart.

A persistent worry, however, was that as premium pet food grew into a larger category, premium pet food manufacturers would open their distribution to supermarkets and warehouse clubs. However, PetSmart grew so fast—both organically and through acquiring its major competition—that the balance of power in the manufacturer-retailer relationship quickly shifted in PetSmart's favor. Even in its early years, PetSmart was able to leverage its extensive selection of premium brands and knowledgeable customer associates to ensure that it was not dependent on a single brand. In one example, PetSmart lost Nutro-Max in Southern California—the brand with the highest premium share in the state—shortly after entering that market in 1992. Yet PetSmart's growth plans in California remained on target, as PetSmart was able to shift customers to other premium brands and compensate for the loss. While PetSmart's total share of the pet supplies market remained small at around 4% in 1996, its much higher premium share (estimated at 19%) meant that "any move by a competitor like

Hills or Iams to broaden distribution could result in a 15% loss of business if PETsMART dropped the brand," whereas at least one analyst doubted "very much whether PETsMART would lose as much as 3% of its total volume if it [discontinued] one of the premium brands, which each [represented] roughly 8% of its total volume and each [had] a 25–30% share of the premium pet food market."[376] In other words, brands were more dependent on PetSmart than the retailer was on them. Nevertheless, to mitigate the risk of losing a brand, PetSmart also introduced private label options early, rolling out the *Authority* brand in premium food and the *Top Paw* brand for supplies in 1992.

PetSmart's Large Market Share Keeps Premium Food Brands in Channel

After PetSmart had opened the door to premium pet food, a number of clone competitors tried to walk through it. However, competition was slow to get started, perhaps because PetSmart had relied on private funding for its first five years and its early success may have gone unnoticed. In any event, the company had developed a substantial lead on its competition. In 1993, the year PetSmart went public, it operated three times the square footage of Petco (the pet retailer with the most stores) and almost four times as many stores as Petzazz, PetSmart's largest superstore competitor. It was also the only national pet retailer. Major retailers in the pet vertical and their size characteristics in 1993 are shown in Figure 7.10.

Company	Store Count	Average Store Size	Square Footage	Region(s)
PetSmart	72	25,000	1,800,000	West, Southwest, South, Southeast, Central, East
Petzazz	19	22,000	418,000	Midwest
Petstuff	12	18,000	216,000	East
Petco	200	3,000	600,000	South, West, East
Pet Care Superstores		3,000-8,000		Midwest
Pet Supply Plus	30	8,000	240,000	Midwest
Pet Food Warehouse	6	18,000	108,000	Midwest
Premium Pet Mart	3			West
Pet Food Supermarket	7			West

Figure 7.10 Source: Balter, Gary, "PETSMART, INC.," *Donaldson, Lufkin & Jenrette*, September 10, 1993, accessed via *Thomson One,* August 30, 2013.

After its public offering, PetSmart cemented its industry-dominating position by acquiring its closest competition in all-stock transactions. Petzazz was merged into PetSmart in 1994, and PetStuff in 1995. So dominant was PetSmart in this space that PetStuff, which began operations in 1992, was, according to its marketing agency, actually formed specifically to be acquired by PetSmart.[377]

Outside of the pet superstore channel, PetSmart won market share over supermarkets and independent pet retailers through greater (and often exclusive) selection, lower prices, and higher service, and by creating a destination for the emerging market segment of "pet parents." While grocery stores with their mass brands and independent pet stores with their premium products had long co-existed, the arrival of PetSmart, which stocked both these assortments at significantly lower prices, significantly changed the industry. A radical shift in channel share followed PetSmart's rapid expansion, with pet superstores displacing both supermarkets and specialty stores. Supermarkets declined from a 95% share of the pet food market in the mid-80s[378] to a 55% share in the mid-90s,[379] and continue to lose ground into the present day (Figure 7.11).

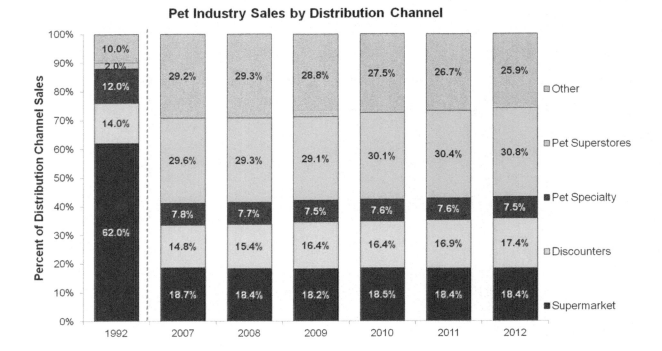

Figure 7.11 Sources: Vroom, Christopher E. and Miller, Barbara E., "PETsMART, Inc.," *Alex, Brown & Sons,* September 8, 1993, accessed via *Thomson One*, August 30, 2013 and Euromonitor International, 2013, Passport GMID. Notes: Other includes non-grocery and non-pet-specific retailing, such as non-store retailing, and veterinary clinics. Discounters includes hypermarkets.

PetSmart's large share of the category killer retail channel, and of the pet supply industry as a whole, helps explain the stickiness of premium brands.

The Advantages of a Category Killer

The characteristics of a category killer superstore (assortment, price, service, and the creation of a destination store) gave PetSmart large advantages over the competing specialty pet and supermarket channels. The small specialty pet stores of the late 1980s were exemplified by Petco's original 3,000 square foot format. These stores carried premium products, virtually no grocery brands, and lacked the space to widely exhibit live animals. Supermarkets and mass merchandisers, for their part, did not devote a substantial amount of space to the pet category, carrying just grocery-brand pet food and little in the way of supplies and accessories. For comparison, the stock-keeping unit (SKU) count in the early 1990s in each of these channels is presented in Figure 7.12.

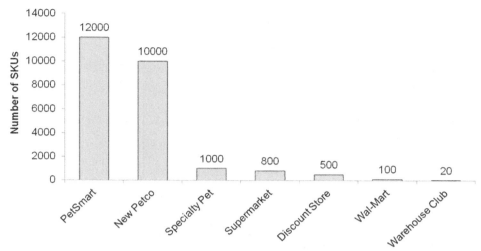

SKU Count in Pet Distribution Channels, Early/Mid 90's

Figure 7.12 Sources: Balter, Gary, "PETSMART, INC.," *Donaldson, Lufkin & Jenrette*, September 10, 1993, accessed via Thomson One, August 30, 2013 and Kully, Thomas, "PETsMART, Inc.," *William Blair & Company*, November 7, 1994, accessed via Thomson One, August 30, 2013.

In addition to the SKU discrepancy, supermarkets were not committed to the pet food department. Despite pet food's growing importance to almost two-thirds of American households, pet food earned a below-average gross margin for the supermarkets and achieved "less-than-optimal inventory turnover," making for a low gross margin return on investment in the category.[380] Pets in the mid-1980s were also only a small part of supermarkets' business, with pet food only accounting for 1.84% of total supermarket sales and pet accessories forming just 0.14%.[381] The pet category's relative unimportance and poor sales, as well as the channel exclusivity of premium pet food manufacturers, perhaps explains why supermarkets did not put up much of a fight to keep their market share.

The humanization of pets and the tailoring of their diets enabled the assortment gap described above to get much larger. From 1988 to 1993, for instance, the number of SKUs in the pet food and supply category increased from 5,000 SKUs to between 8,000 and 10,000 SKUs.[382] SKU counts would continue to expand as the humanization trend continued and as pet superstores helped manufacturers find niches for their products. As a result, independent pet stores and other channels had even more difficulty presenting assortments to rival the pet superstores.

In addition to its assortment advantages at both ends of the spectrum, PetSmart also benefitted from price advantages versus other channels. In premium pet food, the superstores' competitors were smaller pet stores that were independently run or organized in small chains. With their small formats, these stores could not receive direct from manufacturer shipments and often purchased through distributors, resulting in a distributor markup.[383] In addition, small pet stores located closer to town centers and so paid higher rent.[384] With their small formats and low sales volumes, small pet stores did not have as much leverage on their labor costs. These attributes resulted in higher cost structures, and so higher prices, for these small pet stores as compared to PetSmart as shown in the sample pro forma provided in Figure 7.13.

1992	Traditional Pet Store	% Sales	PetSmart	% Sales	Difference
Gross Retail Sales	$203,440		$3,684,000		
Cost of Goods	$122,920	60.4%	$2,696,320	73.2%	
Gross Profit	$80,520	39.6%	$987,680	26.8%	12.8%
Store Op. Expense	$51,000	25.1%	$640,279	17.4%	7.7%
Store Op. Profit	**$29,520**	**14.5%**	**$347,401**	**9.4%**	**5.1%**

Figure 7.13 Source: Vroom, Christopher E. and Miller, Barbara E., "PETsMART, Inc.," *Alex, Brown & Sons,* September 8, 1993, accessed via *Thomson One,* August 30, 2013.

Because supermarkets carried just a fraction of PetSmart's assortment, and none of its premium brands, there wasn't much of an assortment overlap on which to price-compete. Well over half of PetSmart's sales came from product categories not carried by leading competitors. One-third of its sales were in premium products carried mainly by traditional small pet stores and veterinarians who charged much higher prices and 39% of sales consisted of non-branded, less price-sensitive supplies.[385] Even when priced substantially lower than small-format pet stores, these other categories generated much higher margins than grocery-brand pet food, and with pet superstores' high customer service levels, impulse-oriented merchandising, and open invitation to bring pets into the store, upsells to and attachment sales of these categories were frequent. As summarized by one Petco employee, "They'll [customers] come in to just buy dog food and end up buying toys and treats." With these cross-subsidies, PetSmart was able to price its grocery-brand pet food almost 20% less than supermarkets in order to attract customers, and made up the difference through higher-margin attachment sales or by steering customers towards premium pet food.[386]

PetSmart's service offering was also a critical differentiator and needs to be defined in two parts: (1) the product knowledge and salesmanship of its associates and (2) the actual, fee-based services PetSmart came to offer in its stores. Independent pet stores could offer similar levels of product knowledge and help in selecting pet food and products but, due to limited space and lower traffic, could not offer in-store services such as grooming and vet clinics. Supermarkets and mass merchandisers lacked the specialization to train associates in any kind of service. In fee-based pet services, Pet Superstores largely competed against independent contractors[387] and the neighbor's kid. Professionalizing these services at pet superstores contributed to their status as destination stores for pet lovers.

The superstores strengthened their image as destination stores in a number of other ways as well. Pet owners were allowed to bring their pets with them, which created "an atmosphere in which customers [would] stop and swap pet stories, prolonging the visit and increasing the probability of incremental sales."[388] Pet superstores gave pet owners a place to belong with their pets, something supermarkets could not do given that pets are considered a health risk for human food. PetSmart also created "an interactive shopping experience by relying heavily on informational displays, periodic events and active and available assistance by highly trained associates."[389] PetSmart's Discovery Centers and Whisker Cities created stores-within-stores tailored to children and cat owners specifically.[390] In so doing, PetSmart became the store to go to for informed advice and learning opportunities. Petco, for its part, created up-market displays such as a pet treat bar modeled after salad bars for humans, which quickly became an industry standard. Both chains used expanded fish areas, with floor to ceiling tanks on the perimeter of the stores and a tremendous amount of species diversity, to create enthralling displays.

While a fundamental part of its growth story, PetSmart's wide assortment merchandising and price discounting will be familiar to anyone who has seen a category killer at work. What has really distinguished PetSmart, especially in recent years, has been the high service focus of its employees and its ability to leverage its large store size to provide services within its stores. Both of these service offerings have been aided by its customer base's high discretionary income and evolving views on their pets. The services aspect of its business creates traffic and positions PetSmart as a value-added partner to premium brands, and so is where its defense against online retailers rests. Rare among retailers, PetSmart has successfully and consistently introduced services into its stores, and its service organization could be a model for other retailers.

PetSmart's Service Organization

While PetSmart's early names (PetFood Warehouse in 1986, PETsMART in 1989) emphasized the big box aspect of the chain—low prices, wide assortment, no frills, etc.—the company began incorporating services early in its history. In 1988, only two years after its founding, the company began working with local animal welfare groups to hold fundraising and pet adoption events. One year later, in 1989, PETsMART opened its first, store-based full-service grooming salon. In 1992, PETsMART opened its first permanent in-store adoption center and veterinary clinic. In-store pet training programs were introduced in 1994.

Together with these service programs, PetSmart also used these early years to adjust its offering and presentation. The stores remained large and the focus on discounting was still readily apparent—customers bought at prices 10% to 50% below other retail channels, most product was purchased directly from manufacturers and shipped straight to stores, and an everyday-low-pricing (EDLP) policy was in place— but the format had been modified from stark warehouses into a "hybrid retail/warehouse-oriented configuration." In order to create "a specialty store feel," bright lighting and tiled floors had been added to the front halves of the stores where live animals and exotic pet food, supplies, and accessories were sold, while the rear of the stores retained their concrete floors, steel shelving, and trip-driving, price-focused pet food merchandising. As always, the sales floor was staffed by well-trained employees.[391] PetSmart had learned that selling to pet owners was not just about low prices, but was also about the experience and service offered. Due to these renovated stores and services, PetSmart's operating metrics were significantly better than its competitors in the early

90s, with Petzazz stores doing just half the volume of PetSmart's only slightly larger stores[392] and PetStuff unable to match PetSmart prices.[393]

This combined discount and high service model was reaffirmed in the year 2000, when PetSmart introduced a new vision statement "to provide Total Lifetime Care (SM) for every pet, every parent, every time." PETsMART aimed to accomplish this goal by "offering superior products, unmatched services, and superb customer service to pet parents and their pets." PETsMART changed its name to PetSmart in 2005 to signify its move away from the "'mart' mentality" and towards "'smart' solutions."[394] Today, PetSmart's service solutions include PetsHotels for boarding pets (introduced in 2002), day camps where pet owners can drop off their pets when they go to work or need to run errands, grooming services, pet pharmacies and veterinary clinics, pet training classes, and adoption services. We've summarized these service developments in the timeline in Figure 7.14.

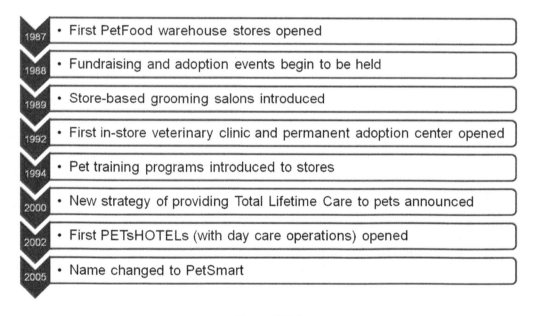

1987 • First PetFood warehouse stores opened

1988 • Fundraising and adoption events begin to be held

1989 • Store-based grooming salons introduced

1992 • First in-store veterinary clinic and permanent adoption center opened

1994 • Pet training programs introduced to stores

2000 • New strategy of providing Total Lifetime Care to pets announced

2002 • First PETsHOTELs (with day care operations) opened

2005 • Name changed to PetSmart

Figure 7.14

PetSmart's renewed service focus as part of its "Total Lifetime Care" vision was just the right response to its first defense, exclusivity in premium brands, coming under threat. On August 11, 1999, Procter & Gamble bought Iams, the largest specialty pet food brand at that time, and declared their intention to grow the brand by expanding distribution.[395] In March of 2000, P&G, in the biggest product launch of its history, delivered Iams products to supermarkets and discount stores nationwide, more than doubling the number of outlets carrying Iams.[396] Iams' market share at the mass channels raced from zero to over 6% within three months, but fell 15% to 20% at specialty stores. This specialty store drop was partly due to the specialty channel losing customers to the convenience of the mass channels, but also to specialty stores ceasing promotion of the Iams brand. While PetSmart shareholders worried Hills' Science Diet (owned by Colgate-Palmolive) would follow Iams into mass channels, Science Diet instead took advantage of the channel switch to encourage specialty stores to make Science Diet "your No. 1 endorsed brand," promising "to ensure our consumer stays in our channel."[397] To date, Iams remains the only major specialty store food brand to move into the mass market. Even so, however, the move by Iams into mass channels was damaging for PetSmart. The company's comp sales fell from mid-single digit gains to barely growing as the effects of Iams' switch, and the dot-com bust, took hold through 2000 (Figure 7.15).

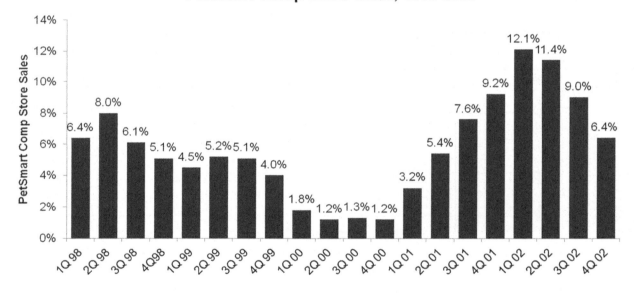

Figure 7.15 Sources: Company Reports.

Total Lifetime Care sought to "align each aspect of [PetSmart's] business with the needs, desires, and aspirations of pet enthusiasts." Services were a cornerstone of this new strategy. In 2000, PETsMART was already the largest provider of professional grooming and pet training in the US, and was working to expand this business by setting up partnerships with pet grooming education institutions to train PETsMART groomers.[398] The company also introduced its new 'Eagle' store refresh that emphasized PetSmart's "highly differentiated training and adoption services."[399] Grooming departments and the new PetsHotel concept were brought to the front of the store and decorated attractively. The Banfield Pet Hospitals, PetSmart's in-store veterinary clinics, were prominently advertised outside the stores. Improvements to the chain's distribution strategy—chiefly the buildout of mixing centers and computerizing inventory and demand planning—enabled PetSmart to reduce the inventory per store by almost half between 1999 and 2003. This created a more efficient operation and also eliminated the need for warehouse-style steel racking to hold large, direct-from-manufacturer deliveries. Consequently, the Eagle reformat allowed for a higher-end specialty feel throughout the store to match the increased focus on service offerings. PetSmart also built on its original Whiskers store-within-store for cat owners and introduced category management into its stores, grouping products by species rather than by product type, and doing deep dives within each category to make sure the merchandise mix was tailored to customer needs and wants.[400] In many ways, the Eagle format was the final stage of the discounter/service provider transformation that began in the early 90s.

PetSmart's renewed emphasis on services also helped make up for lagging same-store sales and productivity issues. The chain was shifting its new stores to a 19,000 square foot format from its traditional 26,000 square foot format to improve store productivity, but the increased focus on services enabled PetSmart to retain many of its larger, older stores by replacing a portion of the selling area with added services space. After the Eagle renovations, older, larger stores with a PetsHotel actually had less selling space than PetSmart's newer, smaller stores. These two formats are compared in Figure 7.16.

	'Eagle'-ized Old Store	New Store Format
Total Square Footage	26,000	19,000
Banfield Vet Clinic	1,800	-
PETsHOTEL	7,500	-
Grooming and Training	700	700
Total Selling Area	**16,000**	**18,300**

Figure 7.16 Sources: Wewer, Dan and Ma, Vivian, "PETsMART, Inc.," CIBC World Markets, August 12, 2003, accessed via Thomson One, September 3, 2013; Rifkin, Alan et. al, "PETsMART, Inc.," Lehman Brothers, November 17, 2003, accessed via Thomson One, August 30, 2013; FY1Q 2002 earnings call; Balter, Gary and Nagel, Brian, "AM CALL: PETM: PETM Sheds Its Fleas," Credit Suisse, April 24, 2002, accessed via Thomson One, August 30, 2013.

Because PetSmart was able to generate materially the same amount of food and supplies sales out of a smaller space in these older stores, services were very much an incremental improvement. Not only did the associated fees generate direct revenue, services replaced unproductive space in the store, drew in new customers, and caused existing customers to increase their trip frequency.[401] PetsHotels had the potential to add 25% to a $5 million annual sales store.[402] In addition, offering services like adoption and pet training cast PetSmart as a knowledgeable educator early on in customers' relationships. This created a "valuable link between PETsMART associates, the customer and the customer's pet that [could] extend beyond the training period, a positive for customer traffic."[403] Referring to the company's larger store formats, CEO Phil Francis commented that they were an "undeniable strategic advantage ... larger stores give us the flexibility to grow our existing services and to test new ones."[404]

This move towards services became even more important as grocery, mass merchandiser, and dollar store channels increasingly moved into the pet category as part of their remerchandising towards baby boomers, and as Petco market areas increasingly overlapped with PetSmart. The emphasis of 'Total Lifetime Care' on specialized services, experiences, products, and the store improvements to support them differentiated PetSmart by solidifying its status as a destination and taking the commodity feel out of its stores.[405] Services also replaced unproductive space and lost Iams sales, provided additional cross-sells to pet owners, and deepened customers' relationships with PetSmart.

Though the benefits are clear and a market need is often present, many retailers have tried to implement services and failed. Understanding how PetSmart implemented the company's services program is as helpful as witnessing its effects. PetSmart's services model is an interesting mix of owning what it can, creating partnerships where it can't own, and finding ways to improve the economics of services that clearly attract customers.

One of the challenges retailers face when trying to offer services is guaranteeing consistent quality, particularly when services are provided by third-party contractors. By directly employing its own groomers, PetSmart overcame this first hurdle. However, the company initially trained these groomers through outside agencies. In 1994, PetSmart brought its grooming training in-house in order to maintain consistency of service, and also began to directly employ and train its own animal trainers as well for obedience school classes. In an effort to quickly implement grooming and training programs in nearly all of its stores as part of the mission to create Total Lifetime Care solutions, PetSmart returned to outside trainers.

PetSmart uses its services to introduce customers to its private label brands early on in their relationship with their pets and throughout their pets' lives. For example, under the *Authority* training system in use at PetSmart, *Authority* private label treats are used as rewards for good pet behavior. Since PetSmart makes higher gross margins on its private label goods than its branded goods, creating loyal customers of its private label brands improves the economics of the service.

PetSmart vet clinics are a fantastic example of how a retailer was able to bring skills it didn't have, and may never have been able to employ directly, into their stores. The vet clinics were originally just wellness clinics—capable of offering low-priced check-ups, vaccinations, heartworm tests, therapeutic foods, and basic operations such as spaying and neutering, but not the full range of veterinary clinic services. In 1994, that began to change when PetSmart moved to full-service, high-tech veterinary clinics and began to roll these clinics out to the majority of its stores. PetSmart's new veterinarian clinics would offer a much broader range, including orthopedic work and other services which together made up 90% of the veterinary market, but excluding those that required multiple days of hospital care.[406] However, due to legal and service reasons, PetSmart couldn't own these veterinary clinics. Instead, PetSmart set up a series of partnerships with both a large veterinary service organization (Medical Management International, or MMI) and a number of veterinarians. Under the arrangement, PetSmart would lease out 1,600 square feet, later 1,800-2,000 square feet, adjacent to its stores.

The costs of these high-tech veterinary clinics were substantial, possibly exceeding $100,000 per clinic. To attract great veterinarians, and because many independent veterinarians were not able to afford this package, PetSmart made it available to them on a leased basis. The exception was MMI, who, already well-capitalized, signed on to the program in order to take advantage of the customer traffic PetSmart stores generated. While PetSmart couldn't own the vet clinics, they did ensure consistent quality of service through a "very extensive" vet recruitment and selection process. Additionally, because these new vet clinics offered near full service and a suite of new technology, they were better able to partner with experienced veterinarians with superior training than were the predecessor wellness clinics.[407] These established veterinarians would also benefit financially as at the time "only 7% of current vet clinics realize[d] $1 million of volume; yet that [was] a reasonable objective for a VETsMART clinic in its fourth or fifth year"[408] and Scott Campbell, MMI's founder, predicted annual veterinary clinic revenues closer to $2 to $2.5 million. PetSmart rapidly built out a number of veterinary clinics in its stores, but had trouble filling them because of the limited pool of veterinarians from which to hire. Only 2,200 veterinarians graduated from vet school each year in the late 90s, and PetSmart's tense relationships with veterinarians—many of whom competed in the sale of premium pet food—meant that seasoned vets were sometimes unwilling to join PetSmart. The large amount of empty space and unused capital assets weighed down productivity.

To fill these clinics, PetSmart made MMI its exclusive veterinary clinic partner, and as part of the deal, MMI acquired other PetSmart veterinary clinics. MMI was able to fill the empty space both because, as a veterinary clinic operator, it had more credibility with veterinarians than a retailer, and because it offered base pay several thousand dollars higher than the industry's average, in addition to stock options, bonus packages, and additional bonus incentives.[409] At MMI, veterinarians also could focus more fully on providing care, as PetSmart took care of the more business-oriented activities. For instance, PetSmart provided advertising for the Banfield Pet Hospitals as part of its media campaigns.

PetSmart, for its part, was able to benefit from the clinic customers both directly and indirectly. Directly, PetSmart was able to charge rent on a portion of its stores, and its leasing arrangement with its veterinarians included a profit participation formula for PetSmart.[410] Indirectly, PetSmart benefitted from customers' trips to the vets when they browsed the rest of the store as well. Veterinary clinics at PetSmart specifically did not have a waiting room, instead, visitors to the clinic (both human and animal) could wander PetSmart while they waited for their appointment. Veterinarians were also able to direct customers to suggested supplies or food in the very accessible PetSmart next door. PetSmart also bolstered its historic strengths in premium food, as very high-end food was sold best by an 'influencer' such as a breeder, dealer, groomer, obedience trainer, or vet. With these new veterinary clinics, "PETsMART stores now [contained] four of these five influencers."[411]

The success of services at PetSmart is admirable. From only 3.6% of total sales in 1999, PetSmart's share of revenue from services grew to 11% in 2012, not including MMI's revenue from operating Banfield vet clinics (Figure 7.17).

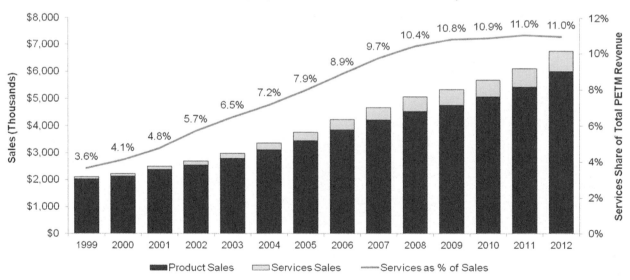

Figure 7.17 Sources: PetSmart 10Ks.

PetSmart's diverse set of services and varied ways of implementing and paying for them created a fantastic services offering that greatly benefitted customers and complemented PetSmart's food and supply offerings. This services offering has been an important defense against online retailers.

Online Threats

Online retail is not a new challenger in the pet industry: one of the greatest failures of the dot-com bubble was Pets.com. Despite Pets.com's failure, however, eCommerce is a threat to the pet industry. Despite PetSmart's introduction of services, routine trips for pet food are still important in driving traffic. If online retailers could succeed in selling pet food, taking those purchases out of the store, PetSmart's profitable attachment sales would suffer significantly.

The source of Pets.com's failure was an industry structure where food accounted for a near majority of sales. The simple fact was that the cost of moving heavy bags of food and litter, particularly for low-margin grocery brands, directly to a customer far exceeded the price customers were willing to pay for the service.[412] To make up for loss-leading on pet food, Pets.com had to be able to sell a large number of high gross-margin pet supplies and accessories. However, with food being the dominant product category in the industry, there weren't enough attachment sales to make this work. PetSmart does better with this strategy as brick-and-mortar stores are better at making impulse and attachment sales. In PetSmart's case, customers come to buy food or use a service, and end up leaving with a high-margin toy or accessory they buy on impulse or from a service provider's suggestion.

However, the industry is different today. Specialty store retailers' hold on exclusivity is slipping as premium pet brands find themselves victim to supply chain leaks that shuttle their goods into the Amazon third-party seller channel. One premium food brand, Blue Buffalo, already sells to Amazon and its subsidiary Wag.com, and the allure of the online channel may be great enough to woo more premium food brands to the Amazon platform. It should be noted, however, that Blue Buffalo still recognizes the value of brick-and-mortar retailers as it employs its own team of more than 1,300 promoters to educate pet parents about their brand in retail stores. If Amazon can sign up more premium brands, its endless aisle will provide a greater assortment than pet superstores. Supply chain improvements, such as Amazon's Subscribe n' Save program and extensive distribution network, have reduced the cost of shipping. With higher gross margins in premium, and especially super-premium, pet food, online retailers may be able to ship this food profitably. If this comes to pass, the impact on the pet superstores could be even more significant than when Iams left for the mass channels.

At the same time, however, online retailers find cross-selling difficult. Online shoppers are generally mission-driven and want to purchase the target of their search, not browse a store. Their baskets contain fewer items as a result. PetSmart's advantage in being able to better bundle attachment sales may help it keep pricing in line with Amazon. Even if some pet food sales do move online, PetSmart's service sales continue to grow, and provide important routine trip generators. Online retailers are at a loss for providing services like grooming, training, or vet check-ups. While a potential future threat, today, prices at PetSmart.com are 5-10% lower than prices at Wag.com,[413] and online retail of pet food accounts for only 0.2% of the market. eCommerce's channel share gains have been largely in non-food sales, as seen in Figure 7.18.

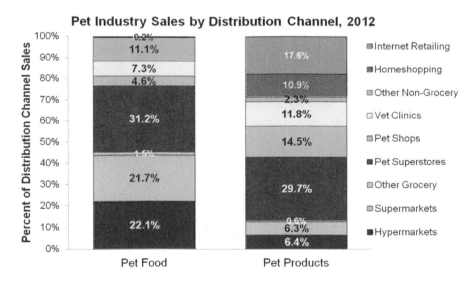

Figure 7.18 Source: Euromonitor International, 2012, Passport GMID.

Non-pet food products, with their high gross margins and endless variety, have grown rapidly online. It's unclear, however, whether or not this matters to PetSmart outside of one category. To the extent that online retail has damaged brick-and-mortar sales, it appears to be confined to pet pharmaceuticals. Over 40% of online pet supply purchases are high ticket, low weight, and high margin pet medications, compared to less than 15% of purchases for pet superstores.[414] The two leading pure-play online retailers in the pet supply vertical are anchored in this category: PetMed Express and Drs Foster & Smith.[415] Many of PetSmart's other pet supply sales occur as an impulse or at the suggestion of a store associate, and it's not certain that these store-driven sales would be hurt by online retailers, so long as PetSmart can keep the traffic coming. Outside of pet pharmaceuticals, it's possible that online sales of pet products are largely incremental to the industry, that is, they don't substitute for in-store sales of pet products. The result is that the majority of PetSmart's store is composed of categories that have online penetration rates of less than 5%; this is very much a defensible store (Figure 7.19).

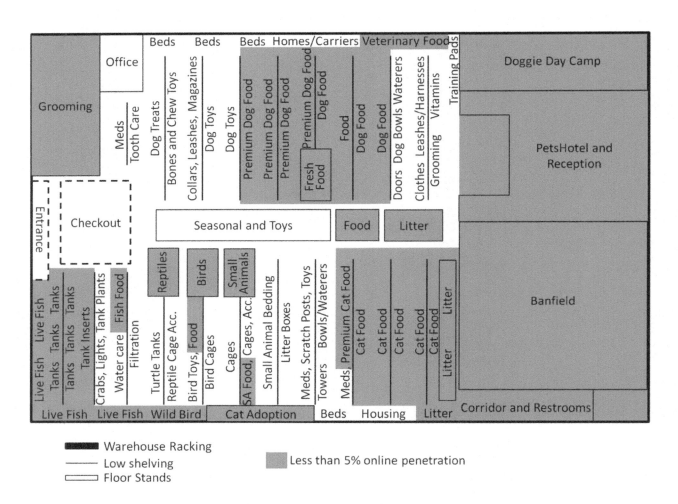

Figure 7.19 Source: Author visit.

PetSmart does have a history in non-store retailing, having acquired catalog companies like Sporting Dog and State Line Tack (an equine catalog) in the mid-90s, and set up in-store kiosks for these catalogs to extend store SKUs from 12,000 to 80,000. Through these acquisitions, PETsMART Direct became the largest catalog retailer of pet and equine-related products in North America.[416] PetSmart also moved into online retail early, partnering with pet online retailer idealab! in a joint venture that merged idealab!'s[417] online pet retail domains and e-tailing prowess with PetSmart's buying and catalog fulfillment network and own domains. This joint venture quickly became the dominant online pet supply site with more unique visitors than any other competitor.[418] PetSmart eventually acquired the entire operation. Even so, however, online retail accounts for less than one percent of PetSmart sales.

Once premium pet food became widespread at competing online retailers, PetSmart.com extended its online merchandising to include this category as well. PetSmart is now in an interesting dilemma: to prevent food brands from exploring other online retail partners, it's in PetSmart's interest to prove to premium and super-premium brands that PetSmart can expand their market online as well. However, PetSmart's margins on food sales are much better when they are purchased in-store because the company saves the cost of shipping and because customers are more likely to make other purchases in-store.[419] It's important for PetSmart to both meet customers where they want to shop, as well as prepare for a future where Amazon is a stronger competitor, and so acting as an online retailer makes perfect sense. However, as part of the "Enhance the Value of the Box" strategy, PetSmart should also be making every effort to direct customer traffic from its website into its stores. Many PetSmart stores have desk staff that serve the grooming department, the training department, the PetsHotel service, and the Banfield clinics. To roll out an online fulfillment model, these staffed areas could double as pick-up-in-store locations. For PetSmart's attachment sale model, pick-up-in-store fulfillment is far more useful than delivery to a customer's home. To encourage these trips, PetSmart could experiment with providing some type of reward for buying or picking up food in-store. Alternatively, PetSmart could experiment with methods to routinize its customers' use of its service offerings in line with their purchase habits of dog food. For example, selling an annual package of 8 grooming trips at once could result in a customer coming to the store every six weeks for grooming, and then purchasing food and attachment sales at the same time.

Petco and PetSmart: Differing Strategies

Since PetSmart's founding, Petco and PetSmart have pursued very different strategies, and their differences have become more pronounced as PetSmart has moved heavily into services. Petco never quite abandoned its roots as a chain of small-format specialty stores, and its legacy store sizes have dictated much of its subsequent actions, and constrain Petco from reinventing itself into a full-service provider like PetSmart.

Though Petco expanded its store size from its traditional 3,500 square foot stores to new, 10,000 square foot (and later 15,000 square foot) prototypes,[420] its average store size has always been below that of PetSmart. Today, Petco's average store size is still significantly smaller than PetSmart's, at 13,500 square feet compared to 24,200 square feet for PetSmart. Petco's expanded format allowed it to merchandise a greater variety of live animals and premium merchandise, but not enough to include the kinds of in-store services that PetSmart finds so useful. Rather than try to serve every pet owner, Petco sought to operate pure-play premium specialty stores without grocery channel products. Petco stores feature premium food almost exclusively, and without the category share of mass market brands, have a higher percentage of high-margin sales, leading to a higher gross margin overall.[421] To better sell these supplies, Petco also has a more specialty feel to its stores which, in addition to their smaller footprint, have lower shelving and feature a greater variety of live small animals and birds.[422] With its greater store size, PetSmart pursues the mass market share more heavily, with 20% of its SKUs and 50% of its sales overlapping with the grocery channel.

While the two chains' stores overlap significantly (more than 50% of PetSmart stores have a Petco store within five miles), the two companies' approaches to real estate are very different. PetSmart chooses to locate near other superstores and warehouse clubs in power centers outside of town. Petco, instead, leverages its smaller store format to locate closer to town centers in small shopping areas anchored by upscale supermarkets and Starbucks.[423] PetSmart uses services and pet food to drive traffic, but

Petco relies instead on its proximity to high-traffic retailers and its more convenient locations to encourage footfall.

Despite their size, merchandise, and location differences, both stores pursue the same target demographic of middle to higher income households, and their primary shoppers are women.[424] PetSmart is less expensive than Petco, with various pricing studies putting the PetSmart discount at 6%[425] to 13%[426] of Petco.

Recently, Petco has doubled down on its small store convenience advantages. Its new store format, Unleashed by Petco, is only 2,000-2,500 square feet in size, and Petco has grown the store count from 13 locations in September of 2010 to 87 stores in 2013. PetSmart has just recently begun experimenting with microstores. Petco has used the smaller stores to locate in residential neighborhood strips near major urban centers (e.g. Boston and New York City), close to supermarkets and their constant high-volume foot traffic. Unleashed has only 20% of the SKUs of its big box peers, and focuses only on dogs and cats, to the exclusion of other species. The stores carry exclusively premium and natural pet foods, and have a strong penetration of high-velocity hard good items.[427] With the smaller format, services at the stores are even less common than in Petco's traditional stores. While seminars, classes, and vaccination clinics are offered on a scheduled basis in the stores' small community areas, they are not full-time service centers like PetSmart stores. Grooming is available only at one Unleashed store, while self-service washing is present at 15 others. Overall, the stores are designed to fulfill a convenience need in affluent areas.

With high gross margins from premium pet food and carrying only high-velocity hard goods, Unleashed stores probably do make a good return on their limited real estate. However, we feel this model leaves Petco more exposed to potential threats from premium pet food channel expansion and online retailers. While PetSmart's model makes it less expensive than Wag.com (and Petco), Petco is priced comparably to Wag.com. At that point, it's up to the consumer to decide if the convenience of lugging 20-lbs bags of pet food home after a grocery store shopping trip is greater than having them delivered. As well, Unleashed, with its very low penetration of services, relies almost exclusively on premium brands to attract customers. If these brands were to broadly expand their distribution to grocery stores or online retailers, Unleashed could see a dramatic decrease in traffic—which would in turn make it unable to sell its high-margin pet product attachments. In contrast, PetSmart's rollout of services early on gives the company more options today.

What Can We Learn From These Examples?

Overall, we believe the PetSmart model is one that has great staying power. The lessons from PetSmart's experience with Iams broadening distribution are very applicable to brick-and-mortar retailers' present day battle with online retailers. Just as when Amazon enters a category and brick-and-mortar retailers see volume sucked out of their stores, Iams volume departed PetSmart stores for other channels. To compete with more efficient retailers (i.e. Walmart), PetSmart made its back-end, non-customer-facing operations much leaner. While obviously not as efficient a distributor as Walmart, PetSmart found other ways to defend itself through focusing on services, exclusivity, and by remodeling itself as a pet destination.

PetSmart continues to stay ahead of the curve today, following the same principles it used to build a wall against the mass channels. It uses its assets in a cohesive strategy to support these principles. A store has a unique set of assets, namely technology, inventory, people, and the brick-and-mortar store itself which provides location advantages and store space. Stores that create unique value for their customers or their suppliers through these assets are likely to succeed against the onslaught of internet-based retailers. PetSmart has done just that.

PetSmart's human assets, primarily its well-trained sales associates and service providers, establish relationships with their customers, offer advice and education and do, actually, have the power to influence PetSmart's customers' choice of pet food brands. Because of this, PetSmart's brand partners, for the most part, recognize the benefits of channel exclusivity and maintain it. With PetSmart's large market share and channel exclusivity guarantees, close relationships with brand partners have concentrated paybacks, and PetSmart is able to share the benefits of its customer insights and retail store launch platform to drive innovation in the category with its brand partners.

PetSmart's store assets, with their large footprints, inviting ambiance, trained service providers, and open-door policy for customers' pets, support PetSmart's multitude of service offerings. Services and service providers attract customers, generate their own revenue, build PetSmart's authority, and deepen customer relationships. They are also an offering that neither online retailers nor mass merchandisers can duplicate.

PetSmart has also made careful inventory decisions, and benefits from the nature of the pet food category itself. Aside from fresh product, its food inventory is long-lived and subject to routine purchases. In the event of a stock-out, trained associates can assist customers with finding another, similar product. Stores carry few, fast-changing 'fashion' type goods which have a high cost of obsolescence, and most items in the store have a low value density. This means that inventory levels can be planned, the costs of both overstocks and stock-outs are relatively low, and that online retailers' typical strengths against brick-and-mortar stores are substantially weakened. PetSmart furthered its advantages relative to online retailers by building a leaner supply chain in the early 2000s. In addition, the company's focus on premium food over standard food has led to exclusivity agreements that protect its business, and PetSmart is able to match its trip-generating food and service sales with profit-generating, often impulse-oriented toy and accessories sales.

PetSmart's actions have built defensible walls around its stores, and have made it one of the few retailers who can adopt the "Enhance the Value of the Box" strategy. PetSmart's next challenge is to continue to increase the productivity of its stores, and it will likely best do so by drawing on its least-used asset, technology. Better use of its website, product, service, and store portfolios could help to drive traffic from online sources into the store, or keep it from going online to begin with. PetSmart's size and channel exclusivity allows it to capture many of the benefits of its innovations, and the company should continue its efforts to turn its website into an educational center similar to its stores. Most recently, PetSmart acquired Pet360 which controls several eCommerce operations as well as information sites and online community groups. Overall, PetSmart's current and past actions have positioned it well to succeed in a world where online retailers pose such a threat to many others. This position is summarized in Figure 7.20.

Pet Supplies

1) Which threat do you face?	**Products and/or customer purchase behavior does not lend itself to online retail**
3) Strategic Imperative:	**Enhance the value of the box: services, ambiance, highly-trained associates, and exclusive/private label goods draw customers**

T Need to develop strong eCommerce platform to drive web traffic to stores and heighten the engagement of pet parents with the brand (education and health).

I Exclusive brand relationships and private label act as a defense for brick-and-mortar stores. High-end food capitalizes on pet humanization trend.

P High quality, knowledgeable store associates with specialized training provide services, cater to pet parents, and support brands.

S Inviting store ambiance that attracts pet parents.

Figure 7.20

In closing, it should be noted that PetSmart's ability to create such a strong service offering was partly dependent on its circumstances. PetSmart's customers have relatively high income and could afford to pay for services many other pet owners choose to do themselves or forego altogether. The trends in the humanization of pets, and PetSmart's role in building and feeding this trend, created a demand for precisely the services PetSmart offers. These trends aren't necessarily exclusive to the pets category, however, and PetSmart is by no means a special case. In Home Improvement, for instance, we discuss the 'Do-It-For-Me' trend where customers prefer to be the decision maker for what work gets done, but have others carry it out. There are many retail categories where people are passionate about their involvement, though perhaps not to quite as high a degree as pet owners. For any retailer in the position to create a service-aided store format, PetSmart's history and its implementation of its service offering provide useful lessons.

One key part of the "Enhance the Value of the Box" strategy that PetSmart has been missing is a compelling approach to eCommerce. This has led to the company's recent pressure from activist investors. Retailers, however, should distinguish between chasing high eCommerce market shares and building a useful online presence. When a retailer's goods are most efficiently fulfilled from a store, and the retailer may in fact lose attachment sales and profits by selling key goods, like pet food, online, the point of an eCommerce model isn't to convert those goods to internet fulfillment, but to encourage customers to revisit the store and make these purchases there. Our next focus retailer, Home Depot, has developed strategies that do exactly that as it inspires its customers with new home projects and helps customers achieve their dreams with its store-based inventory.

Chapter 8

Embracing eCommerce, a New Retail Model for Customer Engagement

While eCommerce, showrooming, and mobile retail have taken their toll across a wide swath of retailing verticals, Home Improvement stores like Home Depot and Lowe's aren't often associated with an online threat. One analyst goes so far as to call the industry "AMZN-proof."[428] In this chapter we make the case that Home Depot, like PetSmart, finds itself in an enviable position: its key product categories aren't easily shipped and they benefit strongly from knowledgeable store associates. But Home Depot's success is more than luck. Rather than succumb to complacency, Home Depot management expends considerable time and energy differentiating itself from Amazon.[429] The company has taken the inherent advantages of its product categories, and combined them with a logistical infrastructure that non-home improvement retailers simply haven't built, and has created a proactive approach to online customer service, eCommerce, and even online customer cultivation that makes them the preeminent brick-and-mortar retailer from which to learn. Home Depot's eCommerce operation, particularly the way it was built to not only sell goods but to also actively support Home Depot's brick-and-mortar stores, are the final leg of the "Enhance the Value of the Box" strategy.

Home Depot's natural advantages are considerable. Many of its products are bulky, heavy, and have low value-density (low price per weight and size), making them expensive to ship to a customer's home. Home delivery of a subset of these categories (e.g. lumber, sheet rock, and CMU blocks) requires specialized delivery trucks and equipment. Online-only retailers cannot price-compete on these goods as Home Depot's and Lowe's multitude of disaggregated building material warehouses have lower stem miles (the distance between the distribution point and the customer's location) than Amazon's far fewer fulfillment centers. Inventory aggregation does not yield significant advantages in these basic goods either. Because customers often buy their building material goods by the project, rather than a la carte, these protected categories provide a shield behind which Home Depot's more at-risk categories shelter. In highly contested categories, like décor and power tools, where Home Depot sales are at risk, the company has built its own well-regarded and exclusive brands that customers often favor. Across all of its categories, Home Depot's non-professional customers often need help and education from knowledgeable Home Depot sales associates to complete their projects, which draws customers to the store and also protects store sales. Its services to professional contractors (Pros), such as vehicle loading, have built a customer base that Home Depot knows how to satisfy. Also, the company has built a vast do-it-yourself (DIY) toolset online that supports the brick-and-mortar model. This is critical to the strategy as online research and pick-up-in-store purchases drive brick-and-mortar sales, and brick-and-mortar interactions drive the use of DIY digital tools.

These defenses have resulted in very low eCommerce penetration in the vertical relative to retail as a whole. In fact, online sales penetration in the home improvement category (electrical supplies, hardware, paint, etc.) averaged just 2.2% in 2012 (including online sales by Lowe's and Home Depot) and in the broader Home and Garden category averaged just 3.2%, compared to 5.2% for US retailing overall (Figure 8.1).[430]

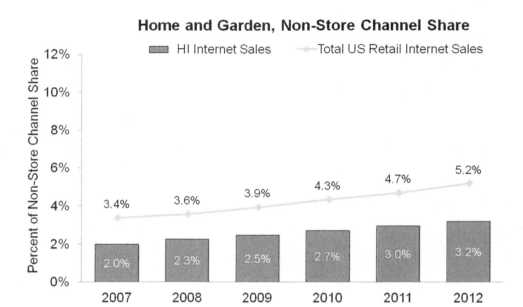

Figure 8.1 Sources: Euromonitor International, Passport GMID; Compiled from 'Estimated Quarterly U.S. Retail Sales (Adjusted): Total and e-Commerce,' *Monthly and Annual Retail Trade*, US Economic Census. Notes: Home and Garden penetration a weighted average of Home Depot relevant categories: Home Improvement, Gardening, Outdoor Living, and Lighting.

However, Home Depot is not invulnerable. While still small, internet retailing has consistently gained channel share. Large online retailers have made inroads in the industry. Amazon, for instance, has dramatically grown its initial assortment of 6,000 home improvement stock-keeping units (SKUs) in 1999 to over eight million today through both its own efforts and by hosting third party sellers on its platform. In other verticals, like Consumer Packaged Goods, online retailers are figuring out ways to extend their models into categories once thought untouchable. While eCommerce has a low overall channel share, it is widely distributed and some categories are more in line with retail trends as a whole. For instance, eCommerce had a 5.0% channel share of window coverings and a 6.8% share of outdoor living products in 2012. Education in a wide range of hobbies and pursuits is increasingly moving online through learning platforms that leverage third party contributors. Pros, who account for a majority of Home Depot sales, have certainly switched retailers in the past, and could switch again in the future for price or service advantages.

For our part, we believe Home Depot is part of a group of retailers with a format that is protected from an online threat (notwithstanding the fact that there are some vulnerable categories sold within the store). Other retailers that appear largely protected, at least for now, are pet stores, auto parts stores, and crafts stores. Key categories in these retailing verticals are shielded through a number of mechanisms: specialized supply chains, physical properties and pricing that render many items too expensive to deliver to customers, a need for customers to interact with the products before purchase (often combined with an exclusive supply or at least pricing parity with online retailers), and customers' need for immediate fulfillment. Category by category, we'll highlight these issues, examining Home Depot's defenses and weaknesses, and then consider potential threats to its model. Throughout this process, we'll also focus on Home Depot's approach to developing its strategy against online retailers, which we consider a defining example of the "Enhance the Value of the Box" strategy. As part of this strategy, we'll explore one of the most powerful initiatives going on at Home Depot. This is the way in which Home Depot is leveraging the internet to bring innovation to its model, categories, and customers, and draw sales from the internet into its stores. Although pressed in some categories, Home Depot has created a strong proposition with enough degrees of freedom to allow it to thrive.

These defenses, and Home Depot's revamped online strategy, have enabled the company to gain business from the increase in housing starts during the recovery, rather than losing it to online retailers. Increasing leverage of fixed assets and stronger gross margins have resulted in increasing returns since the beginning of the recession as shown in Figure 8.2.

	FY 2005	FY 2006	FY 2007	FY 2011	FY 2012	FY 2013
Same-store sales growth	3.8%	-2.8%	-6.7%	3.4%	4.6%	6.8%
ROIC (Op Leases Not Capitalized)	20.0%	16.2%	13.1%	14.5%	17.5%	21.2%
Gross Margin	33.7%	33.6%	33.6%	34.5%	34.6%	34.8%
SG&A Expense Ratio	21.9%	22.4%	24.2%	25.0%	24.2%	23.1%

Figure 8.2 Sources: Company reports accessed through Thomson One.

Home Depot's approach is to inspire home owners to dream while protecting its core categories. This approach is working to both bring more customers into its stores and to defend these stores against online retailers. In order to understand how these defenses work in practice, we'll explore the nature of the threat—and the store's defenses—in each of Home Depot's categories, concluding that Home Depot's stores are not currently in danger of becoming unproductive.

Online Threat in the Home Improvement Industry and Home Depot's Near-Term Response

In talking about brick-and-mortar safety and defensibility, we must address the often discussed threat of showrooming. Part of the reason why online retailing has been slow to penetrate the home improvement industry is that when customers shop online for better prices than they find at Home Depot, they're unlikely to find any. In Figure 8.3, we compare pricing across the Home and Garden subcategories and see interesting clusters emerge.

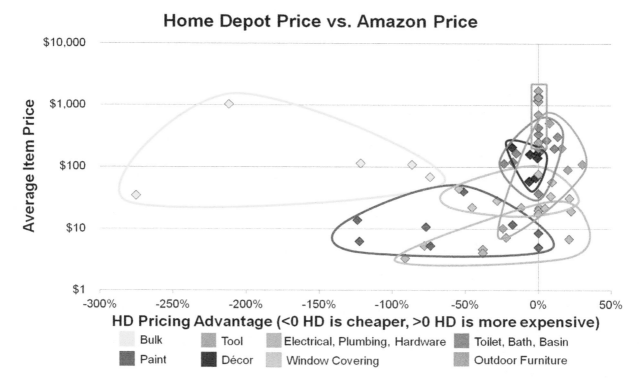

Figure 8.3 Source: Price comparisons between HomeDepot.com and Amazon.com. Notes: Average Item Price is the average of the prices found at Home Depot and Amazon. Price difference calculated as the difference between Home Depot's and Amazon's prices, divided by Home Depot's price. When the item was not already in a Home Depot store, the lowest priced shipping option was selected, including ship-to-store, bundled shipping options, and Amazon Prime. Prime products were preferred, though where the only product available was from a third-party vendor, that price (with shipping) was used. We infer from the nature of Home Depot's project-based sales that bundled shipping is used frequently. When brands could not be matched (e.g. in lumber), equivalent product was compared. All prices are sales tax neutral as our prediction is that online retailers will be subject to sales tax.

Home Depot often wins price comparison tests. In bulk goods like gypsum board and lumber, Home Depot's store-based inventory and pickup gives it a clear and substantial pricing advantage over Amazon's own and its third-party sellers' use of delivery companies like FedEx, USPS, etc. Assorted hardware, electrical, and plumbing pieces, with low average price points, are often cheaper at a Home Depot store than ordered online. This likely reflects Amazon's need to cover its shipping and picking expense on low-priced individual items where these costs are a high percentage of the items' price. Home Depot's customers, meanwhile, do the each-picking themselves in the bulk hardware bins. Paint is a special case, because in many states it is considered a hazardous material and is difficult or impossible for online retailers to ship.

Interestingly, in décor items like lighting and faucets, Home Depot is often able to price below or equivalent to Amazon, perhaps reflecting its scale in these categories, better vendor relationships, the lower cost of shipping to stores versus customers' homes, and a low-cost online-only/special order model in many décor items. Window Coverings (curtains, blinds, and shades) tell a similar story, with prices above, equal to, and less than Amazon. Surprisingly, heavy and fragile items in toilet, bath, and basin like porcelain toilets are sometimes priced more competitively online. Outdoor Furniture, almost universally, is consistently priced the same, perhaps reflecting that for all retailers, this category is drop-shipped from third parties.

Tools, specifically higher-priced power tools, would seem to be the category where Amazon can best leverage its online-only model. Home Depot's omnichannel pricing strategy is to match online pricing to in-store pricing by locality. Home Depot carries many power tools in-store so as to have tools immediately available for Pros whose equipment breaks and in order to offer a one-stop-shop for DIYers. Consequently, power tool prices in Home Depot stores and on HomeDepot.com bear the overhead of the store, resulting in higher prices versus pure online retailers. On high-priced items where shipping cost becomes a smaller percentage of total item cost, Amazon's online-only model is well positioned.

However, even in these categories where Amazon maintains a pricing advantage, the fact that Home Depot customers are often buying items across categories in order to complete a project serves as a defense. For instance, while online retailers like Wayfair appear, on occasion, to be able to price more competitively on toilets, installation requires other assorted materials necessary to the project, like plumber's putty. These small consumables are cheaper at Home Depot due to their low price and the high relative cost of shipping. For these cross-category projects, once the total bill is added up, Home Depot is often less expensive. This ability to bundle products across categories into integrated projects is a critical advantage that retailers who cultivate their customers can exploit.

Conceptually speaking, these price advantages and disadvantages are driven by the item's brand importance and its weight, cube (the item's physical size), velocity, and price level, as well as its potential need for professional installation, education, and its chance of being returned. We present these dynamics graphically in Figure 8.4.

	B&M Price Advantage	Online Price Advantage
Item Price Increases	⬇	⬆
Velocity Increases	⬆	⬇
Weight Increases	⬆	⬇
Cube Increases	⬆	⬇
Brand Importance Increases	⬇	⬆
Installation Need Increases	⬆	⬇
Education Need Increases	⬆	⬇
Chance of Return Increases	⬆	⬇

Figure 8.4

While these attributes are often related (for instance, online retailers do very well in high-priced, low-velocity, low-weight, low-size, and brand-important consumer electronics), holding everything else constant, each attribute has a predictable effect. As an item's price increases, the cost of holding inventory increases and online retailers have the advantage due to the efficiency of online fulfillment operations, while at the same time picking and shipping become a smaller percentage of the overall price. As velocity (the rate at which a SKU is purchased) increases, brick-and-mortar retailers have the advantage due to the fixed cost nature of their business. While online retailers incur additional picking and shipping costs every time an item is ordered (i.e. their costs are variable depending on sales), brick-and-mortar retailers' have a fixed cost for their shelf space. As the velocity of a SKU increases, brick-and-mortar retailers sell more without having to spend any more on the SKU's shelf space. Hence, online retailers often specialize in the long tail of customer purchases and in categories with wide assortments. As an item's weight and cube increase, its delivery cost also increases, disadvantaging online retailers. As brand importance increases, brick-and-mortar retailers provide less value as a showroom, and online retailers, without store expenses, gain pricing advantage. As the need for an in-person service arises, such as installation or education in how to use a product, brick-and-mortar retailers are able to better attract customers to stores, leverage store-based assets, and extract concessions from suppliers, giving them the pricing advantage. Finally, as the chance of an item being returned increases, brick-and-mortar retailers have the pricing advantage due to their stores acting as collection points, whereas returns to online retailers generate another last-mile trip.

Home Depot, which carries many low-priced, heavy, bulky, routinely purchased, commodity goods that customers often don't understand, benefits from these product attributes. Retailers with similar product profiles to Home Depot will likely also find themselves relatively safe from an online showrooming threat.

Beyond price, there are other reasons certain categories at Home Depot are protected. Home Depot has evaluated these defenses and threats in a category-specific way via their "Interconnected Portfolio Strategy," which we show in Figure 8.5. This matrix compares a category's propensity to be researched online to its propensity to be bought online, and examines the reasons for this customer behavior. This analysis suggests ways in which Home Depot can react to the various threats to its merchandise portfolio.

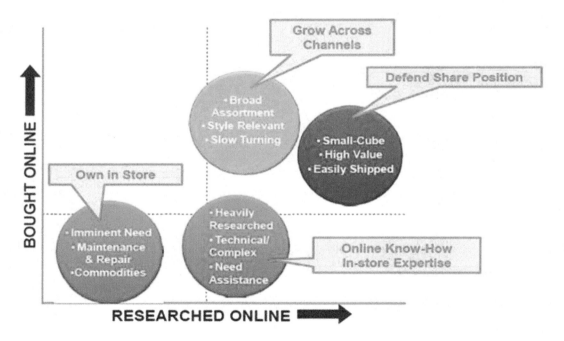

Figure 8.5 Source: 'Home Depot Inc Investor & Analyst Conference, June 6, 2012,' Transcript compiled by Thomson Reuters Streetevents, accessed via Thomson One, July 9, 2013.

In the lower left of the chart are commodities like lumber and also imminent need and maintenance and repair items like a new valve to fix a running toilet. While we've seen that prices in these categories are generally better in-store, there are other reasons these categories are defensible against online retailers. For instant need items, like that toilet valve, customers can't wait for an online delivery to repair their running toilet or leaky pipes; they want it now. In bulk materials, like lumber and gypsum board, online-only retailers are physically incapable of delivering the product out of their parcel-post oriented fulfillment centers. Bulk products make up over 20% of Home Depot sales. They are warehoused in special bulk distribution centers, and then moved to stores on flatbed trucks. In the case of goods like cement block, they are shipped directly from the manufacturer to Home Depot's warehouse-like stores. Fresh goods like house plants are also delivered straight to the store.[431]

The downstream supply chain for bulk goods is no less difficult to duplicate. Home Depot's stores function as working warehouses, with each serving as forward inventory very close to the customers. These 2,000+ inventory points mean that Home Depot is able to deliver critical goods more quickly to its customers and with fewer stem miles. Delivery from these stores utilizes a variety of vehicles, from box trucks, to forklift trucks, to boom and crane trucks depending on the needs and job lot quantity of the delivery. Online retailers like Amazon often use third-party carriers for last leg delivery, and it's difficult to see FedEx loading and fitting cut lumber lengths or pre-fabricated patio stairs next to hair dryers and computers in their standard delivery vehicles—not to mention the fact that a job lot order of sheetrock would very quickly weigh out a typical neighborhood delivery van. Even if online retailers could somehow solve these problems, many Pros are comfortable picking up these materials in-store with their own work vehicles, and paying more for last-mile delivery may not be compelling to them.

To deliver bulk goods, an online retailer would need to invest in recreating Home Depot's bulk DCs, and find a way to efficiently deliver small to job-lot quantities of heavy commodities like cinder blocks directly to the customer. Paint is difficult or impossible to ship due to its hazardous materials designation in many states. Live plants are too fragile to be shipped parcel-post. The competition in this category, therefore, is other brick-and-mortar retailers, rather than online ones. Home Depot is competing by "owning the store:" making it very quick for Pros to get in and get out of their stores through special Pro Desks, Pro loaders, etc. and making sure that DIYers can find what they need and get help from Home Depot associates, who are aided by First Phones and

First Phone Juniors (mobile devices that simplify and bring technology to many in-store tasks such as finding products in the store, checking out customers, and recording inventory, among others).

In the second green circle in Figure 8.5 are product groups like kitchens, HVAC, doors, and windows where the installation is complex and customers (especially DIYers) need help understanding the technical aspects of how to install and seal these items. Home Depot associates can teach customers these techniques and what to look out for in a way that online retailers can't. After going through this training, customers are unlikely to showroom these projects. In addition, DIYers may even need to have some tasks, like cutting lumber or pipe, performed for them in-store. These projects also often involve purchasing many items from multiple categories. For example, besides being heavy, some flooring materials like hardwood, marble, and tile require special tools like wood floor edgers or tile saws. These items are often rented by DIYers, making Home Depot and Lowe's more convenient one-stop shops.

Home Depot is serving do-it-yourselfers' need for online education in this category through online associate Q&A, project guides, and other online initiatives. In the stores, its automation of many in-store processes frees up more associate time for customer service and education. Home Depot would also like to introduce more services to address 'Do-It-For-Me' (DIFM) customers, i.e. those customers who want to be involved in the planning and product selection phases of their projects but not in the construction. However, Home Depot faces challenges and competition in this area that we will discuss later.

In the yellow circle of Home Depot's online research and purchase matrix above are mostly décor items, like lighting and faucets, where the slow-turn nature of the long-tail of design means that the broad assortments necessary to serve this category are best hosted online. The color, style, and material choices are large and varied; much more so than any brick-and-mortar store would be able to contain.

However, the impact to Home Depot of a shift in these categories may be limited. The amount of floor space dedicated to these categories within Home Depot stores is already relatively small and often features exclusive brands, limiting the impact of a broad shift online. Even within this category, the need to also purchase low-price and costly-to-ship commodity products to complete the project, like silicone sealant for a faucet installation, helps keep purchases in the store. Installing window coverings and décor items, while simple tasks, require a modicum of DIY experience, such as the ability to correctly measure window space, cut blinds, or install a faucet. Customers may need to be educated on how to perform these tasks, or Home Depot can do the tasks for them, providing a measure of defense for Home Depot's stores. Meanwhile, Pros are less concerned with the endless selection online, and more concerned with being able to pick up an adequate product for the job quickly.

Still, Home Depot is taking measures to defend itself in these categories. While Home Depot carries some of these SKUs in-store, they're creating an endless aisle online at HomeDepot.com and at Home Decorators Collection, Home Depot's separate décor website, to complement their store operations. Home Depot is thus growing across channels. However, with a plethora of online décor portals, the largest issue is how to ensure that Home Depot is the online portal customers will choose, as points of differentiation are few. Many online retailers use the same inventoryless drop shipping model, so shipping times and prices are often identical. Because building products, such as tiles, are often ordered in quantity, shipping costs are seen as manageable,[432] and a cost advantage for the brick-and-mortar store isn't clear unless the pick-up-in-store option allows Home Depot to use its own distribution network or capitalize on less expensive shipping rates for commercial addresses. Home Depot has invested in search engine optimization (SEO), online ads, and other forms of internet promotion; however, most online retailers use the same tools.

Finally, in the red circle of Home Depot's online research and purchase matrix above are items like power tools, where brand matters, products have high value in a small box, and they are easily shipped. While Home Depot is still the largest retailer of power tools in the country, Amazon has shown greater pricing advantage in this category.[433] Power tools are not unlike the TV category at Best Buy. Best Buy has responded by taking lower-end TVs out-of-store and putting them online, saving just the higher-end TVs, often with vendor enforced minimum pricing, for its in-store assortment. This approach likely won't work for Home Depot, where power tools across the price spectrum must be a part of the Home Depot store assortment. For both Pros and DIYers, power tools are sometimes purchased under significant time pressure. For the high-end power tools that Pros favor, a replacement is needed right away if a

Pro's tool goes down on site. With its large number of store outlets, many Pros treat Home Depot as a convenience stop for these critical needs. For lower-end power tools meant for DIYers, these purchases might be part of a weekend project, and for convenience's sake, they want to get all of their purchases in one place. Consequently, Home Depot's power tool offering bears the price of in-store inventory.

Cheaper online rivals are also not the only threat to this business. On the DIY side, at least, peer-to-peer tool sharing services facilitated by the internet are becoming increasingly prevalent. Tool libraries have popped up in many American cities,[434] and while tool libraries are generally small, limited communities of people sharing tools for free in their generosity of spirit, online marketplaces like SnapGoods and Neighbor Goods enable users to make money off their unused tools by renting them out online. The ability for tool owners to make money by loaning their tools may substantially grow the market.

While Home Depot offers tool rental, renting a power tool directly from a neighbor down the street is likely more convenient than having to drive to a Home Depot to both borrow and return a tool. However, these online communities are still limited in reach, and they face large hurdles to growing market share. The online, peer-to-peer tool rental market likely works for small tools like cordless screwdrivers, but it's the rare DIYer whose neighbor owns a tile saw. Certain more dangerous tools, like chainsaws, could involve a liability issue, so DIYers may be unwilling to rent these to each other. While Pros usually have more substantial tool inventories, they may be too busy working on actual job sites and too protective of their tools to loan them out and fill this gap. The user bases of these online communities are also uncertain, and it's possible that the supply-demand fit may not be there. From our survey of Snap Goods, it appears that renters of goods appear to often be looking for a very cheap price ($5-$10) to make it worth renting instead of buying a low-priced tool, whereas the loaners of goods are looking for a higher price ($10-$20) to make it worth their while to engage in the transaction and incur its associated time costs: posting inventory online, meeting someone to deliver the good, receiving the good back and checking to see if it's undamaged, etc.

This red circle is an area where online retailers have considerable opportunity, and Home Depot has responded by hosting more SKUs exclusively online (these online-only SKUs do not bear the cost of in-store inventory, and so Home Depot can price compete on these items), entering the tool repair business, and emphasizing exclusive brands that can't be found elsewhere. Using management estimates, we get an idea for how much of the Home Depot business is considered at risk from online competition. The colors in the chart on the left of Figure 8.6 correspond to Home Depot's online research and purchase matrix above. With only 15% of the business at serious risk currently, online threats don't loom particularly large. In the chart on the right of Figure 8.6, one sees just how stable Home Depot's mix has been over the last three years. It does not appear as if the category differences and threats described above have resulted in Home Depot's mix shifting significantly.

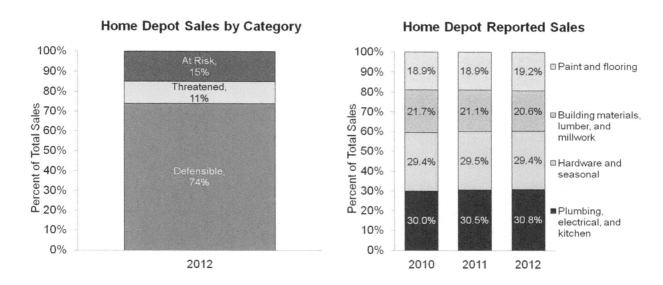

Figure 8.6 Sources: 'The Home Depot, Inc. at Jefferies Group, Inc. Global Consumer Conference,' June 19, 2012, Transcript compiled by Thomson Reuters Streetevents, accessed via Thomson One, July 9, 2013 and Home Depot Annual Report and 10-K, 2012.

When we apply this same coloring and risk assessment to a sample Home Depot store layout in Figure 8.7, we see that most of the store is not at risk of becoming unproductive, and is considered, if not safe, at least defensible.

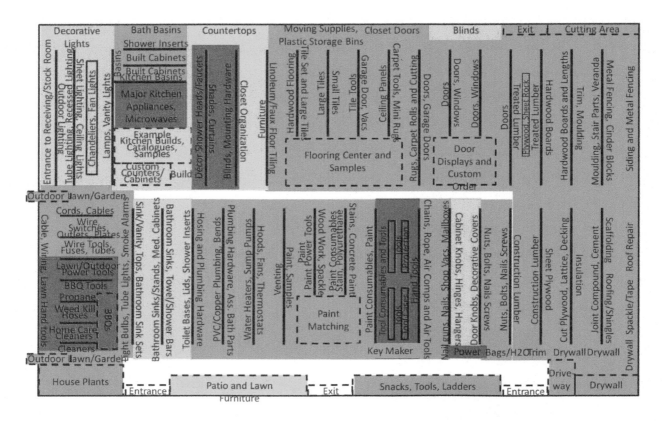

Figure 8.7 Source: Author visit to a Home Depot store.

The relative safety of Home Depot's footprint is important, as despite the large footprint and warehouse aspect of the store, the format itself has proven inflexible in the past. At one time, the company attempted to emphasize décor in its stores. The remodeling for these stores took six to nine months and was very expensive. More importantly though, during the remodeling period, Pro customers, who value ease and being able to get in and out quickly—and who visit Home Depots frequently—were significantly dislocated. Merchandise was moved around and Pros no longer knew where in the store to go to find what they needed. This added time to their shopping, and many Pros abandoned the stores during the remodeling period, and were slow to return once the changes were complete. With this kind of customer behavior, the US market already at saturation, and no immediate need to reduce store size, format changes are not and should not be an immediate or even medium-term option for Home Depot.

In our view, Home Depot's stores are eminently defensible from an online threat. Because of this, Home Depot's additional online and in-store investments are not wasted, as showrooming is unlikely to affect the company. Many of these efforts rely on Home Depot's ability to educate customers and turn novices or casual DIYers into accomplished home experts. This ability has been central to Home Depot's success throughout the company's history, and we believe it is still as relevant today. To illustrate this point, we'll briefly discuss Home Depot's service orientation and people systems, and highlight the negative consequences of CEO Bob Nardelli's decision to reduce the company's investment in service.

Expanding the Early Home Improvement Market

Do-It-Yourself as a concept was limited in the 1970s before Home Depot opened its first, education-focused stores. Small, regional chains like Grossman's in New England catered to DIYers through service programs that paired homeowners with competent workmen, but many homeowners lacked the skills they needed to accomplish home projects on their own. The "tinkerers of the 1940s and 1950s" had given way to the "baby-boomers who grew up with the disposable income to go out and replace what was broken" or to hire someone to do it for them.[435] As the founders of Home Depot describe it, "When we first got to Atlanta, do-it-yourselfers were people who mowed their own lawns and maybe painted once in a while."[436]

Homeowners not only lacked the knowledge to take on their own projects, they also lacked access to supplies, as many building supplies retailers focused on contractors. Lowe's, one of the early leaders in the field, had a customer mix that was 60% professionals and 40% homeowners.[437] Retailers "didn't sell merchandise. They sold pieces. Buy some lumber here, toilets there," without providing instructions on how to work with these pieces.[438] For example, when homeowners "wanted to redo a bathroom, they would call a contractor. The homeowner would give instructions about color, style, and perhaps name brands, then the contractor would pick up the plumbing and flooring items, sinks, tubs, medicine cabinets, and light bars at different places."[439] The situation wasn't much better for the contractor, who, in addition to having to shop at all these different places, contended with stores that "were set up like oversize Woolworth's. Low shelves, low ceilings, and inadequate inventory. They might not even have had what you wanted when you wanted it; chances were 50-50 that they would have to order what you need [*sic*] you'd wait two weeks."[440]

Contributing to this in-stock problem was that many chains' stores were relatively small (compared to the warehouse stores that would come later), at about 30,000 square feet with an attached open-air lumber yard. There just wasn't enough space to host a broad assortment or to warehouse product inventory. Consequently, stores bought through distributors, generating an additional step in the supply chain that added to the cost of product. Traditional home center retailers had a price markup of around 35%.[441] The entire home supply industry was constrained by price, availability, and a wall—composed of ignorance and infrastructure—between the homeowner and the product. Many products "were either too expensive or available only through contractors. Contractors could only get them from distributors or wholesalers and, after all of the markups, many home improvement projects were beyond the means of many middle-class people."[442]

After years spent in the home improvement industry, first in fans and appliances at discount store chain Two Guys, and later serving the contractor market as President at Handy Dan Home Improvement, Bernie Marcus dreamed of creating a store that would solve these problems. When he and Handy Dan's CFO, Arthur Blank, were fired from Handy Dan as the result of a power struggle between Marcus and the head of Handy Dan's parent company, Daylin, the two men struck out to build Marcus's dream.

Marcus and Blank envisioned a large warehouse store, one that would be 55,000 to 75,000 square feet in size with high ceilings, compared to Handy Dan's 35,000 square feet format. This extra square footage would be used to merchandise a broad assortment of goods as compared to Handy Dan's limited on-hand supply of just the top sellers in every category. The broad assortment in the store would be supported by the extra space created by the high ceilings, backed up with steel racking as opposed to short gondolas,[viii] which would enable the store to carry massive inventory levels. A broad assortment and deep inventory ensured that customers would no longer have to wait two weeks for a specially-ordered product, but could count on finding it on the shelf, ready to buy. The extra holding space would also enable the store to buy directly from manufacturers and

---

[viii] A gondola is a store fixture with shelving used to display merchandise.

avoid the costs of using distribution centers and distributors; savings which could be passed on to the customer. To keep this extra inventory productive, Marcus and Blank knew they would have to sell in large volumes, and they planned to do so by pricing at low margins. Whereas the traditional price markup at home center retailers was about 35%, Home Depot kept its markup at 26% through the 1990s.[443] These low margins, combined with buying directly from manufacturers, would fund lower prices than the competition, which, in turn, would attract the volume needed to sustain them.

Marcus and Blank also desired to open home improvement up to the regular home owner. Other home improvement retailers had tried customer education programs in the past. For instance, in the 1950s, Grossman's implemented the "Build-It-Yourself" home program, which sold blueprints, instructions, and materials for building a house, and the "Do It Yourself—Or We'll Do It For You" and the "We Start It—You Finish It" concepts that provided plans, advice, and skilled workers for homeowners who wanted to improve their homes.[444] Rather than sell defined plans like previous retailers, however, Home Depot wanted to enable customers to create their own plans and build their own customized dreams. The store would be staffed by highly trained employees, with history in the trades themselves, so DIYers could get expert advice. The expert staff would be supported by a culture and employee system that cared about customer service above all else.[445] Finally, the store was first envisioned as a place for the DIY customer, rather than the professional contractor, where DIYers could find the service they needed to learn about and complete their projects.

Marcus and Blank were joined by many former colleagues from Handy Dan, as well as Pat Farrah, who had earlier opened a failed store that embodied much of Marcus's vision. The team opened the first Home Depot stores in Atlanta in 1979. The chain gradually expanded into Florida, then on west through the remaining states in the Sun Belt, and eventually all across the United States and abroad to become the largest retailer of home improvement goods and services in North America. Home Depot's sales and store growth, and its position compared to its competitors, are shown in Figure 8.8.

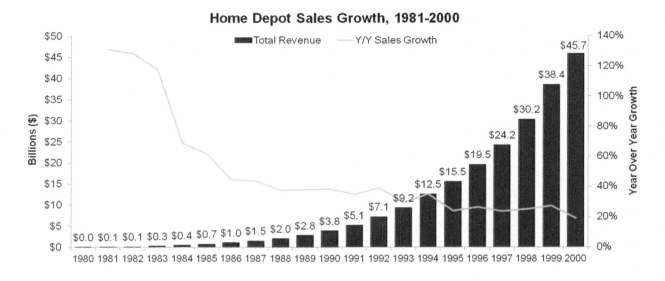

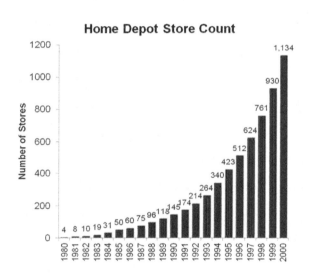

Rank		Company	Sales (millions)		1990 Market Share
1990	1980		1990	1980	
1	NA	The Home Depot	$3,815	$22	4.1%
2	2	Lowe's	2,833	884	3.0
3	7	Payless Cashways	2,226	316	2.4
4	NM	Builder's Square	1,900	NM	2.0
5	19	Hechinger Co.	1,450	172	1.6
6	NM	Home Club	1,260	NM	1.4
7	1	Wickes Lumber	850	1,300	0.9
8	5	Grossman's	810	650	0.9
9	30	Menard	800	99	0.9
10	6	84 Lumber	785	555	0.8%

NM = Not Meaningful NA= Not Available

Figure 8.8 Sources: *ThomsonOne* and Company Reports.

Home Depot's story mirrors other big box chains' histories in its rapid growth, industry disruption, displacement of competitors, and the mechanical aspects of lower prices, broader assortments, and one-stop shopping through warehouse-style retailing. The big difference is in the customer service model that Home Depot built. While much of what Home Depot did in merchandising, assortment, store format, etc. could be, and was, cloned by competitors, the company's people system was the secret to creating more productive stores, more loyal employees and customers, and ultimately, a much larger market for DIY home improvement goods. This people system was the part of the company that was difficult to copy, and was also a source of Home Depot's success from its first store openings in Atlanta in 1979 until Bob Nardelli's appointment as CEO in 2000. Given Home Depot's unrivaled leadership in the building materials category throughout the 1980s and 1990s, we'll focus on Home Depot throughout our examination of this period.

Home Depot's People System

Home Depot's people system from 1980-2000 was a structure built on purposeful decisions to ensure that the highest quality customer service was delivered. It included policies on associate wages and compensation, hiring qualities, executive activities, store operations, organizational structure, and culture, all of which made it possible for associates at the store level to make meaningful decisions to help customers. What was this service philosophy? In the words of Bernie Marcus, it was "'Whatever it takes.'" This simple phrase meant that Home Depot would "do whatever it [took] to satisfy a customer within all human reason" and was about "taking ownership of customer problem resolutions, even if it [meant] going far out of our way to do it."[446]

What did this level of service look like? It was an associate at an out-of-stock store personally driving to other Home Depots to get products customers needed. It was an associate correctly diagnosing a customer's problem as a leaky faucet and not a broken one, and selling them a low-cost replacement part as opposed to a high-priced new faucet. It was an associate stopping by a customer's home, for free, to switch out a fan after the customer realized that the fan she bought was too small. This service, paired with the store advantages discussed in the previous section, stood out from the competition. The results of a 1994 test are illuminating. In one challenge, employees at leading chains Home Depot, Lowe's, Home Quarters, and Builders Square were challenged to find a 5½ by ½ inch wedge concrete anchor bolt, which is used to fasten wood to masonry. It took a minute for the Home Depot associate to come up with the part. At the competitors, it was a different story: "After searching for nine minutes, a Lowe's clerk gave up and suggested a 5-inch lag screw instead. At the Builders Square, the employee gave up after six minutes and called a local hardware store." [447]

The impact of Home Depot's service philosophy and structure created an organization that was amongst the most admired in the United States, as seen in Figure 8.9.

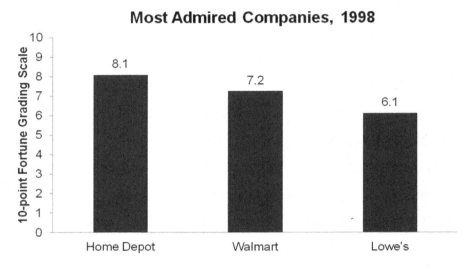

Most Admired Companies, 1998

Figure 8.9 Source: Roush, Chris, *Inside Home Depot*, New York, New York: McGraw-Hill, 1999, p 5. Notes: Ranking from Fortune Magazine ranking of Most Admired Companies in America. Overall score based on survey responses from 12,000 senior executives, outside directors, and Wall Street analysts, covering seven categories: quality of management, quality of products and services, innovation, investment value, financial soundness, talent, and corporate responsibility.

These anecdotes, though out of date now that online retailers can search a database for a part faster than a Home Depot associate can find it on the shelves, capture the service organization that is a prerequisite for the higher-order level of service that Home Depot offers in educating and cultivating customers as long-term loyalists. Every aspect of the service organization described here, no matter how mundane, was a building block in Home Depot's strategy of customer cultivation.

As part of its service philosophy, Home Depot wanted to be sure that store associates spent as much time as possible serving customers face to face. In order to achieve this profitably, Home Depot removed a number of common tasks from store operations to free up associate time. Other retailers, like Hechinger's, strove to keep their stores sparkling and well-presented. Home Depot associates, in contrast, didn't 'front' the shelves by bringing merchandise forward to the edge of the shelf, and they didn't 'face' merchandise by turning the product so that labels always faced customers.[448]

While Home Depot's stores didn't look as well-presented as other retailers, Home Depot associates had more time to actually serve customers.

Home Depot's founders believed that store associates, as front-line employees, had the most impact on whether or not an individual customer left the store satisfied. Consequently, Home Depot empowered its associates to make decisions at the individual level to satisfy a customer.[449] Associates during this period were not just register clerks or shelf stockers, they were well-trained, committed, and hard-working individuals who believed in the company's service mission and were encouraged to think and make decisions.[450] They were the element that differentiated Home Depot from its competition. As Bernie Marcus put it in 1998, "those who shop our stores know our people are different. These are people who are concerned, that do get involved with the customer, that do treat the customer a lot differently [from] other retail environments."[451]

Home Depot associates, then, were special, and Home Depot would go to great lengths to attract and train them. The company wanted, searched for, and paid for the best.[452] In Home Depot's aisles, DIYers and Pros could find licensed electricians and plumbers to help them with their projects, and contractors that, over their career, had built multiple homes. These experts were there because they had the experience to answer any question a customer might bring them. In one example of Home Depot's pursuit of the most-qualified store associates, the store manager of a newly-opened location in Evanston, IL, searched for associates at the local Builders Square and Menard's, where she would "feign ignorance of products, trying to uncover the competition's best, smartest, and friendliest people." When she had found the best, Home Depot hired them.[453] Like store associates, store managers also had wide discretion over decisions that fell in their span of control, such as hiring and firing. If they found someone they felt they needed in the store, it was up to the store manager to set a wage or salary package that would convince them to come on board.

The founders recognized that, when looking for the best, it was necessary to pay the best, and that serving their associates well was a prerequisite to serving their customers well. It may have been relatively easy for managers to lure competitors' best people away, as, during this period, Home Depot associates earned up to 20-25% more than employees at Lowe's, Hechinger, and Builders Square.[454] Employees at all levels were encouraged to own stock, and salaried staff received stock options while associates received a compelling stock purchase plan. This plan encouraged ownership of the company down to the hourly level. Under the stock purchase plan, associates could purchase company stock at a 15% discount off the market price, and, if the stock price dropped below the price they had paid, they could "get a refund of their money at any time before the plan ends."[455] This high level of remuneration and equity ownership not only attracted the best, but also led to a low turnover rate among associates who'd been with Home Depot for more than a year.[456] This low turnover manifested itself in the fact that many of Home Depot's executives in the 1990s had started out as hourly associates with Marcus, Blank, and Farrah when Home Depot was just getting started.

Low turnover was a good thing, because Home Depot not only paid for the best, the company invested a lot in making the best better. In 1999, new hires' training started with a week of classes on everything from company history to greeting customers, followed by three more weeks shadowing a department manager.[457] Training didn't end for associates after their onboarding, but was continuous throughout their careers at Home Depot. Arthur Blank emphasized this approach, stating that "training is not an event ... training is a way of life."[458] After their initial training, associates were "constantly being trained, either about new products or about how the store is run." Each employee was "required to have one hour of training each week." Marcus called this emphasis on training "the best investment we'll make," asking "How do you make people qualified if you don't train them?"[459] The founders backed up these statements by setting the example. Marcus and Blank traveled to stores throughout the country to lead training sessions in the stores and talk with associates, and they both personally took part in new assistant manager and store manager training. While Blank was CEO of Home Depot, he spent a full third of his time training employees—an unusually large proportion for a CEO. But Blank believed that it was "a significant part of our jobs to reinforce the culture and keep the training up."[460]

Home Depot made sure it supported these high-caliber, highly trained associates. The organization as a whole subscribed to an inverted pyramid structure that placed customers at the very top, with associates just beneath them. We reproduce this inverted pyramid in Figure 8.10.

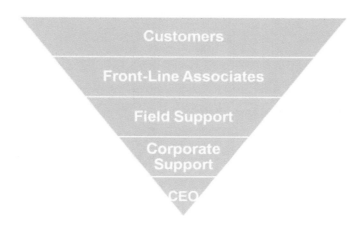

Figure 8.10 Source: Reproduction from company documents.

Unlike traditional organization charts, which are organized by level of authority, Home Depot's version privileged the employee category's proximity to the customer. Under this structure, the company and its entire infrastructure existed to support the sales associates in the store, so that they could support the customers. The company's customers were the ultimate "bosses." Home Depot backed up the inverted pyramid with both public statements and policy. As an example, when Home Depot constructed their headquarters in Atlanta, they named it the Store Support Center. The founders' instructions to everyone at the Store Support Center were that if a store called them, "stop what you are doing and take the store call."[461] New executives without experience at Home Depot stores were required to work in the stores before assuming their official duties. This experience in the store was required so that, when these executives assumed the roles for which they were hired, they would realize the impact of their actions on stores and associates. This organizational structure, and the policies backing it, focused the company on ensuring that store associates received the support they needed to serve customers.

An important part of instituting and perpetuating any organizational structure, system, and culture is to show that everyone believes in it, from the top down, and to model the appropriate behavior. Senior executives at the Home Depot demonstrated through their own actions what they expected of store associates, sometimes in ways that were sure to make a point. For instance, in a store acquired from Bowater, a Home Depot manager drove a forklift through the walls of the store manager's office, to make the point that Home Depot store managers belong on the floor, serving customers and training associates. In more common examples, Marcus, Blank, and Farrah routinely donned orange aprons in the stores, performing all the same tasks and service requests as new associates. In Home Depot's early days, if the stores didn't have a product customers were looking for, Bernie would drive out, find the product, buy it, and deliver it to a customer's home.

Taken together, the company's policies of hiring the best associates, paying them well, training them deeply, supporting them, and modeling the desired behavior led to the creation of the 'Bleeding Orange' culture that was so strong throughout this period. To the founders, Bleeding Orange meant taking care of people—both customers and employees, teaching customers, taking ownership and responsibility, trusting each other to make the right decisions, instilling teamwork, inviting a flat hierarchy where management treated associates as equals and sought to learn from them, and encouraging entrepreneurialism and risk-taking in the company.462 The customer interactions and educational opportunities that Marcus and Blank targeted took place in mere minutes on the sales floor, and were unplanned and unpredictable. Consequently, the founders needed to have expert, capable, and well-paid associates make customer service decisions in real-time, and the values-led culture at Home Depot provided associates the freedom and motivation to do so.

The culture extended beyond store operations as well. It carried Home Depot through sometimes bitter competition with rivals as the company grew. The culture of doing what's right for the customer motivated management to hold 'Issues and Answers' gatherings for soliciting suggestions from employees ways to improve the company. Merchandisers channeled this culture when they worked in partnership with vendors to develop products that better served Home Depot customers. The other aspects of Home Depot's people system laid the foundation for superior customer service, but the Bleeding Orange culture is what pushed associates to deploy those skills, and aligned everyone in the organization towards serving the customer.

While the financial impacts of this culture and the system that formed it are hard to measure and isolate, anecdotal evidence implies that the impact was real and significant. Bernie Marcus is fond of telling a story about a faucet. The condensed version is that one of Marcus's golf partners went into Home Depot to buy a replacement for a broken faucet. He was ready to spend $200 on a new faucet, but the

Home Depot associate he was talking to showed him how to fix his old faucet for $1.50, thus losing a high-priced sale and a substantial amount of gross margin dollars. Marcus's golf partner believed that Home Depot was "stupid" for encouraging this kind of behavior. However, Marcus then asked him where he was going to go the next time he had a plumbing issue, and his golf partner said he'd go right back to that Home Depot associate.463 With one empowered associate, Home Depot gained a customer for life.

Did every superior service experience customers had at the Home Depot inspire this kind of loyalty? Probably not. However, if Home Depot hadn't hired the best associates, trained them well, and instilled in them a passion for customer service and the Home Depot way, this event, and many others like it, would not have happened at all. To further attempt to quantify the financial impact of its superior customer service, it's worth asking why Home Depot succeeded, when numerous clones with similar formats, product assortments, locations, and financial backing failed, and why, in the 1990s, when Lowe's adopted Home Depot's operating mechanics wholesale, Home Depot consistently operated better performing stores, as seen in the charts in Figure 8.11.

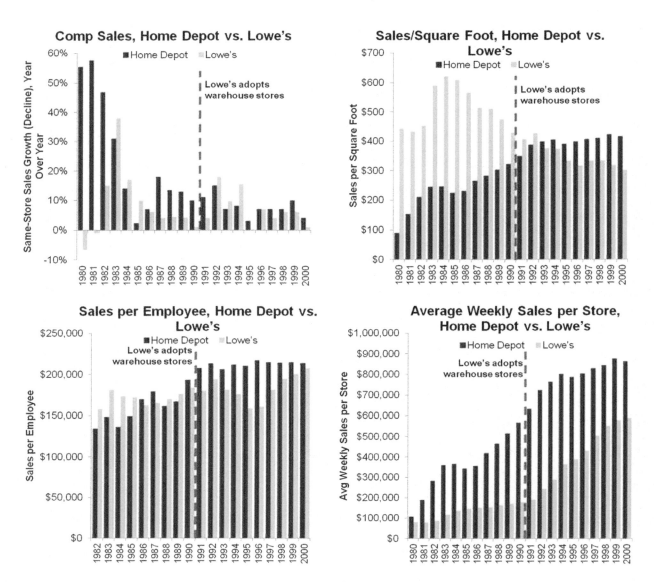

Figure 8.11 Sources: Company reports. Note: While Lowe's operated higher comping stores in the early 1990's, these strong comparable sales were driven by the large amount of new or substantially remodeled stores the company was introducing, creating a store base similar to Home Depot's early years.

With all else being near equal across its clone competitors and against the 1990s era Lowe's, the most likely reason is that Home Depot's culture and employee systems drove this performance.

Customer Cultivation

Home Depot didn't stop at superior customer service. They used it as a base and turned it into customer cultivation. While customer service at Home Depot was about satisfying a customer's immediate need—such as the right product and installation for a chandelier or a faucet—customer cultivation was about teaching the customer how to perform a home improvement project, encouraging them in the process, and helping them move along the spectrum from novice to weekend warrior—and thus expanding the DIY market itself. Arthur Blank described Home Depot's goal in teaching customers as taking someone who was a "light do-it-yourselfer" and turning him into "a serious do-it-yourselfer."[464] Richard Mayo, who joined as Home Depot's first buyer after being Handy Dan's merchandising manager in Texas, and was later promoted to vice president of merchandising, described the process thus: "We were going to enlighten the customer ... maybe we'd start with paint and wallpaper," and when that customer experienced success at his first, simple project, and felt both pride and an inspiration to do more, he became "the next best customer to take on low-voltage lighting outside or that leaky faucet."[465] Throughout the process, the education and expert advice at the Home Depot "took the fear out of a lot of projects."[466]

Home Depot encouraged its customers to try both new projects and better ways of accomplishing existing projects in many ways. First, Home Depot focused its associates on solution-selling. The company trained managers, assistant managers, and associates to ask "What are you building today?" and to discover the customer's ultimate goal. If there were better materials to use in the project, or if there was a better way to complete it, the associate would teach that to the customer. Associates made sure that before a DIYer left the store, they had everything they needed to finish their project. This was not limited to tools and merchandise, but included knowledge and confidence as well.[467]

In addition to this spontaneous one-on-one instruction in its stores' aisles, Home Depot also provided group instruction through classes. Marcus and Blank had held a few classes at Handy Dan, but found they failed to generate enthusiasm and were unsuccessful because "they were taught by manufacturer representatives who thought the sessions were a waste of time" or because the classes focused on tasks that were too simple or crafty, like finishing furniture.[468] Drawing again on their expert and well-trained associates, many of whom had been plumbers, electricians, and craftspeople before joining Home Depot, the company hosted How-To Clinics (which covered topics like installing flooring and staining a deck) to formalize instruction and attract customers to the stores.[469]

The classes were successful, and as Home Depot grew, the company looked at other ways to further educate their customers. One-page print-outs were positioned next to many products, so that customers could take step-by-step instructions home with them. In the company's first try at multimedia, Pat Farrah hosted a radio show on home improvement in the early 1980s. The company followed that up with *Home Improvement 1-2-3*, a 480-page tome on home improvement and also published other books in this series such as *Outdoor Projects 1-2-3*. These books were created by polling Home Depot's own associates about the projects they heard about most and the best solutions they taught customers. *HouseSmart*, a Discovery Channel show sponsored by Home Depot, premiered in 1995. Home Depot also introduced *Weekend*, a home improvement magazine that could introduce customers to seasonal repairs like taking care of poinsettias in the winter. Adding to *Home Improvement 1-2-3*, *Outdoor Projects 1-2-3*, and *Weekend*, Home Depot published a CD-ROM offering DIY advice as well.[470] In 1997, Home Depot introduced Kids' Workshop, which taught children handy skills by means of projects such as building birdhouses. All these teaching tools drew on the experience and expertise of Home Depot's associates, and in many cases, relied on Home Depot's associates to teach the lessons themselves. They were all part of Home Depot's efforts to help more people progressively understand home improvement, and they played a role in encouraging beginning DIYers to take on more advanced projects.

Home Depot's return policy played a role in customer cultivation as well. Home Depot would let customers bring a product back for any reason in order to engender trust. Associates encouraged customers to buy more supplies than necessary, and return the leftovers for a full refund. This return policy took both the fear and the hassle of missing supplies out of DIY work, and so encouraged "people to do projects."[471]

These customer cultivation efforts had real impact in building the home improvement market of the late 1900s. While traditional lumberyards had always done a small amount of business with final consumers, the movement to do-it-yourself home improvement really began in the post-World War II housing boom. It was helped along by a precipitous fall in housing starts (caused by high interest rates) in 1978 that dried up the contactor business and encouraged traditional lumberyards like Grossman's, Scotty's, Central Hardware, and Lowe's to cater more to DIY consumers.[472] The DIY movement may have happened with or without Home Depot, but as one of the first, and by far the most successful, DIY-centric home improvement centers, the company's customer cultivation efforts certainly helped the movement along. Its expert staff, emphasis on teaching, and open return policy encouraged more homeowners to try projects out for themselves; and, after Home Depot's sales passed industry leader Lowe's in 1989, Home Depot stood to gain the most from the increasing DIY trend shown in Figure 8.12.

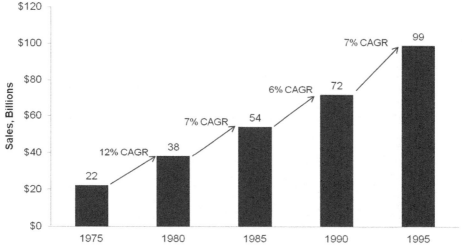

Figure 8.12 Source: Salmon, Walter and Wylie, David, 'Lowe's,' case number 9-590-013, Boston: Harvard Business School Publishing, 1997.

As it entered the end of the 1990s, Home Depot continued to educate the customer and was pursuing new service offerings. For customers still hesitant to do their own installations, Home Depot was gradually adding installation services; taking it slowly after first rushing in too fast and engaging less than perfect third party contractors. After realizing that the company was only capturing 10% of the Pro market, Home Depot began actively catering to small contractors through opening the first Pro desks and the creation of Pro-only services. However, Home Depot was soon about to lose its way.

2000-2007: The Nardelli Years

By the early 2000s, parts of Home Depot's model were beginning to appear dated. The company was approaching store saturation in the United States, growth was slowing, and it was unclear where future growth would come from. After years of double-digit comp store sales growth, the mid to late 1990s brought a string of single digit same-store sales growth numbers. The company had grown significantly, yet, prioritizing decentralization, had failed to capture substantial efficiencies. Competition from Lowe's was also a concern as it became apparent that Lowe's' brighter, cleaner stores were "stealing customers, particularly women."[473]

The Board of Directors, "citing a need for better efficiency, better use of resources, and more operational discipline,"[474] hired Bob Nardelli as CEO in December 2000. Nardelli, coming from General Electric, was well known for process improvements and systems implementations; he was said to be expert at jump-starting businesses that appeared to be stalled at maturity.

Nardelli quickly took charge of the company. He focused Home Depot on extending the business into new lines, expanding into new markets and customer segments, and, in existing operations, driving efficiency, eliminating waste, and ensuring safe, clean stores. Nardelli slowed store growth and redirected resources to the creation of a wholesale building supplies business through acquisitions and investments. This new business, called HD Supply, moved beyond small contractors to target large real estate developers, maintenance staff, industrial contractors, and construction crews and carried supplies not found in the stores like fire hydrants, huge pipes, and steel beams. HD Supply grew quickly, becoming a $12 billion company by 2006.

Yet Nardelli was also responsible for nearly snuffing out the Bleeding Orange culture. In an effort to improve store operations, he instituted a number of cost-cutting measures that ran contrary to the values and people system installed by Marcus and Blank, and reduced the ability of store associates to provide high levels of service and customer education. [475] We've summarized many of these changes and their impact to the stores in Figure 8.13.

People System	Marcus and Blank	Nardelli
Tasks	• Eliminated traditional non-service store tasks that took up associate time	• Introduced a number of non customer-facing reports and paperwork • Attempted to introduce technology to speed up tasks but poor execution negated efficiency gains
People Type	• Full-time experts	• Part-time novices
Store Autonomy	• Store managers had discretion over associate wages and many inventory decisions	• Merchandising centralized, store inventory mismatched to local communities • Wages limited, incentives and reports detracted from customer service
Training	• Marcus and Blank trained managers who disseminated training to associates	• Nardelli more removed from stores, many top managers left company • Little training available
Inverted Pyramid	• Hung in every break room • Behavior often modeled	• Out of favor • Private lunches for senior execs
Bleeding Orange Culture	• Reinforced by above, and by ranks of managers with long tenure	• Exodus of talent as 98% of the top 170 positions turned over) • New workers not invested in culture or career
Return Policy	• Cash on Demand	• Store Credit Only

Figure 8.13 Sources: Sellers, Patricia, "Something to Prove," Fortune, June 24, 2002; Alvarez, José B., Zeynep Ton, and Ryan Johnson, "Home Depot and Interconnected Retail," HBS case number 512-036, Boston: Harvard Business School Publishing, March 2012.

Between 2000 and 2005, profitability did improve at Home Depot, while sales improved 12% a year, largely driven by HD Supply. However, sales at Lowe's increased 19% a year, partly at the expense of Home Depot's retail business. Lowe's stock doubled over the period, while Home Depot experienced a slight fall in stock price. Most importantly, customer satisfaction in Home Depot's core retail operation fell significantly while Home Depot was distracted with HD Supply (Figure 8.14).

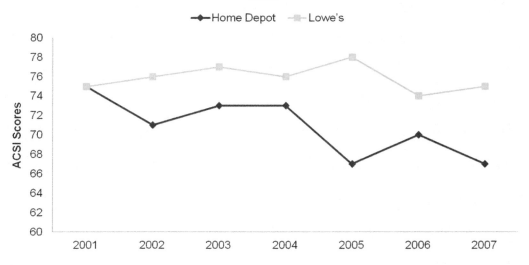

Figure 8.14 Source: American Customer Satisfaction Index. Note: ACSI is the American Customer Satisfaction Index.

As one analyst commented, "They've got people in there working for less money and are less knowledgeable and less experienced. It's all about profitability at the cost of serving the customer." This drop in customer service and satisfaction had huge impacts on the retail business, with Lowe's gaining ground in every important store operating metric, as well as growing its market share relative to Home Depot, as depicted in Figure 8.15.

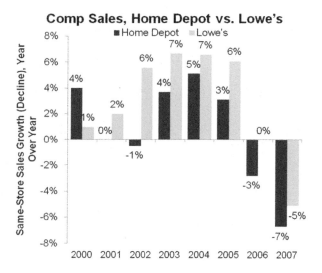

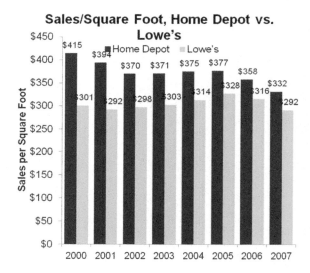

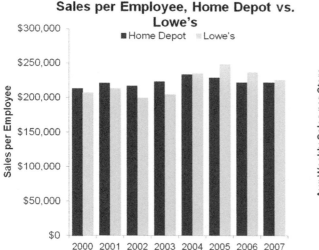

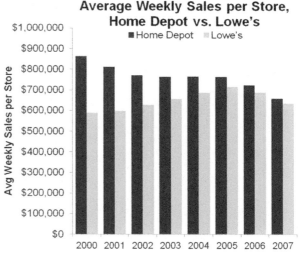

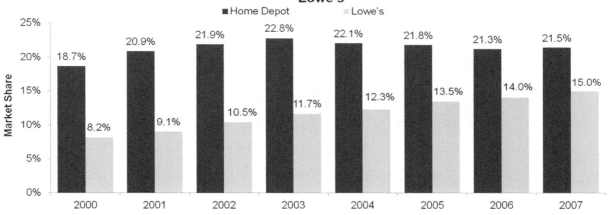

Figure 8.15 Sources: Company Reports, Author Calculations, and US Census of Retail Trade.

2007-Present: Frank Blake's Tenure

In light of the declining retail operations and a stagnant stock price, the Home Depot Board of Directors replaced Nardelli in 2007 with Frank Blake, Home Depot's Vice Chairman of the Board and Executive Vice President of Business Development. Blake made it clear from the start that he would lead Home Depot back to its roots. He publicly brought back the inverted pyramid, announced a return to superior customer service, and emphasized that he planned to return Home Depot to its founders' vision. He also built the "foundational retail building blocks" Nardelli had been unable to produce: "IT, merchandising, supply chain and store operations." With upgraded systems, Blake could return the local feel to stores while "centralizing with more nuance." Blake also quickly sold HD Supply in order to focus on retail operations.

Unfortunately, the US housing market began to falter in 2006, and Home Depot faced negative comp sales and declining sales per employee, store, and square foot. The global financial crisis and the Great Recession followed the housing market collapse. Home improvement retail sales dropped more than 21% between 2006 and 2009 before beginning to recover (Figure 8.16).

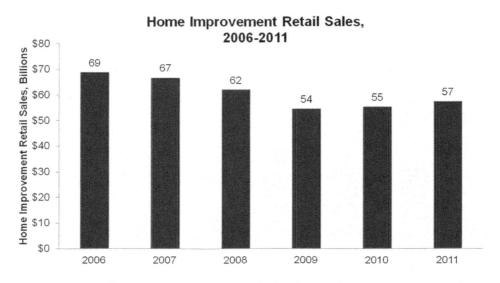

Figure 8.16 Source: "Home Improvement in the US," *Passport*, Euromonitor, July, 2012.

Blake used the recession as a platform for change at Home Depot. Understanding that future income growth would not come from square footage increases but would have to come from operating efficiencies, increased service, and same-store sales, Home Depot under Blake invested over $3 billion in "systems, IT, supply chain, and our people" and tried to get "more out of what we've already got."[476] With many of these investments, Blake effectively used technology to make store operations more efficient, and in other cases, adjusted Nardelli's store operations plan to improve customer service.

As a result of Nardelli's metrics and report introductions, only 40% of store hourly payroll time was allocated to service and selling while 60% was focused on tasking—doing reports, stocking shelves, and dealing with requests from headquarters. Home Depot introduced the '60/40 initiative' which aimed to flip these numbers. To meet this target, Home Depot cut a number of reports introduced under Nardelli's leadership and made it, in EVP of US Stores Marvin Ellison's words, "virtually impossible for people in the stores not to understand that customer service was the most important thing. Service became the number one measure." Home Depot effectively used IT to automate other tasks that were taking up associate and manager time. For example, Home Depot introduced a new scheduling system that automated the assignment of employees to specific departments and time slots based on their training levels and availability. Through this new system, Home Depot eliminated about 30 hours per week of non-customer facing scheduling activity from stores.[477]

The company also used technology to make associates more effective in customer-facing activity as well. The scheduling system operated dynamically, allowing Home Depot to implement activity-based staffing, matching staffing levels with sales. Home Depot also introduced power hours during peak customer sales periods. Associates were expected to only serve customers and avoid administrative tasks in these periods. Both of these initiatives sought to ensure that customers were being served by an appropriate number of associates. Home Depot rolled out the First Phone which gave store associates six tools in one: "phone, walkie-talkie, mobile register, rapid register, inventory management, and business analytics." With the First Phone, and a later scaled-down model called the First Phone Junior, associates could easily locate items on the shelves for customers, call other associates for application-specific help, and check customers out while they waited in line at traditional registers. It also made administrative tasks more efficient, such as determining inventory needs and reordering merchandise.[478] By the end of 2012, Home Depot had made great progress on its 60/40 initiative, with approximately 57% of store labor hours dedicated to customer-facing activity, and was on track to meet its 60/40 goal by the end of 2013.[479]

Home Depot also reemphasized training and learning to make the part-time, non-career path associates hired under Nardelli into "experts in the products and projects that Home Depot sold." Tom Spahr, newly appointed Vice President of Learning at Home Depot, emphasized the importance of educated associates. Customers, he explained, "don't come to Home Depot to buy just a thing; [they] are buying a dream ... so it's not just, 'Here let me take you over to the aisle and here's the item,' but it's 'Let's spend the next 30 minutes together talking about all the parts, pieces, and tools you need and how to use the tools and the techniques you need to do this project.'" Under the new training program, 300,000 associates were trained in 10 weeks, a feat accomplished by leveraging technology to broadcast lessons via webinars, which also allowed participants to chat and ask questions via computer or on the phone. In keeping with the Bleeding Orange culture, Blake also made sure that Home Depot took care of its associates during the recession, increasing the payout of success-sharing checks, introducing additional merit-based pay increases and bonuses, and maintaining its 401k match.

While Nardelli attempted to centralize merchandising and supply chain in order to benefit from economies of scale, he failed due to outdated IT systems and infrastructure and an unwillingness to include store-level input. Under Blake, the merchandising strategy shifted to centralizing "with more nuance." Rather than buying the same things for every store, regionalization was made possible through an "assortment management tool that clustered products and stores based on customer purchasing patterns and inventory turnover." Stores were also granted merchandising control of about 25% of their assortments to capitalize on local knowledge. This merchandising control ranged from deciding how much inventory was required in a reorder to sourcing and negotiating contracts with local suppliers. Thus, Home Depot was able to achieve significant efficiencies while maintaining localized community-based stores.

To support centralized merchandising, Home Depot dramatically improved its supply chain. At the beginning of Blake's tenure as CEO, Home Depot stores were both over-inventoried and frequently out of stock, at the same time. According to Mark Holifield, Senior Vice President of Supply Chain: "37,000 people had the ability to order product from suppliers and 75% of the SKUs were being sent directly from suppliers to stores. Associates were burdened with supply chain tasks."[480] Home Depot built RDCs (rapid deployment centers) that aggregated merchandise for 100 to 130 stores and then distributed the product as needed. This system allowed the company to better respond to high quantity sales of a certain item, often driven by large purchases by Pros. Home Depot also built a central inventory management tool to track the movement of products at each individual store and ensure stores had needed products on the shelves. Even during the Great Recession, the investments in merchandising IT and physical supply chain assets allowed Home Depot to capture the benefits of centralized merchandising and reallocate associate time without disrupting the stores. As a result of these initiatives, Home Depot began to earn ACSI scores closer to its Marcus and Blank era zenith, and, while the end of the Great Recession certainly had an impact, began to realize improvements in sales growth, customer transactions, market share, and gross margin.[481] We show these improvements in Figure 8.17.

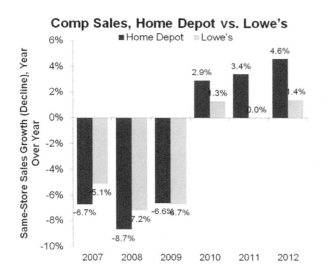

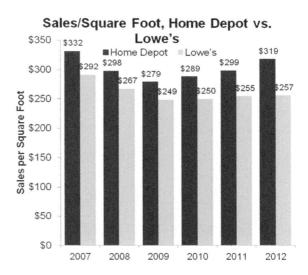

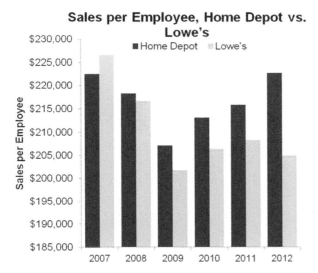

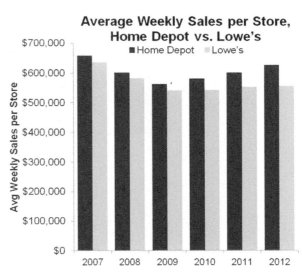

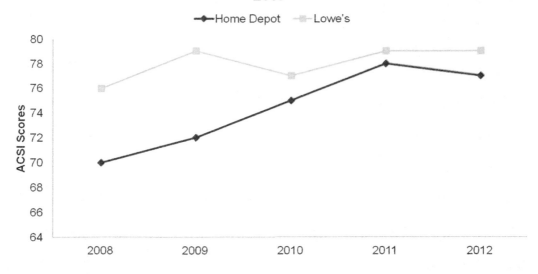

Figure 8.17 Source: Company Reports.

Blake's achievements in increasing customer-facing hours, making associates more efficient, matching associates to sales levels, educating Home Depot's part-time employees, and reinvigorating the Bleeding Orange culture certainly yielded positive results. It should be noted, however, that the employee model under Blake is not the same as it was under Marcus and Blank. In many ways, under Blake, Home Depot is doing more with less: fewer employees in the store and fewer full-time employees. The reduction in employees in the store is not because the stores are getting smaller; store size is actually stable. Rather, employees are now covering more square feet of the store than in the past. Blake has also increasingly relied on the part-time model that began in the last years of Marcus and Blank. We show these trends in Figure 8.18.

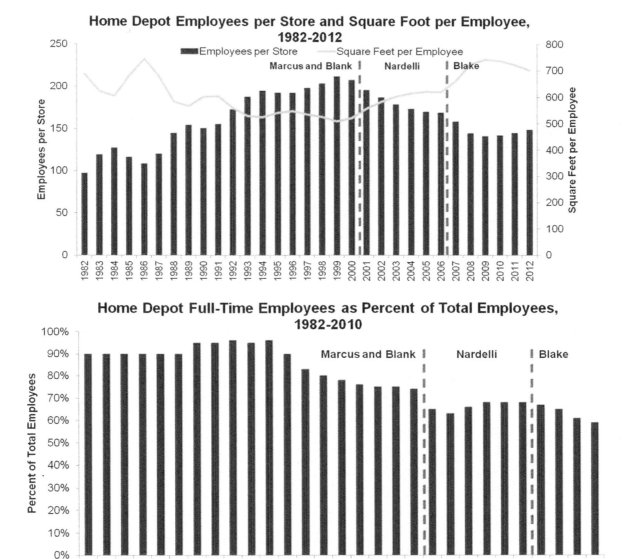

Figure 8.18 Sources: Home Depot 10-Ks. Note: Employees refers to total employees, full-time and part-time, and makes no adjustments to reach full-time equivalents.

Lowe's meanwhile, continues to edge out Home Depot on customer satisfaction, if not profitability. While Lowe's has its employees covering more square feet, it also uses a greater proportion of full-time employees, with 69% of its employees full-time in 2010, compared to 59% for Home Depot. Lowe's' greater use of full-time employees may be the reason for the 2 point advantage it holds over Home Depot on the ACSI score.

Categorizing Home Depot's Response to the Online Threat

We've covered Home Depot's history in such depth to show one thing: service, especially customer education, is very important in this category. Marcus, Blank, and Farrah created the DIY home improvement industry almost from scratch by emphasizing service and customer education. Nardelli did a lot of damage to the retail organization by deemphasizing service in preference for control. Blake has recovered the business by finding new ways to provide high quality service at a lower cost.

However, in an online world, many brick-and-mortar retailers shrink from offering service out of fear that service offered is money wasted if customers leave the store to purchase at a lower-priced online retailer. Many retailers shrink from making investments in online education and service for the same reason. Home Depot, however, is recreating its customer education and cultivation practices on the internet. It is precisely because Home Depot has a protected format that the company can use its online efforts to draw web users to its stores, and can create entirely new business by helping its customers dream. As we discussed earlier, an online threat is present in the Home Improvement space, but it is relatively contained across categories. We think that Home Depot has done a superior job of insulating themselves from customer showrooming behavior while benefiting from the nature of products in their vertical.

For other retailers, who, like Home Depot, have defensible brick-and-mortar stores, Home Depot serves as an exemplar for how to build additional walls around these stores by adding in-store services and exclusive lines, and then leveraging the internet to both expand selection beyond the store and drive new sales through online customer cultivation. Retailers should recognize that just because their category may be viewed as safe or defensible doesn't mean that eCommerce cannot be leveraged to improve the customer experience in the category and further defend the retailer's position. This is the contribution of the "Enhance the Value of the Box" strategy. We will explore how Home Depot is using the following category-specific as well as cross-category and interconnecting tactics to leverage eCommerce: inspiring customers to do more and larger products, extending product advantages through bundling, creating a network of service providers, expanding its online assortment, pairing store assets with eCommerce, and partnering with brands. These tactics draw on the four primary store assets: physical space, people, inventory, and technology that Home Depot is using to strengthen its position across its stores.

To inspire homeowners to undertake DIY projects, Home Depot is in the process of recreating its in-store experience online, and becoming the preeminent online "destination for customers thinking about, planning or starting projects." Home Depot's online site hosts information on products, how-to guides, project plans, and product purchase checklists. Home Depot also created a team of experienced and knowledgeable associates trained to blog, create how-to videos, build links back to the Home Depot site, and film instructional videos. These associates create content for Home Depot's online home improvement forum.

All of these efforts are part of bringing Home Depot's former growth strategy of customer cultivation online. Under Marcus and Blank, Home Depot's stores and associates inspired homeowners to take on bigger and bigger projects themselves, and gave them the confidence, expertise, materials, and tools to do so successfully. The online world gives Home Depot the tools to take this customer cultivation to another level, helping people dream bigger and accomplish those dreams faster.

In the gardening category, Home Depot has taken a compelling approach to customer cultivation online. Through the launch of Garden Club, Home Depot has assembled five million plant enthusiasts in a place where they can trade information, source project ideas and how-to advice, and engage in a community. This community serves as an important customer cultivation tool, as customers educate themselves on different projects they can undertake with materials found at the Home Depot and become more confident in their gardening abilities. In the past, Home Depot was almost a passive cultivator. If a customer came in to build a chicken coop, it was up to the customer to later come in and decide to build a shed. With the Garden Club, however, Home Depot can influence people to begin a new project by emailing exclusive savings or examples of projects made entirely with materials available at Home Depot. This spurs Garden Club members to start and complete a project they may otherwise not have done, or take on a project they would not have even thought about. In effect, Home Depot has turned Garden Club into a demand generation tool. At the same time, Home Depot has satisfied its customers by helping them achieve their gardening dreams through project guides, helpful hints, and online associate advice. While Home Depot may not have online competitors in this category, they definitely compete for a share of a household's overall budget, and this type of customer education and partnership helps them win.

Home Depot can extend the ideas behind its Garden Club strategy to other areas of the store, and has started to do so. It is already taking steps to systematically suggest projects to its customers, which is a way of creating an active, instead of a passive, customer cultivation effort. Through its acquisition of MeasureComp, a floor plan measuring service provider, Home Depot learned that after buying flooring, homeowners often buy different types of supplies (e.g. paint and window treatments) at similar intervals.[482] With this fuller understanding of customers' project lifecycles, Home Depot is better able to time and target messages to customers that suggest projects they're likely to undertake. Also, if a customer is already planning the next project, these messages place Home Depot at the top of their minds. Recognizing this capability, Home Depot continues to invest in customer relationship management capabilities that enable it to communicate with customers in a timely and effective manner.

As part of its effort to inspire DIYers to begin new projects, Home Depot is using its online platforms to remove pain points from customers' projects. Through Home Depot's How-To Community, customers can ask questions of Home Depot associates or other forum members before they get to the store or after they've already left. For instance, a customer who wants to make sure they have everything they need for a project can ask the forum for a checklist before leaving home. A customer who has forgotten a step in their installation process can post to the forum rather than drive back to the store to speak to an associate. These service efforts take Home Depot's customer cultivation efforts onto the internet and save customers time and money. The tools Home Depot has created are a springboard to even greater customer satisfaction.

Introducing customers to more complicated DIY home repairs through efforts like CRM services may be an avenue through which Home Depot can sell its service or

Redbeacon offerings. Redbeacon is an online platform that Home Depot acquired to match homeowners with peer-reviewed and recommended contractors and tradesmen in their areas. Between Redbeacon and the services Home Depot offers directly, the company provides multiple installation and service options. If customers begin to dream, and decide that they'd like extra help accomplishing those dreams, these two Do-It-For-Me service options are great pairings. Customer cultivation that expands a homeowner's dream to include services or categories where Home Depot wins on price and/or delivery creates project-based bundling that further defends the store. Most of all though, customer cultivation online is a chance to show Home Depot's customers what is within their reach, both financially and in terms of their skills.

While inspiration has a valuable role to play going forward, much as customer cultivation did throughout Home Depot's early history, Home Depot will have to strike a balance between perspiration (getting it done) and inspiration (dreaming about getting it done) online. A store associate can quickly distinguish between a Pro customer who is looking to buy 50 panels of sheetrock instantly and a DIYer who is in the store to browse the ceiling fan selection. The distinction is harder to make online. However, Home Depot is addressing this problem by tailoring its online and mobile channels to specific users, and allowing them to self-segregate to the channel of their choice. For instance, through the Pro mobile app, Pro customers can quickly search for products they need, choose products from past receipts to pre-order, and have these items picked and ready for them at the store closest to their current job-site. They can also choose same-day delivery to have their order delivered directly to their job site. The app is designed to help Pros get what they need quickly. Home Depot's website contains a number of features for DIYers, such as the project guides and checklists described above, as well as reviews for projects they may be considering. Home Decorators Collection, on the other hand, is set up for décor-minded homeowners to browse collections. These customers can buy products they like now, or save their favorite items to a Wish List they can return to later as they complete their home decoration designs. This ability to take what, in many cases, is the same inventory, and tailor its presentation to specific customer types and needs, is a powerful and useful way to make the distinction between perspiration and inspiration for Home Depot's online and mobile efforts.

After inspiring DIYers to take on a project, Home Depot has to ensure that it gets the business. Part of the way Home Depot does this is by extending the price, supply chain, and customer behavior advantages it has in certain categories (e.g. building materials, small hardware pieces, installation consumables, paint, and live plants) to less competitive ones (e.g. décor items and power tools) through purchase bundling. By bundling items where it is strong with items where it is pressured, Home Depot is better able to defend itself in at-risk categories. This tactic utilizes Home Depot's complete line of home improvement products, its knowledgeable associates, its strengths as a project—versus a product—retailer, and its position as an omnichannel retailer that can offer everything in one place within the same delivery window.

To extend the shield formed by the building materials, paint, small hardware, and installation consumables categories around other products in its merchandise mix, Home Depot uses the internet to help customers plan projects and bundle product purchases. At homedepot.com, visitors can find a number of project guides to teach them how to perform any number of small tasks around their home. They can also find printable checklists to ensure that they don't forget anything on their store trip. In addition, visitors can create lists to which they can save products while browsing the online assortment. For example, DIYers who want to learn how to install a kitchen faucet can go to this project guide and play a video that will walk them through the process in just over three minutes. If they prefer, they can scroll down the page to read about the installation step-by-step. This is the kind of investment that Home Depot, with its team of merchandisers, will make but that online retailers like Amazon, with its thin teams of category managers and data-driven product rankings, would either rely on brands to do or not undertake in the first place.

These holistic instructional guides also reorient the customer to the project, and not just to the centerpiece. By doing so, the guides pair products for which Home Depot may not win a price war, like faucets, with items that they virtually always win in, like small hand tools, bolts, and consumables. If the customer is buying multiple items, is getting a good price on the total cost, and Home Depot has made it easy for them to buy these items, they are less likely to cross-shop each individual item at online vendors.

A third Home Depot tactic is furthering the service advantage it has built over decades through the use of online and mobile tools. Home Depot has long served Pros well, and Home Depot is now using technology to improve its Pro services in-store and extend its in-store service to online and mobile channels. For Pros, time is money, and they often want to get the supplies they need from Home Depot and get out as fast as possible. With the investments Home Depot has made in automating administrative tasks, they've freed up substantial amounts of associate time that they have reallocated to customer-facing initiatives. With the introduction of First Phone and First Phone Junior, they've also made this associate time more efficient when it comes to tasks like finding product on the shelves. In the past, to collect an order for his job-site, a Pro would either bring his own team or search out help at the Pro Desk. Now, while on the job-site, Pros can order online or through the Pro app on their smartphones, and have all of their materials picked and waiting for them to pick up within two hours of placing their orders. They can also request same-day job-site delivery. Both options save Pros a substantial amount of time, which is very important to them in their choice of where to shop. To order online or via a smartphone, Pros must first set up an account with Home Depot. These installed accounts may increase Pro stickiness against both traditional and online competitors. An added benefit of these accounts is that the user manuals for Pros' power tool purchases are stored online in their accounts, making it easy for them to troubleshoot any issues on a job-site, easily replace a broken tool at the closest Home Depot store, or have a replacement delivered.

On the DIY side, services are particularly vital and Home Depot has long excelled with its in-store services. DIYers in Home Depot stores can get materials cut, fitted, and otherwise altered before leaving the store, saving them from having to purchase another piece of equipment and lowering the cost of their overall project. At-home services have been harder to implement, yet we feel that they are critical to protecting Home Depot's position in many categories. Creating a successful at-home services program at Home Depot could make up for falling productivity in the most at-risk categories, establish a more defensible business, and attract more DIFM customers. We feel that the real threat in many Home Depot categories, particularly those in the yellow bubble of Home Depot's Interconnected Portfolio Strategy in Figure 8.5, isn't from pure-play online retailers. Rather, it is from traditional direct sellers or installers who are now leveraging the internet and their own private label lines, and who have long histories of operating in this space. Renewal by Andersen is the installation arm of the largest window and door manufacturer in North America, with over a century of manufacturing experience. While Andersen sells windows and doors through Home Depot, Renewal by Andersen relies on a brand of windows and doors only available through its installation arm. Empire Today has been installing flooring for over fifty years and focuses on national advertising to convince homeowners to invite salesmen in for a visit. Re-Bath and similar bathroom makeover companies use a franchise model to sell and install bathroom makeovers to homeowners, and can use their own private label lines or well-known brands in the installation. Increasingly, all of these companies are featuring more of their selection online, enabling homeowners to browse and choose product online before contacting a salesperson for a quote.

Home Depot's logistics advantage against online retailers fades in these combined service and product sales. When an installer from ReBath or any of these direct seller/installer companies arrives at a customer's house in his work van or truck, he solves the weight and last leg logistics problems faced by pure-play online retailers by bringing everything with him. Indeed, the steps that Home Depot engages in to sell these services—visiting a home, looking through samples together, measuring and evaluating the area, etc.—are the same steps that these direct sellers/installers take. With the service steps the same, and with many of these installers using their own private labels, it's difficult to see a cost advantage for Home Depot.

It's also difficult to see a service advantage. As many retailers have found, doing service well is hard to accomplish. Home Depot's history in selling services has been no different. The company has been trying to grow its home services business since the mid-1990s, and services are still only 4% of Home Depot sales today. In its initial push, it had so much success in its first combined product-installation sales that it rapidly expanded its services offerings through third party contractors. Many of these contractors did not live up to Home Depot's service standards and the company eventually pulled installation services from many of its products. From that point in the late 1990s, Home Depot slowly expanded its offerings, and tried to choose its third-party contractors with more care. One of Nardelli's growth platforms was to try to expand this services business significantly, but services have stubbornly remained a small share of Home Depot's overall revenue. Former Sears CEO Arthur Martinez, who led a similar failed effort to grow Sears' home services business to $10 billion, has explained the difficulty of the initiative. Centralizing services, he explained, was "an extraordinarily difficult executional challenge. The biggest misjudgment I made was that we could bring scale to this business. It's an intensely local business—dealing with the repairman, technician, carpet cleaner." [483] Ensuring quality and reliability is difficult when the installers are contractors and not employees. Many installers that work for one company are reported to also contract for others, including Home Depot. If the base of installers is the same, it's unlikely any company has a service advantage.

To establish a service advantage in a pool of third-party contractors, Home Depot can either employ installers directly rather than sub-contracting the business, or enable customers to easily choose whom they regard as the best quality contractors. It has taken steps along both paths. Employing installers directly means that Home Depot can instill customer satisfaction training, institute customer service metrics, and in general more closely control customer outcomes. Home Depot has gradually brought some services in house through its acquisition of Measure Comp, as well as its earlier acquisitions of companies such as RMA Home Services, a contract installer of replacement windows and siding, and Installed Products USA, a contract installer of roofing. Home Depot has also made it easier for customers to choose their own tradesmen through its acquisition of Redbeacon. Through this service, Home Depot is using the internet to help its customers find highly rated contractors.

It's important that Home Depot gets the services part of its business right. An installation or service job can apply to almost every aisle in Home Depot, and is critical to defending itself against online retailers and direct sellers. Aside from being potential profit sources, good service experiences also result in increased customer loyalty. In addition, solving the services puzzle removes one more pain point for Home Depot customers. Reliable, trustworthy service providers make it easy for Do-It-For-Me customers to dream about and complete home improvement projects.

A fourth tactic Home Depot has used is to expand its assortment within home improvement by selling additional products online. To accomplish this channel expansion, Home Depot added online merchants that were responsible for "the very fringe stuff, the accessories on the patio furniture that will never be stocked in the store, and maybe custom-made patio furniture that [Home Depot] couldn't have offered before." Merchant teams took a hard look at how to divide assortments between physical stores and online eCommerce portals, and were "constantly evaluating what products were being bought online and what products were sold in stores" to create better online offerings as well as better space allocation, floor layout, and product mix in the store.[484]

Within Home Depot, the company has digitized its special-order catalogs in order to make it more convenient for customers to shop beyond the store assortment. Home Depot also launched a décor-focused site separate from the main Home Depot site by acquiring Home Decorators Collection in 2006. Home Depot has grown this business from around 130,000 products[485] in 2006 to 500,000 SKUs in mid-2012 (as compared to the 35,000 SKUs total, across all categories, available in-store), and had plans to offer 200,000 more.[486] By comparison, Wayfair, a home décor etailer, is reported to have offered over 4.5 million items for the home in 2012.[487]

Despite the larger assortment at other online retailers, HomeDepot.com and Home Decorators Collection are very important platforms for Home Depot. In the two threatened categories at Home Depot, the yellow and red bubbles on Home Depot's Interconnected Portfolio Matrix, Home Depot has responded to eCommerce with expanded online-only assortments. For décor items and the yellow bubble in general, the online assortment opens up choices to customers that they wouldn't see in store. For the red bubble, especially power tools, creating online-only SKUs allows Home Depot to price-compete on these SKUs without the burden of store overhead. Across the store, the online assortment allows Home Depot to enter new categories that stores may not have been able to support otherwise. Items like shower handholds are important to older customers, but brick-and-mortar stores can only carry basic products as they lack the volume to stock a full assortment within the category.[488] However, HomeDepot.com can carry a broad assortment, and, by picking up their online orders in-store or by using the Home Depot community forum, customers can get the advice they need to install these products much as if they were bought from within a store.

Engaging in online power tool sales is proving both a good defense and a good offense for Home Depot. By expanding Home Depot's online assortment and introducing new brands in the online channel exclusively, Home Depot grew market share faster than the leading online retailer in the first half of 2012.[489] Home Decorators Collection is a central location to find all of the more 'finishing touch' items, and, as a separate portal from HomeDepot.com, can target customers more interested in design and style than HomeDepot.com's Pro and weekend warrior customers. In many ways, Home Decorators Collection is providing Home Depot an entrance into the space it tried to penetrate with EXPO by giving customers a different shopping experience than HomeDepot.com or Home Depot stores can. With the massive assortments available at online retailers, having an endless aisle online is really just table stakes for brick-and-mortar retailers. The real issues are how to attract visitors to these websites and convert them to customers, and what to do with the floor space dedicated to these categories in-store.

To become the eCommerce portal of choice for these goods, Home Depot's efforts to build its educational presence online are very important to customer acquisition. For example, Home Depot's How-To Community (the company's online DIY forum) is a source of constantly new material, with part of the attraction being that responses are often written by store associates. This forum and its contents, as well as Home Depot's project guides, serve as valuable search engine optimization tools. Because of these resources, when potential customers search for a phrase like "How to install a faucet?" they have a high likelihood of landing at HomeDepot.com.

Additionally, Home Depot is able to match its online assortment with its in-store services. Ship-to-store enables customers to tap into Home Depot's store-based expertise. Home Depot also deploys its services and installation offerings to help customers use the décor items they've purchased online, an important differentiator relative to online-only retailers.

As high-value, branded, parcel-shipped goods are increasingly sold online, the floor space devoted to these goods will become increasingly unproductive. Power tools, lighting, faucets, window coverings, tiles, and seasonal items like barbecues and patio furniture are all categories threatened by online retailers, and together take up approximately 20% of Home Depot's floor space. It is our belief that the space devoted to these categories will eventually become almost entirely a show space for Home Depot's private label offerings like Hampton Bay.

As the competition for these products moves online and showrooming behavior becomes more widely adopted, Home Depot will need to price-compete with online retailers to win customers. To do so effectively, Home Depot will have to reduce its in-store assortment of branded goods in these categories so that prices online don't reflect the overhead of hosting these items in stores. Price competition with online-only retailers will drive down prices and margin, and Home Depot's exclusive private label collections may become the only items in these categories with enough gross margin to support store overhead. Home Depot prevents showrooming and online price competition in these product lines by controlling the supply, and so protects the margin. What branded goods are left in-store would likely be limited to just the top movers in each design theme (e.g. classic, modern, etc.). It's necessary to keep this limited branded selection in-store for DIYers who are in need of an immediate replacement and may just want to match their previous brand, and for brand-loyal Pros who want to buy brands they have experienced success with in the past and desire in-and-out convenience. In both of these customer cases, design and brand selection just needs to be adequate, but not extensive. Customers wishing to browse décor products in store will be limited to private label products and this small branded assortment.

Many of Home Depot's tactics have paired online and in-store assets. A final in-store asset Home Depot could use is its reverse logistics infrastructure. Any time a customer trip to a store can substitute for a costly last-mile pick-up for an online retailer is an advantage for the brick-and-mortar store. One example of this is power tool rental and repair, where Home Depot is increasing its capabilities in its tool rental department. Rather than customers having to mail a tool out for repair, they can just bring it to a store. Supplementing this in-store ability, Home Depot has also created a reverse logistics supply chain so that tool repairs that are too complicated for in-store repairs can be sent to central facilities for repair. This results in lower costs for customers. It also benefits Home Depot in that even if the company loses share in new tools, it hopes to extend its ownership and authority over the life of the tool, no matter from where it was purchased.

A final tactic Home Depot has used is creating deeper partnerships with brands. While minimum advertised pricing policies (or MAPP, which are policies brands put in place to ensure a price floor exists in the marketplace, the violation of which can result in brands restricting shipments to retailers) have been slow to materialize in the power tools space, Home Depot is using its "strategic relationships with key suppliers" to "bring innovation and brands to market exclusively with us," especially in the power tool category.[490] This exclusivity extends beyond product launches to also include Home Depot's private label and exclusive brands such as Husky, Ridgid, Ryobi, and Milwaukee Tools that can only be found at Home Depot. By controlling the supply, especially among brand-conscious customers such as Pros, Home Depot hopes to pre-empt retailers like Amazon from entering the market in a large way. In the future, Lowe's and Home Depot together may be able to convince their brand partners to adopt minimum pricing and level the playing field between online and store-based retailers. If Home Depot is successful at moving most brands to its online channels in favor of keeping private label in-store, this is especially likely to happen.

Summing Up Home Depot's Response

The examples above are used to outline Home Depot's response to online threats in its industry. The "Enhance the Value of the Box" strategy requires that retailers further defend their stores (through product bundling, services, leveraging store assets, and brand partnerships), while also using the internet to bring more business into their stores (through online inspiration, an expanded online assortment, and technology and cultivation efforts that link these two channels). By no means are these examples exhaustive, there is certainly more that Home Depot could do or experiment with.

For example, the project guides discussed earlier mostly focus on small DIY projects or disaggregated tasks, which are great for the weekend warrior. But, for homeowners looking at larger remodels, online tools to help them define their project, estimate their budget, and suggest ideas would translate their dreams into visible, cost-estimated steps, whether they do the work themselves or rely on Home Depot's installers. Home Depot could also try using its stores to better support its online décor selection. For example, Home Depot could take the approach used in its own paint and flooring sections and show color tabs, fabric swatches, and sample frames to customers buying outdoor furniture. Alternatively, Home Depot could take a CarMax approach where customers can view the company's entire inventory online, and have the cars they are interested in delivered to the CarMax store closest to them. Home Depot could do the same by offering to deliver an assortment of online-only products to a conveniently located store so that customers could see their choices in-person before buying. The pricing structure could be similar to that of Home Depot's pre-installation services: the company could charge a small fee for these preliminary services, which would then be deducted from the final cost of the product if the customer buys one of the pieces. Because customers of online retailers don't have a chance to physically view products before purchasing, and face hefty costs for exchanges or returns, either of these options could save customers money and increase their purchase satisfaction.

While the implementation of its strategy is still evolving, Home Depot's category-specific approach to evaluating the online threat and determining its online strategy has given us a chance to evaluate a range of options that overlap categories and seek to establish a stronger overall position based on the varied mix within Home Depot stores. We've summarized the strategies and categories discussed in Figure 8.19 (organized by strategy) and Figure 8.20 (organized by product category). It's clear that Home Depot has taken many steps in its category-specific approach, but likely needs to take many more to both defend against online retailers and leverage the internet to increase the options available in its stores.

Strategy	Category Characteristics	Categories Affected	How it Works
Bundling	• Heavy, difficult to ship • Low-priced, relatively expensive to ship • Hazardous to ship • Fragile, live goods	• Building materials and building consumables (e.g. spackle) • Small hardware pieces and installation consumables (e.g. plumber's putty) • Paint • Garden	• By pairing products where Home Depot has a pricing advantage with those where it doesn't, Home Depot shows it can get the overall project done for less.
Inspiration	• Entire store save for repair and maintenance products	• Everything from a paint job to a new addition	• By being the source customers go to for help dreaming, Home Depot both encourages new business and stands the best chance of capturing this new business
Services	• Complicated projects • Arduous or difficult tasks • Dangerous installations	• Roofing, framing, etc. • Painting, flooring installation, etc. • Lighting, fan, etc. installation	• Engender loyalty among users with mobile accounts (Pros) • Create a more defensible business against online retailers and make up for lost sales floor productivity • Support customer inspiration by removing technical skills as a prerequisite to building
Balance Online and In-Store Assortment	• High-priced • Low weight • Small size • Branded • Wide assortment critical	• Independent living • Window coverings • Lighting • Faucets • Tiling • Other décor • Outdoor furniture • Power tools	• Supports categories customers want but that can't be hosted in-store • Puts product where it's most productive, and aligns sales channels to customer needs • Competes on same playing field as online retailers • Puts pressure on brands

Leverage Store Assets	• Touch and sight are important purchase criteria • Expensive to ship	• Décor products • Bulky products (e.g. furniture) • Power tools (and rentals)	• Easy returns or ability to see in-store gives customers comfort • Extending focus to lifecycle of product increases authority in category
Partner with Brands	• Brands important in category • Online retailers particularly strong	• Décor products • Power tools	• Brand-enforced minimum pricing or exclusive partnerships provides defense against online retailers

Figure 8.19

Category	Online Threat	Ways to Improve Customer Experience and Defend Against Online Retailers
Bulk Building Materials	Low—heavy, bulky and expensive to ship; complicated inbound and outbound logistics	• Use online tools to encourage customers to dream, and dream big • Inspire projects that bring in less competitive areas of Home Depot's mix • Make Pro ordering more convenient
Countertops and Cabinets	Low—heavy, bulky and expensive to ship	• Inspire projects that bring in less competitive areas of Home Depot's mix • Expand assortment by emphasizing special order capabilities and online browsing
Paint	Low—Hazardous material and so difficult to ship	• Inspire projects that bring in less competitive areas of Home Depot's mix
Nuts, Bolts Hardware	Low—Expensive to each-pick and mail low price pieces. Online more competitive if bought in bulk.	• Bundle with other products (e.g. toilets with plumber's putty) to reduce shipping cost and/or encourage customers to come to store
Garden	Low—Live plants are fragile when shipped	• Creation of online community encourages gardeners to dream and take on projects drawing from the rest of the Home Depot store (e.g. raised beds with lumber, sheds, etc.)
Doors and Windows, Bath Inserts, Basins, and Toilets	Low to Medium—Direct Sellers/Installers increasingly using internet to compete for Do-It-For-Me customers	• Need to own service: either bring contractors in-house or leverage Redbeacon to pair DIFM customers with well-regarded contractors
Flooring	Medium—While bulky and heavy, if ordered in quantity shipping costs are manageable; customers appreciate wide assortments available online	• Bundle with tool rental (e.g. floor edgers, tile saws, etc.) to create a more compelling total purchase • Expand assortment online and leverage ability to ship-to-store to keep cost down • Use service offerings to create a distinction between Home Depot and online product-only retailers
Window Coverings	Medium—Somewhat of a technical product; window must be accurately measured before product is purchased	• Expand assortment online and leverage ability to ship-to-store to keep cost down • Use service offerings to create a distinction between Home Depot and online product-only retailers
Outdoor Living—Patio Furniture	High—High price points and industry standard of drop-shipping; everyone has the same price	• Use store shipping capabilities to enable customers to view in person before buying • Guarantee satisfaction by emphasizing store returns

Décor (Faucets, Lighting, etc.)	High—High brand importance and price, low weight and cube, and ability to carry online makes category perfect for online retailer	• Extend online assortment to compete with online retailers selling branded goods • Use store shipping capabilities to enable customers to view in person before buying • Emphasize higher gross-margin private label items in store, reserving branded goods for online assortment
Powertools	High—High brand importance and price, low weight and cube, and ability to carry online makes category perfect for online retailer	• Control supply through new exclusive brand partners and product introductions • Extend online assortment and price compete on items not carried in stores • Own more of the tool business overall, e.g. repair • Make tool replacement fast and convenient

Figure 8.20

Conclusion

In the context of the "Enhance the Value of the Box" strategy, Home Depot is a study in marshalling assets (stores, inventory, people, and technology) to defend its value proposition and, from this secure base, leveraging technology and expertise to expand its market. Home Depot's store base and inventory of bulk product provides the most efficient way to deliver a large portion of its mix. Its committed sales associates both ensure that Pros are able to get in and out quickly and that DIYers can get the education they need. For convenience and product assistance, the in-store abilities at Home Depot are strong, and getting stronger as management focuses on increasing training and automating manual store processes as well as mobile ordering and delivery options for professionals.

Home Depot associates' ability to deliver education and their customers' need for it, both in-store and online, becomes even more compelling when one understands the innovation occurring in this industry. Even in an industry selling staples like lumber and spackle, innovation is occurring in the parcel post categories online retailers target. For instance, Sharkbite push-fit plumbing fittings can eliminate the need to solder copper pipes, and new power tool launches happen regularly. In the Home Improvement vertical, likely more than in any other retail vertical, customers across the spectrum come in looking for advice and education. This puts these retailers in a unique position to introduce customers to new tools, supplies, and methods. Given that Lowe's and Home Depot between them control 36% of the US DIY, home improvement, and garden retail market,[491] and other formats are chiefly of the small hardware store variety that are unable to stock deep assortments or dedicate associate time to store displays, these two retailers would seem to have a duopoly on the ability to introduce new products. Home Depot is doubling down on this ability through its exclusive brand and product launches.

With solid store defenses in place, Home Depot can launch initiatives to both further build the wall around its stores as well as expand its market, again with the four key assets we've discussed. Pairing the benefits of a broad online assortment for décor items with the ability to see and touch them before taking final ownership would be a benefit to customers. Bundling these online-exclusive items with store-based price benefits on the consumables required to install them and with savings from store pickup drives down the overall project cost. Service offerings paired with online assortments provide complete solutions for the DIFM segment. Carefully balancing online and in-store assortments assures that inventory is placed where it can best be of use. How-to guides and other education tools online help DIYers accomplish their dreams in-store, while online communities like Garden Club drive demand at brick-and-mortar stores in categories where items can't be shipped. A combination of supplier power and new ways of looking at its tool and rental business may help Home Depot defend even its most endangered category against online competition. Above all, the internet provides a way to continue the customer education and cultivation efforts begun under Marcus and Blank. Online videos show homeowners that adding an addition or a deck patio is within their ability, and interactive room designers allow homeowners to virtually repaint their room. Many other online tools to inspire homeowners are also possible. The TIPS assets discussed in this chapter are summarized in Figure 8.21.

Home Building and DIY

1) Which threat do you face?	Products and/or customer purchase behavior does not lend itself to online retail
3) Strategic Imperative:	Enhance the value of the box: help customers dream about home projects and then achieve them

T   Online sales used to expand in-store assortment. Ordering platforms make Pro shopping quick and help to bundle items to offer lowest total project cost. Online education, forums, and groups inspire customers to take on projects. Online network of contractors help DIFMers achieve their dreams.

I   Exclusive brand relationships and private label products act as a defense for brick-and-mortar stores. eCommerce-resistant categories protect threatened ones.

P   High quality, specialized labor provide services. Knowledgeable store associates help customers through projects. Delivery personnel achieve timely order fulfillment for Pros.

S   Warehouse stores act as important node in distribution system that creates competitive advantage with Pros who request job lot orders. Format provides a classroom for DIYers.

Figure 8.21

Importantly, the varied sales mix across the store gives Home Depot a number of options to bring the internet into its business through an interconnected approach and create a better experience for Pros and DIYers alike. It provides opportunities to take strengths in some areas, and extend them to others. By comparing Home Depot's categories with those of other retailers, learnings exist across the entire retailing industry.

Chapter 9
Conclusion

We've attempted to describe three eCommerce-related challenges that brick-and-mortar retailers face and potential responses to each. The first challenge is a fundamental shift in a retailer's core product to digital content and distribution, such as experienced by Blockbuster, Barnes & Noble, and the office supply superstores. The second challenge is that of online retailers' advantages in cost, inventory, and selection, and is most applicable to brick-and-mortar retailers with high value density products that require a deep assortment, such as Best Buy, apparel retailers, and sporting goods retailers. The third challenge is for retailers who, for a variety of both product and customer reasons, run stores that are mostly protected from the eCommerce threats described in the first two challenges, but still must find ways to both build more defenses for their stores and leverage their online presences to drive more traffic to their brick-and-mortar operations. Home Depot and PetSmart are exemplars of retailers successfully meeting this third challenge. Broad assortment, high volume retailers like Walmart, Target, and supermarkets who face all of these challenges are striving to maintain the one-stop shop nature of their stores.

Going from challenge to solution is not a straight line, however. The options available to retailers facing these challenges depend on retailers' individual histories, legacy assets, competencies, customer and brand relationships, and merchandise mixes. Best Buy, for example, will need to convince its brand partners to transform their relationship from that of a customer-supplier to that of a marketing partner. Thanks to past bankruptcies in this space, most notably Circuit City's, which served to both disrupt brands' distribution and leave Best Buy as the last technology showroom, there is a strong chance that brands will be receptive to this new strategy. Conversely, while office superstores sell technology products as well, their smaller market share and limited assortment likely mean that brands will not partner with them in the same way. PetSmart built its store defenses of exclusive products, services, and expert help as a reaction to the threat of mass merchandisers and as a way to take advantage of the pet humanization trend. When eCommerce presented itself as a serious threat to other retailers, PetSmart was already well prepared to defend itself. Walmart's massive scale and existing strength in the grocery retail vertical provides it with a significant opportunity over Amazon and other mass merchandisers like Target as it builds out its next generation fulfillment network of small grocery stores. For retailers without any such advantages, the threat of eCommerce looms much larger, and these are the retailers who should most strongly consider the "Wind Down" strategy. We've presented three solutions retailers are employing to combat the eCommerce threat. This framework is summarized for all the retailers we've discussed in Figure 9.1.

Office Supplies

1) Which threat do you face? — Digitization or disappearance of core product: offices and consumers use less paper

2) Do you have a compelling advantage? — No

3) Strategic Imperative: — Wind Down: Consolidate network and downsize stores to maximize cash flow

T — Bolster cash flow with incremental online sales.

I — Concentrate on basic items and jettison uncompetitive/unprofitable categories; combine store and services group logistics systems.

P — As an order taker, can survive with a bare bones, low-skilled, low-paid workforce whose chief jobs are to stock shelves and checkout customers.

S — Shrink store formats to reflect fewer product categories, maintain flexible leases, create store network consolidation strategy

Consumer Electronics

1) Which threat do you face? — Online retailers have large cost, inventory, and selection advantages

2) Do you have a compelling advantage? — Yes. Brands need a physical showroom for their products

3) Strategic Imperative: — Shrink and transform the format: provide a high-end brand-supported showroom experience relying on eCommerce fulfillment

T — Improve eCommerce operation so that chain can rely predominantly on online fulfillment

I — Stock commodity products online and display high-end electronics in-store, few, if any, items sold in-store

P — Brands provide hyper-informed sales associates for their products, where brands are too small to support a SWAS, Best Buy provides high-end experience with knowledgeable associates. Best Buy Geek Squad functions as cross-brand support network.

S — Shrink store formats to reflect fewer product categories and renovate stores to feature high-end SWAS and product displays.

Supermarkets

1) Which threat do you face? — Digitization or disappearance of core product: Americans eating out more and cooking less

2) Do you have a compelling advantage? — Yes. Regional density and distribution networks good locations, experience selling perishable items and prepared meals

3) Strategic Imperative: — Shrink and transform the format: technology used to make shopping CPG easier, stores refocused to provide meals and education

T — Introduce automated picking systems and mobile ordering platforms

I — Fresh goods and prepared meals displayed for customers, CPG goods in warehouse fulfillment.

P — Better trained, higher quality store labor to help customers with selection, meal planning, and preparation.

S — Shrink store formats to locate closer to customers, gain greater leverage on occupancy costs (e.g. lease fallow space), and make grocery shopping easier and more convenient for customers

Walmart

1) Which threat do you face? — Online retailers have large cost, inventory, and selection advantages

2) Do you have a compelling advantage? — Yes. Massive scale and logistics expertise

3) Strategic Imperative: — Shrink and transform the format: supercenters act as nodes in distribution network for eCommerce and small format stores

T — Develop strong eCommerce platform to compete with Amazon.

I — Products competitive with eCommerce (i.e. dollar store merchandise and food) stocked in small formats, larger assortment stocked in supercenters and distribution centers.

P — Investments in eCommerce personnel required, small format employees may need different skills

S — Expansion of small format stores is essential. Rethink viability and customer experience of 180,000 square foot supercenters to accommodate eCommerce, a new role as distribution centers for small stores, and an eCommerce-driven shift in categories

PetSmart

1) Which threat do you face? — Products and/or customer purchase behavior does not lend itself to online retail

3) Strategic Imperative: — Enhance the value of the box: services, ambiance, highly-trained associates, and exclusive/private label goods draw customers

T — Need to develop strong eCommerce platform to drive web traffic to stores and heighten the engagement of pet parents with the brand (education and health).

I — Exclusive brand relationships and private label act as a defense for brick-and-mortar stores. High-end food capitalizes on pet humanization trend.

P — High quality, knowledgeable store associates with specialized training provide services, cater to pet parents, and support brands.

S — Inviting store ambiance that attracts pet parents

Home Depot

1) Which threat do you face? — Products and/or customer purchase behavior does not lend itself to online retail

3) Strategic Imperative: — Enhance the value of the box: help customers dream about home projects and then achieve them

T — Online sales used to expand in-store assortment. Ordering platforms make Pro shopping quick and help to bundle items to offer lowest total project cost. Online education, forums, and groups inspire customers to take on projects. Online network of contractors help DIFMers achieve their dreams.

I — Exclusive brand relationships and private label products act as a defense for brick-and-mortar stores. eCommerce-resistant categories protect threatened ones.

P — High quality, specialized labor provide services. Knowledgeable store associates help customers through projects. Delivery personnel achieve timely order fulfillment for Pros.

S — Warehouse stores act as important node in distribution system that creates competitive advantage with Pros who request job lot orders. Format provides a classroom for DIYers.

Figure 9.1

Retailers who should "Wind Down" and manage for cash flow undoubtedly would rather find themselves in another solution category. The decision to manage for cash flow necessitates a variety of difficult decisions: possibly seeking a private equity sponsor, shutting down stores, finding employees willing to work in short-lived positions, and most of all admitting that the path forward is not one of growth but rather of retrenchment. However, trying to pursue a different path is reckless. Retailers in this category face the digitization and eCommerce-superiority challenges described above. Using physical outlets to fight a head-to-head battle with online retailers over goods that are now (1) digital, (2) disappearing altogether, or (3) dramatically less expensive online; and that possess no customer preference for in-store help, experimentation, or immediate fulfillment is pointless. Brick-and-mortar retailers who should "Wind Down" will find the "Shrink and Transform" strategy to be either a mere delaying action or a waste of resources. There is simply no unique advantage around which to build a new, permanent format. JC Penney attempted a transformation under Ron Johnson, using stores-within-a-store (SWAS) to generate traffic. However, the SWAS were a poor fit with JC Penney's legacy locations and customers, and enormous amounts of time and billions of dollars were wasted. Some may point out that bank branches face a similar digitization threat as office supply superstores, but may survive by rebuilding the branch around personal account executives and more sophisticated services rather than transactions. Yet this example fails to hold much promise for formats like office supply superstores, which don't have a comparable service offering to make up for the loss of foot traffic-generating office supplies.

The "Enhance the Value of the Box" strategy is also not an option for retailers with stores that should be wound down, as their large store legacy formats will drag these companies under. There is nothing these stores can build from as physical product sales evaporate because of changing consumption habits or are sucked out of the store by eCommerce. Any investment in online education, from the perspective of these brick-and-mortar stores, is wasted as those sales migrate to online retailers. Circuit City is an exemplar of this tactic's misuse. It maintained high-service operations while bare bones Best Buy stores, often located very close by, vacuumed up the sales when Circuit City-educated customers walked across the parking lot to compare prices. By the time Circuit City realized its predicament, it was too late to turn the company around. Blockbuster also attempted the "Enhance the Value of the Box" strategy, but by the time Blockbuster acted, it probably should have wound down its stores. Blockbuster's misplaced effort squandered a large amount of investors' cash. In contrast, Netflix is doing a great job of winding down its DVD-by-mail business as its streaming operation cannibalizes customers. Toys 'R Us is attempting to use private label toys to defend its stores, but fickle and fast-growing children are not life-long customers like Home Depot's contractors, and without brands' national advertising, it's unclear that this is an effective barrier to online competitors. The best solution for retailers with disappearing or uncompetitive categories and no enduring advantages is to wind down the stores and manage the businesses for cash flow, in effect turning the business into a declining annuity for its shareholders.

The strategies of those retailers in the "Shrink and Transform the Format" solution category may look disparate, but in reality are just different implementations of the "Shrink and Transform the Format" strategy. These different implementations share commonalities in the threats they address and in the ability of their respective retailers to focus on a compelling advantage. Best Buy will focus on its ability to act as a showroom for retailers in its transformation; supermarkets will capitalize on their locations, distribution networks, existing customer bases, and perishables experience as their stores transform into more Drive-like operations; and Walmart will leverage its scale and logistics as it builds out its small store eCommerce pickup points. For all these retailers, there is value to be both created and captured into the future, and consequently winding down is likely not the value-maximizing solution.

However, these retailers also can't maintain their current store bases against online competitors—pure-play online retailers have too many advantages in price, selection, and service. Consequently, they cannot adopt the "Enhance the Value of the Box" strategy. Best Buy and other retailers have tried to compete directly through price-matching policies and have suffered the consequences in plummeting gross margins. We don't pretend that this group has an easy road ahead: it will be a herculean and expensive effort to transform store formats, store networks, supplier relationships, and customer expectations and behavior—and the outcome may result in lower absolute profits than during these category killers' heyday.

Facing this difficult path, retailers could be forgiven for thinking that they can work themselves into a position where the "Enhance the Value of the Box" strategy is viable. When comparing PetSmart to Petco, they might think they can get there by introducing private label products, exclusive brands, educated in-store help, and services. These retailers should very carefully consider whether this is a viable option. Many retailers in the "Shrink and Transform the Format" solution category participate in retail verticals where online retailers have already gained so much market share that brands would be reluctant to cut off online distribution in order to favor an exclusive relationship. With strong national brand presence, the ability of retailers to introduce private labels that people care about is questionable. In verticals with short product cycles, the ability of retailers to innovate given the amount of research and complexity involved is also in doubt. Few verticals lend themselves as well to services as pets. If a wall cannot be built around the brick-and-mortar store, investing in online education makes little sense as sales generated by these efforts can be siphoned off by more efficient online-only retailers. It's important to remember that PetSmart's and Home Depot's current enviable positions are the results of many years of guided evolution and experimentation to create their significant private label offerings, dedicated customers, brand reputation, educated employees, and service offerings. Given the continuing rapid advance of eCommerce and the limited margin for experimentation described in the gross margin and same-store sales threshold figures in the introduction to this book, most retailers probably need to take immediate action to right-size their store formats and lack the time to find a solution that permits them to keep their legacy square footage. It's most likely that a slimmed down and focused retail format, combined with renegotiated brand relationships, serves customers, brands, and shareholders best.

Many retailers adopting the "Shrink and Transform the Format" strategy won't be competing with online retailers directly by selling goods, instead they will opt to act as showrooms or service centers. Those that can compete head-to-head, however, like Walmart and supermarkets, may have no other choice but to do so. For retailers with broad merchandise assortments, dropping a non-productive merchandise line would damage their one-stop-shop promise and possibly lose them customer segments who may go online or to other retailers for the convenience of shopping at a single portal. Broad-assortment retailers are also often dealing in commodity products, and they have little to build a store around besides assortment and low prices, as JC Penney discovered. With little category expertise, they would function poorly as showrooms, and their customers likely require little in the way of education for products that are so widely understood. If they do nothing, declining sales in even a few categories will eventually reach a point where they threaten to overwhelm the positive aspects of the store, and at this point these retailers would find themselves faced with adopting a Wind Down strategy. Broad-assortment retailers, enabled by technology, do, however, have significant opportunities to solve persistent customer problems with their current formats, such as long checkout lines, difficult-to-navigate stores, and a lack of service, by a wholesale reimagining of what their brick-and-mortar stores, supply chain, and employees can do. By engaging in this transformation, it's possible that they can beat online retailers at their own game.

Retailers in the "Enhance the Value of the Box" solution category, like Home Depot and PetSmart, should not be searching for another option. They have no reason to shut down stores, trim store sizes, or reimagine their offer as their brick-and-mortar stores will experience negligible negative impacts from eCommerce. They should, however, be prepared to further defend their brick-and-mortar stores with brand partnerships and/or private label products, expanded in-store fee-for-service offerings, and possible new business models such as Home Depot's online contractor platform. In the last extreme, they could consider substituting out threatened merchandise lines for more defensible ones. The main challenge for these retailers will be to imagine the internet not only as a way to sell goods online, but as a way to serve customers better and generate more interest in their stores, such as Home Depot has done with its Pro smartphone apps and Garden Club group. With their deep product and customer expertise compared to many pure-play online retailers, they should be capable of doing so.

Readers should also note that the retail environment is changing rapidly. Many of the trends we speak of are already upon us and technological capabilities are advancing quickly. Retailers facing a given threat today may face new ones tomorrow. For instance, retailers that currently have little to fear from an online threat due to current customer purchasing behavior will need to monitor this behavior closely to ensure that it cannot be conducted online. To accommodate this unstable environment, retailers must create much more flexible operations than they have been accustomed to in the past regarding all of their TIPS assets, but especially their store real estate.

Because of the different core competencies of brick-and-mortar and online retailers, the strategies discussed above try to leverage the existing abilities of brick-and-mortar retailers. However, many retailers, particularly those pursuing the "Shrink and Transform the Format" and "Enhance the Value of the Box" strategies, will be forced to build new competencies. Figure 9.2 can serve as a roadmap for these retailers to understand what capabilities they are missing.

	Traditional Retailer	Internet Retailer	eComm Platform/Enabler
How They Create Value	• Break bulk • Reduce transport costs for customers (e.g. act as one stop shop) • Create showroom and selling point for brands • Provide services to customers for which they are willing to pay • Provide channel for convenience and impulse buying	• Lower operating costs than B&M (people, occupancy, depreciation) • Lower working capital than B&M (consolidated inventory + payment days) • Efficient transport to end consumer • Lowest prices • Widest assortment for customers • Create place for small brands to thrive	• Become first point of consideration (i.e. drive traffic to site) • Charge vendors for use of platform • Keep platform costs low while continuing to develop capabilities • Eliminate risk: weather, obsolescence, execution, and real estate
Key Decisions	• Format design • Store location and network design • Determination of curated assortment • Negotiation of buys and determination of buy volumes • Determination of pricing • Allocation of buys to stores • Scheduling of store personnel • Warehouse locations • Transportation infrastructure • Hiring and development of buyers • Hiring and development of store operations personnel	• Fulfillment center locations • Shipping partners (e.g. UPS vs. USPS vs. FedEx) • Negotiation of buys • Determination of pricing • Fulfillment center technology development and infrastructure • Hiring of key management for intellectual property development (e.g. CRM algorithm developers, machine learning experts)	• Platform technology • Partner acquisition • Hiring of relationship managers for platform customers • Hiring of key management for intellectual property development (e.g. CRM algorithm developers, machine learning experts)
Risks Inherent in Model	• Real estate • Missed sales from out of stocks • Inventory obsolescence (perishability/fashion as well as customer traffic issues) • Weather • Theft and robbery • Execution: store locations as multiple points of failure and under/over allocation of store personnel	• Fulfillment center location • Inventory obsolescence (but significantly reduced from B&M) • Technology obsolescence • Hacking of site • Loss of consumer appeal • Missed sales from out of stocks (but significantly reduced from B&M)	• Technology obsolescence • Loss of consumer appeal • Hacking of site

Figure 9.2

Identifying the challenges they face, exploring what advantages they have versus online retailers, and developing strategies such as those suggested by our framework are near-term, three- to five-year problems for brick-and-mortar retailers. Beyond this timeframe, the challenges posed by eCommerce, and the strategies that these challenges will force upon brick-and-mortar retailers, will also be responsible for broader trends within the retail industry. In addition, we see future customer trends among Millennials, driven by their close connection to technology and their generation's coming-of-age during the Great Recession, that retailers will need to pay close attention to in order to ensure that their long-term strategies are aligned with their future customers.

The Trends Shaping Retail's Future

While some of these trends are mostly relevant just for Millennials and the retailers that will serve them, many will have important ramifications for customers, suppliers, and the United States as a whole. We'll first discuss these trends on their own as we describe our vision of the broad future of retail, and end with the impacts that these trends and the implementation of the strategies we have posited will have on all stakeholders within the retail system.

Since the rise of department stores in the late 1800s, the broad trend in retail has been towards one-stop shops. Early department stores tried to capture all the trips a consumer might possibly need to take. Michael Cullen's grocery store combined the separate functions of a butcher, a green grocer, and a dry goods merchant in one store. Walmart combined its discount department store with a supermarket. Category-killers sought to answer any need or desire a customer might have within their category in one spot. Now, however, we are witnessing a fragmentation in retail across channels as stores do what stores do best, and eCommerce picks up the rest. For instance, Best Buy has moved lower-priced TVs out of its stores and into the online channel where it is better able to compete, reserving store space for MAPP compliant products. Office Depot and other office supply retailers are shrinking their footprints and moving technology and furniture products online. Home Depot is limiting décor assortment in the store to its proprietary and exclusive brands and using its eCommerce operation to provide a broader assortment. This can be frightening for retailers who delivered a brand promise of one-stop convenience to customers. Without that promise, could they lose sales, traffic, and relevance with customers? Many supermarkets, for instance, would gladly drop loss-leading diapers from their aisles, if not for the fact that parents, a key customer segment, would probably abandon the stores in droves. This one-stop promise, however, appears to be losing its relevance with consumers. This could be liberating for many retailers.

As demonstrated by the subculture of bargain-hunting coupon clippers, customers today are getting very good at using technology to determine just where to go to get the best price, and have no problem shopping multiple outlets when most of the pre-work has already been done at home. Smartphone apps and subscription programs are also making it simple for customers to purchase items on the go or set up specific deliveries for routine purchases. This makes it very easy for customers to segregate their purchases between different outlets. This, of course, raises the question of whether the one-stop promise will remain relevant to customers. Could all those retailers with products on the shelves that just don't make sense on a stand-alone basis, but are needed to provide a full assortment, abandon those products to online retailers or their own online operations and focus their brick-and-mortar stores on just what they're good at without losing customers? Walmart's plan to base its future growth on narrow-assortment supermarkets and dollar stores, backed up with online fulfillment for everything else, may help customers adjust to this new mindset. For retailers hesitant to slim down their stores, jettison poorly performing categories, and otherwise engage in the "Shrink and Transform the Format" strategy out of fear of losing their one-stop-shop promise, a close watch of this consumer trend may give them the confidence to adopt this approach.

The rise in the popularity of "extreme couponing"—the extensive and focused use of coupons and other special offers to save money when shopping—is related to the recent recession which forced many families and individuals to adopt more frugal practices. Millennials have come of age during the worst macroeconomic conditions since the Great Depression. In 2010, 37% of 18-29 year-olds were either unemployed or out of the workforce, the highest rate in 30 years. Graduating from college in a bad economy also has long-lasting negative consequences.[492] As a result, many Millennials may remain price-conscious even as they age and move into higher-paying jobs. This attitude will likely manifest itself in greater price transparency and continuing price pressure for retailers. In a survey of online shopping behavior, displayed in Figure 9.3, SymphonyIRI found that Millennials were far more likely than other generations to have engaged in online couponing activities like downloading coupons when shopping for CPG products.

Online CPG Shopping Behaviors of US Online Shoppers by Age, Q4 2012			
Age Range	18-34	35-54	55+
Download coupons from couponing sites	55%	38%	21%
Download coupons from retailer websites	53%	40%	24%
Download coupons from manufacturer websites	53%	42%	25%
Use social media sources to get coupons	40%	22%	4%
Visit online deal sites	38%	27%	12%

Figure 9.3 Source: "MarketPulse Survey Q4 2012," *SymphonyIRI,* as cited in "2012 CPG Year in Review: Finding the New Normal," Feb 20, 2013; accessed via *eMarketer.*

Even if Millennials grow out of what may be just a frugal life stage, they will likely flatten prices due to their widespread digital access and comfort with technology.

Outside of technology, another trend in retail has also been responsible for flattening prices. Category killers and other retailers have been actively blurring the line between retail and wholesale as they have sought to maximize the asset productivity of their brick-and-mortar stores. Best Buy services both small businesses and consumers with its Geek Squad service. Costco blends both customer groups together in its warehouse club with the only difference being the membership tier. Office supply retailers have long had customers from across the spectrum. Building material retailers like Home Depot have set up special services for their professional customers, while their consumer customers benefit greatly from associates' experience.

All these retailers have succeeded in pushing the retail price closer and closer to the wholesale price. The online environment promises to narrow this gap further. With the transparency and efficiency of eCommerce, customers are able to connect directly with manufacturers and brands. Platforms like Alibaba make it simple for a customer in the US to buy directly from a manufacturer in China. eCommerce operations have enabled many brands, such as P&G, to connect directly with customers. Amazon is increasingly in the business of providing these services to brands and third-party sellers rather than acting as a retailer itself. These developments often remove the retailer from the equation, and can create universally similar, generally lower, prices. Over two-thirds of digital natives, for their part, can envision purchasing directly from manufacturers in the future in order to save money, according to an Oracle report.[493]

These eCommerce developments will also likely shift the balance of power between retailers and brands. A 2013 Harris poll makes the case that webrooming (examining or researching a product online before purchasing it at a brick-and-mortar store) has a significantly higher penetration than showrooming across all generations.[494] Product discovery has also changed, with Millennial internet users rating word-of-mouth and social networks as far more important influence sources in their purchases of apparel, packaged foods, and travel than the Baby Boomer population. Word-of-mouth specifically was the most influential source for Millennials while it was generally one of the least influential sources for Baby Boomers.[495] While Best Buy has a compelling case in its transformation to a brand-sponsored showroom, brands may be better positioned to act as the source of and sponsor for word-of-mouth and social marketing content.

Millennials also want to be more engaged with the brands they buy. In an Edelman Berland study, the Millennials' top answer, given by 40% of respondents, to the question of "How do you wish to be entertained by brands?" was to allow the Millennial to influence the product in a co-creation relationship.[496] This may be a result of Millennials' greater drive to express themselves, as implied by their higher-than-average tattoo and piercing rates, or simply a result of Millennials having more media in which to communicate given the wide-spread adoption of social media and brands' desire to engage with this customer segment. Whatever the reason, closer relationships between brands and customers may weaken part of the retailer's value-add in the brand-retailer relationship if brands no longer rely on retailers to help them understand what customers want, where it's selling, and how to market it.

In an environment of flatter prices and greater brand power, retailers of all sorts must constantly evaluate the added value that they can contribute to their ecosystem and answer the question of "What reason do customers and suppliers have to come to my company?" in order to identify and cultivate their points of differentiation from competitors. This introduces another key development in retail, which is the choice of being a destination store or a convenience store. Category killers have long been destination stores—they located outside of residential zones, and customers knew that if they had a need or want within a category, they could resolve it at a category killer, making the trip worthwhile. Retailers like Best Buy and PetSmart are attempting to reinvent the meaning of a destination store within the category killer context by making destination less about a one-stop-shop and more about some unique, defining characteristics. Best Buy's store-within-a-store program provides customers a unique space to browse technology they won't find anywhere else. PetSmart has increased the relevance of the destination definition with the services it offers in its stores. Other category killers, however, are reducing their footprints in order to compete with convenience. Office Depot's 5,000 square foot stores are one example, PetCo's small format, urban neighborhood-located Unleashed by Petco model is another. The Best Buy Mobile format is an interesting blend of both, created to satisfy consumers' need to see expensive electronics in person before they buy them in the most conveniently located setting possible.

What Millennials think of convenience, however, is somewhat contradictory. On the one hand, convenience-oriented apps like Uber, HomeJoy, Instacart, Postmates, eBay Now, and many others will perform all manner of tasks for users at the push of a button, usually for a premium over what customers would pay to do it themselves. These apps are being driven by young, wealthy, Millennial users. Such customers would probably gladly pay a premium at the small-format store close to them in order to have something they wanted right away (or even pay someone else to go get it for them). On the other hand, customers' overwhelming preference is for free, rather than fast, shipping, as shown in Figure 9.4.

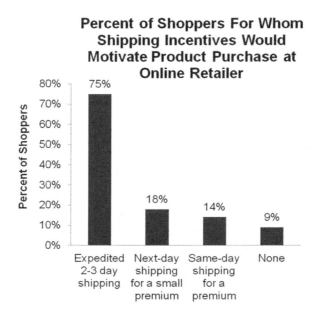

Figure 9.4 Source: eMarketer; Note: Assumes product price is the same across all retailers; survey conducted in December, 2013 in France, Germany, the UK, and the US.

Price-conscious customers, i.e. the majority of Americans, will likely wait on their orders, or price-shop them at stores further away and pick them up as part of their weekly errands. The question of whether convenience is a defensible strategy remains open.

It's also a very important question to Amazon and Walmart as their solutions envision two very different futures. In the convenience-maximizing future led by Amazon, so much volume has been sucked out of stores that, from an ROIC-perspective, large numbers of retail verticals, including grocery, cannot support their store base. In this future, consumers are relatively sedentary creatures content to have their purchases delivered right to their door, and have few, if any, other purchasing options. They don't go shopping as we know the term today. Even for retailers recreating destination stores, such a future virtually eliminates any walk-in traffic they may have attracted. These retailers will have to create a very compelling destination store to convince customers to leave their homes. In the price-focused Walmart future, rather than stay at home, customers will leave their homes and visit supermarkets and dollar stores to pick up their packages. Retailers can then cluster around these collection points in order to benefit from cross-traffic. While other retailers have for years competed with Walmart, Walmart may actually be their saving grace in the future.

The contrasting views among Millennials regarding convenience point to another trend, which is the bifurcation of customers across income. We explored this development in depth in the supermarket chapter, and the income inequality that drives these differences will likely become even worse as Millennials' current unemployment and divergent career paths play out. What this means for retailers is that occupying a position in the middle of the market, like supermarkets have done for so long, may be a tough position to hold.

All of these trends have important ramifications for parties besides retailers themselves.

Brands will need to evaluate what functions they can take on, and what is better left to retailers themselves. It is likely that more and more brands will find themselves involved in more parts of the industry value chain. eCommerce has helped small brands that don't have the volume to merit shelf space in main-stream retailers tremendously. Larger brands will need to determine if distribution relationships are still important. Product innovation could benefit from real-world marketplace testing much more quickly. Brands may choose to focus more on niche development, one level up from mass customization, in order to pursue new growth markets. New product introductions could become less expensive with resources invested in new forms of advertising rather than purchasing shelf space. The entire concept of physical shelf-space and inventory may be rendered obsolete if 3D printing becomes a form of on-demand product fulfillment.

It's notable that two of the three strategic options retailers have involve store closures and/or shrinking formats. Retail property developers will face a continuing glut of retail space on the market. This will lead to falling rental rates in most segments of retail. Category-killers, seeking the ability to adapt more quickly, will also want shorter lease terms, and, given the abundance of available space, will likely get them. Retailers will also become competitors to their landlords. Many retailers, unable to get out of store leases, will try to sublease out some percentage of their floorspace or entire stores as they seek to either shrink formats or shut down stores. This will make the above problems worse for retail property owners. In looking for new tenants, retail property owners will need to carefully evaluate retailers using the framework we've described.

The largest impact from these trends, however, will be felt on a national scale. Eleven percent of jobs in the US are in store-based retail, with many more jobs indirectly supported by retail stores.[497] Given that online retailers are as much as four times as efficient as brick-and-mortar stores from a sales per employee perspective, massive cuts in retail employment are inevitable. Using just the example of supermarkets, we can identify many functions and activities that would cease to exist in the Drive model:

- Fronting and facing merchandise
- Reduced walk paths due to smaller store footprints and more efficient product storage
- Reduced touch points as merchandise is loaded onto shelves in cases rather than by individual item
- Time spent assisting customers in-aisle
- Greater efficiency from inventory tracking and product location

Retail jobs are also of critical importance in the contexts of the larger economy, questions of public policy, and the career paths of many workers. These jobs have been some of the few available for people with low education levels and low skills. Before the most recent recession, they were also opportunities that served as a training ground and a stepping stone to better jobs. Often, individuals without a great amount of formal training or education could advance quite far in their careers within a retailer. In recent years, the average education level in retail has been rising significantly as a reflection of the greater economic difficulties faced by many Americans. Retail jobs have become the last resort for many Americans facing hard times. When many of these jobs evaporate, a large and fundamental piece of the American dream and safety net will disappear. Income inequality will grow measurably worse as a direct result.

Retail's value-added contribution to the US economy makes up six percent of US GDP. If eCommerce successfully disintermediates a significant portion of brick-and-mortar stores, this transition could lead to slight productivity-related deflationary pressure as increased efficiency decreases the value-added contribution and brings the general price level of retail goods down. This is the same effect with which Walmart has been credited in the past.

Mild, productivity-driven deflation is really of negligible concern, however. More worrying to retailers and to policy-makers is what will happen to the 27% of US GDP that is the end-result of retail sales if consumers, specifically Millennials, reduce their consumption.[498] As Millennials take over the high-spending, middle-aged cohort, a number of factors may limit their consumption: more targeted shopping patterns, a rise in the renting/sharing economy, delayed major life events, a general lack of desire for possessions, and continued underemployment and lower incomes coupled with high student loan debt. While internet-led productivity gains may cause a fall in prices, they are unlikely to lead to a fall in the quantity of things consumed. The dynamics just listed, however, could.

Shoppers' buying behavior online is much different than it is in-store. Trends among Millennials are exacerbating this outcome. Millennials are more likely to research products online than other generations.[499] Millennials are also more likely to click on search ads (Figure 9.5).

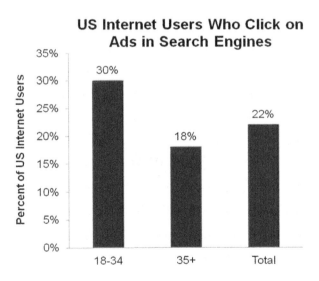

Figure 9.5 Source: eMarketer.

The result is that Millennials' purchases are more carefully researched and targeted, leading to a decline in trips, smaller baskets, and, ultimately, lower consumption.

Millennials are also finding new ways to consume that don't require purchasing products. While it may just be a temporary result of the Great Recession, and there are signs that it may tick up, home ownership among 29-34 year olds is a little over half of what it was between 1999 and 2001. Millennials, at least right now, are more likely to be renters. If this is an intentional choice not to own things, it is reflected in the rise of the sharing economy. The sharing economy, aided by ubiquitous internet and mobile access, online trust creation mechanisms, and Millennials' greater confidence with technology, is removing the need to own consumer goods when they can instead be rented or bought as a service. By increasing the utilization of products already produced, from cars to power tools, Millennials are eliminating the need to individually purchase these items.

Millennials' lower rate of home ownership also points to a Millennial trend of pushing major life events, such as marriage and having children, back into later adulthood. This leaves Millennials with less time to form families and create dependents. Part of the reason that middle-aged households spend more is because they have more people in them, but Millennial-led households may not experience this same consumption uptick until later in life, and when it happens, the uptick may be smaller.

Millennials are also showing signs that they may simply not want to consume as much, at least per capita, as previous generations. What Millennials want materially may be less than what everyone else thinks they need. When asked what will be one of the most important things in their lives, Millennials, like other generations, often respond with intangible goals like "being a good parent" and "having a successful marriage" rather than financial criteria like "Having a high-paying career." However, Millennials also say that, despite their wide-spread unemployment, they will have "enough money or will eventually meet their financial goals," and, unlike every previous generation, they leave out "work ethic" as a distinctive feature of their generation.[500] If Millennials hope to achieve their goals without working diligently, they are either ever-hopeful optimists, or have accepted a lower standard of living, at least from a consumption perspective. Coming of age in the Great Recession, they may have learned to make do with less.

Given all of these factors limiting demand among Millennials, the question arises of how Millennials will spend the money they save through more targeted purchasing, renting vs. buying, delaying major life events, and choosing to consume less. They could buy nicer things, different things entirely, save it, or have never had the money to spend in the first place. This latter case seems increasingly likely. Young Millennials, according to research done by Lisa Kahn at the Yale School of Management, have not only graduated from college into high unemployment rates and relatively lower wages, but their incomes may never catch up. All together, more targeted shopping; a reduced need to spend due to the option of renting, the postponement of child-bearing, and a possible lack of desire to consume; and lower incomes may mean less retail consumption for this generation, and consequently lower GDP for the nation.

In addition to a broad, nation-wide impact on GDP, we will also feel the effects of these transitions in our communities. Based on retailers' strategic options, we see a future with many empty former big box stores. Empty buildings inevitably lead to blight. With stores closing and downsizing, and inevitable layoffs on the horizon, local communities will also face erosion in their tax bases as property, sales, and income taxes decline. This will leave fewer public resources to deal with the blight left by departed brick-and-mortar stores.

Despite this negative picture, there are some reasons to hope that the future for brick-and-mortar retail is not, as some venture capitalists believe, certain death. In addition to the TIPS-focused strategies we've described and the retail verticals that are defensible, there are also bright spots in Millennials' shopping habits. Millennials have not cut the cord with brick-and-mortar stores, and a much higher number than other generations shop in these outlets daily (Figure 9.6).

Frequency with which US consumers shop in-store, by age (% of respondents)						
	18-20	21-29	30-39	40-49	50-59	60+
Daily	13%	16%	10%	12%	7%	6%
2-3 times per week	34%	36%	43%	42%	39%	43%
Once per week	25%	25%	26%	24%	30%	29%
2-3 times per month	22%	15%	18%	17%	19%	20%
Once per month	4%	3%	3%	4%	5%	1%
Less than once per month	1%	3%	1%	1%	0%	1%
Never	1%	1%	0%	1%	0%	0%

Figure 9.6 Source: eMarketer.

Millennials also treat in-store shopping as social and experiential activities, and retailers who provide showrooms, personal relationships, or some other important customer criteria satisfy this need. And, while Millennials do rely on word-of-mouth more than other generations, they are still heavily influenced by salespeople, so some power remains with stores to affect customers' buying decisions.

Brick-and-mortar retailers face a host of challenges in the years ahead. For some retailers, eCommerce threatens to digitize the products they sell and leave them without anything meaningful to stock in their stores. For others, hyper-competitive online retailers with operating, price, selection, and convenience advantages render their brick-and-mortar formats unable to earn their cost of capital. A few retailers face the challenge of successfully capturing the opportunities eCommerce presents to increase the productivity of their existing brick-and-mortar stores.

The vast majority of shoppers, aided by the transparency of technology and conditioned by the Great Recession, are becoming more price-driven causing many brick-and-mortar retailers to become unable to compete. Furthermore, some hyper-informed customers now connect directly with manufacturers, cutting retailers out of the transaction entirely. As shopping trips, both online and in-store, become more targeted and baskets shrink, retail continues to fragment between brick-and-mortar stores and eCommerce. As consumers, too, fragment along income lines, retailers that have depended on a broad middle class are finding that their one-size-fits-all formats now fit only a narrow segment of the population. Finally, much of retail growth over the last three decades has relied on aggregating volume to support a large store infrastructure. However, this volume may not materialize in any channel in the coming years. Millennials, who are soon to become the main consumer segment in the economy, are expressing decreased consumption due to better utilization of existing goods, lower spending capacity, lower desire to consume, and delays in key life events that drive consumption (e.g. marriage, children).

A key tenet of this book is that retailers are not all equal in facing these threats. While some retailers will manage through this revolution, many will perish. The old strategy of containing shrink and growing incremental store traffic two percent per year will not save stores. Rather, we are at an inflection point for brick-and-mortar retail, and survival requires comprehensive strategies that in many cases will transform and revolutionize brick-and-mortar retail as we know it. The strategies outlined in this book are a good starting point for retailers to rethink their businesses.

This retail revolution will not occur in a vacuum. Brick-and-mortar retail is at the center of many parts of our society—it bridges the gap between consumers and brands, brings Americans into the workforce and helps them advance their careers, attracts traffic and a sense of community to our towns and cities, and plays a very important role in America's local and national economies. The shifts in retail that we have described will likely shrink store counts, square footage, and retail employment. Municipal, state, and federal governments will need to pay close attention and find solutions to the increased blight and decreased tax base and employment that are unavoidable consequences of survival strategies on the part of retailers. The new retail landscape requires strategic thinking not just from retailers and landlords but from policy makers as well.

Chapter 10
Technical Appendix

This appendix will explain the calculations used to estimate the impacts to same-store sales and gross margin the retailers in our sample could withstand before either facing bankruptcy or being unable to meet the return rates required by their investors. We will use Autozone as an example throughout this appendix to further illustrate these calculations.

Impact to Bankruptcy

To estimate the same-store sales and gross margin impacts a retailer can withstand before facing bankruptcy, we look at when the average store can no longer make an EBITDA contribution to the corporation. As a result, we exclude any corporate expenses such as interest and taxes, and we use EBITDA to approximate a cash contribution. In the case of Autozone, depreciation and amortization are accounted for in both COGS (from warehouses) and SG&A (from stores). The bulk of this depreciation comes from the store base, so to simplify, we've reduced the SG&A expense by the amount of D&A. Figure 10.1 provides the inputs for the bankruptcy estimates.

Calendar Year 2013	(000)
Sales	$9,208,282
COGS	$4,430,345
Gross Margin	*52%*
SG&A	$2,757,518

Figure 10.1 Note: Autozone had 53 weeks over this time period and we've removed the effect of the extra week.

Same-Store Sales Impact Leading to Zero EBITDA Contribution (Bankruptcy)

Setting contribution to zero (the point at which a retailer would be entering bankruptcy), we first solve for what new sales would be in this scenario, assuming

SG&A costs and gross margin are fixed. Then, we convert this equation to percentage terms and calculate the percentage impact to sales. With our assumption that retail stores are saturated, the percentage impact to total sales is the same as the percentage impact to same-store sales.

$$Contribution = Sales * Gross\ Margin - SG\&A$$

$$\frac{SGA}{Gross\ Margin} = Sales_{at\ zero\ EBITDA\ contribution}$$

$$\frac{SG\&A}{Gross\ Margin * Sales_{current}} - 1 = Same\ Store\ Sales\ Impact\ (\%)$$

In Autozone's case, this yields a same-store sales impact of -42%.

$$\frac{\$2,757,518}{52\% * \$9,208,282} - 1 = -42\%$$

Gross Margin Impact Leading to Zero EBITDA Contribution (Bankruptcy)

To calculate the gross margin impact to bankruptcy, we again set the contribution equation to zero, but this time solve for gross margin, and leave sales and SG&A fixed. We then calculate the gross margin impact.

$$Contribution = Sales * Gross\ Margin - SG\&A$$

$$\frac{SGA}{Sales} = Gross\ Margin_{at\ zero\ EBITDA\ contribution}$$

$$Gross\ Margin_{at\ zero\ EBITDA\ contribution} - Gross\ Margin_{current} = Gross\ Margin\ Impact\ (\%)$$

In Autozone's case, this yields a gross margin impact of -22%.

$$\frac{\$2,757,518}{\$9,208,282} - 52\% = -22\%$$

Impact to Hurdle Rate of 10%

To estimate the same-store sales and gross margin impacts a retailer can withstand before its ROIC no longer meets its cost of capital, we look at when the corporation will no longer be able to generate this return. These calculations are similar to the ones above, with the added complications of tax and invested capital. In this calculation, we include taxes, depreciation, and amortization, but exclude interest payments as we are interested in the returns to total capital, rather than to any one capital source. To capture the tax impact but ignore which type of capital (debt or equity) the company has employed to purchase its assets, we use NOPAT, or $EBIT * (1 - t)$, where t is the tax rate. As we're interested in these retailers' long-term survival, we use what we believe is an effective long-term tax rate of 35%, rather than each retailer's current effective tax rate. The inputs for NOPAT are shown in Figure 10.2.

Calendar Year 2013	(000)
Sales	$9,208,282
COGS	$4,430,345
Gross Margin	*52%*
SG&A	$2,998,830
Tax Rate	35%
NOPAT	$1,156,419

Figure 10.2

We use invested capital to capture just the operating assets that a retailer has actually had to directly pay for, either through debt or equity. To arrive at this number, we begin with total assets, subtract cash as a non-operating asset, and subtract non-interest bearing current liabilities as this is free financing that retailers have not had to pay for. Because we are looking at the return rate, we've made assumptions that fixed assets take a year to yield any return, while current assets and liabilities have a more immediate effect, so we average their balances over the previous four quarters. Figure 10.3 presents a simplified balance sheet for Autozone, and shows which asset and liability types are averaged and which are based in the beginning of the period.

Quarter ending	15/02/2014	23/11/2013	31/08/2013	4/5/2013	9/2/2013	Inputs to Invested Capital
Cash	$139,755	$125,852	$142,191	$133,685	$115,548	$131,406
Accounts Receivable	$191,115	$173,114	$171,638	$155,550	$160,420	$170,367
Inventory	$3,089,245	$2,947,556	$2,861,014	$2,796,782	$2,758,543	$2,890,628
Other Current Assets	$118,383	$123,713	$103,170	$92,306	$88,857	$105,286
Net PP&E	$3,135,255	$3,108,770	$3,071,361	$3,002,823	$2,944,549	$2,944,549
Net Intangible Assets	$436,768	$409,029	$409,845	$433,542	$385,985	$385,985
Other Long-term Assets	$152,371	$135,389	$132,870	$168,353	$208,286	$208,286
Total Assets	**$7,262,892**	**$7,023,423**	**$6,892,089**	**$6,783,041**	**$6,662,188**	**$6,836,507**
Accounts Payable	$3,477,697	$3,407,286	$3,307,535	$3,116,557	$3,034,017	$3,268,618
Accrued Expenses	$459,227	$462,263	$467,831	$469,942	$462,858	$464,424
Income Taxes Payable	$104,628	$95,466	$17,129	$63,161	$69,063	$69,889
Deferred Tax	$199,318	$207,554	$202,922	$186,389	$181,337	$195,504
Noninterest Bearing Current Liabilities	**$4,240,870**	**$4,172,569**	**$3,995,417**	**$3,836,049**	**$3,747,275**	**$3,998,436**

Quarterly Average   Beginning of Period

Figure 10.3 Autozone Balance Sheet

From this balance sheet, we arrive at invested capital as shown in Figure 10.4.

	Invested Capital
Total Assets	$6,836,507
Less Cash	-$131,406
Less Noninterest Bearing Current Liabilities	-$3,998,436
Invested Capital	$2,706,665

Figure 10.4

Same-Store Sales Impact Leading to 10% Hurdle Rate

To calculate the impact to the 10% hurdle rate, we lay out the ROIC equation but set the result to 10% and solve for what new sales would be in this scenario, assuming SG&A costs and gross margin are fixed. Then, we convert this equation to percentage terms and calculate the sales impact.

$$10\% = \frac{(Sales * Gross\ Margin - SG\&A)(1-t)}{Invested\ Capital}$$

$$\frac{\frac{10\% * Invested\ Capital}{(1-t)} + SG\&A}{Gross\ Margin} = Sales_{at\ 10\%\ ROIC}$$

$$\frac{\frac{10\% * Invested\ Capital}{(1-t)} + SG\&A}{Gross\ Margin * Sales_{current}} - 1 = Same\ Store\ Sales\ Impact\ (\%)$$

In Autozone's case, this yields a same-store sales impact of -29%.

$$\frac{\dfrac{10\% * \$2,706,665}{(1 - 35\%)} + \$2,998,830}{52\% * \$9,208,282} - 1 = -29\%$$

Gross Margin Impact Leading to 10% Hurdle Rate

To calculate the gross margin impact to a 10% hurdle rate, we again set the return rate to 10%, but this time solve for gross margin, and leave sales and SG&A fixed. We then calculate the gross margin impact.

$$10\% = \frac{(Sales * Gross\ Margin - SG\&A)(1 - t)}{Invested\ Capital}$$

$$\frac{\dfrac{10\% * Invested\ Capital}{(1 - t)} + SG\&A}{Sales} = Gross\ Margin_{at\ 10\%\ ROIC}$$

$$Gross\ Margin\ Impact\ (\%) = Gross\ Margin_{at\ 10\%\ ROIC} - Gross\ Margin_{current}$$

In Autozone's case, this yields a gross margin impact of -15%.

$$\frac{\dfrac{10\% * \$2,706,665}{(1 - 35\%)} + \$2,998,830}{\$9,208,282} - 52\% = -15\%$$

Capitalized Operating Leases

To take into account the effect of operating leases on these metrics, we capitalize them using the following method. Operating lease commitments are reported in companies' financial statements for each of the next five years. The cumulative value of any operating lease commitments after five years is also reported. To estimate the annual operating lease commitments after year five, the cumulative amount for this period is divided by the operating lease commitments in year five to give the period over which these lease commitments are to be paid, and the commitments are expected to be paid in equal installments over this period. Then, these commitments are converted to their cumulative present value using the company's pre-tax cost of debt. For Autozone, this process is presented in Figure 10.5.

Year	Nominal Value of Operating Leases	Present Value of Operating Leases
1	$217,844	$208,547
2	$209,300	$191,816
3	$192,296	$168,712
4	$174,844	$146,853
5	$157,691	$126,794
Years After Five	$958,435	
Period	6	
6	$159,739	$122,959
7	$159,739	$117,712
8	$159,739	$112,688
9	$159,739	$107,879
10	$159,739	$103,275
11	$159,739	$98,867
Cost of Debt		4.5%
Present Value of Operating Lease Commitments		$1,506,101
Interest Charge		$67,142

Figure 10.5

The inputs into the equations detailed above are then adjusted to capture the effect of the capitalized operating leases. The present value of operating lease commitments, $1.5 billion in Autozone's case, are added to total assets. The interest charge (reached by multiplying the present value of operating lease commitments by the company's cost of debt), $67 million in Autozone's case, is treated as a contra-expense to either SG&A or COGS depending on where the retailer has chosen to book its store costs. For Autozone, these changes are shown in Figure 10.6.

NOPAT	Non-Capitalized Op Leases		Change	Capitalized Op Leases	
Sales	$9,208,282			$9,208,282	
COGS	$4,430,345			$4,430,345	
Gross Margin		52%			52%
SG&A	$2,998,830		-$67,142	$2,931,688	
Tax Rate		35%			35%
NOPAT	**$1,156,419**			**$1,200,062**	
Invested Capital	**Non-Capitalized Op Leases**		**Change**	**Capitalized Op Leases**	
Total Assets	$6,836,507		+$1,506,101	$8,342,609	
Less Cash	-$131,406			-$131,406	
Less Noninterest Bearing Current Liabilities	-$3,998,436			-$3,998,436	
Invested Capital	**$2,706,665**			**$4,212,767**	

Figure 10.6

The equations detailed earlier are then recalculated with these new inputs. With capitalized operating leases, Autozone's same-store sales impact until it reaches a 10% ROIC is estimated at -25%.

$$\frac{\frac{10\% * \$4,212,767}{(1-35\%)} + \$2,931,688}{52\% * \$9,208,282} - 1 = -25\%$$

With capitalized operating leases, Autozone's gross margin impact until it reaches a 10% ROIC is estimated at -13%.

$$\frac{\frac{10\% * \$4,212,767}{(1-35\%)} + \$2,931,688}{\$9,208,282} - 52\% = -13\%$$

Notes

[1] Hansell, Saul, "Money Starts to Show in Internet Shopping," *New York Times*, December 1, 1997, accessed via *Lexis-Nexis*.

[2] Laseter, Tim and Turner, Martha, "Operations at the Core: What Amazon Offers Category Killers," *Strategy+Business*, May 18, 2001.

[3] Thomas, Ian et. al, "Quarterly Retail E-Commerce Sales, 3rd Quarter 2013," *U.S. Census Bureau News*, US Department of Commerce, November 22, 2013.

[4] GMV estimated as a combination of owned and operated sales and grossed up third-party sales, total retail sales drawn from 2012 US Census Annual Retail Trade Report, and excludes food services and motor vehicle and parts dealers.

[5] Estimated using US Department of Commerce Quarterly Retail eCommece Sales Reports and company reports

[6] Horvers, Christopher et. al, "Big Box Retail: The Reports of Its Death are Greatly Exaggerated; Retail Can Thrive in an AMZN World," *JP Morgan*, April 29, 2013.

[7] "Macy's, Inc. Same-Store Sales Up 11.7% in January," February 7, 2013, available at http://pressroom.macysinc.com/press.aspx?catid=0&pcatid=0&mkid=360&pid=15636

[8] Nordstrom FY 2013 10-K

[9] Walmart Annual Conference for the Investment Community, October 24, 2013.

[10] Lal, Rajiv and Alvarez, José, "Retailing Revolution: Category Killers on the Brink," *Harvard Business School Working Knowledge*, October 10, 2011, available at http://hbswk.hbs.edu/item/6813.html

[11] Banjo, Shelly and Fitzgerald, Drew, "Stores Confront New World of Reduced Shopper Traffic," *Wall Street Journal*, January 16, 2014.

[12] Jargon, Julie et al, "Private Equity Firms Show Supervalu Who is the Boss," *The Wall Street Journal*, January 10, 2013, available at http://online.wsj.com/news/articles/SB10001424127887324081704578234092523748504

[13] Horovitz, Jacques et al, "Amazon: Success, survival or suicide?," IMD case number IMD097, Lausanne: International Institute for Management Development, February 21, 2003.

[14] Parry, Mark E., "Jeff Bezos and Amazon.com," Darden School of Business case number UV0319, Charlottesville: University of Virginia Darden School Foundation, 1999.

[15] Horovitz, Jacques et al, "Amazon: Success, survival or suicide?," IMD case number IMD097, Lausanne: International Institute for Management Development, February 21, 2003.

[16] Parry, Mark E., "Jeff Bezos and Amazon.com," UV0319, Charlottesville: University of Virginia Darden School Foundation, 1999.

[17] Swerdlow, Fiona, "Forrester's Mulpuru: 2013 Great Year for eCommerce; 2014 Even Better," *National Retail Federation*, January 14, 2014, available at https://nrf.com/news/forresters-mulpuru-2013-great-year-e-commerce-2014-even-better

[18] Del Rey, Jason, "ShopRunner's Scott Thompson: We're Building So Much More Than an Amazon Prime Competitor," *All Things D*, October 12, 2013, available at http://allthingsd.com/20131012/shoprunners-scott-thompson-were-building-so-much-more-than-an-amazon-prime-competitor/

[19] Hottovy, R.J., "Amazon is uniquely positioned to be a disruptive force to the traditional retail channel for years to come," March 4, 2013, *Morningstar*, accessed via *Thomson One*, October 30, 2013.

[20] Applegate, Linda, "Amazon.com: 1994-2000," HBS case number 9-801-194, Boston: Harvard Business School Publishing, 2002.

[21] Leschly, Stig, et. al, "Amazon.com – 2002," HBS case number 9-803-098, Boston: Harvard Business School Publishing, 2003.

[22] *ibid*

[23] *ibid*

[24] Bensinger, Greg, "Competing with Amazon on Amazon," *The Wall Street Journal*, June 27, 2012, available at http://online.wsj.com/news/articles/SB10001424052702304441404577482902055882264.

[25] Bensinger, Greg, "Competing with Amazon on Amazon," *The Wall Street Journal*, June 27, 2012, available at http://online.wsj.com/news/articles/SB10001424052702304441404577482902055882264.

[26] Lunden, Ingrid, "Amazon Offers 'Amazon Pages' For Brands to Customize With Their Own URLs, And 'Amazon Posts' for Social Media Marketing," *TechCrunch*, November 20, 2012, available at http://techcrunch.com/2012/11/20/amazon-offers-amazon-pages-for-brands-to-customize-with-their-own-urls-and-amazon-posts-for-social-media-marketing/.

[27] Neff, Jack, "Fast-Rising E-Commerce Could Jolt Package-Goods Giants," *Advertising Age*, September 26, 2013, available at http://adage.com/article/news/cpg-e-commerce-sales-pose-risks-big-brands/244381/.

[28] Anderson, George, "Brands Skip Retailers, Go Direct to Consumers," *Retailwire*, March 1, 2012, available at http://www.retailwire.com/discussion/15850/brands-skip-retailers-go-direct-to-consumers.

[29] Barr, Alistair, "Amazon is Getting Heat Over Third-Party Sellers," *Reuters and Huffington Post,* October 23, 2012, available at http://www.huffingtonpost.com/2012/10/23/amazon-third-party-sellers_n_2006783.html.

[30] Ng, Serena, "Soap Opera: Amazon Moves in with P&G," *Wall Street Journal*, October 14, 2013, available at http://online.wsj.com/news/articles/SB10001424052702304330904579135840230674458.

[31] *ibid*

[32] *ibid*

[33] Stone, Brad, "What's in Amazon's Box? Instant Gratification," *BloombergBusinessweek*, November 24, 2010, available at http://www.businessweek.com/magazine/content/10_49/b4206039292096.htm.

[34] Tuttle, Brad, "Amazon Prime: Bigger, More Powerful, More Profitable than Anyone Imagined," *Time*, March 18, 2013, available at http://business.time.com/2013/03/18/amazon-prime-bigger-more-powerful-more-profitable-than-anyone-imagined/.

[35] Stone, Brad, "What's in Amazon's Box? Instant Gratification," *BloombergBusinessweek*, November 24, 2010, available at http://www.businessweek.com/magazine/content/10_49/b4206039292096.htm.

[36] Tuttle, Brad, "Amazon Prime: Bigger, More Powerful, More Profitable than Anyone Imagined," *Time*, March 18, 2013, available at http://business.time.com/2013/03/18/amazon-prime-bigger-more-powerful-more-profitable-than-anyone-imagined/.

[37] Stone, Brad, "What's in Amazon's Box? Instant Gratification," *BloombergBusinessweek*, November 24, 2010, available at http://www.businessweek.com/magazine/content/10_49/b4206039292096.htm.

[38] Tuttle, Brad, "Amazon Prime: Bigger, More Powerful, More Profitable than Anyone Imagined," *Time*, March 18, 2013, available at http://business.time.com/2013/03/18/amazon-prime-bigger-more-powerful-more-profitable-than-anyone-imagined/.

[39] Schachter, Ben et. al, "Amazon Confirms 20mm+ Prime Members," *Macquarie Equities Research,* January 6, 2014, accessed via *ThomsonOne.*

[40] "Record-Setting Holiday Season for Amazon Prime," Company Press Release, December 26, 2013, available at http://phx.corporate-ir.net/phoenix.zhtml?c=176060&p=irol-newsArticle&ID=1886961

[41] "Amazon.com Management Discusses Q3 2013 Results - Earnings Call Transcript," http://seekingalpha.com/article/1771612-amazon-coms-management-discusses-q3-2013-results-earnings-call-transcript?part=single

[42] Pace, Mark, "Attention Retailers: Amazon Prime members are located in aisle 5," *Compete Pulse*, available at https://blog.compete.com/2013/04/17/attention-retailers-amazon-prime-members-are-located-in-aisle-5/.

[43] Blackledge, John and Champion, Thomas, "Cowen Amazon Tracker: February Data", *Cowen and Company,* March 22, 2013, accessed via *Thomson One.*

[44] Pachter, Michael, et. al, "Q2:14 Preview: Hardware Launches Expected to Drain Earnings in Q2 and Q3," *WedBush,* July 16, 2014 and MacKay, Joscelyn, "Amazon is a uniquely disruptive force across the traditional retail and technology industries," *MorningStar,* June 2, 2014; WedBush estimates 25 million worldwide Prime members and MorningStar estimates over three-fourths are in the United States.

[45] Per company reports, Costco had 71.2 million total members as of Sept. 1, 2013 per Company reports (http://phx.corporate-ir.net/phoenix.zhtml?c=83830&p=irol-homeprofile). US members estimated by multiplying Costco's total members against its share of revenue from the United States, ~72%.

[46] Netflix Second Quarter 2014 Letter to Shareholders, hosted by Netflix at http://ir.netflix.com/results.cfm

[47] Mahaney, Mark et al, "Amazon.com," *RBC Capital Markets*, September 18, 2014.

[48] Edwards, Cliff, "Netflix Seen Cracking Down on Sharing to Bolster Profit," *Bloomberg*, April 22, 2013, available at http://www.bloomberg.com/news/2013-04-22/netflix-seen-cracking-down-on-sharing-to-bolster-profit.html.

[49] Amazon Customer Letter

[50] Noguchi, Yuki, "Moving in with Manufacturers, Amazon Delivers a New Approach," *NPR News*, October 28, 2013, available at http://www.npr.org/2013/10/28/240742832/moving-in-with-manufacturers-amazon-delivers-a-new-approach

[51] Beswick, Paul et. al., "How can category killers cope with an online world?" *Oliver Wyman*, 2013. http://www.oliverwyman.com/insights/publications/2013/sep/how-can-category-killers-cope-with-an-online-world-.html#.VHN9DEgo7Dc

[52] "Total retail shopping trips in the United States in 2008 and 2012," *Statista*.

[53] Banjo, Shelly and Fitzgerald, Drew, "Stores Confront New World of Reduced Shopper Traffic," *Wall Street Journal*, January 16, 2014.

[54] Louie, Dickson L. and Rayport, Jeffrey F., "Amazon.com (A)," HBS case number 9-897-128, Harvard Business School Publishing: Boston, 1997

[55] Applegate, Linda, "Amazon.com: 1994-2000," HBS case number 9-801-194, Boston: Harvard Business School Publishing, 2002.

[56] Applegate, Linda, "Amazon.com: 1994-2000," HBS case number 9-801-194, Boston: Harvard Business School Publishing, 2002.

[57] Louie, Dickson L. and Rayport, Jeffrey F., "Amazon.com (A)," HBS case number 9-897-128, Harvard Business School Publishing: Boston, 1997

[58] Stone, Brad, "In a Grocery Face-Off, Is Costco Amazon-Proof," *BloombergBusinessweek,* June 6, 2013, available at http://www.businessweek.com/articles/2013-06-06/in-a-grocery-faceoff-is-costco-amazon-proof.

[59] Yglesias, Matthew, "Amazon Profits Fall More than 45 Percent, Still the Most Amazing Company in the World," *Slate.com,* January 29, 2013, available at http://www.slate.com/blogs/moneybox/2013/01/29/amazon_q4_profits_fall_45_percent.html

[60] Parry, Mark E., "Jeff Bezos and Amazon.com," Darden School of Business case number UV0319, Charlottesville: University of Virginia Darden School Foundation, 1999.

[61] eMarketer

[62] New Media Trend Watch, *European Travel Commission*, available at http://www.newmediatrendwatch.com/markets-by-country/17-usa/123-demographics?showall=1 and accessed 11/20/2013.

[63] *Compete,* "Online Shopper Intelligence Study," April 12, 2011 in Garcia, Krista, "Driving CPG Sales Online: Brands Get Closer to Consumers," *eMarketer,* December 2011.

[64] Nawaguna, Elvina, "No more mailman at the door under U.S. Postal Service plan," *Reuters,* July 23, 2013, available at http://www.reuters.com/article/2013/07/23/usa-postal-delivery-idUSL1N0FT14T20130723

[65] SJ Consulting Group, *"Report on Measuring the Benefits of Rural Postal Service,"* August, 2011.

[66] SJ Consulting Group, *"Report on Measuring the Benefits of Rural Postal Service,"* August, 2011.

[67] Miller, Mark et. al, "Amazon Model Evolving to Higher Profitability; Expanding Selection and Price Gap Persist as Challenges for Retailers," *William Blair*, October 3, 2013, accessed via *ThomsonOne*.

[68] *HBR Ideacast*, "Jeff Bezos on Leading for the Long-term at Amazon," *HBR Blog Network*, January 3, 2013, available at http://blogs.hbr.org/2013/01/jeff-bezos-on-leading-for-the-/.

[69] Ben-David, Itzhak et al, "The 'Amazon Tax:' Emprical Evidence from Amazon and Main Street Retailers," *NBER Working Paper Series,* April, 2014.

[70] Author conversation

[71] Lal, Rajiv et al, "Netflix: Competitive Dynamics in the Consumer Video Market," HBS case number 9-712-459, Harvard Business School Publishing: Boston, 2013.

[72] Lal, Rajiv et al, "Netflix: Competitive Dynamics in the Consumer Video Market," HBS case number 9-712-459, Harvard Business School Publishing: Boston, 2013.

[73] Gandel, Stephen, "How Blockbuster Failed at Failing," *Time Magazine*, October 17, 2010, available at http://content.time.com/time/magazine/article/0,9171,2022624-1,00.html

[74] Binder, Daniel et. al, *Jefferies*, 'Office Depot', report dated February 20, 2013.

[75] Hart, Myra et al., "Staples: A Year in the Life of a Start-up," HBS case number 9-800-241, (Boston: Harvard Business School Publishing, 2012).

[76] "Supplies and Demand", Harvard Business School Alumni Bulletin, December 1996, http://www.alumni.hbs.edu/bulletin/1996/december/entre.html#stemberg, accessed December 2012.

[77] Rodengen, Jeffrey L. *Office Depot: taking care of business: the first 20 years*. Fort Lauderdale, FL: Write Stuff Enterprises, 2006, p 12.

[78] Hart, Myra et al., "Staples: A Year in the Life of a Start-up," HBS case number 9-800-241, (Boston: Harvard Business School Publishing, 2012).

[79] Martin, Douglas, "Leo Kahn, Trailblazer in Big-Box Retailing, Dies at 94", *New York Times,* May 12, 2011, http://www.nytimes.com/2011/05/13/business/13kahn.html, accessed December 2012.

[80] Rodengen, Jeffrey L. *Office Depot: taking care of business: the first 20 years*. Fort Lauderdale, FL: Write Stuff Enterprises, 2006, pgs. 21-22.

[81] Stemberg, Thomas G. *Staples for success: from business plan to billion-dollar business in just a decade*. Santa Monica, CA: Knowledge Exchange, 1996.

[82] 'Merchandise by Kind of Business' in Merchandise Line Sales, Retail Trade Subject Series, US Economic Census, for year 1992 and author's calculations. For Stationery Stores, SIC 5943, total sales of stationery stores were divided by the number of establishments in the stationery SIC code.

[83] Stemberg, Thomas G. *Staples for success: from business plan to billion-dollar business in just a decade*. Santa Monica, CA: Knowledge Exchange, 1996, p. 44.

[84] Rodengen, Jeffrey L. *Office Depot: taking care of business: the first 20 years*. Fort Lauderdale, FL: Write Stuff Enterprises, 2006, p 15.

[85] Stemberg, Thomas G. *Staples for success: from business plan to billion-dollar business in just a decade*. Santa Monica, CA: Knowledge Exchange, 1996.

[86] Stemberg, Thomas G. *Staples for success: from business plan to billion-dollar business in just a decade*. Santa Monica, CA: Knowledge Exchange, 1996, p. 56.

[87] Stemberg, Thomas G. *Staples for success: from business plan to billion-dollar business in just a decade*. Santa Monica, CA: Knowledge Exchange, 1996, p. 50.

[88] McCormack, P.F., *Dean Witter Reynolds*, report dated July 2, 1992.

[89] McGlade, M., *PaineWebber*, report dated October 7, 1992.

[90] Stemberg, Thomas G. *Staples for success: from business plan to billion-dollar business in just a decade*. Santa Monica, CA: Knowledge Exchange, 1996, p. 10.

[91] Hart, Myra et al., "Staples: A Year in the Life of a Start-up," HBS case number 9-800-241, (Boston: Harvard Business School Publishing, 2012).

[92] Rodengen, Jeffrey L. *Office Depot: taking care of business: the first 20 years*. Fort Lauderdale, FL: Write Stuff Enterprises, 2006, pgs. 21-22.

[93] Stemberg, Thomas G. *Staples for success: from business plan to billion-dollar business in just a decade*. Santa Monica, CA: Knowledge Exchange, 1996, pgs. 92-93.

[94] Hart, Myra et al., "Staples: A Year in the Life of a Start-up," HBS case number 9-800-241, (Boston: Harvard Business School Publishing, 2012).

[95] Hart, Myra et al., "Staples: A Year in the Life of a Start-up," HBS case number 9-800-241, (Boston: Harvard Business School Publishing, 2012).

[96] Stemberg, Thomas G. *Staples for success: from business plan to billion-dollar business in just a decade*. Santa Monica, CA: Knowledge Exchange, 1996, p. 68.

[97] Consolidated from company reports – some store counts estimated from earlier and later dates than 1990.

[98] Rodengen, Jeffrey L. *Office Depot: taking care of business: the first 20 years*. Fort Lauderdale, FL: Write Stuff Enterprises, 2006, pgs. 31.

[99] Stemberg, Thomas G. *Staples for success: from business plan to billion-dollar business in just a decade*. Santa Monica, CA: Knowledge Exchange, 1996, p. 141.

[100] Rodengen, Jeffrey L. *Office Depot: taking care of business: the first 20 years*. Fort Lauderdale, FL: Write Stuff Enterprises, 2006, pgs. 40.

[101] Vroom, C.E. et al, *Alex Brown & Sons*, 'Office Depot', February 14 1994.

[102] L Keith Mullins and James P. Stoeffel, *Smith Barney*, 'Office Depot', report dated January 30, 1995.

[103] Staples Company, *News Center Milestones*,
http://staples.newshq.businesswire.com/about/milestones?page=1#axzz2HP0N4Irq, accessed January 2012.

[104] Office Depot Company, *Company Info, Company Facts Timeline*,
http://www.officedepot.com/specialLinks.do?file=/companyinfo/companyfacts/timeline.jsp&template=companyInfo, accessed January 2012.

[105] Rodengen, Jeffrey L. *Office Depot: taking care of business: the first 20 years*. Fort Lauderdale, FL: Write Stuff Enterprises, 2006, pgs 101-102.

[106] Stemberg, Thomas G. *Staples for success: from business plan to billion-dollar business in just a decade*. Santa Monica, CA: Knowledge Exchange, 1996, p. 67.

[107] Stemberg, Thomas G. *Staples for success: from business plan to billion-dollar business in just a decade*. Santa Monica, CA: Knowledge Exchange, 1996, p. 75.

[108] Thayer, J.L., *Bear, Stearns & Co.*, 'Office Depot', report dated April 16, 1990.

[109] Thayer, J.L., *Bear, Stearns & Co.*, 'Office Depot', report dated April 16, 1990.

[110] Binder, Daniel et. al, *Jefferies*, 'Office Depot', report dated February 20, 2013.

[111] Lal, Rajiv et al. "Staples: Back to the Future," HBS case number N2-505-044, (Boston: Harvard Business School Publishing, 2012).

[112] Lal, Rajiv et al. "Staples: Back to the Future," HBS case number N2-505-044, (Boston: Harvard Business School Publishing, 2012).

[113] US Economic Census, Office and Stationery Supplies Category, 1997.

[114] Thomson, Sheelagh McCaughey, *Morgan Stanley Dean Witter*, 'Office Depot', report dated Feb. 3, 1998.

[115] Julian, William et al, *Salomon Smith Barney*, 'Office Depot', Feb. 13, 2003.

[116] Rodengen, Jeffrey L. *Office Depot: taking care of business: the first 20 years*. Fort Lauderdale, FL: Write Stuff Enterprises, 2006, pg 82.

[117] Rodengen, Jeffrey L. *Office Depot: taking care of business: the first 20 years*. Fort Lauderdale, FL: Write Stuff Enterprises, 2006, pg 82.

[118] Rodengen, Jeffrey L. *Office Depot: taking care of business: the first 20 years*. Fort Lauderdale, FL: Write Stuff Enterprises, 2006, pg 87.

[119] Rodengen, Jeffrey L. *Office Depot: taking care of business: the first 20 years*. Fort Lauderdale, FL: Write Stuff Enterprises, 2006, pg 91.

[120] Rodengen, Jeffrey L. *Office Depot: taking care of business: the first 20 years*. Fort Lauderdale, FL: Write Stuff Enterprises, 2006, pgs 100-101.

[121] Rodengen, Jeffrey L. *Office Depot: taking care of business: the first 20 years*. Fort Lauderdale, FL: Write Stuff Enterprises, 2006, pg 91.

[122] Tesley, Dana et. al, *Bear, Stearns, & Co.*, 'Office Depot', report dated February 11, 2005.

[123] Baker, Mike and West, Jason, *Deutsche Bank*, 'Office Depot', report dated March 12, 2007

[124] Tesley, Dana et. al, *Bear, Stearns, & Co.*, 'Office Depot', report dated February 11, 2005.

[125] Wintermantel, Oliver and Melich, Gregory, *Morgan Stanley*, 'Office Depot', Feb 26 2009

[126] Rodengen, Jeffrey L. *Office Depot: taking care of business: the first 20 years*. Fort Lauderdale, FL: Write Stuff Enterprises, 2006, pg 64.

[127] Binder, Daniel T., *Brown Brothers Harriman & Co.*, 'Office Depot', report dated Feb 24, 1999.

[128] Binder, Daniel T., *Brown Brothers Harriman & Co.*, 'Office Depot', report dated Feb 24, 1999.

[129] Binder, Daniel T., *Brown Brothers Harriman & Co.*, 'Office Depot', report dated Feb 24, 1999.

[130] Rodengen, Jeffrey L. *Office Depot: taking care of business: the first 20 years*. Fort Lauderdale, FL: Write Stuff Enterprises, 2006, pg 107.

[131] Conversation with Colin McGranahan, April 15, 2013.

[132] Conversation with Colin McGranahan, April 15, 2013.

[133] Finaldi, Laura, 'Staples ties for first for fastest delivery time among top 25 online retailers', Boston Globe, December 18, 2012, (http://www.boston.com/businessupdates/2012/12/18/staples-ties-for-first-for-fastest-delivery-time-among-top-online-retailers/mEwyuAESpSweUf8OLJPtjM/story.html, accessed on May 20, 2013).

[134] Conversation with Colin McGranahan, April 15, 2013.

[135] "Staples, Inc. at Sanford C Bernstein Strategic Decisions Conference," *Thomson Reuters StreetEvents,* May 29, 2013, accessed via ThomsonOne.

[136] 'Merchandise by Kind of Business' in Merchandise Line Sales, Retail Trade Subject Series, US Economic Census, for year 2007 and author's calculations.

[137] Yochim, Dayana, "6 Recession Strategies from Staples' CEO," *Motley Fool,* September 18, 2009, available at http://www.fool.com/investing/general/2009/09/18/6-recession-strategies-from-staples-ceo.aspx

[138] Dawson, Mike, "Talk with Staples CEO Ronald Sargent," *German Retail Blog*, January 16, 2009, available at http://www.german-retail-blog.com/topic/past-blogs/talk-with-staples-42

[139] Stambor, Zak, "Small-box stores for the internet era," *Internet Retailer*, September 4, 2013, available at http://www.internetretailer.com/2013/09/04/big-box-stores-internet-era?p=1

[140] Company Reports, accessed via *Thomson One*

[141] Moylan, Martin, "More competition could cut into Best Buy's lucrative Geek Squad service," *MPR News*, May 30, 2012, available at http://www.mprnews.org/story/2012/05/30/business/best-buy-geek-squad-baby-boomers

[142] Gober, David et al, *Morgan Stanley*, 'Office Depot', report dated January 20, 2012.

[143] McGranahan, Colin et al, *Bernstein Research*, 'Office Depot: Leading the Office Supply Sector Towards a Small Store Strategy?' report dated January 23, 2012.

[144] Conversation with Colin McGranahan, April 15, 2013.

[145] Gober, David et al, *Morgan Stanley*, 'Office Depot', report dated January 20, 2012.

[146] Kimes, Mina, "At Sears, Eddie Lampert's Warring Divisions Model Adds to the Troubles," *Bloomberg Businessweek,* July 11, 2013, available at http://www.businessweek.com/articles/2013-07-11/at-sears-eddie-lamperts-warring-divisions-model-adds-to-the-troubles#p6

[147] Wells, John, "Best Buy in Crisis," HBS case number 9-713-403, Boston: Harvard Business School Publishing, 2012.

[148] Jannarone, John, "Forecast for Best Buy: Worst is Yet to Come," *Wall Street Journal*, March 4, 2011.

[149] Wells, John, "Best Buy in Crisis," HBS case number 9-713-403, Boston: Harvard Business School Publishing, 2012.

[150] Fitzgerald, Drew, "Fear of Showrooming Fades," *Wall Street Journal,* November 3, 2013.

[151] Consumer Electronics Distribution Statistics, Passport GMID, 2013, Euromonitor International.

[152] Circuit City 1989 Annual Report

[153] Unless otherwise noted, many of the examples of convergence in this paragraph are consolidated from industry reports written by Passport, Euromonitor International.

[154] "Food Preparation Appliances in the US," *Passport, Euromonitor International*, May, 2014.

[155] 2011 FDIC National Survey of Unbanked and Underbanked Households, Federal Deposit Insurance Corporation, September, 2012, available at http://www.fdic.gov/householdsurvey/2012_unbankedreport.pdf, accessed June 26, 2013.

[156] Circuit City 1987 Annual Report

[157] Chakravarthy, Balaji and Rangan, V. Kasturi, "Best Buy," HBS case number 9-598-016 Boston: Harvard Business School Publishing, 1997.

[158] Circuit City 1985 Annual Report

[159] Circuit City 1987 Annual Report

[160] Circuit City 1987 Annual Report

[161] *International Directory of Company Histories*, Vol.63. St. James Press, 2004.

[162] Circuit City 1985 Annual Report

[163] Circuit City 1989 Annual Report

[164] Gibson, Elizabeth and Billings, Andy, Big Change at Best Buy, pgs 4-5, Davies-Black Publishing: Palo Alto, CA, 2003.

[165] *International Directory of Company Histories*, Vol.63. St. James Press, 2004.

[166] Chakravarthy, Balaji and Rangan, V. Kasturi, "Best Buy," HBS case number 9-598-016 Boston: Harvard Business School Publishing, 1997.

[167] Chakravarthy, Balaji and Rangan, V. Kasturi, "Best Buy," HBS case number 9-598-016 Boston: Harvard Business School Publishing, 1997.

[168] *International Directory of Company Histories*, Vol.63. St. James Press, 2004.

[169] *International Directory of Company Histories*, Vol.63. St. James Press, 2004.

[170] *International Directory of Company Histories*, Vol.63. St. James Press, 2004.

[171] Wells, John R. and Danskin, Galen, "The Rise of Circuit City Stores, Inc.," HBS case number 9-713-401 Boston: Harvard Business School Publishing, 2012.

[172] Murphy, H. Lee, 'Electronics Superstore Battle: Watch the Sequel,' *Crains Chicago Business*, August 31, 1992, available on Factiva, accessed June 8, 2013.

[173] Circuit City 1987 Annual Report

[174] Wells, John R. and Haglock, Travis, "Best Buy Co., Inc.: Competing on the Edge," HBS case number 9-706-417 Boston: Harvard Business School Publishing, 2007.

[175] Wells John R. and Danskin, Galen, "The Fall of Circuit City Stores, Inc.," HBS case number 9-713-402 Boston: Harvard Business School Publishing, 2012.

[176] Wells John R. and Danskin, Galen, "The Rise of Circuit City Stores, Inc.," HBS case number 9-713-401 Boston: Harvard Business School Publishing, 2012.

[177] Lal, Rajiv et al., "Best Buy Co., Inc.: Customer Centricity," HBS case number 9-506-055, Boston: Harvard Business School Publishing, 2006.

[178] Wells, John, "Best Buy in Crisis," HBS case number 9-713-403, Boston: Harvard Business School Publishing, 2012.

[179] Wells, John, "Best Buy in Crisis," HBS case number 9-713-403, Boston: Harvard Business School Publishing, 2012.

[180] Gourville, John et. al, "Tweeter etc.," HBS case number 9-597-028, Boston: Harvard Business School Publishing, 1996.

[181] Gourville, John et. al, "Tweeter etc.," HBS case number 9-597-028, Boston: Harvard Business School Publishing, 1996.

[182] Ren et al.: *Managing Product Variety and Collocation in a Competitive Environment*, Management Science 57(6), pp. 1009-1024.

[183] 'Stereo Stores Slipping, See Survival in 'Supermarkets,'' *Wall Street Journal*, March 8, 1983, available on Factiva, accessed June 11, 2013.

[184] Circuit City 1985 Annual Report

[185] Gibson, Elizabeth and Billings, Andy, Big Change at Best Buy, page 4, Davies-Black Publishing: Palo Alto, CA, 2003; Circuit City 1985 Annual Report

[186] Circuit City 1991 Annual Report

[187] Harrington, Mark, 'Disappearing storefronts: Consumer electronics retail consolidation accelerates in '91,' *The Weekly Home Furnishings Newspaper*, August 19, 1991, available on Factiva, accessed June 6, 2013.

[188] Harrington, Mark, 'Disappearing storefronts: Consumer electronics retail consolidation accelerates in '91,' *The Weekly Home Furnishings Newspaper*, August 19, 1991, available on Factiva, accessed June 6, 2013.

[189] *International Directory of Company Histories*, Vol. 63. St. James Press, 2004.

[190] Drolet, Danielle, 'An Interview with Tim Brenner,' eMarketer, September 14, 2012, accessed: June 11, 2013.

[191] Author conversation, September 12, 2013.

[192] Strasser, David et. al, 'A Basis for Discussion Instead of Hysteria: TV Pricing at BBY vs. AMZN', *Janney Capital Markets,* Report Dated: April 5, 2011.

[193] Ciccarelli, Scot, et. al, 'Best Buy Co, Inc.: Well, at least they warned us … Margin Performance highlights pricing challenges,' *RBC Capital Markets*, report dated November 20, 2012.

[194] "Best Buy Holds Analyst and Investor Day to Provide Assessment of the Company and to Outline Priorities to Reinvigorate Performance and Rejuvenate Its Business," *Best Buy Financial News Release,* November 13, 2012, available at http://phx.corporate-ir.net/phoenix.zhtml?c=83192&p=irol-newsArticle&ID=1758167&highlight=

[195] Binder, Daniel et. al, 'Best Buy: BBY Protects Share With Price, FCF Miss On WC Timing,' Jefferies, report dated January 11, 2013.

[196] Binder, Daniel et. al, 'Best Buy: BBY Protects Share With Price, FCF Miss On WC Timing,' Jefferies, report dated January 11, 2013.

[197] Horvers, Christopher et al, 'Best Buy: BBY and Samsung Partnership: Big Step in Right Direction,' J.P. Morgan, April 4, 2013.

[198] Pachter, Michael and McKay, Nick, "Best Buy: 10 Reasons to Love Best Buy, and Why We Reject Each One," WedBush, report dated April 22, 2013.

[199] Chukumba, Anthony and Cohen, Eric, "BBY: Microsoft Windows Shop-In-Shops Another Positive Development," BB&T Capital Markets, report dated June 13, 2013.

[200] Brooker, Ira, "We visit a Best Buy Connected Store," *Best Buy Mobile* blog post, August 3, 2012, available at http://blog.bestbuymobile.com/2012/08/03/we-visit-a-best-buy-connected-store/

[201] Gruley, Bryan and McCracken, Jeffrey, "The Battle for Best Buy, the Incredibly Shrinking Box," *Bloomberg Businessweek,* October 18, 2012.

[202] Wells, John, "Best Buy in Crisis," HBS case number 9-713-403, Boston: Harvard Business School Publishing, 2012.

[203] Berg, Jonathan N., 'Best Buy: Q4 Tops Consensus; Mobile, Appliances and Gaming Focus in F12; Maintain OW,' *Piper Jaffray, Report Dated: March 25, 2011.*

[204] Strasser, David et al., 'Preparing to Own the Future', *Janney Capital Markets*, Report Dated: April 15, 2011.

[205] Strasser, David et. al, 'BBY: SG&A Cuts So Yesterday – Remerchandising is the New, New Thing,' Janney Capital Markets, report dated April 3, 2013.

[206] Berg, Jonathan N., 'Best Buy: Q4 Tops Consensus; Mobile, Appliances and Gaming Focus in F12; Maintain OW,' *Piper Jaffray, Report Dated: March 25, 2011.*

[207] Strasser, David, et. al, 'The Dislike of Best Buy is Out of Control', *Janney Capital Markets,* Report Dated: March 25, 2011.

[208] 'Inside Best Buy's Connected Store,' *StarTribune*, June 29, 2012, available at http://www.startribune.com/business/160917095.html, accessed June 27, 2013.

[209] Balter, Gary et al., 'BBY Adapting To a Changing World, Will They Leave Wall Street In The Dust?', *Credit Suisse*, Report Dated: April 15, 2011.

[210] Ciccarelli, Scot, 'Best Buy Co., Inc.: Comps Improved and GMs Stabilized; Solid Early Signs of Turnaround Efforts,' RBC Capital Markets, report dated March 1, 2013.

[211] Binder, Daniel and Gugliuzza, John, 'Best Buy: Upgrade to Buy: Seven Reasons to Own BBY,' Jefferies, report dated March 6, 2013.

[212] Binder, Daniel and Gugliuzza, John, 'Best Buy: Upgrade to Buy: Seven Reasons to Own BBY,' Jefferies, report dated March 6, 2013.

[213] Best Buy 4th Quarter 2014 and 1st Quarter 2015 Earnings Call Transcripts, accessed through Morningstar.

[214] Pachter, Michael, "*Q3 Review: Eroding Business Model Unlikely to Rebound; Reiterate UNDERPERFORM, Lowering PT to $9", WedBush,* Report Dated: November 20, 2012.

[215] Bensinger, Greg, "New Year Rings in Sales Tax for Amazon Shoppers in Three States," *Wall Street Journal,* January 1, 2014.

[216] "Nielsen: U.S. Consumers Making Fewer Shopping Trips," Nielsen press release, March 17, 2008, on Nielsen website,http://www.nielsen.com/content/dam/nielsen/en_us/documents/pdf/Press%20Releases/2008/Mar/Nielsen%20U.S.%20Consumers%20Making%20Fewer%20Shopping%20Trips.pdf, accessed July 2012.

[217] Consumer Expenditure Survey, Bureau of Labor Statistics, United States Department of Labor, 1990-2010, and author's calculations – real average Frozen Prepared Foods expenditure for all consumer units (categorized under Miscellaneous Foods) indexed to BLS CPI for Frozen and Freeze Dried Prepared Foods divided by real average Food At Home expenditure for all consumer units indexed to relevant food categories within BLS CPI.

[218] *ibid*

[219] The NPD Group, Eating Patterns in America (25th edition), September 2009.

[220] Compiled from 'Appliances', Housing Characteristics Tables, Residential Energy Consumption Survey Data, US Energy Information Administration, Years 1993, 1997, 2001, 2005, 2009 and author's calculations.

[221] The NPD Group, Eating Patterns in America (25th edition), September 2009.

[222] *ibid*

[223] Compiled from Table 7, Food Expenditure Series, Economic Research Service, United States Department of Agriculture.

[224] The NPD Group, Eating Patterns in America (25th edition), September 2009.

[225] *ibid*

[226] MacFayden, Tevere, "The Rise of the Supermarket," *American Heritage*, October/November 1985, Volume 36:6, http://www.americanheritage.com/content/rise-supermarket, accessed November 2012.

[227] *ibid*

[228] Swift, Tammy, "The everchanging marketplace; From the neighborhood grocery to the hyperstores of today," *The Forum,* August 18, 1999, http://legacy.inforum.com/specials/century/jan3/week34.html accessed October, 2012.

[229] Compiled from 'Merchandise by Kind of Business' and 'Kinds of Business by Broad Merchandise Line' in Merchandise Line Sales, Retail Trade Subject Series, Economic Census, for years 1992, 1997, 2002, and 2007 and author's calculations. Specialty Stores included as non-supermarket volume. Dollar volumes brought to real terms by indexing against relevant CPI categories.

[230] "NPD Finds Nearly Every U.S. Household Consumes Private Label and Store Brand Foods," NPD Group press release, April 21, 2009, on NPD Group website https://www.npd.com/wps/portal/npd/us/news/press-releases/pr_090421/ , accessed July, 2012.

[231] "Store Brands Growing Across All Channels," in *Market Profile*, Private Label Manufacturers Association, 2011.

[232] Hanna, Julia, "How Mercadona Fixes Retail's 'Last 10 Yards,'" *Working Knowledge, Harvard Business School*, July 19, 2010, available at http://hbswk.hbs.edu/item/6440.html

[233] Zeynep, Ton, *The Good Jobs Strategy: How the Smartest Companies Invest in Employees to Lower Costs & Boost Profits*. Boston: New Harvest, Houghton Mifflin Harcourt, 2014.

[234] "Mercadona Invests 650 Million Euros and Creates 4,000 New Permanent Jobs in 2012," *Mercadona Press Release,* March 7, 2013, available at http://www.mercadona.es/corp/ing-html/noticias.html

[235] Zeynep, Ton, *The Good Jobs Strategy: How the Smartest Companies Invest in Employees to Lower Costs & Boost Profits*. Boston: New Harvest, Houghton Mifflin Harcourt, 2014.

[236] Company Financial Statements, via Thomson One, accessed July, 2012.

[237] Measured using FMI's median average transaction tables in the 'Food Retailing Industry Speaks' series as well as Walmart's reported contributions of ticket gains to Walmart US and Sam's Club comp sales.

[238] Schwartz, Shelly K, "As Waistlines Grow, So Do Refrigerator Sizes," *CNBC*, October 8, 2012, available at http://www.cnbc.com/id/49101730#.

[239] Natunewicz, Ann T, "Dollar Days: How Dollar Stores are Growing in a Weak Economy," Colliers International white paper, December 2011, on Colliers International website,http://www.colliers.com/~/media/Files/Global/ResearchReports/Colliers_whitepaper_DollarDays_120611.ashx, accessed September 2012.

[240] Tuttle, Brad, "Why Shoppers and Shopping Centers Alike Now Embrace the Dollar Store," *Time*, January 27, 2012, http://business.time.com/2012/01/27/why-shoppers-and-shopping-centers-alike-now-embrace-the-dollar-store/, accessed September 2012.

[241] Natunewicz, Ann T, "Dollar Days: How Dollar Stores are Growing in a Weak Economy," Colliers International white paper, December 2011, on Colliers International website,http://www.colliers.com/~/media/Files/Global/ResearchReports/Colliers_whitepaper_DollarDays_120611.ashx, accessed September 2012.

[242] Wilson, Marianne, "Kantar Retail survey: Dollar General offers least expensive basket price," *Chain Store Age*, October 5, 2012, http://www.chainstoreage.com/article/kantar-retail-survey-dollar-general-offers-least-expensive-basket-price, accessed October, 2012.

[243] "Family Dollar Stores' CEO Discusses Q2 2012 Results – Earnings Call Transcript," via Seeking Alpha, March 28, 2012, http://seekingalpha.com/article/464121-family-dollar-stores-ceo-discusses-q2-2012-results-earnings-call-transcript?part=single, accessed October 2012.

[244] "Dollar General's CEO Discusses Q1 2012 Results – Earnings Call Transcript," via Seeking Alpha, June 5, 2012, http://seekingalpha.com/article/636891-dollar-general-s-ceo-discusses-q1-2012-results-earnings-call-transcript, accessed October 2012.

[245] Family Dollar Stores, 2012 10K, page 6, via Thomson One, accessed October 2012.

[246] Natunewicz, Ann T, "Dollar Days: How Dollar Stores are Growing in a Weak Economy," Colliers International white paper, December 2011, on Colliers International website,http://www.colliers.com/~/media/Files/Global/ResearchReports/Colliers_whitepaper_DollarDays_12061 1.ashx, accessed September 2012.

[247] Tuttle, Brad, "Why Shoppers and Shopping Centers Alike Now Embrace the Dollar Store," *Time*, January 27, 2012, http://business.time.com/2012/01/27/why-shoppers-and-shopping-centers-alike-now-embrace-the-dollar-store/, accessed September 2012.

[248] Natunewicz, Ann T, "Dollar Days: How Dollar Stores are Growing in a Weak Economy," Colliers International white paper, December 2011, on Colliers International website,http://www.colliers.com/~/media/Files/Global/ResearchReports/Colliers_whitepaper_DollarDays_12061 1.ashx, accessed September 2012.

[249] Dollar General Corporation, 2011 10K, pages 6 and 7, via Thomson One, accessed October 2012.

[250] Dollar General Corporation, *News Center Company Facts*, http://newscenter.dollargeneral.com/company+facts/, accessed October 2012.

[251] Natunewicz, Ann T, "Dollar Days: How Dollar Stores are Growing in a Weak Economy," Colliers International white paper, December 2011, on Colliers International website,http://www.colliers.com/~/media/Files/Global/ResearchReports/Colliers_whitepaper_DollarDays_12061 1.ashx, accessed September 2012.

[252] Tuttle, Brad, "Why Shoppers and Shopping Centers Alike Now Embrace the Dollar Store," *Time*, January 27, 2012, http://business.time.com/2012/01/27/why-shoppers-and-shopping-centers-alike-now-embrace-the-dollar-store/, accessed September 2012.

[253] Anderson, Tania, "Is Online Grocery Shopping Worth the Fee?" *The Washington Post*, July 9, 2008, http://voices.washingtonpost.com/shoptoit/2008/07/is_online_grocery_shopping_wor.html accessed October, 2012.

[254] Lewis, Mike, "Taking Amazon Fresh for a Spin," *Puget Sound Business Journal*, October 2, 2009, http://www.bizjournals.com/seattle/blog/techflash/2009/10/taking_amazon_fresh_for_a_spin.html?page=all, accessed October, 2012.

[255] McClain, Alan, "Is Grocery Delivery/Pick-Up Finally Ready for Prime Time?" *Retail Wire*, September 10, 2012, available at http://www.retailwire.com/discussion/16261/is-grocery-delivery-pick-up-finally-ready-for-prime-time

[256] Cruz, Julie, "FreshDirect vs. Peapod: New York's Online Food Fight," *Bloomberg Businessweek*, March 14, 2013, available at http://www.businessweek.com/articles/2013-03-14/freshdirect-vs-dot-peapod-new-yorks-online-food-fight

[257] Moore, Stefany, "Can Amazon Sell Groceries in the Big Apple?" *Internet Retailer*, December 13, 2013, available at http://www.internetretailer.com/2013/12/13/can-amazon-sell-groceries-big-apple

[258] Penetration levels calculated by applying average American at-home food expenditures from Consumer Expenditure Survey (expenditure per consumer unit divided by persons per consumer unit) to the population of online retailers' market areas.

[259] Bell, David E., and Leamon, Ann, "Costco Companies, Inc.", HBS case number 599-041 (Boston: Harvard Business School Publishing, 1998).

[260] Glassdor, *Best Places to Work 2013*, http://www.glassdoor.com/Best-Places-to-Work-LST_KQ0,19.htm, accessed January 2012.

[261] Palmeri, Christopher, "Trader Joe's Recipe for Success," *Businessweek*, February 20, 2008, http://www.businessweek.com/stories/2008-02-20/trader-joes-recipe-for-success, accessed October 2012.

[262] Beswick, Paul et. al., "Winning at Home: How retailers can win a greater share of their natural customers," *Oliver Wyman*, 2008.

[263] *ibid*

[264] *ibid*

[265] Dawson, Mike, "Talk with Dansk Supermarked," *German Retail Blog* (blog), June 22, 2007, http://www.german-retail-blog.com/2007/06/22/talk-with-dansk-supermarked, accessed October 2012.

[266] *ibid*

[267] *ibid*

[268] *ibid*

[269] *ibid*

[270] Geldmacher, Christopher, et. al., "Keeping it simple, getting it right," *McKinsey & Company*, February, 2012, http://csi.mckinsey.com/knowledge_by_region/europe_africa_middle_east/discount_retail_stores_in_europe, accessed October, 2012.

[271] Consumer Reports, *Supermarket Buying Guide*, July 2012, http://www.consumerreports.org/cro/supermarkets/buying-guide.htm, accessed October 2012.

[272] "What's Keeping Americans Out of Their Kitchens? National Survey Reveals the Top Excuses for Not Cooking," Bosch press release, September 8, 2011, on Market Wire website, http://www.marketwire.com/press-release/whats-keeping-americans-out-their-kitchens-national-survey-reveals-top-excuses-not-cooking-1558601.htm, accessed July 2012.

[273] *Food Retailing Industry Speaks*, by Food Marketing Institute. Various years.

[274] SKUs listed in Amazon's Grocery, Health & Beauty Department, www.amazon.com, accessed: May 2014.

[275] Author calculations based on data found in *Food Retailing Industry Speaks*, by Food Marketing Institute. Various years.

[276] MacDonald, Shawn, "Will Supermarkets Come Full Circle?", *Strategy & Analytics Blog* (blog), *Pitney Bowes Software Strategy & Analytics Blog*, January 6, 2011, http://analytics.pbbiblogs.com/2011/01/06/will-supermarkets-come-full-circle/, accessed: November 2012.

[277] Rohde, David, "The Anti-Walmart: The Secret Sauce of Wegmans is People", *The Atlantic*, March 23, 2012, http://www.theatlantic.com/business/archive/2012/03/the-anti-walmart-the-secret-sauce-of-wegmans-is-people/254994/, accessed September 2012.

[278] Merrefield, David, "FOODELECTRIC", *Supermarket News,* Oct. 23, 1995, http://supermarketnews.com/archive/foodelectric, accessed January 2013.

[279] Braddock, Richard, "Lessons of Internet Marketing from FreshDirect", *The Wall Street Journal*, May 11, 2009, http://online.wsj.com/article/SB124205175154206817.html accessed July 2012.

[280] Safeway Corporation, 2011 10K, page 22, via Thomson One, accessed October 2012.

[281] Tracey, James and de Speville, Marc, "Ocado: Coming of Age," *Redburn*, May 13, 2013.

[282] Warschun, Mirko, "A Fresh Look at Online Grocery," *AT Kearney*, March, 2012.

[283] Dauvers, Olivier, "Drive et Rentabilité," *Les Dossiers Grande Conso*, November, 2013.

[284] "Drive Format Powers French Hybrid Retail," *The Economist Intelligence Unit*, April 28, 2014, available at http://www.eiu.com/industry/article/311766015/drive-format-powers-french-hybrid-retail/2014-04-28

[285] Garnier, Juliette, "Le drive menace-t-il l'hypermarché?" *La Tribune*, January 6, 2012, available at http://www.latribune.fr/entreprises-finance/services/distribution/20120601trib000701562/le-drive-menace-t-il-l-hypermarche-.html

[286] Tesco Terms and Conditions, available at http://www.tesco.com/termsandconditions/termsconditionsgroc.htm, accessed June 3, 2014.

[287] Debouté, Alexandre, "Auchan crée un nouveau type de centre commercial," *Le Figaro,* August 10, 2010.

[288] MacDaid, Donal, "What's In Store for Click & Collect, Part 2?" *Symphony EYC,* April 8, 2014, available at http://www.eyc.com/blog/what-s-in-store-for-click-collect-part-2

[289] O'Connor, Tim, "Drive Through Retail in France," *Retail Net Group,* November, 2010, available at http://www.retailnetgroup.com/public/FrenchDrive.pdf

[290] Thomasson, Emma and Vidalon, Dominique, "Analysis: Retailers Look to Click & Collect Online Profits," *Reuters,* September 6, 2013, available at http://www.reuters.com/article/2013/09/06/us-retail-online-collect-analysis-idUSBRE9850DC20130906

[291] Dauvers, Olivier, *Mag Drive*, 4th volume, February, 2014.

[292] "Grocery Retailers in France," *Euromonitor International,* June, 2014.

[293] Dauvers, Olivier, *Mag Drive*, 4th volume, February, 2014.

[294] Dauvers, Olivier, "Exclu: 1926 drives au 6 décembre, + 90 en un mois!" December 10, 2012, available at http://www.olivierdauvers.fr/2012/12/10/exclu-1926-drives-au-6-decembre-90-en-un-mois/ and Dauvers, Olivier, "DRIVE INSIGHTS décembre est dispo!" December 18, 2013, available at http://www.olivierdauvers.fr/2013/12/18/drive-insights-decembre-est-dispo/.

[295] If store openings are evenly spaced throughout the year, each new store could only provide, on average, half a year's worth of sales. The balance of the sales growth would have to come from increases in same-store sales and sales from the previous year's new stores that have not been open for at least a year.

[296] Popa, Tudor, "Will Leclerc's Strong 2013 Carry Into 2014?" *Kantar Retail iQ,* February 19, 2014, available at http://www.kriq.com/ContentIndex/ArticleDetails.aspx?key=BlgDyrQrbCLgY2XCgaCpwg==&id=615506

[297] Thomasson, Emma and Vidalon, Dominique, "Analysis: Retailers Look to Click & Collect Online Profits," *Reuters,* September 6, 2013, available at http://www.reuters.com/article/2013/09/06/us-retail-online-collect-analysis-idUSBRE9850DC20130906

[298] Dauvers, Olivier, *Mag Drive,* 4th volume, February, 2014.

[299] *Access to Affordable Food: Measuring and Understanding Food Deserts and Their Consequences*, Report to Congress, Economic Research Service, United States Department of Agriculture, June 2009.

[300] Ehrenhalt, Alan, "The Grocery Gap," in *Governing*, April 2006, http://www.governing.com/topics/mgmt/Grocery-Gap.html, accessed: October 2012.

[301] "What's Keeping Americans Out of Their Kitchens? National Survey Reveals the Top Excuses for Not Cooking," Bosch press release, September 8, 2011, on Market Wire website, http://www.marketwire.com/press-release/whats-keeping-americans-out-their-kitchens-national-survey-reveals-top-excuses-not-cooking-1558601.htm, accessed July 2012.

[302] Alpi, Jean-Claude, "Picard: The Frozen Food Specialist," *PL Magazine*, Spring 2010, http://www.plstorebrands.com/plmag-article-picard__the_frozen_food_specialist-4818.html, accessed September 2012.

[303] Societe Generale Corporate and Investment Banking, Offering Memorandum, Picard Bondco S.A., November 4, 2010.

[304] *ibid*

[305] Alvarez, José et al., "H-E-B: Creating a Movement to Reduce Obesity in Texas," HBS case number 512-034, (Boston: Harvard Business School Publishing, 2012).

[306] Vance, Sandra and Scott, Roy, *Wal-Mart: A History of Sam Walton's Retail Phenomenon*. New York, New York: Twayne Publishers, 1994.

[307] *ibid*

[308] *ibid*

[309] *ibid*

[310] *ibid*

[311] *ibid*

[312] *ibid*

[313] *ibid*

[314] *ibid*

[315] *ibid*

[316] *ibid*

[317] *ibid*

[318] *ibid*

[319] *ibid*

[320] Holmes, Thomas J, "*The Diffusion of Wal-Mart and Economics of Density*," Econometrica, Vol 79, No. 1, January, 2011.

[321] Vance, Sandra and Scott, Roy, *Wal-Mart: A History of Sam Walton's Retail Phenomenon*. New York, New York: Twayne Publishers, 1994.

[322] Johnson, Fraser P, "Supply Chain Management at Wal-Mart," Ivey case number 907D01, London, Ontario: Richard Ivey School of Business Foundation, 2013.

[323] *ibid*

[324] Ortmeyer, G. K., J. A. Quelch, and W. J. Salmon. "Restoring Credibility to Retail Pricing." *MIT Sloan Management Review* 33, no. 1 (fall 1991): 55–66.

[325] Johnson, Fraser P, "Supply Chain Management at Wal-Mart," Ivey case number 907D01, London, Ontario: Richard Ivey School of Business Foundation, 2013.

[326] Ortmeyer, G. K., J. A. Quelch, and W. J. Salmon. "Restoring Credibility to Retail Pricing." *MIT Sloan Management Review* 33, no. 1 (fall 1991): 55–66.

[327] 'Walmart U.S. Logistics," *Walmart*, available at http://corporate.walmart.com/our-story/our-business/logistics and 'The Walmart Distribution Center Network in the United States,' *MWPVL*, available at http://www.mwpvl.com/html/walmart.html

[328] Souza, Kim, "Wal-mart distribution centers key to revenue growth," *The City Wire*, June 10, 2013, available at http://www.thecitywire.com/node/28208#.UqHz9uK0aGV

[329] Vance, Sandra and Scott, Roy, *Wal-Mart: A History of Sam Walton's Retail Phenomenon*. New York, New York: Twayne Publishers, 1994.

[330] *ibid*

[331] *ibid*

[332] Walmart 2013 Annual Report

[333] Fishman, Charles, *The Wal-mart Effect*. New York, New York: Penguin Books, 2006.

[334] Banjo, Shelly, "As Amazon Gets Physical, Walmart Goes Digital," *The Wall Street Journal*, March 26, 2013, available at http://blogs.wsj.com/corporate-intelligence/2013/03/26/as-amazon-gets-physical-wal-mart-goes-digital/

[335] US Census, Department of Commerce, 'ua list all.xls' available at http://www2.census.gov/geo/ua/

[336] 'Dollar General Maintains Overall Opening Price Point Leadership, New Kantar Retail Basket Study Reveals,' *Kantar Retail*, October 13, 2014, available at http://www.kantarretail.com/pressroom/102014_OPP_Press_Release.pdf

[337] Natunewicz, Ann T, "Dollar Days: How Dollar Stores are Growing in a Weak Economy," *Colliers International*, December, 2011, available at http://www.colliers.com/~/media/Files/MarketResearch/UnitedStates/MARKETS/2011%20Q4/Colliers_Whitepaper_DollarDays_20111201%281%29.ashx?campaign=DollarDaysReport

[338] McArdle, Megan, "Walmart's New CEO Has to Take on Amazon and Unions," *Bloomberg Opinion*, Nov 26, 2013, available at http://www.bloomberg.com/news/2013-11-26/wal-mart-s-new-ceo-has-to-take-on-amazon-and-unions.html

[339] O'Connor, Clare, "Wal-Mart vs. Amazon: World's Biggest E-Commerce Battle Could Boil Down to Vegetables," *Forbes*, April 23, 2013, available at http://www.forbes.com/sites/clareoconnor/2013/04/23/wal-mart-vs-amazon-worlds-biggest-e-commerce-battle-could-boil-down-to-vegetables/.

[340] Florida, Richard, "What Dollar Store Locations Reveal About America," *The Atlantic Cities*, February 7, 2012, available at http://www.theatlanticcities.com/jobs-and-economy/2012/02/what-dollar-store-locations-reveal-about-america/1115/ and Hitt, Jack, "The Dollar-Store Economy," *New York Times*, August 18, 2011 available at http://www.nytimes.com/2011/08/21/magazine/the-dollar-store-economy.html?pagewanted=all&_r=0

[341] Wiltamuth, Mark and Mandeville, Christopher, "Kroger, Initiating at Hold: Bet in Class; Solid 10-12% Grower, Fairly Valued," *Jefferies*, October 7, 2013, available via *Thomson One* and Gara, Tom, "As Grocer Prices Rise, Wal-Mart Gets Cheaper," *Wall Street Journal,* October 15, 2012.

[342] Company Pre-Recorded Conference Calls, FY 2004-FY2010, compiled by *Thomson Reuters*, available via *Thomson One*.

[343] 'Kroger Outlines Growth Strategy, Raises Long Term EPS Growth Target to 8-11%,' *Kroger News Release*, October 16, 2012, available at http://ir.kroger.com/phoenix.zhtml?c=106409&p=irol-newsArticle&ID=1745982

[344] Kantar Retail ShopperScape data, May 2014 and Senzamici, Kate, "ShopperScape Snapshot: Why are Shoppers Shopping Walmart, Target Less Often?", June 2013, *Kantar Retail Shopper Insights*.

[345] McGuire, Rachel, "Walmart Shoppers, Inside and Out," *Kantar Retail,* April 2014

[346] "The 20th Annual Meeting for the Investment Community," *Walmart*, October 16, 2013.

[347] DeRise, Jason and Carden, Mark, "Wal-Mart Stores: Now, Later and Long Term," *UBS Investment Research*, April 15, 2013, accessed via *Thomson One*.

[348] 'The Walmart Distribution Center Network in the United States,' *MWPVL*, available at http://www.mwpvl.com/html/walmart.html

[349] "Adapting to a Showrooming World: How Retailers are Earning Customer Loyalty," eMarketer

[350] Zybowski, Anne et al, "Walmart-Amazon Pricing Study: The Gap Narrows," *Kantar Retail*, October 27, 2014.

[351] Kantar Retail ShopperScape data, May 2014 and Senzamici, Kate, "ShopperScape Snapshot: Why are Shoppers Shopping Walmart, Target Less Often?", June 2013, *Kantar Retail.*

[352] Souza, Kim, "Wal-mart distribution centers key to revenue growth," *The City Wire*, June 10, 2013.

[353] De DeRise, Jason and Carden, Mark, "Wal-Mart Stores: Now, Later and Long Term," *UBS Investment Research*, April 15, 2013, accessed via *Thomson One.*

[354] "Share of Shopping Trips of US Consumers by Channel, 2013," *IRI*, accessed through Statista.

[355] Dishman, Lydia, "Why Walmart is Betting Big on Small Stores," *Forbes*, March 6, 2013, available at http://www.forbes.com/sites/lydiadishman/2013/03/06/why-walmart-is-betting-big-on-small-stores/

[356] Sandler, Ross et. al, "Moving Closer to Customers – The Good, Bad, & Not At All Ugly," *Deutsche Bank,* March 22, 2013.

[357] "Glass Half Empty?", *Progressive Grocer's 79th Annual Report of the Grocery Industry*, April 2012.

[358] "For the Eighth Consecutive Year, Amazon Ranks #1 in Customer Satisfaction During the Holiday Shopping Season," Amazon Press Release, December 27, 2012, available at http://phx.corporate-ir.net/phoenix.zhtml?c=176060&p=irol-newsArticle&ID=1769785. North American order volume estimated by applying North American retail sales share to global order volume.

[359] Bell, David E. and Feiner, Jeffrey M., "Wal-Mart Neighborhood Markets," HBS case number 9-503-034, Harvard Business School Publishing: Boston, MA, November 22, 2003.

[360] Fishman, Charles, *The Wal-Mart Effect.* New York, New York: The Penguin Press, 2006.

[361] Quinn, Kirsten, "National, Local Pet Industry a Steady Growing Market," *Santa Clarita Valley Signal*, June 21, 2013, accessed August 30, 2013 at http://www.signalscv.com/section/434/article/99026/.

[362] Brady, Diane et al, "The Pet Economy," *Bloomberg Businessweek*, August 5, 2007, accessed on August 30, 2013 at http://www.businessweek.com/stories/2007-08-05/the-pet-economy.

[363] Lummis, David, "U.S. Pet Market Outlook, 2013-2014," *Packaged Facts*, June 2013.

[364] Ryan, Amy, 'PetSmart Inc, Initiating Coverage with a Pawsitive Rating,' *Oppenheimer & Co. Inc.,* November 8, 2005, accessed via *Thomson One*, August 30, 2013.

[365] Average food expenditures per person in the US calculated from Table 1 of the USDA's food expenditure's statistics, available at http://www.ers.usda.gov/data-products/food-expenditures.aspx#26634 and does not include donations or home-grown produce. Total expenses per cat and dog calculated from APPA's 2013-2014 APPA National Pet Owners Survey basic annual expenses for dog-owners and cat-owners, and the average number of dogs and cats per dog and cat owning household. These basic annual expenses are not comprehensive.

[366] "PETsMART, Inc.," *William Blair & Company*, November, 1995, accessed via *Thomson One*, August 30, 2013.

[367] "PETsMART, Inc.," *William Blair & Company*, November, 1995, accessed via *Thomson One*, August 30, 2013.

[368] Vroom, Christopher E. and Miller, Barbara E., "PETsMART, Inc.," *Alex, Brown & Sons,* September 8, 1993, accessed via *Thomson One*, August 30, 2013.

[369] *ibid*

[370] *ibid*

[371] *ibid*

[372] Vroom, C.E., et al, "PETsMART, Inc.," *Alex, Brown & Sons, Inc.,* May 2, 1994, accessed via *Thomson One*, August 30, 2013.

[373] Kully, Thomas, "PETsMART, Inc.," *William Blair & Company*, November 7, 1994, accessed via *Thomson One,* August 30, 2013.

[374] Vroom, Christopher E. and Miller, Barbara E., "PETsMART, Inc.," *Alex, Brown & Sons,* September 8, 1993, accessed via *Thomson One*, August 30, 2013.

[375] Mandel, Mark, "PETM: Initiate Coverage With A Buy Rating And $53 Price Target," *ThinkEquity LLC,* October 17, 2011, accessed via *Thomson One*, September 3, 2013.

[376] "PETsMART, Inc.," *William Blair & Company*, November, 1995.

[377] "Created to Sell," *McCulloch + Company,* available at http://mccull.com/petstuff.swf, accessed September 17, 2013.

[378] Eaton, Leslie, "Hey Big Spenders," *New York Times*, September 11, 1994, available at http://www.nytimes.com/1994/09/11/business/hey-big-spenders.html?pagewanted=all&src=pm, accessed September 16, 2013.

[379] *ibid*

[380] Vroom, Christopher E. and Miller, Barbara E., "PETsMART, Inc.," *Alex, Brown & Sons,* September 8, 1993, accessed via *Thomson One*, August 30, 2013.

[381] *ibid*

[382] *ibid*

[383] *ibid*

[384] Balter, Gary, "PETSMART, INC.," *Donaldson, Lufkin & Jenrette*, September 10, 1993, accessed via *Thomson One,* August 30, 2013.

[385] *ibid*

[386] Vroom, Christopher E. and Miller, Barbara E., "PETsMART, Inc.," *Alex, Brown & Sons,* September 8, 1993, accessed via *Thomson One*, August 30, 2013.

[387] *ibid*

[388] *ibid*

[389] Balter, Gary, "PETSMART, INC.," *Donaldson, Lufkin & Jenrette*, September 10, 1993, accessed via *Thomson One,* August 30, 2013.

[390] Vroom, C.E., et al, "PETsMART, Inc.," *Alex, Brown & Sons, Inc.,* October 7, 1994, accessed via *Thomson One*, August 30, 2013.

[391] Vroom, Christopher E. and Miller, Barbara E., "PETsMART, Inc.," *Alex, Brown & Sons,* September 8, 1993, accessed via *Thomson One*, August 30, 2013.

[392] Vroom, C.E., et al, "PETsMART, Inc.," *Alex, Brown & Sons, Inc.,* January 31, 1994, accessed via *Thomson One*, August 30, 2013.

[393] Vroom, Christopher E. and Miller, Barbara E., "PETsMART, Inc.," *Alex, Brown & Sons,* September 8, 1993, accessed via *Thomson One*, August 30, 2013 and Kully, Thomas, "PETsMART, Inc.," *William Blair & Company*, November 7, 1994, accessed via *Thomson One,* August 30, 2013.

[394] 'Company History,' PetSmart.com, http://phx.corporate-ir.net/phoenix.zhtml?c=93506&p=irol-timeline, accessed August 31, 2013.

[395] Balter, Gary, "PETSMART: P&G Acquisition of Iams Potential Negative To PETsMART," *Donaldson, Lufkin & Jenrette,* August 12, 1999, accessed via *Thomson One*, September 3, 2013.

[396] Nelson, Emily, "After Racing Ahead with Iams, P&G Finds Itself on the Defensive," *The Wall Street Journal*, June 14, 2000, available at http://online.wsj.com/article/SB960938323187091851.html.

[397] *ibid*

[398] PETsMART Annual Report, FY 2000, filed January 28, 2001.

[399] PETsMART Annual Report, FY 2005, filed January 29, 2006.

[400] Holdsworth, Gary, "PETsMART," *Wedbush Morgan Securities*, April 20, 2004, accessed via *Thomson One,* August 30, 2013.

[401] Wewer, Dan and Ma, Vivian, "PETsMART, Inc.," *CIBC World Markets,* August 12, 2003, accessed via *Thomson One*, September 3, 2013.

[402] Ryan, Amy, 'PetSmart Inc, Initiating Coverage with a Pawsitive Rating,' *Oppenheimer & Co. Inc.,* November 8, 2005, accessed via *Thomson One*, August 30, 2013.

[403] Vroom, C.E., et al, "PETsMART, Inc.," *Alex, Brown & Sons, Inc.,* May 2, 1994, accessed via *Thomson One*, August 30, 2013.

[404] "Q1 2002 PetSmart Earnings Call," *Thomson Street Events*, accessed September 1, 2013 via *Thomson One.*

[405] "Q2 2005 PetsMart Earnings Conference Call," August 24, 2005, *Thomson Streetevents,* accessed September 1, 2013 via *Thomson One.*.

[406] Kully, Thomas, "PETsMART, Inc.," *William Blair & Company*, November 7, 1994, accessed via *Thomson One,* August 30, 2013.

[407] *ibid*

[408] "PETsMART, Inc.," *William Blair & Company*, November, 1995.

[409] Make, Jonathan, "The Scott Thomason of Veterinarians," *Portland Business Journal*, July 6, 1997, available at http://www.bizjournals.com/portland/stories/1997/07/07/story3.html?page=all and accessed September 23, 2013.

[410] Kully, Thomas, "PETsMART, Inc.," *William Blair & Company*, November 7, 1994, accessed via *Thomson One*, August 30, 2013.

[411] "PETsMART, Inc.," *William Blair & Company*, November, 1995, accessed via *Thomson One*, August 30, 2013.

[412] Holdsworth, Gary, "PETsMART," *Wedbush Morgan Securities*, April 20, 2004, accessed via *Thomson One*, August 30, 2013.

[413] Horvers, Christopher, "PetSmart, Inc., Management Meeting Highlights," *JP Morgan*, June 26, 2013, accessed via *Thomson One*, August 31, 2013.

[414] Gober, David and Rupeka, Cynthia, "PetSmart, Inc, This Puppy's Growing Fast; Initiating at Overweight," *Morgan Stanley*, June 13, 2012.

[415] *ibid*

[416] Glass, John S. and Hone, David F., "PETsMART, Inc.," March 12, 1999, *Bankers Trust Alex Brown*, accessed via *Thomson One*, August 30, 2013.

[417] Glass, John S. and Hone, David F., "PETsMART, Inc.," May 14, 1999, *Bankers Trust Alex Brown*, accessed via *Thomson One*, August 30, 2013.

[418] Balter, Gary and Gandhi, Neel, "PETSMART: PETsMART Reported Q3 EPS Of $0.03, Penny Below Our Estimate," *Donaldson, Lufkin & Jenrette*, November 24, 1999, accessed via *Thomson One*, August 31, 2013.

[419] 'PetSmart's CEO presents at 2013 Consumer & Retail Conference,' March 12, 2013, transcript available at Seeking Alpha.

[420] Kully, Thomas, "PETsMART, Inc.," *William Blair & Company*, November 7, 1994, accessed via *Thomson One*, August 30, 2013.

[421] Wewer, Dan and Ma, Vivian, "PETsMART, Inc.," *CIBC World Markets,* August 12, 2003, accessed via *Thomson One*, September 3, 2013.

[422] Holdsworth, Gary, "PETsMART," *Wedbush Morgan Securities*, April 20, 2004, accessed via *Thomson One*, August 30, 2013.

[423] Wewer, Dan and Ma, Vivian, "PETsMART, Inc.," *CIBC World Markets,* August 12, 2003, accessed via *Thomson One*, September 3, 2013.

[424] Vroom, Christopher E. and Miller, Barbara E., "PETsMART, Inc.," *Alex, Brown & Sons,* September 8, 1993, accessed via *Thomson One*, August 30, 2013.

[425] Ciccarelli, Scot et. al, "PetSmart, Inc: Compelling Long-Term Growth Potential With Some Downside Protection," *RBC Capital Markets*, July 25, 2011, accessed via *Thomson One, September 4, 2013.*

[426] Ryan, Amy, 'PetSmart Inc, Initiating Coverage with a Pawsitive Rating,' *Oppenheimer & Co. Inc.,* November 8, 2005, accessed via *Thomson One*, August 30, 2013.

[427] Buss, Christian, "PETM: Initiate Coverage with a Buy Rating and $41 Price Target," *Think Equity LLC,* September 13, 2010, accessed via *Thomson One, September 5, 2013.*

[428] Horvers, Christopher, et. al., 'The Home Depot: Big Orange Crush; Reiterate Overweight,' *J.P. Morgan*, February 27, 2013.

[429] Alvarez, José et. al, 'Home Depot and Interconnected Retail,' HBS case number N9-512-036, Boston: Harvard Business School Publishing, 2012.

[430] Thomas, Ian et. al, 'Quarterly Retail E-Commerce Sales, 1st Quarter 2013,' *US Census Bureau News*, US Department of Commerce, May 15, 2013, available at http://www.census.gov/retail/mrts/www/data/pdf/ec_current.pdf and accessed July 13, 2013.

[431] 'Home Depot Inc Investor & Analyst Conference, June 6, 2012,' Transcript compiled by Thomson Reuters StreetEvents, accessed via Thomson One, July 9, 2013.

[432] Conversation with Niraj Shah, CEO of Wayfair, August 9, 2013.

[433] *ibid*

[434] Shore, Damian, 'Social Sharing and Hand and Power Tools – a Dangerous Combination for Manufacturers,' *Passport,* March 26, 2013.

[435] Roush, Chris, *Inside Home Depot*, New York, New York: McGraw-Hill, 1999, p 101-102.

[436] Marcus, Bernie, Blank, Arthur, and Andelman, Bob, *Built From Scratch*, New York, New York: Times Books, 1999, p 205.

[437] Lowe's annual report, Fiscal Year 1982, accessed via *Thomson*, August 12, 2013.

[438] Marcus, Bernie, Blank, Arthur, and Andelman, Bob, *Built From Scratch*, New York, New York: Times Books, 1999, p 194.

[439] Marcus, Bernie, Blank, Arthur, and Andelman, Bob, *Built From Scratch*, New York, New York: Times Books, 1999, p 137.

[440] Marcus, Bernie, Blank, Arthur, and Andelman, Bob, *Built From Scratch*, New York, New York: Times Books, 1999, p 194.

[441] Roush, Chris, *Inside Home Depot*, New York, New York: McGraw-Hill, 1999, p 11.

[442] Marcus, Bernie, Blank, Arthur, and Andelman, Bob, *Built From Scratch*, New York, New York: Times Books, 1999, p xviii.

[443] Roush, Chris, *Inside Home Depot*, New York, New York: McGraw-Hill, 1999, p 11.

[444] "Grossman's Inc. History," *International Directory of Company Histories*, Volume 13, St. James Press, 1996.

[445] Marcus, Bernie, Blank, Arthur, and Andelman, Bob, *Built From Scratch*, New York, New York: Times Books, 1999, p 41.

[446] Marcus, Bernie, Blank, Arthur, and Andelman, Bob, *Built From Scratch*, New York, New York: Times Books, 1999, p 135.

[447] Roush, Chris, *Inside Home Depot*, New York, New York: McGraw-Hill, 1999, p 82.

[448] Marcus, Bernie, Blank, Arthur, and Andelman, Bob, *Built From Scratch*, New York, New York: Times Books, 1999, p 81.

[449] Marcus, Bernie, Blank, Arthur, and Andelman, Bob, *Built From Scratch*, New York, New York: Times Books, 1999, p 106.

[450] Roush, Chris, *Inside Home Depot*, New York, New York: McGraw-Hill, 1999, p 7.

[451] Roush, Chris, *Inside Home Depot*, New York, New York: McGraw-Hill, 1999, p 8.

[452] Marcus, Bernie, Blank, Arthur, and Andelman, Bob, *Built From Scratch*, New York, New York: Times Books, 1999, p 106.

[453] Marcus, Bernie, Blank, Arthur, and Andelman, Bob, *Built From Scratch*, New York, New York: Times Books, 1999, p 113.

[454] Roush, Chris, *Inside Home Depot*, New York, New York: McGraw-Hill, 1999, p 15.

[455] Marcus, Bernie, Blank, Arthur, and Andelman, Bob, *Built From Scratch*, New York, New York: Times Books, 1999, p 106.

[456] Marcus, Bernie, Blank, Arthur, and Andelman, Bob, *Built From Scratch*, New York, New York: Times Books, 1999, p 106.

[457] Roush, Chris, *Inside Home Depot*, New York, New York: McGraw-Hill, 1999, p 12.

[458] Roush, Chris, *Inside Home Depot*, New York, New York: McGraw-Hill, 1999, p 11.

[459] Roush, Chris, *Inside Home Depot*, New York, New York: McGraw-Hill, 1999, p 12.

[460] Roush, Chris, *Inside Home Depot*, New York, New York: McGraw-Hill, 1999, p 15.

[461] Marcus, Bernie, Blank, Arthur, and Andelman, Bob, *Built From Scratch*, New York, New York: Times Books, 1999, p 271.

[462] Roush, Chris, *Inside Home Depot*, New York, New York: McGraw-Hill, 1999, p 28-32.

[463] Marcus, Bernie, Blank, Arthur, and Andelman, Bob, *Built From Scratch*, New York, New York: Times Books, 1999, p 103-104.

[464] Roush, Chris, *Inside Home Depot*, New York, New York: McGraw-Hill, 1999, p 101.

[465] Roush, Chris, *Inside Home Depot*, New York, New York: McGraw-Hill, 1999, p 104.

[466] Marcus, Bernie, Blank, Arthur, and Andelman, Bob, *Built From Scratch*, New York, New York: Times Books, 1999, p 205.

[467] Roush, Chris, *Inside Home Depot*, New York, New York: McGraw-Hill, 1999, p 10.

[468] Roush, Chris, *Inside Home Depot*, New York, New York: McGraw-Hill, 1999, p 103.

[469] Marcus, Bernie, Blank, Arthur, and Andelman, Bob, *Built From Scratch*, New York, New York: Times Books, 1999, p 137.

[470] Roush, Chris, *Inside Home Depot*, New York, New York: McGraw-Hill, 1999, p 102-109.

[471] Marcus, Bernie, Blank, Arthur, and Andelman, Bob, *Built From Scratch*, New York, New York: Times Books, 1999, p 139.

[472] Salmon, Walter and Wylie, David, 'Lowe's,' HBS case number 9-590-013, Boston: Harvard Business School Publishing, 1997.

[473] Sellers, Patricia, "Something to Prove," *Fortune*, June 24, 2002, http://money.cnn.com/magazines/fortune/fortune_archive/2002/06/24/325190/.

[474] Alvarez, José et. al, 'Home Depot and Interconnected Retail,' HBS case number N9-512-036, Boston: Harvard Business School Publishing, 2012.

[475] Sellers, Patricia, "Something to Prove," *Fortune*, June 24, 2002, http://money.cnn.com/magazines/fortune/fortune_archive/2002/06/24/325190/.

[476] Alvarez, José et. al, 'Home Depot and Interconnected Retail,' HBS case number N9-512-036, Boston: Harvard Business School Publishing, 2012.

[477] "The Home Depot's CEO Discusses Q2 2011 Results – Earnings Call Transcript," *Seeking Alpha,* accessed August 11, 2013, http://seekingalpha.com/article/287741-the-home-depots-ceo-discusses-q2-2011-results-earnings-call-transcript?part=single.

[478] "A Look at Home Depot's First Phone," *Retail Industry,* March, 2011, http://www.retailindustry.com/retail-tech/articles/2011/homedepot-first-phone.html.

[479] Home Depot 10-K, 2012, accessed via *Thomson*, August 23, 2013.

[480] Alvarez, José et. al, 'Home Depot and Interconnected Retail,' HBS case number N9-512-036, Boston: Harvard Business School Publishing, 2012.

[481] *ibid*

[482] 'Home Depot Inc Investor & Analyst Conference, June 6, 2012,' Transcript compiled by Thomson Reuters StreetEvents, accessed via Thomson One, July 9, 2013.

[483] Sellers, Patricia, "Something to Prove," *Fortune*, June 24, 2002, http://money.cnn.com/magazines/fortune/fortune_archive/2002/06/24/325190/.

[484] Alvarez, José et. al, 'Home Depot and Interconnected Retail,' HBS case number N9-512-036, Boston: Harvard Business School Publishing, 2012.

[485] Johnson, Julia M., "Knight's Direct Sells Unit to Home Depot," *St. Louis Business Journal,* April 26, 2006, http://www.bizjournals.com/stlouis/stories/2006/04/24/daily30.html?page=all.

[486] 'Home Depot Inc Investor & Analyst Conference, June 6, 2012,' Transcript compiled by Thomson Reuters StreetEvents, accessed via Thomson One, July 9, 2013.

[487] Wehrum, Kasey, "Special Report: Wayfair's Road to $1 Billion," *Inc.*, April, 2012, http://www.inc.com/magazine/201204/kasey-wehrum/the-road-to-1-billion-growth-special-report.html.

[488] 'Home Depot Inc Investor & Analyst Conference, June 6, 2012,' Transcript compiled by Thomson Reuters StreetEvents, accessed via Thomson One, July 9, 2013.

[489] *ibid*

[490] *ibid*

[491] 'The Home Depot Inc in Retailing,' Euromonitor International, Passport, April 2012.

[492] "Millennials: a Portrait of Generation Next," *Pew Research Center*, February, 2010.

[493] "The Future of Retail," *Oracle Retail,* September, 2011.

[494] "The Harris Poll," *Harris Interactive,* accessed via *eMarketer*.

[495] "Generations Study: Millennials & Boomers," *Radius Global Market Research,* December 3, 2013; accessed via *eMarketer*.

[496] "The Future of Retail," *eMarketer.*

[497] "Gross Domestic Product by Industry Data," US Department of Commerce, Bureau of Economic Analysis, 2012. Note: Retail Trade Employment over All Employment.

[498] "Total US Retail Sales Top $4.5 Trillion in 2013, Outpace GDP Growth," *eMarketer*, April 10, 2014, available at http://www.emarketer.com/Article/Total-US-Retail-Sales-Top-3645-Trillion-2013-Outpace-GDP-Growth/1010756

[499] "MarketPulse Survey Q4 2012," *SymphonyIRI*, as cited in "2012 CPG Year in Review: Finding the New Normal," February 20, 2013, accessed via *eMarketer*.

[500] "Millennials: a Portrait of Generation Next," *Pew Research Center*, February, 2010.

CPSIA information can be obtained
at www.ICGtesting.com
Printed in the USA
BVOW05*0931140717
489260BV00023B/287/P